World War I
A Visual Encyclopedia

World War I
A Visual Encyclopedia

General Editor: Simon Forty

World War I: A Visual Encyclopedia was written by a team of specialist authors under the general editorship of Simon Forty. The authors are identified by their initials under each entry. They are:

STEPHEN BULL, who provided the entries covering land warfare and weaponry, and the Western Front.

DUNCAN CLARKE, who covered the politics and political events.

MARK COWARD, who detailed the battles.

ANGUS KONSTAM, who covered the war at sea and other naval entries.

JERRY SCUTTS, who covered the air war and aviation subjects.

MICHAEL SWIFT, who wrote the biographies.

IAN WESTWELL, who covered the war outside the Western Front.

BILL YENNE, who covered the American involvement in the war.

The publisher wishes to thank all those who kindly supplied the photographs and maps for this book. All picture credits are located under each caption inside the book. The photographs on the front and back covers were all supplied courtesy of the Chrysalis Photo Library.

This edition produced by
PRC Publishing Ltd,
64 Brewery Road, London N7 9NT
A member of the Chrysalis Group plc

Published 2002 by Greenwich Editions
64 Brewery Road, London, N7 9NT

A member of **Chrysalis** Books plc

© 2002 PRC Publishing Ltd.

ISBN 0 86288 487 X

Printed and bound in China

ABBREVIATIONS

AF of L	American Federation of Labor
ANZAC	Australian and New Zealand Army Corps
AEF	American Expeditionary Force
BAR	Browning Automatic Rifle
BEF	British Expeditionary Force
CO	Commanding Officer
(H/L)MG	(Heavy/Light) Machine gun
MP	Member of Parliament
NCO	Non-commissioned officer
NSDAP	*Nationalsozialistische Deutsche Arbeiterpartei* = Nazi
OC	Officer Commanding
RFC	Royal Flying Corps
RHA	Royal Horse Artillery
RN	Royal Navy
RNAS	Royal Naval Air Service
SS	Submarine Scout
VAD	Volunteer Aid Detachment

Title Page: Men of the 369th Infantry, 93rd Division in trenches outside Maffrecourt, May 5, 1918. *Chrysalis Photo Library*

Right: Fokker Triplanes being wheeled back to their sheds after a patrol, March 1918. *Chrysalis Photo Library*

Overleaf: Mud was always a problem on the World War I battlefields. Here men haul an eighteen-pounder during the Flanders Offensive, August 9, 1917. *Chrysalis Photo Library*

PREFACE

Today we don't see World War I as the "war to end all wars," but the first part of a conflict that would flare up again twenty years later under the Nazis. Its causes are hard to define briefly and had to do with mindsets difficult to understand today. It is hard to believe that the assassination of the Hapsburg Archduke Ferdinand in Sarajevo on June 28, 1914, would set in motion a confrontation that would see nearly thirty million military casualties. It is hard to believe that European societies could tolerate the horror of some four years of trench warfare. It is hard to believe that the European ruling powers could allow the war to continue for so long, effectively breaking the power of the old world.

World War I: A Visual Encyclopedia does not attempt to discover the rationale for these events but to catalog them in a way that will be useful to the researcher, illustrating as many entries as possible. The alphabetical nature of the encyclopedia makes it difficult to follow events chronologically, and so the index below is provided for continuity.

CHRONOLOGICAL INDEX BY WAR THEATER

A

Abdullah ibn Hussein (1882–1951)

Born in Mecca, Abdullah ibn Hussein was the second son of Hussein ibn Ali. One of the leaders of the Arab revolt against Turkey in the years between 1916 and 1918, he was to become the Emir of Transjordan in 1921. The area was called Occupied Enemy Territory (East) initially and was part of the Kingdom of Syria, under Emir Faisal, between March and July 1920. On April 25, 1920, the Supreme Council of the Allies assigned to Britain a mandate to govern both Palestine and Transjordan. The British mandate over Transjordan continued until 1946, although it was recognized as an autonomous state in 1923 and granted a limited degree of independence five years later. In 1946, at the end of the British mandate, Abdullah ibn Hussein became the first king of Jordan; he was also briefly declared king of Palestine in 1948, but the creation of Israel resulted in his realm being much diminished. He was assassinated in 1951. *MS*

Aces

The French Air Service was the first to recommend that pilots who showed exceptional prowess in destroying five enemy aircraft in combat had won the honor of being known as aces. All five victories were subject to a strict rule of independent confirmation, without which no credit would be given, although victories shared with another pilot (or other pilots) were allowed. The Germans made their baseline score ten victories, while the British authorities followed much the same rule as the French but allowed probable claims. American air leaders based their system on that imposed by their French comrades. All countries publicized their successful pilots accordingly. *JS*

The top 20 aces

Richthofen, Rittmeister Manfred Freiherr von	80
Fonck, Captain Rene	75
Bishop, Major William A.	72
Mannock, Major Edward approx.	68
Udet, Oberleutnant Ernst	62
Collishaw, Major Raymond	62
McCudden Major T. B.	57
Guynemer, Captain Georges	54
Beauchamp-Proctor, Captain Anthony W.	54
Lowenhardt, Oberleutnant Erich	53
Barker, Captain William G.	52
Dallas, Major Roderic S.	51
McElroy, Captain George E. H.	49
Jacobs, Lieutenant Josef	48
Voss, Leutnant Werner	48
Ball, Captain Albert	47
Little, Captain Robert A	47
Nungesser, Lieutenant Charles	45
Rumey, Leutnant Fritz	45
Berthold, Hauptmann Rudolph	44

JS

Adriatic Sea, Operations in the

Although the Austro-Hungarian Navy was a reasonably powerful force, with dreadnought and predreadnought battleships, it never undertook any major operations. Allied control of the Straits of Otranto prevented access into the

Right: Captain Albert Ball, VC, DSO, MC, RFC, who would end the war with forty-seven kills.
Chrysalis Photo Library

Far Right: Canadian Captain William Bishop, VC, RFC, after his thirty-seventh kill had been confirmed. He would end the war a major with seventy-two kills to his name.
Chrysalis Photo Library

Mediterranean and limited Austrian surface naval activity to hit-and-run sorties. Following the entrance of Italy into the war on the Allied side in May 1915, the Italian Navy helped ensure the Allies retained naval supremacy in the region. The Otranto Barrage consisted of nets and patrolling warships, but it was unable to completely prevent the movement of Austrian submarines, and in December 1914 an Austrian U-boat south of the barrier sank a French battleship. Although the main Italian base was at Taranto, in southern Italy, submarines and light forces operated from Venice, and much of the naval war involved actions by submarines or coastal forces. This was particularly evident during the Allied evacuation of the defeated Serbian Army from Albania during the winter of 1915–16. On the night of October 31, 1918, an Italian miniature submarine penetrated the naval defenses of the principal Austrian base at Pola and sank the battleship *Viribus Unitis* at anchor, only to find that Austria had already surrendered. *AK*

Aegean Sea, Operations in the

The Aegean Sea should have been a backwater during the war, as the Turkish Navy was almost nonexistent. The flight of the German battlecruiser *Goeben* and the cruiser *Breslau* to Constantinople in August 1914, providing two powerful units to the Turkish fleet, but in December 1914 the British submarine *B11* penetrated the Dardanelles and sank the Turkish cruiser *Messudiyeh*. The Gallipoli expedition of 1915 meant that Allied warships were required to bombard invasion beaches, but the risks of close support were heavy, and four battleships were lost to mines, shore batteries or torpedo attacks during May alone. For the rest of the year, Allied submarines penetrated the Sea of Marmara, sinking the Turkish battleship *Hairedin Barbarossa* together with several smaller targets. The submarine offensive halved Turkey's merchant fleet. Following the Allies' withdrawal from Gallipoli, the Aegean theater became quiet, apart from antisubmarine actions, as the Allies tried to prevent the U-boats slipping into the Mediterranean. The last action of the *Goeben* and *Breslau* came in January 1918, when they slipped through the Dardanelles, and sank two British monitors anchored off Imbros. The *Breslau* struck a mine and sank during the action. *AK*

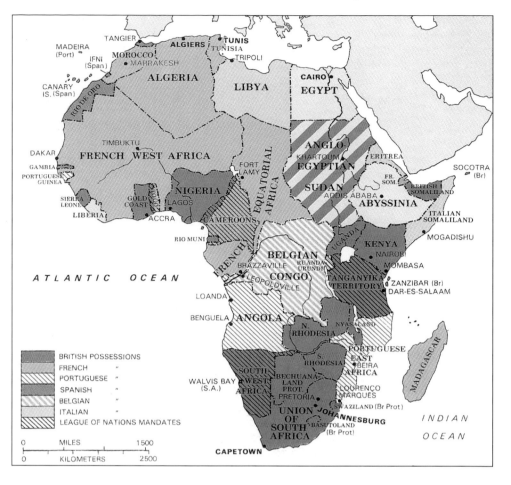

Africa, World War I in

The greater part of Africa had been carved up between various European colonial powers before World War I, with the lion's share going to the Allied countries, chiefly Britain. Germany, one of the later colonial powers, held just four possessions—Togoland, Cameroon, German Southwest Africa, and German East Africa—and these were highly vulnerable to capture for a number of reasons. First, their links with Germany were tenuous, because the German Navy lacked the ships to offer them full protection or bring in vital supplies, whereas the Allied navies could spare resources to interdict German shipping. Second, the forces available to protect them, a mixture of German colonial troops and local levies, were of good quality but limited in quantity. Third, the individual German colonies were so far apart that they would have to fight in isolation. Fourth, all were surrounded by the colonies of Germany's enemies, chiefly Britain and France. Finally, Britain in particular was willing to commit huge resources to protect its colonies for as much a matter of national honor as strategic necessity. Germany's many disadvantages were revealed in the first months of the war. Togoland,

Above: European colonies in Africa.
Richard Natkiel

defended by 300 German and 1,200 local troops, fell to a joint Anglo-French invasion from their neighboring colonies, with the local commander surrendering on August 26, 1914. German Southwest Africa came under Allied attack when two columns of South African troops, under the command of Louis Botha and Jan Christiaan Smuts, invaded in February 1915 and moved on its capital, Windhoek, which fell on May 20. Surviving German forces surrendered on July 9. Cameroon was assailed by British and French forces from August 1914. However, after initial successes, progress slowed until late 1915. This was due to disagreements between the British and French, the country's difficult terrain and lack of good communications, rampant disease, and a skillfully conducted German guerrilla campaign. The Allies reinforced their forces and captured the key town of Yuande on January 1, 1916, but many German troops escaped capture, preferring to withdraw into the neighboring Spanish enclave of Rio Muni. The Allied takeover of Cameroon was completed on March 4. German East

Left: An abandoned German 4.1-inch naval gun on the road near Masassi, East Africa, November 24, 1917. *Chrysalis Photo Library*

Africa proved much more difficult to subdue. Surrounded and outnumbered, with little hope of resupply from his homeland, the local German commander, General Paul von Lettow-Vorbeck, resorted to waging an aggressive and wide-ranging guerrilla war that tied up more and more enemy forces. Living off the land or on captured supplies, his small forces ranged across East Africa, launching hit-and-run raids at strategic targets, such as railroads. Try as they might, the Allies never fully countered the threat and Lettow-Vorbeck only surrendered after the Armistice had been signed. Aside from these major campaigns, the war in Africa saw both sides attempt to foster revolts among the local peoples. Germany provoked anti-British Boer nationalists to rebel in South Africa in October 1914. Pro-British South African forces inflicted defeats on the rebels, but the revolt simmered until February 1915. Elsewhere, there was a minor British-sponsored revolt in German East Africa and a Turkish-backed one in Sudan, but neither were of consequence, chiefly because all of the colonial powers feared widespread outbreaks of violent anticolonialism. *IW*

Air war during World War I

During the first decade of the twentieth century a practical use for airpower was only slowly being appreciated by the army staffs, which invariably controlled aviation. Few combat-worthy aircraft were available to any nation when war broke out in 1914, and those aircrew who went aloft began carrying revolvers and carbines to defend themselves in the event of a close encounter with an enemy machine. Both sides answered the enormous demand for aerial reconnaissance with regular flights by balloons and photographic sorties by airplanes. Spotting for their own guns and identifying those of the enemy occupied pilots on many dangerous sorties, but the results obtained increasingly formed an integral part of planning new ground offensives. Protecting these all-important reconnaissance flights brought about clashes with the front-line patrols mounted by opposing forces, which were often aloft for exactly the same reason. When machine guns were fitted to aircraft, aerial combat became more deadly and far less personal. There remained, nevertheless, a strand of old-fashioned chivalry which both sides observed to a degree. Respect for the skill of the enemy was reflected in such acts as the dropping of a wreath when news was received that a famous pilot on the other side had been downed. Linking the combatants was an undeniable comradeship of the air at a time when flying remained the province of very few compared to the vast numbers serving in the ground armies. Flying was not without its inherent risks, for although the structure of the airplanes of 1914-18 made for light weight, speed, and maneuverability, aero engine development in just over a decade of peacetime conditions, had hardly proceeded at the same pace. Many aircraft were, therefore, terribly slow and vulnerable to enemy fire—nor could they be very adequately protected without a prohibitive drop in performance. Numbers tended to make up for such deficiencies, and in numerous instances such superiority did indeed win the day. Development of formation tactics, including providing a high-flying top cover, as well as lower-altitude escort to PR aircraft, was possible when an increased number of pilots produced by the training schools reached the front. As second-generation fighters—such as the Spad and Nieuport series, the Sopwith Pup, Camel, and the SE5 on the Allied side and the Pfalz and Albatros series plus the Fokker Dr I and DVII of the German air forces—came into service, dogfights became more equal. The skill of the opposing pilots came much more into play as they were flying types that were more evenly matched than before. As fighters became technically more capable, more ambitious air operations

Below: The OC of No. 15 Squadron, RFC, Major Walker, outside his office receiving reports from his pilots. Photo taken on March 20, 1918, during the Second Battle of Bapaume.
Chrysalis Photo Library

Left: Dramatic landing—General de Lisle (center) and an American artillery general check out a crash near Langemarck, September 12, 1917. *Chrysalis Photo Library*

could be executed with larger formations ranging further afield and deploying over contested sectors of the front. Attacks on enemy airfields and supply lines whittled down strength and had a significant psychological effect. Tactical ground strafing and bombing brought about a new dimension in air warfare, one in which the deadly potential of the airplane to almost dictate the course of ground campaigns was decisively demonstrated. Against soft targets—such as vehicles, railways, trench positions, and troop concentrations—even the two or three machine guns carried by the majority of World War I aircraft could be highly effective. The vastness of Imperial Russia led to the development of some of the world's first large multiengined aircraft, able to bomb distant targets. The munitions' factories of Germany's foes also lay hundreds of miles distant and the air service initially deployed airships and later conventional bombers to carry out strategic bombing attacks. More or less surrounded by hostile nations, the Kaiser had little choice but to strike at both continental European targets and those in England in an attempt to bring about at least a compromise peace. This was the first demonstration of the fatally flawed belief that a powerful enemy's morale could be cowed by air raids. Nobody knew, of course, exactly what the reaction would be. German airships had begun such raids in daylight but the reaction from guns and interceptor fighters was such that a heavy concentration of bombs was rarely achieved. Switching to night bombing brought the German Army and Navy Zeppelins some initial success as, again, this was another entirely new method of waging war. In Britain the

raids led to the first night interception sorties, and the makeshift beginnings of a cohesive defense. In time, losses of the huge airships became prohibitive and the offensive was abandoned. Air tactics gradually evolved over the Western Front trench system with its numerous small-scale offensives and probing attacks on enemy positions. Air operations were invariably connected with events on the battlefield and the first aircraft were developed specifically to carry out ground attacks. Thus the concept of air support to the ground armies was born. The continuing pattern of virtually static trench warfare punctuated by frustratingly small advances—at appalling cost in human life—could be broken by the astute deployment of airplanes. By 1918 air superiority was beginning to be a prerequisite to a successful ground offensive and the Allies were at last in a position to deploy tactical aircraft to that end. Although equally confident, the Germans, very aware of

the importance that air operations had assumed, had suffered some potentially disastrous midwar setbacks. They not only began to lose any numerical edge they had enjoyed, but technical superiority as well. In 1917 when their independent fighter units were reorganized into *Jasta* or squadrons, the balance was temporarily redressed. Numerous German pilots became air aces, their ability to destroy enemy machines at a steady rate making some of them famous on both sides of the lines. The same was true of French and British pilots, who became aces and the pin-ups of their day. In some four years of war, both the Allies and the Central Powers had experienced enormous, near-crippling losses in army manpower—from the ranks of which most aircrew were still recruited—that the 1917 involvement of America promised to tip the balance in the Allies' favor. For their part, the Germans anticipated that after the October Revolution, men released from fighting the Russians and transferred to boost the Western Front armies could win the war before American troops were committed in overwhelming strength. Von Ludendorff's Spring Offensive of 1918 so nearly achieved that goal, and it is not overstating the case to say that Allied *combined* operations, on land, in the air, and at sea (in that order) were responsible for the final defeat of the Central Powers. *JS*

Below: Fokker EIII. *Chrysalis Photo Library*

Aircraft carriers

A handful of naval officers understood the potential offered by aircraft as early as 1914, and plans were developed to launch aircraft from warships. The first carriers were vessels converted to carry floatplanes, such as the British seaplane tender *Engadine*, which had to lower its aircraft into the water using cranes before they could take off. The floats also degraded performance, so a system was devised where a wooden "flying-off deck" was mounted to the forecastle of an existing ship. Aircraft could take off from these vessels, but were unable to land back on board. Landing attempts onto HMS *Furious* in August 1917 resulted in fatal accidents, so it was decided to redesign the flying-off platform, adding a landing-on deck. The result was HMS *Argus*, a former liner converted into the first aircraft carrier with a full-length flightdeck. She entered service in December 1917. The following year the *Hermes*, a specialist aircraft carrier, was laid down. The effectiveness of naval air-power was demonstrated in July 1918, when seven aircraft launched from *Furious* attacked a German Zeppelin station at Tondern in Belgium. Within three years both the United States and Japan had commissioned their own purpose-built aircraft carriers. *AK*

Below: HMS *Furious*, 1918. *Chrysalis Photo Library*

Right: HMS *Argus* in dazzle camouflage scheme. *Chrysalis Photo Library*

Below Right: Example of a "flying-off deck." *Chrysalis Photo Library*

Aircraft, Development of

When the European powers went to war just eleven years on from man's first powered flight by the Wright Brothers, the airplanes supporting the opposing armies were flimsy, generally low-powered, and quite unsuitable for combat. They bore a strong family resemblance to the very first generation of aircraft, with much of the basic airframe structure uncovered and visible. Minimal fabric covering was obvious, along with numerous bracing wires to hold wings and tail surfaces in place—and in military terms, there was a distinct lack of any form of armament. But from modest beginnings the aircraft that fought the first air war in history gradually became more capable military machines, often as a direct counter to enemy developments. The lightweight wooden kite-like structures of the type purchased by military forces in 1914 attained top speeds of less than 100mph from engines rated at around 80–120hp. The limitations of the rotary engine were soon appreciated, although for the time it was efficient enough and widely used. Whether they were of pusher or tractor configuration, had one or more engines, or could carry bombs, airplanes evolved under the impetus of war and became quite deadly instruments of destruction. No types

exemplified this progress more than four-engined bombers with wingspans of 120ft or more. Such monsters began to demonstrate the awesome potential for bombing war factories—and non-combatants—far beyond the battlefield. In what largely remained a biplane and triplane era—although monoplanes were developed and operated by each side—World War I saw aeronautical engineering advance to an unprecedented level, with factories establishing assembly lines to rival the mass-production techniques of the automobile industry. Aircraft operated during the war's early "stick and string" months evolved into more streamlined designs with the structure completely covered in fabric or wood. Monoplanes began to demonstrate the performance gains from adopting less drag-inducing wire bracing in cantilever wings and floats. Externally there was a strong similarity between the leading aircraft types in each class and most proved to be capable of surviving air combat. By 1918 fighter speeds had more than doubled compared to those of 1914 but streamlining, with a cleaner design approach was in its infancy. Armament remained modest, generally two to three machine guns—in fighters these were invariably synchronized to fire straight ahead. Two guns were more than adequate in aerial combat but

Above: BE2c biplane. *Chrysalis Photo Library*

Above Right: Early tractor biplane of No. 2 Squadron, RFC, at Montrose, Scotland. *Chrysalis Photo Library*

Right: Sopwith Camel leaving the deck of HMS *Furious*. *Chrysalis Photo Library*

aircrew survival, in a period when items such as self-sealing fuel tanks were virtually unheard of and pilots generally shunned parachutes, was something of a lottery. Had it been possible to add greater protection to the aircraft structure, many pilots would undoubtedly have been saved, along with their aircraft. Some armor plate protection was, however, available on certain types, and oxygen systems had made their appearance. It speaks volumes for the technical strides made in World War I military aviation that development slowed after 1918; apart from adopting all-metal structures, the biplane ruled for nearly two more decades while international air arms all but forgot some of the vital lessons learned the hard way in the "war to end wars." *JS*

Airships

Several nations built airships for military purposes, but Germany led both in production and deployment with 115 airships in various classes up to the giant Zeppelin *L71* of 1918 which was nearly 700ft long. Italy developed the M-series of semi-rigid dirigibles, nineteen of which were completed and used mainly for night bombing. Britain's small, non-rigid airships, such as the Coastal, North Sea, and SS (Submarine Scout) classes, were primarily used for maritime reconnaissance; many examples of the SS-3 of 1915 were supplied to France and Italy. By August 1917 the first of three Vickers N23 rigid airships had flown. Used mainly for patrols and training, the 534ft long N23 was small compared to the Zeppelins. *JS*

Right: German naval airship *L70*. It was shot down in 1918. *Chrysalis Photo Library*

Below: The Zeppelins were extremely large— some nearly 700ft long—and required substantial hangars.
Chrysalis Photo Library

Left: Inside a Zeppelin—this remarkable photograph shows the skeleton of one of these giant airships. *Chrysalis Photo Library*

Below: The British *R33* airship. *Chrysalis Photo Library*

WORLD WAR I: A VISUAL ENCYCLOPEDIA

Aisne (1914), First Battle of the

From September 14–18, 1914, the river Aisne became the most critical front of the Western Front. The German First, Second, Third, Fourth, and Fifth Armies retreated to positions above the Aisne following their repulsion from the Marne, under orders to "fortify and defend" the lines there. Thus the First Battle of the Aisne marked the end of the war of movement, prefiguring the trench warfare of First Ypres. On September 12 the BEF crossed the river in a bid to exploit an opening that had developed between the German First and Second Armies, but the German Seventh Army arrived in time to plug the gap and repel the assault. The French Fourth Army managed some small gains on September 14, but German resistance sent them back to their starting positions and both forces soon discovered that frontal assaults without artillery support were no longer proving tactically effective. After four days of largely static fighting, it became evident that any opportunity that was to be won from the battle lay in the 100-mile gap between the Aisne positions and the North Sea. The Allied and German armies began the series of attempts to outflank one another known as the "Race to the Sea." *MC*

Aisne (1917), Second Battle of the

Coming a week after the British diversionary attack at Arras, the Second Battle of the Aisne was masterminded by the French Commander-in-Chief Robert Nivelle. Contested between April 16 and May 9, 1917, it represented an overly ambitious attempt to break through the Hindenburg Line, and would end with the loss of 187,000 French and 163,000 German lives, demoralizing French forces to the point of mutiny. The French attack began on April 16 along a fifty-

Above: The Third Battle of the Aisne—men of the Worcesters holding the southern flank at Maizy, May 27, 1918. *Chrysalis Photo Library*

mile front, involving the Sixth and Fifth Armies under the overall direction of Micheler. The first day of advance alone cost the French 150 tanks, as the German Seventh and First Armies resisted determinedly. By April 20 some modest gains had been made, with the Fort Malmaison salient abandoned, the Aisne valley cleared, the Rheims-Soissons railway freed, and 20,000 prisoners taken. French reinforcements arrived in the form of the Tenth Army, bringing Nivelle's forces up to 1,200,000 men and 7,000 guns, but the height of their achievements was the capture of no more than two miles of the Hindenburg Line on the Chemin des Dames ridge. The final attack was launched on May 5, but the promised breakthrough remained elusive and little had been achieved when the attack ended four days later. *MC*

Aisne (1918), Third Battle of the

The superbly planned German attack on the Aisne of May 27–June 5, 1918, code-named "Blücher," was so successful that the Germans themselves were taken by surprise. A blitzkrieg without the panzers, the Third Battle of the Aisne represented a return to the war of movement that had ended with the 1914 "Race to the Sea." Coming at a time when the Allied forces were still reeling from von Ludendorff's Spring Offensive, "Blücher" combined carefully deployed infantry with pulverizing artillery under a sky dominated by German *Jagdgeschwader*. The opening day of the assault saw three British divisions all but destroyed, as they and the French XI Corps were forced down the ridges of Chemin des Dames. Two more British divisions were beaten on May 28, and the German Seventh Army under General von Bohn seized the bridges controlling the Aisne river and canal, threatening the cities of Rheims and Soissons on either side of a salient twenty-five miles wide and eleven miles deep. Over the coming weeks, the Germans continued to push deeper into the Champagne region, capturing Soissons. "Blücher" finally ended on June 5 on the banks of the Marne, halted through lack of German reserves to consolidate the gains of the vanguard. *MC*

Aitken, William Maxwell (1870–1964)

Born in Canada, Aitken made his fortune through the amalgamation of the Canadian cement industry. He moved to Britain in 1910, being elected to the House of Commons in 1911 as a Conservative. He served as Bonar Law's private secretary and as an observer on the Western Front until he was appointed Minister of Information under Lloyd George in 1918 (having been created the first Baron Beaverbrook the previous year). The following year, he acquired the *Daily Express*, which marked the start of his career as a press baron. He launched the *Sunday Express* and bought the London *Evening Standard*. He again served as a minister in World War II as Minister of Supply (1941–42) and later

as Lord Privy Seal. Lord Beaverbrook died in 1964. *MS*

"Alberich," Operation

Following the British Somme offensives of 1916 and the battle of attrition around Verdun, fearing further Allied offensives in 1917, General von Ludendorff opted to voluntarily withdraw the German forces from a considerable stretch of the line between Arras and Rheims in an effort to free vital reserve divisions from his front-line forces. This operation, known as "Alberich" after the dwarf from the Niebelung Saga, was carried out starting on March 16. Von Ludendorff had previously ensured that there was a formidable position prepared for the German defenders. This line, known to the Allies as the Hindenburg Line and the Germans as the Siegfried line, had been constructed during the winter of 1916–17 and reflected the summit of defensive technology. The front line was based on the reverse slopes of hills in order to protect the defenders from artillery fire, and there were further reserve lines and machine-gun posts located to the rear to break up enemy attacks and form a more flexible defensive front. The Allies did not realize that the Germans had withdrawn until March 25, and when they slowly advanced they discovered that the entire area left by the Germans had been devastated: villages were razed, water sources contaminated, and the area was littered with booby traps. *MC*

Albert I, King (1875–1934)

King of Belgium, Albert I reigned from 1909 until 1934, having succeeded his uncle Leopold II to the throne. It was in August 1914, when the Germans invaded France through supposedly neutral Belgium following the king's refusal to allow them to transit his country, that Albert invoked the various treaties that had guaranteed Belgian neutrality when the country was first established in 1831. Britain, one of these guarantors, was thus drawn into the war. After helping the Belgian army in its resistance to the German onslaught, he retreated with his defeated forces to Flanders. He remained active as a commander, leading the French and Belgian forces in their Courtrai Offensive up the Belgian coast in 1918. He reentered Brussels on November 22, 1918, and remained

popular until his death in a climbing accident. *MS*

Albrecht, Duke of Württemberg (1865–1939)

The Duke of Württemberg was one of the early German commanders, leading the Fourth Army through the Ardennes in August 1914, reaching the Marne by September. The Fourth Army was then transferred to Flanders, where it served in the "Race to the Sea" and led the German assaults on Ypres. He was promoted field marshal in August 1916, taking command of Army Group Albrecht in February 1917. Retiring after the war, he died in 1939. *MS*

Aleppo, Capture of

The fall of Aleppo in Turkish-controlled northern Palestine during late October 1918 brought the fighting in the theater to an end. The defending Turks were ravaged by illness and demoralized in the face of overwhelming Allied forces supported by Arab guerrillas. As the British advanced, the defenders simply melted away with only a rearguard under Mustapha Kemal Pasha offering any resistance. *IW*

Alexander, Crown Prince (1888–1934)

The second son of King Peter of Serbia, Alexander became heir apparent in 1909 when his elder brother, George, renounced his claims to the throne. Alexander became regent when his father was forced into exile in June 1914. Notionally commander-in-chief of the Serbian Army, he was forced out of his homeland following the "Great Retreat" of November 1915. From his capital in exile on Corfu he continued to ensure Serbia's role in the anti-Central Powers coalition, and in the fall of 1918, he created the new federal kingdom of Serbs, Croats, and Slovenes—this was the future Yugoslavia. Alexander became king on the death of his father in 1921, and from 1929, effectively ruled as a dictator following the dissolution of parliament. He was assassinated in 1934. *MS*

Alexandra, Tsarina (1872–1917)

The daughter of Grand Duke Louis of Hesse-Darmstadt and Princess Alice Maud Mary (the daughter of Queen Victoria), Alexandra was born in

Darmstadt. In 1894 she married Tsar Nicholas II of Russia, who had just inherited the throne. She had a number of unfortunate traits—a tendency to dominate her husband and a misguided belief in others—that were to ultimately lead to disaster. She bore Nicholas one son—Alexis, who was tragically afflicted with hemophilia—as well as a number of daughters. Her son's illness led her to be influenced by figures such as Rasputin, who were instrumental in the growing unpopularity of the Russian royal family at the time and the growing alienation of much of the aristocracy. With Nicholas away during the war leading his troops, Alexandra meddled in domestic politics, in particular supporting Stürmer's appointment as premier in early 1916, again compounding the growing hatred. With the October Revolution in 1917 she and the rest of the Imperial family, including her husband, the Tsar, were imprisoned by the Bolsheviks and eventually murdered in 1917 at Yekaterinburg. *MS*

Alexeev, Mikhail (1857–1917)

Alexeev served as chief of staff in the Russian Army of Galicia in August 1914, before assuming command of the Army of the Northwest in March 1915. His reluctance to release forces to assist the Carpathian campaign was one factor in Ivanov's defeat. In September 1915 he became chief of staff at Stavka, where, despite poor communications and limited resources, he established much stronger control. In November 1916 he suffered a heart attack, but he returned to his command just prior to the February 1917 revolution. Dismissed by Kerensky in May 1917, he was reappointed briefly in September, and led the anti-Bolshevik forces after the October Revolution prior to his death later in the month. *MS*

Allenby, Sir Edmund Henry Hynman (1861–1936)

Allenby saw service in South Africa between 1884 and 1885 and again in 1888 as well as during the Second Boer War of 1899–1902. At the outbreak of World War I in 1914, he was appointed commander of the cavalry division of the BEF (serving at Mons and at Le Cateau). He then commanded an infantry corps in the Second Battle of Ypres before commanding the Third Army in France from October 1915 until 1917. After the Battle of Arras, in June 1917 he was transferred to the Middle East, where he commanded the march through Palestine that culminated in the capture of Jerusalem in December of that year. Although his forces were weakened by the demands to reinforce the British forces on the Western Front, he was able to launch a further offensive in September 1918 that forced the demoralized Turkish forces northward into Syria prior to the signing of the Armistice of Mudros on October 30, 1918. In 1919 he was ennobled as the first Viscount Allenby and later served—between 1919 and 1925—as British High Commissioner in Egypt prior to his death. *MS*

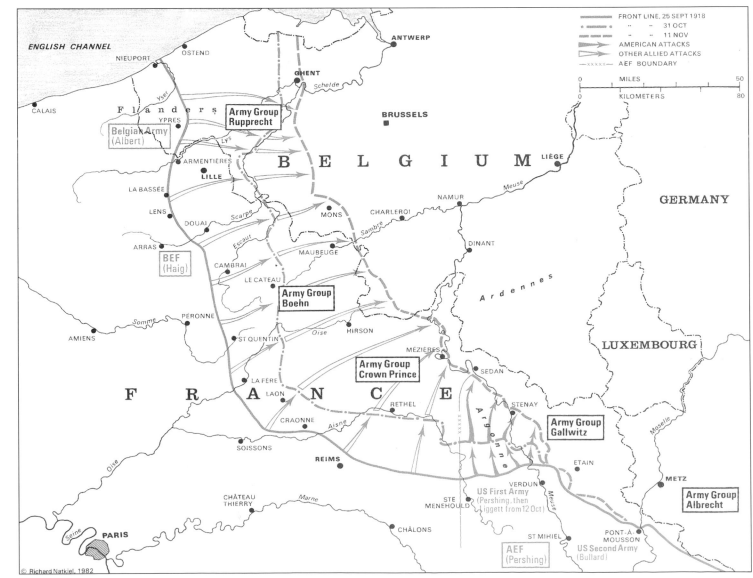

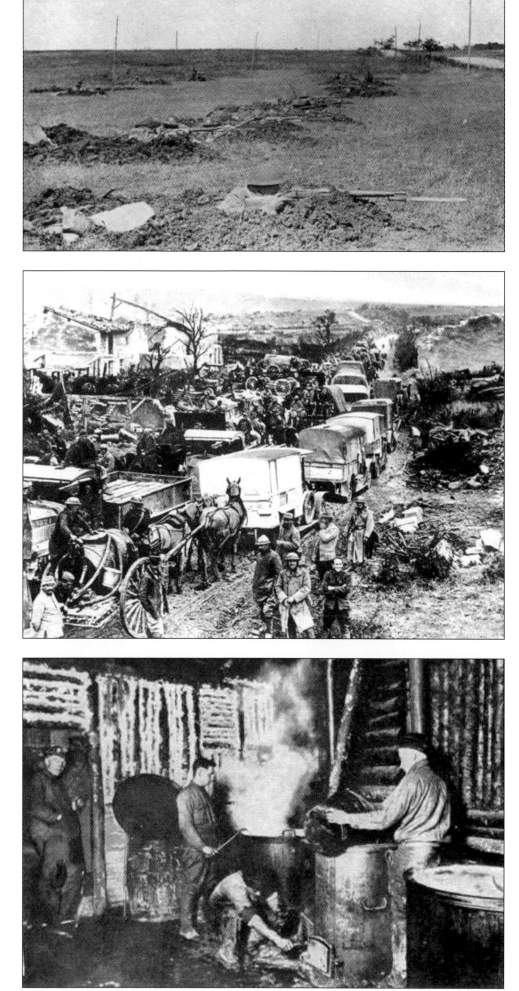

Allied Offensive of 1918

With the failure of von Ludendorff's offensives of spring and early summer 1918, the way lay open for a renewed Allied offensive. "Everyone to the attack," Foch proclaimed. There were 123 Allied divisions, along with fifty-seven in reserve, facing 197 German divisions, of which only fifty-one were considered battleworthy. The first blow to be struck was in the area around Amiens when, on August 8, 1918, the British Fourth and French First Armies attacked, following a short barrage and spearheaded by over 450 tanks. Surprise was absolute; between August 8 and 12 Fourth Army captured over 21,000 prisoners for a loss of 20,000 casualties. In early September the newly formed U.S. First Army launched an attack on the St. Mihiel salient to the south of Verdun, clearing it by September 16 for the loss of 7,000 casualties. The Americans then turned their attention to the area of the Meuse-Argonne, driving northward into the German positions on September 26, 1918. A day later the major Allied offensive of the year opened in the west. Field Marshal Haig's army group, consisting of the British First, Third, Fourth, and Fifth Armies, was launched directly at the Hindenburg Line, which was breached on October 5. King Albert's Belgian Army Group, containing the British Second Army and the Belgian Army, thrust out of the Ypres Salient westward, but was slowed by the swampy ground. Further south the French also attacked, maintaining a constant pressure on the German line and not allowing them to remove any troops to reinforce threatened areas. *MC*

Top: The positions of the AEF's 167th Infantry Regiment, 42nd Infantry Division, near St. Banoit, St. Mihiel salient, September 15, 1918. *Collection of Bill Yenne*

Center: Traffic jam at Esnes on the Meuse-Argonne front, September 1918. *Collection of Bill Yenne*

Bottom: U.S. Army cooks preparing chow in captured German boilers. *Collection of Bill Yenne*

Opposite: The Allied Offensive of 1918. *Richard Natkiel*

American Expeditionary Force (AEF)

The AEF was the umbrella organization, with a fully comprehensive command structure, for U.S. forces (primarily U.S. Army) sent into combat in World War I. As commanding general of the AEF President Wilson and the War Department selected Major General John J. Pershing. In retrospect, the creation of the expeditionary force seems to be a logical organizational move. However, the creation of the AEF was not a foregone conclusion when the United States entered the war in April 1917. Initially, there was stiff opposition in Congress, and even President Wilson was cool to the notion of fielding an all-American expeditionary force. His declaration of war speech had made no mention of how the United States would intervene. Indeed, he hoped that simply the threat of United States' involvement would cause Germany to ask for a ceasefire. Meanwhile, some Allied political leaders saw the United States' intervention as a source of materiel, rather than manpower. They questioned the wisdom of creating the AEF on the grounds that it would divert resources into training Americans that could be used in combat by British and French forces. It was evident to all that the United States faced a staggering challenge in terms of training and equipping an effective expeditionary force to

Above: Recruits at Camp Kearny, in San Diego, California. *Collection of Bill Yenne*

Left: Major General John J. Pershing arrives in London, 1917. *Collection of Bill Yenne*

Left and Below: More views from Camp Kearny. The United States rose to the staggering challenge of training an effective expeditionary force.
Collection of Bill Yenne

months of conflict, the AEF led offensive operations against the best-defended sectors of the front. Of the U.S. Army's total of 4,057,000 soldiers, nearly ten percent were from New York State. Pennsylvania contributed 7.9 percent; Illinois, 6.7 percent; Ohio, 5.3 percent; Texas, 4.3 percent; Michigan 3.6 percent; Missouri, 3.4 percent; and California, 3 percent. Theoretically, the AEF could have been used on any of the several fronts in the conflict, but there was little discussion of committing U.S. ground troops anywhere but on the Western Front in cooperation with the British and French forces. It has been suggested that the Western Front policy was as political as it was military. It would allow the United States to see plenty of action in the war, which would therefore fit well with President Wilson's political goals of playing a role in shaping postwar Europe. The Allies were insistent that some U.S. forces be sent soon and United States' leaders agreed, although only previously trained regular U.S. Army personnel would be sent until conscripts had received proper training. In May 1917, General Pershing was ordered to take a division-strength first

operate overseas—and in convincing the Allies that the task was possible. At the time the United States entered World War I in April 1917, the U.S. Army was essentially a small 127,000-man constabulary force with units stationed across the nation and in the Philippines. Coincidentally, the French Army had suffered approximately that number of casualties during April 1917 alone. Though it had performed well in the Spanish-American War of 1898, and had recent experience in the Mexican Punitive Expedition of 1916, the U.S. Army had little experience in industrial-age warfare. It was on the same level of sophistication in 1917 as most European armies prior to 1914. The most optimistic American estimates concluded that a force of 500,000 would not be available for nearly a year, while the British General Staff estimated that only half that number could be in the field by the middle of 1918. In fact, in the space of nineteen months the number of personnel in the U.S. Army rose from 127,000 to more than 4,057,000. In addition, the U.S. Navy had 599,051 personnel in uniform, and the U.S. Marine Corps—which had just a token force of 3,321 in 1898—had 78,839

under arms in 1918. Of a total of 4,734,991 uniformed personnel, 2,086,000 U.S. troops were sent to France to become part of the AEF in the war zone. In November 1918, the AEF was occupying more of the Western Front than all British Commonwealth forces, including England. In the closing

element of the AEF to France. Also during that month, a draft was initiated to bring men into the U.S. Army and to grow it as quickly as possible. The two million Americans sent overseas arrived in almost equal proportion in Britain in France, with 844,000 passing through Liverpool, 791,000 debarking at Brest, and 62,000 arriving via London. By the end of 1917, the numbers of American soldiers arriving at the front were such that the AEF could take over defensive positions across entire sectors of the front and allow British and French units to rest or redeploy. It also forced the German High Command to undertake an offensive early in 1918 under the theory that the U.S. forces would soon be a decisive obstacle. During the summer and fall of 1918, the AEF did indeed

Above: Camp Kearny.
Collection of Bill Yenne

Right: Troops of the AEF's 165th Infantry Regiment, Croismare, March 2, 1918.
Collection of Bill Yenne

WORLD WAR I: A VISUAL ENCYCLOPEDIA

form the decisive obstacle that turned the German offensive. As for the practical deployment of U.S. troops, Britain and France had proposed using any Americans troops not in larger units under American command, but simply as replacements to be assigned to British or French units. The United States, especially General Pershing, favored the use of a force composed of integral units commanded by American officers. General Pershing was given wide latitude by President Wilson in planning the deployment of U.S. troops. Almost as soon as he arrived, Pershing began asking for more troops and supplies to carry out his mission. He outlined the necessity of shipping the equivalent of four divisions to France monthly for twelve months, and predicted an eventual AEF of three million troops. His idea was for basic training to occur in the United States with advanced training in Europe.

Right: Men of the AEF's 125th Infantry, 32nd Division, Company A, crossing the German frontier at Sentheim, Alsace, May 29, 1918.
Collection of Bill Yenne

Below: The AEF's 7th Machine Gun Battalion, 3rd Division, at a Chateau Thierry bridgehead.
Collection of Bill Yenne

Organizationally, the AEF was theoretically capable of containing several numbered armies as they became administratively necessary in the chain of command between the AEF itself and the constituent divisions. Initially, First Army was created, and it was under General Pershing's direct command. In October 1918, with the First Army embroiled in the Meuse-Argonne Offensive, the Second Army was created and given responsibility for the reduced St. Mihiel salient for an eventual thrust against Metz. General Hunter Liggett was given command of First Army, and General Robert Lee Bullard was given command of the Second Army. In the AEF chain of command both, in turn, reported to General Pershing—who reported to Field Marshal Ferdinand Foch, the supreme Allied commander. During World War I, the U.S. Army

Above: Men of the AEF's 7th Field Artillery.
Collection of Bill Yenne

Right: Troops of the AEF's 308th Infantry, 77th Division, resting after their first advance in the Argonne, September 26, 1918.
Collection of Bill Yenne

Above: Supply train from the AEF's 129th Infantry, 33rd Division, on the road at Bethincourt, September 29, 1918.
Collection of Bill Yenne

Right: Soldiers of the AEF's 132nd Infantry, 33rd Division, holding the line on the west bank of the Meuse, opposite Consenvoye.
Collection of Bill Yenne

consisted of twenty Regular Army divisions, numbered 1st through 20th; seventeen National Guard divisions, numbered 26th through 42nd; and eighteen National Army divisions—these were Regular Army divisions created during and for the war—numbered 76th through 93rd. Of the latter, the 92nd and 93rd were "Colored" or African-American divisions. A total of forty-two of the above divisions had reached the AEF (and its two constituent numbered armies) by the time of the Armistice. The 1st Division was the first to arrive in France (June 1917) and the first to have its troops enter combat (October 1917). The 2nd Division was the second to arrive in France (October 1917), but the fourth to have troops in action (March 1918). Both the 26th and 42nd Divisions arrived in France in November 1917 and

had troops in combat in February 1918. At the end of 1917, the AEF had five divisions in France, the above four plus the 41st Division. The 32nd Division arrived next (February 1918), followed by the 3rd and 77th Divisions in April 1918. Nine divisions (the 5th, 27th, 35th, 82nd, 4th, 28th, 30th, 33rd, and 80th) arrived during May 1918. Though the decision had been made to keep AEF troops as integral units, it was to be several months before division-strength units entered the line. For example, smaller component units of the 1st, 2nd, 26th, and 42nd Divisions had all seen combat though March 1918, but it was not until the end of April that the 1st Division became the first American division to go into combat as a division. Both the 2nd and 3rd Divisions followed in June 1918, and the 26th, 42nd, 32nd, 27th, 4th, 28th, and 30th Divisions were all in the line as complete units by the end of July. By the time of the Armistice, the AEF had twenty-eight divisions that had seen combat. Of these, all but four had, by November 11, entered the line as integral division-strength units. The total casualty figure for the AEF was 300,041, which represented seven percent of total U.S. Army strength and fourteen percent of those sent overseas with the AEF. The U.S. Department of Defense calculates that the United States suffered 53,402 battle deaths, 63,114 deaths from other causes (such as disease), and 204,002 troops were wounded. U.S. Army battle

deaths were the largest, numbering 50,510, followed by 2,461 Marines and 431 sailors. The U.S. Army suffered 193,663 wounded, the U.S. Marine Corps had 9,520 wounded and the U.S. Navy reported 819 battle-related injuries. By comparison, the total casualties suffered in the American Civil War were 646,392 for the Union (north) and approximately 410,000 for the Confederacy (south) for a total of 1.06 million. Battle deaths on the Union side were 138,154 and for the Confederacy,

roughly 200,000. The Civil War lasted roughly forty-eight months, while the AEF was in combat for roughly ten months. Calculated on a monthly basis, therefore, both sides in the Civil War suffered 7,045 killed in action monthly, while the AEF suffered a monthly killed in action average of 5,340. The monthly killed in action average in World War II was 6,338 for all services. The highest number of casualties were suffered during the Meuse-Argonne Offensive. According to Colonel Leonard P. Ayres of the Statistics Division of the U.S. Army General Staff, there were 6,589 battle deaths during the week of September 29 through October 5, the bloodiest of the war. The following two weeks, the second and third bloodiest of the war, saw 6,019 and 5,019 troops killed in action. The war's last seven weeks—beginning with September 29 and concluding with the Armistice on November 11—saw 27,840 battle deaths, more than half the overall total for the war. *BY*

Above: Wounded men of the AEF's 312th Infantry, 78th Division, being carried to an aid station, Bois de Negremont, near Grandpre, October 21, 1918. *Collection of Bill Yenne*

Left: Soldiers of the French 320th Infantry, Fourth Army, with members of the AEF's 312th Infantry, 78th Division. *Collection of Bill Yenne*

Ammunition

An advance in ammunition technology was one of the reasons for the increasing importance of trenches. In the latter part of the nineteenth century, small-arms brass cartridges with integral primers helped to revolutionize magazine-loading belt-feeding ammunition storage, and weapon reliability. British .303-inch Mk. VII cartridges were of solid drawn brass with a pointed, jacketed bullet with a two-part core of lead and aluminum. The charge was thirty-eight grains of cordite. Infantrymen now carried upward

Left: Men of the 102nd Ammunition Train, 33rd Division, AEF, unloading ammo. *Collection of Bill Yenne*

Below: French 75mm in action during the Third Battle of Krithia, Gallipoli, June 4, 1915. Note ammunition stowage. *Chrysalis Photo Library*

of a 100 rounds per man, often in clips or chargers—the usual German allowance was 120 in a pair of 1909 Model leather belt carriers, and thirty in the pack; theBritish, 150 rounds in the ten carriers of the Pattern 1908 webbing). Advances in artillery shells were no less impressive. Shrapnel shells had improved to the point at which they could be set to burst at a predetermined time over the heads of the enemy, showering them with metal shrapnel balls; high-explosive shells were in use with howitzers and larger guns. In the field artillery, quick-firers used fixed brass cartridges which were easy to handle allowing many rounds per minute. By 1912 the Germans were issuing a "universal" shell containing both shrapnel and TNT. Unfortunately, calculations regarding ammunition stocks were based on previous wars, which were generally of short duration, or consisted of brief engagements within longer campaigns. The British Mowatt scale allowed 1,500 rounds per field gun, with an extra 500 should the war last six months. Prewar production facilities were capable of producing only one round per gun per day. Most nations, therefore, suffered a shell scandal during 1915 when ammunition ran out, or batteries were limited to a few rounds per day. Moreover, against entrenchments light shells and shrapnel had but limited impact. There were Herculean efforts to increase production, with controlled labor and what was effectively nationalization of the factories in many nations. In Britain a Ministry of Munitions was created under Lloyd George, and by 1918 British factories had sent 187,342,870 shells to the Western Front alone. *SB*

Left: Shell-filling factory at Chilwell, England.
Chrysalis Photo Library

Right: 9.2-inch shells waiting for a howitzer in action with British 91st Battery during the Arras Offensive, April 1, 1917. Note camouflage netting.
Chrysalis Photo Library

Above: A German truck-mounted antiaircraft gun in action, Flanders, August 1917.
Chrysalis Photo Library

Right: A Lewis gun in action against hostile aircraft near Ypres, September 22, 1917.
Chrysalis Photo Library

Antiaircraft Guns

To use World War I artillery in an anti-aircraft capacity guns were often tethered on suitable inclines to fire at the necessary high angles. Thus able to maintain barrage fire over individual targets, the multiple bursts from German antiaircraft shells were nicknamed "Archie" by RFC pilots. The French "Soixante-Quinze" (7.5cm) was famously mounted on pivots—complete with wheels—both to defend Paris and areas of Belgium over which there was intense air activity. *JS*

Antisubmarine Warfare

In August 1914, the German Navy only had six operational ocean-going diesel submarines available for use, but more were immediately ordered, and 307 German and twenty-seven Austrian U-boats eventually undertook wartime patrols. In the early days of the war, U-boats ambushed their prey by surfacing, then sinking the merchantman with gunfire. As British losses mounted, the Admiralty decided to convert merchantmen into "Q-Ships,"—decoys fitted with a powerful and camouflaged armament. Increasing numbers of destroyers were used to hunt down U-boats in British and Mediterranean waters. In May 1917 the British responded to German "unrestricted"

Right: Setting a depth charge on the USS *Perkins*.
Collection of Bill Yenne

U-boat warfare by instituting a convoy system, which greatly reduced losses. At the same time, antisubmarine forces using depth charges operated successfully in home waters, and accounted for the loss of thirty boats, while surface gunnery accounted for twenty more. Specially developed "hydrophone" listening devices allowed surface warships to locate and depth-charge U-boats, or track them until the drain on their batteries forced the submarines to the surface, when they could be rammed or sunk by gunfire. The most successful antisubmarine weapon of all was the mine, and protective screens in the North Sea and English Channel accounted for the loss of forty-eight U-boats. *AK*

Antwerp, Battle of

Following the German invasion of Belgium, the six divisions of the Belgian Field Army had fallen back upon the fortified city of Antwerp, forming a redoubt to the rear of the main German advance. After September 27, following the halt of actions along the Aisne, the newly appointed German chief of staff, Erich von Falkenhayn, was determined to make a drive for the Channel ports, after reducing the fortress of Antwerp. From September 28 the forts surrounding the city were pounded with artillery and, although the British Royal Naval Division was landed on October 4, the Germans broke through into the ring of forts on October 5. The fortress was surrendered on October 5, with the British and Belgian defenders retreating westward. *MC*

ANZAC at Gallipoli

The Australian and New Zealand Army Corps (ANZAC) played a leading role in the Allied attempt to capture the Gallipoli Peninsula from the Turks as a prelude to an advance on their capital, Constantinople, in 1915–16. The

Right: Making bombs from tin cans—filled with nails, shrapnel, barbed wire, and an explosive charge they made a frightening concoction; Gallipoli, Battle of Krithia, June 4, 1916.
Chrysalis Photo Library

Above: Anzac Cove, Gallipoli.
Chrysalis Photo Library

Right: Representatives of the tribes coming in under cover of white flag to swear allegiance to Sheikh Feisal, Aqaba. *Chrysalis Photo Library*

"ANZACs," as its members were known, were involved from April 25, 1915, the opening day of the bitterly contested and ultimately unsuccessful campaign, establishing a narrow beach-head on the north coast of Gallipoli at what became known as Anzac Cove. Their commander was Britain's General William Birdwood. Over the following weeks, the greatly outnumbered ANZACs fought off a number of Turkish attacks designed to evict them from their positions among difficult mountainous terrain. By late May both sides had dug in, often no more than a few yards apart, and vicious trench warfare ensued. However, Birdwood received a number of reinforcements, not all ANZACs, and was ordered to support a British amphibious assault to the north at Suvla Bay in early August by breaking out of his beach-head to link up with the

WORLD WAR I: A VISUAL ENCYCLOPEDIA

landing force. The attack toward Sari Bair Ridge, which was supported by a diversionary advance on Lone Pine to the south of Anzac Cove, opened on the 6th. The fighting lasted for several days, but despite some successes, the breakout failed, although the Suvla and Anzac Cove positions were eventually united. Stalemate again returned to Anzac Cove, although the fighting was punctuated by frequent raids and occasionally larger actions, including the successful but costly attempt to storm Hill 60 in late August. Nevertheless, it became apparent that the Gallipoli operation was failing and the decision to evacuate was taken in early December. Anzac Cove was abandoned with great skill between the 10th and 19th. *IW*

Arab Revolt

Arab desires to achieve independence from Turkey centered on Feisal Ibn Hussein, third son of Hussein Ibn Ali, who controlled much of the Red Sea coast of Arabia. The British agreed to support the Arabs and began shipping arms to the independence movement in early 1916. The revolt began on June 5 and, despite failing to capture Medina, the Arabs occupied Mecca and Jeddah within a few days. Over the following weeks, the Arab Army emerged, consisting of three main forces each commanded by one of Ali's sons, totaling around 25,000 men. British assistance to the Arabs increased over the following months, not least with the arrival of Lawrence of Arabia, who became a close and respected adviser to Feisal. By the spring of 1917, Arab guerrilla attacks had spread northward in a move to support the British advance through Palestine. The chief strike force was Feisal's Northern Army, which in July captured the port of Aqaba, and then began guerrilla attacks on the Hejaz railroad. As British pressure in southern Palestine increased, the Northern Army operated along its inland flank to draw Turkish troops away from the coastal region. Turkish resistance began to crumble throughout 1918, allowing the Arabs to occupy Damascus and take part in the occupation of Aleppo in the final days of the war. However, British and French support for an independent Arab homeland, which had always remained ambiguous, was not forthcoming and the nationalists' aspirations remained unsatisfied. *IW*

Armies, Organization of

Meticulous military organization was vital to mobilization, transition of orders, movement, and success in battle. Higher formations were designed to combine all the major elements, including headquarters, communications, infantry, cavalry, artillery, supply, and engineers, producing a balanced and flexible force for varied tasks. The biggest commands were army groups, individual armies being comprised of corps. Corps were made up of divisions—usually the smallest formations to have all the supporting arms in their composition. Divisions contained brigades, and brigades were made up of regiments and battalions. Individual infantry battalions were composed of companies. Each company was made of platoons, and platoons of sections. In the artillery, brigades, and regiments were split into batteries of guns; the cavalry regiments into squadrons and troops. In the British Army of 1914 corps commanders were lieutenant generals. The divisions were usually commanded by major generals, with a headquarters that included staff officers, assistant directors for quartermaster, medical, ordnance, and veterinary services. The division included three brigades each of infantry and field artillery (total fifty-four guns); a howitzer brigade (total eighteen howitzers); ammunition columns; divisional train;

Below: British troops marching along a military road near Metz, March 8, 1918. They were probably singing "Tipperary" or one of the other marching songs of the time.
Chrysalis Photo Library

three field ambulances; two field companies of engineers with headquarters; a signal company and a cavalry squadron. The three infantry brigades of the division were commanded by brigadier generals with a much smaller headquarters, and each brigade had four infantry battalions. Each infantry battalion, under a lieutenant colonel, had a fighting strength of thirty officers and 977 men with additional for the MG company and headquarters. Other armies were essentially similar, but there were myriad variations of detail. German infantry divisions were of twelve or thirteen battalions, while two regiments totaling six battalions made up each brigade. French divisions were likewise of twelve battalions in two brigades. Russian

Above: Scottish ration party in the ruins of Beaucourt, May 26, 1917. *Chrysalis Photo Library*

Right: Men collecting in Poperinghe to go on leave (they are waving their leave papers), September 30, 1917. *Chrysalis Photo Library*

Far Right, Top: Woodcoate Park, Epsom, 1918. *Chrysalis Photo Library*

Far Right, Bottom: Hay and petrol being placed among the boxes of stores at West Beach, Sulva Point, to be burnt on evacuation; December 1915. *Chrysalis Photo Library*

divisions had sixteen battalions, organized in two brigades, while the Turks had ten-battalion divisions organized in three regiments. Armies were rapidly expanded. At the same time there was economization on infantry with increased numbers of specialist troops and support services. On the suggestion of von Wrisberg of the Prussian War Ministry, in 1915 the Germans began to reduce their divisions to nine infantry battalions organized in one brigade. British divisions were later reduced to three brigades totaling nine battalions, plus a pioneer battalion. Machine Gun Corps' companies and trench mortar batteries were added to each brigade, while many additional units of heavy artillery and tank battalions were formed. *SB*

Above: Stacks of stores at Rouen, January 15; the logistics involved in keeping so many troops in the trenches were immense. This sort of open-air storage of materiel would become impossible once bombing from the air became more accurate and more regular. *Chrysalis Photo Library*

Left: Army camp in Mesopotamia, with slit trenches dug. *Chrysalis Photo Library*

Armistice

Agreement setting out the terms imposed on the defeated Central Powers pending a final peace treaty. Germany signed the Armistice on November 11, 1919, agreeing to severe conditions that included:

- the evacuation of all occupied territories
- demilitarization of the west bank of the Rhine and three areas on the east bank around Mainz, Koblenz, and Köln.
- surrender of equipment including 5,000 cannon and 2,000 aircraft.
- internment of all submarines and most ships.
- repudiation of the treaties of Brest-Litovsk and Bucharest.
- return of Allied prisoners of war.
- acceptance of the continuation of the Allied naval blockade. *DC*

Opposite, Top: Men of U.S. 64th Regiment, 7th Infantry Division, celebrate the news of the Armistice, November 11, 1918. *National Archives via Chrysalis Photo Library*

Opposite, Bottom: More Armistice celebrations, this time north of Verdun. *National Archives via Chrysalis Photo Library*

Above: President Wilson reading the Armistice terms to Congress in Washington, November 1918. *Chrysalis Photo Library*

Left: British and French military representatives outside the railway carriage in which the Armistice was signed. *Chrysalis Photo Library*

Armored cars

Development of the armored car began in 1896, and it was soon recognized as a useful reconnaissance vehicle and weapons platform. Early models included the Austrian Daimler of 1904, the German Erhardt of 1906, and the French Hotchkiss of 1909. One of the best was the Rolls-Royce of 1914 which was based on a Silver Ghost chassis, weighed 3.5 tons, and mounted a machine gun in a revolving turret. Even so very few armored cars were in the hands of the troops at the outbreak of war. British cavalry units actually purchased a few armored cars privately, while Belgian officers modified touring cars. A Royal Naval Armored Car Division was formed in late 1914, and by 1915 it had squadrons serving in France. Unfortunately poor cross-country performance and trenches would prevent the armored car reaching its full potential on the Western Front until the resumption of open warfare in 1918. More was achieved in Southwest Africa, where a Rolls-Royce squadron was sent in 1915, and in East Africa, where Lanchesters and Leyland lorries were deployed. Perhaps most famously, British armored cars were also operated in North Africa and Palestine—in the latter by Colonel T. E. Lawrence against the Arabs. *SB*

Above: Belgian armored car in 1914; open-topped it has a 37mm armament.
Collection of George Forty

Right: British armored cars during the Battle of Arras, April 1917. *Chrysalis Photo Library*

Arras (1914), First Battle of

Part of the series of encounters known as the "Race to the Sea," the Battle of Arras was planned by Joffre to outflank the German forces by advancing along a line between Arras and Lens. The attack began on October 1 once sufficient troops had been collected to form Maud'huy's new Tenth Army. Tenth Army made good initial progress but Crown Prince Rupprecht's German Sixth Army was thrown into the line, having been transferred north from Lorraine. These extra numbers blunted the attack and the French were obliged to withdraw. The following day the German counterattacked with IV Corps (First Army), Guard Corps (Second Army), and I Bavaria Reserve Corps (Seventh Army). The French were badly battered but managed to hold onto their positions around Arras, though Lens was lost to the Germans on October 4. At this point the line began to stabilize and operations moved further northward toward Flanders and the Ypres salient. *MC*

Arras (1917), Second Battle of

In December 1916 Robert Nivelle replaced Joseph Joffre as commander-in-chief of Allied forces on the Western Front. Nivelle immediately began to plan a major offensive on the German front line, primarily by the French armies under his command, but an important aspect of his offensive was a British attack on the German lines around Arras prior to the main French drive. On April 9 General Edmund Allenby and the British Third Army attacked on both sides of Arras and the Scarpe, and achieved considerable gains north of the river on the first day, mainly through the use of gas. However, progress was much slower south of the river. In an attempt to keep the momentum of the attack going and to stretch the German defenders, General Hubert Gough and the British Fifth Army launched an attack further south. This was repulsed around Bullecourt with the 4th Australian Division suffering particularly heavy casualties. On April 14 the attack was halted to await news of the French Aisne Offensive. When it was realized that this was a failure, the British were ordered to attack again. However, they made limited gains and the offensive was finally halted at the end of May. *MC*

Below: Wiring party crossing a railroad line between Arras and Feuchy, May 1917.
Chrysalis Photo Library

Right: British 12th Division artillery officers observe fire from a forward observation post during the Second Battle of Arras, April 1917.
Chrysalis Photo Library

Below Right: A flurry of activity during the Second Battle of Arras: a tank and infantry pass British eighteen-pounders next to the corrugated-iron roof of an abandoned communication trench.
Chrysalis Photo Library

Artillery

Artillery was easily the greatest killer of the war. German statistics suggest that artillery caused half of wounds in the early part of the war, rising to more than three-quarters toward the end. Detailed British figures for the month of January 1916 similarly show "artillery and trench mortars" as the cause of sixty-three percent of severe wounds and sixty-eight percent of slight wounds. This was—at least in part—because long periods of stalemate gave artillery a static target, but also because artillery technology and tactics had advanced so far. Significant advances in technology in the years prior to 1914 included hydraulic buffers to absorb recoil, fixed charge shells—where the propellant and shell formed a single unit—and quick-acting breech mechanisms which could be thrown open with a single movement. The gun that set the pace was the 75mm French Model 1897 field gun, whose development was pushed through by General Deloye. This had a range of 22,500ft, was towed into action by a team of six horses, and for short periods could fire a round every four seconds. They were organized into four-gun batteries. About 17,000 had been made by the end of the war, and many were supplied to other Allies including America. Though quick-firing field guns were in the numerical majority, and along with light howitzers supplied the field artillery of the armies, other types of artillery were deployed in other ways. Heavier guns were organized into heavy or siege units, known in the German Army as the "foot" artillery. In the British Army only small numbers of sixty-pounders, and five-inch and six-inch howitzers were available in the first few months of the war. The German "foot" artillery had an early lead, having

Above Right: British Gun Carrier Mk. I: when not carrying guns they could carry ten tons of ammunition (some 200 six-inch shells). *Collection of George Forty*

Right: Mud was always a problem on the World War I battlefields. Here men haul an eighteen-pounder during the Flanders Offensive, August 9, 1917. *Chrysalis Photo Library*

Far Right, Top: Twelve-inch howitzer firing near Louez, May 19, 1918. *Chrysalis Photo Library*

Far Right, Bottom: Serbian heavy battery in action against the Austrians in the Balkans. *Chrysalis Photo Library*

forty-eight battalions of heavy guns by 1913. The best German equipment of the period were the 15cm howitzer and 21cm mortar, though many other types were used as the war progressed. The range of the 21cm was about five miles. Particularly noteworthy heavy pieces also included the French 155mm Model 1917, which was the first large-caliber gun to feature a modern split trail, and the British 9.2-inch, twelve-inch, and fifteen-inch howitzers. Railway mountings offered mobility to some of the most unwieldy pieces, including British fourteen-inch guns. It was the fourteen-inch railway gun *Boche-buster* which, in the presence of King George V, fired a first-shot direct-hit on Douai railway station at a range of eighteen miles. Yet the most extraordinary guns of the war were the German Paris guns or *Wilhelmgeschütze*. Consisting of converted giant 38cm *Long Max* naval guns, these were ultimately capable of a range of seventy miles, and rained over 300 shells on Paris in 1918. Coast defense artillery saw relatively little action though the guns of Hartlepool engaged German ships during the raid on the east coast of England in December 1914. The

Opposite, Top: Railroad mountings offered mobility to some of the most unwieldy pieces, including British fourteen-inch guns and the German giant 38cm *Wilhelmgeschütze*.
Chrysalis Photo Library

Opposite, Bottom: The British 39th Siege Battery with eight-inch howitzers, during the Battle of the Somme, August 1916.
Chrysalis Photo Library

Above: British twelve-inch gun on a railroad mounting near Meaulte, August 1916.
Chrysalis Photo Library

Left: British six-inch Mk. VII gun in action near Feuchy, June 5, 1917. *Chrysalis Photo Library*

battlecruiser *Blücher* was slightly damaged. The Germans redeployed some naval and coastal artillery to add weight to the Western Front. Though guns and shells advanced considerably it was artillery tactics that saw the most dramatic development. Improved communications, sound and flash location, and predicted fire made longer-range bombardments practical. Fire plans were related more closely to infantry movement, and fire was made briefer, more intense, and more intelligent. *SB*

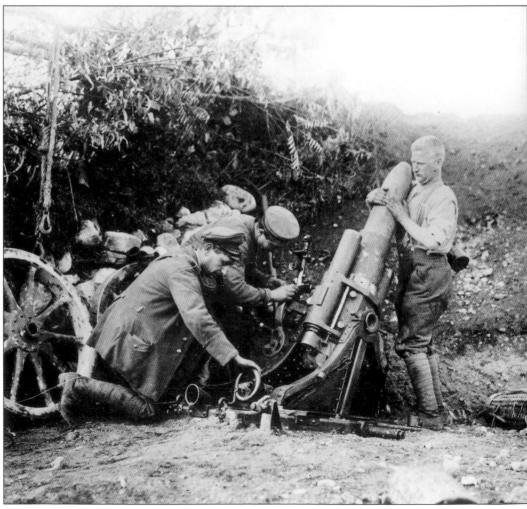

Opposite, Above: German field artillery being manhandled into firing positions. Note the basket of carrier pigeons on the gun's trail. *Chrysalis Photo Library*

Opposite, Below: Oxen towing a German artillery piece in 1914. *Chrysalis Photo Library*

Above: Unusual view of a British tank hauling artillery. *Chrysalis Photo Library*

Right: A German heavy 25cm *Minenwerfer* being loaded. *Chrysalis Photo Library*

Artois Offensive (1915)

Despite the reverses of the early part of the year, Joffre was determined to attempt to break the German lines in 1915. Once the French reserves had started to arrive from the colonies and the first British New Army divisions began to take their place in the front line, he was sure that he now had the forces to hand to attempt a major offensive. The ground chosen was the area around Artois. The plan called for an attack by the French Tenth Army under D'Urbal against the formidable obstacle of Vimy Ridge, while Haig's British First Army attacked the north of the Vimy salient around Loos. Further south there were to be additional attacks by Langle de Cary's Fourth Army and Pétain's Second Army in the Champagne district. The attacks began on September 25, and the French Tenth Army initially made some progress, with one division managing to reach the crest of Vimy Ridge on September 29. However, the German Sixth Army under Rupprecht counter-attacked, denying the French possession of the high ground. The British attack met with a similar fate: initially gains were good and by the end of the first day British troops were on the outskirts of Lens. However, strong German counter-attacks forced the British back. Their position was not helped by a shortage of shells, which was to become a national scandal, or by Sir John French holding the reserves too far from the front line, ensuring that none of the breakthroughs could be adequately exploited. *MC*

Asiago Offensive (1916)

The Asiago, or Trentino, Offensive in 1916 was Austria-Hungary's first major attack on the Italian Front during the war. Chief of staff Field Marshal Franz Conrad von Hötzendorf planned to launch two armies, the Eleventh and Third, southward through the Trentino region on the northern sector of the front. This drive aimed at cutting off the bulk of the Italian Army, which was fighting along the line of the Isonzo River far to the east. The Austro-Hungarians enjoyed a four-to-one superiority in troops and a significant advantage in artillery and, when the offensive began on May 14, the assault units made rapid progress against the Italian First Army. By the 29th, the Italians had retreated some ten miles (16km), and had abandoned the town of Asiago after heavy fighting. However, the Italian chief of staff, General Luigi Cadorna, made good use of his country's rail network to rush 400,000 reinforcements to the Trentino. These troops, coupled with the supply difficulties through mountainous terrain faced by the Austro-Hungarians, who also had to send troops from the Trentino to the Eastern Front to block Russia's Brusilov Offensive, allowed the Italians to recapture most of the lost ground by July 1. Both sides suffered around 150,000 casualties but, more importantly, the Austro-Hungarian failure highlighted the empire's growing military weakness. Henceforth, German troops provided the backbone for the two Central Powers' offensive and defensive operations. *IW*

Asquith, Herbert Henry (1852–1928)

Asquith was a lawyer and, from 1886 until 1918, a Liberal Member of Parliament representing East Fife, Scotland. He served under Gladstone and Rosebery as Home Secretary between 1892 and 1895, but fell out of favor with the Liberal Party through his support of the Boer War. Following the Liberal Party's return to power in 1905 and great election victory of 1906, he became Chancellor of the Exchequer, and in 1908 succeeded Campbell-Bannerman as Prime Minister. His tenure of office was marked by a number of crises. Some were constitutional—it was in response to the budget of 1909 that the 1911 Parliament Act was passed which constrained the powers of the unelected House of Lords—and others political, particularly in relations with Ireland (where Home Rule was proposed in 1913–14). He was British Prime Minister at the outbreak of war in August 1914, and in May of the following year headed the new coalition government, but he was to be ousted in December 1916 by Lloyd George. He lost his parliamentary seat in 1918, but was returned as MP for Paisley in 1920 and again served as Liberal leader between 1923 and 1926. He was created the first Earl of Oxford and Asquith in 1925. *MS*

Australian Army

Although Australia was part of the British Empire, it had enjoyed a degree of political independence since being granted self-governing dominion status in 1901. Despite this semi-independence, the country's ties with Britain remained strong, and there was almost unanimous agreement among its main political parties to offer military assistance in August 1914. However, the country's regular army was insignificant and a large part of the state's defense rested with its part-time volunteer militia, some 45,000 men aged between nineteen and twenty-one. There had been some recent attempts to upgrade Australia's armed forces in the recent past. In 1903–04, for example, an act permitted the call-up of all men aged from eighteen to sixty in wartime, but only for service within the Commonwealth, while the 1909 Defense Act laid the groundwork for universal training. Nevertheless, on August 3, 1914, 20,000 men, later known as the Australian Imperial Force, were made available for overseas service. This was to be an entirely new force and not based on the militia, which was considered too youthful. Popular support for Britain and an intense recruitment campaign led to a large influx of volunteers, and the first troops for service overseas sailed on November 7. The flow of recruits dropped somewhat from 1915, but conscription was never introduced as the rate of volunteering remained more than adequate. This is reflected by the figures. In 1914 Australia had a population of just five million, yet some 320,000 eventually saw service. Australia's forces were ultimately split between five divisions, which in turn were for much of the war part of the two Australian and New Zealand Army Corps (ANZAC). In 1917 the bulk of the Australian units were redesignated the Australian Corps. Overseas service began with a training period in Egypt and some commitment to the defense of the Suez Canal against the Turks. Large-scale Australian involvement in the war really started with the Gallipoli campaign during 1915–16, in which the troops under British General William Birdwood were praised for their fighting skills, if not for

Above Right: Australian troops at Anzac Cove, December 17, 1915. *Chrysalis Photo Library*

Right: The camp and horse lines of "A" Squadron of the 9th Australian Light Horse near Jericho, August 17, 1918. *Chrysalis Photo Library*

their lack of adherence to military regulations and behavior. The horrors of Gallipoli became seared on Australia's national consciousness. After the campaign the bulk of the Australian forces saw service on the Western Front, where they gained a reputation among both Allied and German commanders as elite troops. Consequently, they played a leading role in many of the Allied offensives, especially in 1918. At the forefront of British attacks during the later stages of the war, they won fame for the victory at the Battle of Le Hamel in July, where the Australian Corps was led by one of its own countrymen, General John Monash. Aside from the Western Front, Australian units were deployed to Palestine in 1917–18, where mounted units spearheaded several successful attacks against the Turks. Australia's key role in Britain's war effort can best be summarized by the scale of its losses. Of the 320,000 men who served, some 280,000 became casualties, including 60,000 dead. This rate of casualties was more than eighty percent, a figure unrivaled by any other combatant nation during the whole war. *IW*

Above: Men of 1st Anzac Corps moving in single file over a duckboard track, Ypres, October 12, 1917. *Chrysalis Photo Library*

Left: Men of the 13th Australian Field Ambulance wearing respirators, near Anzac Ridge, Ypres, September 30, 1917. *Chrysalis Photo Library*

Above Right and Right: Australia also provided air forces during the conflict—the Australian Flying Corps (founded in 1914). Here, 69th Australian Squadron aircraft starts off on a night-time raid on October 22, 1917; note machine gun at side of pilot that fired through the propeller using an interruptor gear (see page 203). *Chrysalis Photo Library*

Austro-Hungarian air forces and aircraft

Aligned with the Central Powers, the air arm of the Austro-Hungarian Empire entered combat later than other nations, in spite of declaring war on the Allies in August 1914. The Aviatik works had, however, developed the BI reconnaissance biplane in time for it to be deployed by Germany from the outbreak of hostilities. One reason for Austria's delayed entry into combat was that production of the Aviatik BII proved a lengthy process and it was German pilots that were invariably at the controls of these aircraft encountered in combat. Austria's aero industry produced various designs which flew in German national markings, among them some of the first C category two-seat armed reconnaissance aircraft. The Lloyd CII, a product of the Ungarische Lloyd Flugzeug und Motorenfabrik AG, appeared in 1915, with the Hansa-Brandenburg CI following in 1916. Jakob Lohner AG built the Lohner CI for service that year, with the UFAG CI (Ungarische) and Phoenix CI both remaining in service until the Armistice. Hansa-Brandenburg was probably best known for its distinctive seaplanes, including the biplane W12 and monoplane W29. It was not until 1917 that an Austrian pilot gained the country's first defensive victory when on May 31, Linienschiffleutnant G. Banfield forced down an Italian seaplane whilst flying a Pfalz. *JS*

Austro-Hungarian Army

The Austro-Hungarian Empire's ground forces at the outbreak of war comprised three distinct elements. These were the Common Army, which was made up of recruits from both Austria and Hungary and was originally intended to be deployed outside the empire's frontiers in time of conflict. Supporting this were two other forces that were originally created for the home defense of Austria and Hungary respectively. These were termed the Imperial Royal Landwehr in the case of Austria and the Royal Hungarian Landwehr for the other component of the Dual Monarchy. From the 1890s, however, it was recognized that the Landwehr forces should be upgraded to bolster the empire's war-fighting capabilities. The training of the Landwehr was improved, thereby making them of roughly equal quality to the Common Army, while new home-defense forces, the Austrian and Hungarian *Landsturm*, were created. Following these reforms the peacetime army's strength stood at 325,000 men while the Austrian and Hungarian Landwehr forces totaled some 70,000 men. In 1914, these were divided between forty-nine infantry and eleven cavalry divisions that made up six armies. Officially, overall command of the army rested with the emperor but its chief of staff effectively set military policy. On full mobilization, the total number of troops that the empire could put into the field was 2.25 million men, a comparatively small figure in relation to a population of close to 51.5 million. Recruits to the army were drawn from throughout the empire's various nationalities, although many individuals were exempt for family or occupational reasons. Some thirty percent of the army was of German origin, while another fifty percent were of Slavic origin. However, eighty percent of all officers were German-speakers. The multinational nature of the empire's army was to have profound consequences on its ability to fight as the war progressed, with many of the non-German nationalities viewing the empire as their oppressor. Many became increasingly reluctant to fight in defense of the empire, and rates of surrender (and desertion) were higher in the Austro-Hungarian Army than any other combatant nation during World War I. Once war had been declared, it rapidly became apparent that there were major weakness in the Austro-Hungarian Army. At the top there was friction between the political leaders of Austria and Hungary. Indeed, the Hungarians had stalled Austrian attempts to modernize the armed forces before the conflict, fearing that the latter would come to dominate the empire even more than they already did. Although much of the army's basic equipment was of reasonably modern design, there was a less than adequate provision of some key weapons, notably machine guns, that was never fully rectified. Equally, much of the artillery was

Above: Austrian machine-gun position in the Alps. *Chrysalis Photo Library*

Below Left: A quiet moment in an Austrian trench. *Chrysalis Photo Library*

Below: Austrian troops in a dugout on the Italian Front. *Chrysalis Photo Library*

levels, bad planning, indecision among the high command, and acute shortages of all types of supplies. *IW*

Austro-Hungarian Navy

The Austro-Hungarian fleet was a small force designed for the coastal defense of her relatively small shoreline on the Adriatic Sea. As such, naval operations played a relatively insignificant part in Austrian planning, and their role was limited to the struggle for control of the Adriatic. Faced with a virtually overwhelming preponderance of Allied ships in the Mediterranean in 1914, the Austrians decided to avoid a major clash, which could denude them of naval protection altogether. When the war began the fleet was based at Pola, but it maintained a secondary base at Trieste, and maintained a fleet of river monitors which operated on the River Danube. The pride of the fleet were four dreadnoughts (the "*Viribus Unitis*" class), all of which entered service by 1915, and these powerful units were supported by twelve predreadnought battleships of varying quality, supported by a squadron of cruisers and lighter vessels. Apart from occasional raids against the Italian coastline, or to harass the evacuation of the Serbian army from Albania or to attack the Otranto barrage, offensive operations were limited to the Austrian U-boat fleet, whose twenty-seven boats proved successful in operations in both the Adriatic and the Mediterranean Sea. *AK*

Averescu, General Alexandru
(1859–1938)

The Romanian commander and politician Alexandru Averescu served in the Second Balkan War, and when Romania entered the war in August 1916, became commander of the Third Army in the south of the country, where he led his forces in the unsuccessful attack at Flamanda in September 1916. He then took command in Wallachia, where he planned the unsuccessful River Arges Offensive. He was, however, more successful in his defense at Foscani in August 1917 and, in February 1918, was appointed Romanian Prime Minister for a month. Failure to negotiate a separate peace with Germany led to his dismissal, but he was again to serve twice as Prime Minister of postwar Romania before his death. *MS*

somewhat outdated, although the 305mm howitzer nicknamed *Schlanke Emma* (Skinny Emma) was a potent weapon. In general the Austro-Hungarian Army performed badly during the war, partly for the reasons already outlined, and was increasingly forced to call on Germany for direct military support. Aside from ethnic tensions and equipment difficulties, it was frequently hamstrung by poor leaderships at all

B

Baker, Newton Diehl (1871–1937)

The U.S. Secretary of War during World War I, Newton Baker was born in Martinsburg, West Virginia, and practiced law in Cleveland. He entered politics and served as city solicitor from 1902 to 1912. Elected mayor in 1912, he instituted tax reforms. Though he was an avowed pacifist, Woodrow Wilson picked him as Secretary of War in 1916 to succeed Lindley Garrison, who had served in the job in Wilson's first term. Because of his antiwar position, Baker's management of the War Department was seen initially as being inadequate and he was widely criticized. Ultimately, however, he was credited with having been a good manager. At the end of World War I, he supported Wilson's call for a League of Nations and he continued to urge United States entry into the league even after he and Wilson left office in 1921. After leaving office, Baker returned to private law practice, but in 1928, President Coolidge appointed him to the Permanent Court of Arbitration in the Hague. *BY*

Baku, Taking of

Baku, an important center of oil production on the Caspian Sea, became a focus of German and Turkish operations in the second half of 1918. By late August the town was being defended by a garrison of Russian troops drawn from Persia, local nationalists, and Britain's Dunsterforce, a mixed unit named after its commander, General L. C. Dunsterville, which had also been operating to protect Persia's oilfields. The defense of Baku proved impossible in the face of 14,000 Turkish troops, and Dunsterforce abandoned the town on September 14. Following the armistice with Turkey, the British retook Baku on November 17. *IW*

Balfour, Arthur James (1848–1930)

Balfour was one of the leading Conservative politicians of his generation. From a political family—his uncle Lord Salisbury was also Prime Minister—Balfour's first entered parliament in 1874 and his first political offices were those of Secretary for Scotland in 1886 and Chief Secretary of Ireland between 1887 and 1892. His policies of suppression in the latter were to earn him the nickname "Bloody Balfour." He became Prime Minister in

1902, but was to lose office at the 1906 election. In 1911, as a result of the constitutional crisis caused by the Parliament Act of that year, he had lost the party leadership in favor of Bonar Law, but was to achieve high office again during the coalition government, becoming First Lord of the Admiralty in 1915 and Foreign Secretary from 1916 until 1919. In that role he led a mission to the United States in 1917 and was British signatory to the Treaty of Versailles in 1919. In 1921 he headed the British delegation to the Washington Conference. The following year he was created an earl. *MS*

Balfour Declaration

An official proclamation of British Government support for the establishment of a Jewish state in Israel, the Balfour Declaration was intended to boost Jewish support for Allied war aims, particularly in the then neutral United States. In the longer term it was also hoped that British influence over the strategically vital region of Palestine might be enhanced. Prepared in March 1916 and published in November 1917, the Balfour Declaration expressed the British government's approval of Zionism with "the establishment in Palestine of a national home for the Jewish people" and committed them to use "best endeavors to facilitate the achievement of this object." *DC*

Balkans, War in the

The incident that sparked World War I, the assassination of the heir to the Austro-Hungarian throne in Sarajevo on June 28, 1914, grew out of the Balkan rivalries between the empire and Serbia, and the first fighting of the conflict took place in the region. Following a bombardment of Belgrade by gunboats on the Danube River on July 29, the Austro-Hungarians launched a series of offensives against Serbia, lasting from September to December. Despite their numerical superiority, the Austro-Hungarians were comprehensively beaten, despite occupying Belgrade for a brief period in December, and their commander, General Oskar Potiorek, was replaced by Archduke Eugene on the 22nd. The Balkan theater remained quiet for much of 1915, chiefly due to Austro-Hungarian and German commitments on the Eastern Front, but a new, multi-

Bulgaria, but links with the other Central Power, Turkey, remained blocked as another Balkan power, Romania, had closed its frontiers to Germany in June 1915. The opportunity to reopen this corridor came with Romania's ill-judged declaration of war in support of the Allies in August. Retribution was swift, with Austro-Hungarian, Bulgarian, and German forces overrunning the greater part of the country by December. Thus by the end of 1916, the Central Powers controlled most of the Balkans, with the a multinational Allied force being penned up in Salonika, and Italian troops holding southern parts of Albania. For much of 1917 the Balkan Front remained inactive, with the Allies holding a line than ran through Salonika and southern Albania. Small-scale offensives achieved little due to a number of factors,

including the ambiguous position of Greece (a situation that was only resolved with the country's declaration of war against the Central Powers in late June), infighting between the local British and French senior commanders, Allied commitments on the Western Front and elsewhere, and rampant disease that undermined their troops' strength in the Balkans. By the spring of 1918, many of these issues had been resolved to some extent, but the Allies delayed launching an all-out offensive until mid-September, by which time the Central Powers' forces in the Balkans were short of supplies and demoralized. Their collapse was rapid but the progress of the Allied force was slowed due to their own lack of resources, but the greater part of the Balkans had been captured by the Allies at the end of the war. *IW*

pronged offensive against Serbia was launched in October. Assailed by Austro-Hungarian and German forces to the north and two Bulgarian armies from the east, the Serbian Army was forced out of the greater part of its homeland. In January 1916 it was evacuated by Allied ships to Corfu and then Salonika, which had been occupied by Allied forces the previous October, despite the fluctuating and lukewarm agreement of the Greek authorities. Both Serbia and Montenegro were occupied by the Central Powers, along with the northern and central regions of neighboring Albania, for much of the remainder of the conflict, although they had to face local guerrilla forces in a campaign that was marked by numerous atrocities. The capture of Serbia had eased communications between German, Austria-Hungary, and

Top: Rear Admiral Ernest Troubridge inspects a British gun emplacement on the Danube, summer 1915. *Chrysalis Photo Library*

Above: Eighteen-pounder in action on the Struma Front, Bulgaria, November 1916. *Chrysalis Photo Library*

Left: Austrian supply convoy. *Chrysalis Photo Library*

Balloons

The advantages of small, helium-filled balloons for battlefield observation were fully recognized by 1914 and all combatants used them extensively. Classed as lighter-than-air vehicles, balloons had a suspended basket carrying one or two observers primarily to spot for their own artillery and to observe enemy dispositions. Having the advantage of being completely silent, balloon observers made hundreds of flights quite safely, although they became legitimate targets for enemy guns and airplanes. The courageous observers took to wearing parachutes to give them a slim chance of survival if enemy fighters shot down their balloon. *JS*

Right: A Caquot kite balloon being hauled down near Fricourt. Note observer in basket and trench lines at left. *Chrysalis Photo Library*

Below: Close-up of a Caquot kite balloon near Ypres, October 5, 1917. *Chrysalis Photo Library*

Baltic Sea, Operations in the

Given the limited size of the Russian Baltic Fleet, the German Navy had little need of a powerful fleet in the Baltic Sea, and both sides made extensive use of mines to protect their main ports (Libau, Riga, and Reval for the Russians, and Kiel and Lübeck for the Germans). The German cruiser *Friedrich Karl* was sunk when she struck a Russian mine in November 1918, off the southern tip of Sweden, but for the most part it was the Germans who relied on offensive minelaying as a strategic tool. The Russian cruiser *Minin* was mined in August 1915, a loss which alarmed the Russians and made them hesitant to launch aggressive sorties. In October 1917, a German amphibious assault on the islands off the Gulf of Riga sealed off Riga, while Russian mutinies curtailed any further Russian operations. British submarines penetrated the Baltic in 1914, and based on Dagö Island off the Gulf of Riga, they attacked German cargo vessels transporting vital iron ore from Luleå in the Gulf of Bothnia to Germany. Other successes included the disabling of the battlecruiser *Moltke* in August 1915, and the sinking of the cruiser *Udine*. *AK*

Baracca, Francesco (1888–1918)

When the first Spad VIIs in Italy equipped the 91st Squadriglia, the aircraft proved a deadly weapon in Francesco Baracca's capable hands. Having gained his own (and Italy's) first aerial victory flying a Nieuport 11 on April 7, 1916, Baraccu set out to form his unit into a "squadron of aces." By May 13 he had claimed his first kill in the Spad. Not alone in preferring the lightly armed Spad VII to the later SXIII, Baracca continued to use the former to great effect, eventually scoring twenty-nine victories. *JS*

Battlecruisers

While Admiral "Jackie" Fisher's revolutionary *Dreadnought* was being built, the British Admiralty discovered the Japanese were building fast armored cruisers which carried four twelve-inch guns. Fisher decided that the British needed their own fast "super armored cruiser," capable of keeping pace with the *Dreadnought* and her planned successors, but also capable of outrunning or outgunning any existing cruiser afloat. While original designs favored lighter guns, the Admiralty favored their battlecruisers carrying larger weapons. The result was the "Invincible" class of three warships (*Invincible*, *Inflexible*, and *Indomitable*), which Fisher dubbed "battlecruisers." Displacing 20,000 tons and measuring 567ft long, they were

Below: The British battlecruiser *Invincible* in 1912. *Chrysalis Photo Library*

Bottom: The British battlecruiser HMS *Queen Mary* in 1914. *Chrysalis Photo Library*

Left: The German battlecruiser *Derfflinger*. *Chrysalis Photo Library*

armed with eight twelve-inch guns in four turrets, and could attain speeds of twenty-five knots. Their armored belt of four to six inches was sufficient to protect them against the shells of an armored cruiser. They all entered service in 1907, and although they proved invaluable during operations against isolated German units, they lacked the armor to stand against enemy battleships firing a similar-sized shell. When the Germans began building their own battlecruisers (the first was commissioned in 1909, carrying twelve 8.2-inch guns), it became inevitable that battlecruisers would be involved in a major fleet action if it occurred. The first three British battlecruisers were joined by the more powerful "Indefatigable" class (*Indefatigable* and *New Zealand*) in 1909–11, the "Lion" class (*Lion, Princess Royal*, and *Queen Mary*) in 1910–12, and the one-off *Tiger* in 1913. The last four named battlecruisers carried eight 13.5-inch guns. Further battlecruisers were built during the war, but none saw service, at least in their original role. By 1914 the British battlecruisers were grouped together into a powerful force commanded by Vice-Admiral Beatty. Following the launch of the small battlecruiser *Blücher* in 1909, the Germans added the *Von der Tann* in 1910 (carrying eight eleven-inch guns), the "Moltke" class (*Moltke, Goeben*) in 1911–12, and the *Seydlitz* in 1913. During the war the "Derfflinger" class (*Derfflinger, Lützow, Hindenburg*) was added to the fleet. Unlike previous German battlecruisers, they carried eight twelve-inch guns. While British battlecruisers generally carried a more powerful armament, their German counterparts were better armored (matching gun size with armor thickness), and had improved damage-control and fire-control systems, making them more effective in battle. During the Battle of Jutland (1916), the British lost three battlecruisers, and the Germans one. Ultimately, the battlecruiser experiment was a failure, as the ships were too expensive and too vulnerable to risk. *AK*

Battleships

The notion of the "battleship" had its roots in the American Civil War, when the first clash between ironclad warships demonstrated that the future of naval warfare lay in vessels boasting a combination of powerful guns and armored protection. Gradually the notion of the turret-mounted gun became the standard form of naval mount during the late nineteenth century, and broadside mountings were reserved for smaller, secondary guns. During the period the British maintained their naval supremacy in numbers over rival navies, particularly the French, and the Naval Defence Act of 1889 ensured the addition of eight modern first-class battleships to the fleet. By 1894, the Royal Navy consisted of twenty-six first-class battleships, and over sixty cruisers. During the same period the U.S. Navy underwent a rapid growth, and launched a series of powerful battleships, as did Japan, Russia, Germany, and several other smaller maritime countries. In Britain, naval designer William White produced a series of four battleship classes ("Majestic," "Canopus," "Formidable," and "Duncan"), and these twenty-nine ships entered service between 1895 and 1902, ensuring Britain's preeminence as a naval power. Like most of the battleships in other fleets, they carried a main armament of four twelve-inch guns, mounted in two turrets, one forward, the other aft. Secondary six-inch guns and tertiary twelve-pounders provided extra firepower at close range. These vessels were similar to the American battleships which saw action at the Battle of Santiago (1898), or the Japanese and the more modern Russian battleships which took part in the Battle of the Yellow Sea (1904) and the Battle of Tsushima (1905). Although powerful, the *Dreadnought* would render these powerful warships obsolete. Designed by Admiral "Jackie" Fisher as a "super battleship," the *Dreadnought* carried ten twelve-inch guns and twenty-seven

Below: The British battleship *Canopus* at Mudros. *Chrysalis Photo Library*

BATTLESHIPS

twelve-pounders, and was powered by turbines, giving her a top speed of twenty-one knots. With a displacement of 23,000 tons and an armored protective belt between four and eleven inches thick, she was in a class all of her own. With her improved fire-control systems and suite of powerful homogenous big guns, the *Dreadnought* was the equivalent of four other battleships. Her launch precipitated a worldwide arms race, as navies struggled to replace their existing fleets with dreadnoughts. Similar revolutionary ships were being built in the United States, but they entered service two years after *Dreadnought*. The Royal Navy launched a succession of increasingly more powerful battleships: the "Bellerophon" class (three ships) in 1907, the "St. Vincent" class (three ships) in 1908–09, the *Neptune* in 1909, and the "Colossus" class (two ships) in 1910. The Germans responded with the "Nassau" class (four ships) commissioned in 1909–10, the "Helgoland" class (four ships) in 1911-12, the "Kaiser" class (five ships) in 1912–13, and the "König" class (four ships) in 1914. Apart from the "Nassau" class, all these German ships carried twelve-inch

guns. A later "Bayern" class mounting eight fifteen-inch guns was laid down, but only two entered service during the war. The British augmented their first wave of dreadnoughts with a series of what were dubbed "super dreadnoughts," carrying ten 13.5-inch guns. These, the "Orion" class (four ships, 1910–11), "King George V" class (four ships, 1911–12), and the "Iron Duke" class (four ships, 1912–13), were probably the most powerful vessels afloat when the war began, and were joined soon after by the "Royal Sovereign" class (five ships), commissioned as the war progressed. A final group of five British warships of the "Queen Elizabeth" class were dubbed "fast battleships," as they could steam at twenty-

four knots, three knots faster than most other dreadnoughts. This class also carried eight fifteen-inch guns. Other navies raced to compete with this, and by August 1914 the U.S. Navy had twelve dreadnoughts, the Japanese had one (and four battlecruisers), the French seven, the Italians five, the Austrians two, and the Russians four (although technically they count as battlecruisers), Spain three, Argentina two, and Brazil two. These dreadnought battleships would be the arbiters of naval victory. Although the British and German main battle fleets only clashed once, at the Battle of Jutland (1916), the British superiority in numbers managed to offset any German superiority in armor, damage control, or fire control. Both sides learned lessons

from the engagement, and improvements were made in damage and fire control to the battleships of both sides. The battleship's reason for existence was her ability to engage an enemy at ranges of up to twenty miles with a broadside armament of big guns, usually twelve-inch pieces. A typical dreadnought twelve-inch gun mounted in a twin turret was crewed by thirty-five men, and relied on a complex system of lifts and hydraulics to supply the crew with shells and powder (cordite). World War I was the era where the big gun reigned supreme as a naval weapons system, and victory centered on the accurate firing of these mammoth weapons at an opposing "floating fortress." *AK*

Beatty, David (1871–1936)

Beatty was appointed commander of the Battlecruiser Fleet in 1913, and the dashing officer appeared to be the ideal commander for the force. He fought two successful actions at Heligoland Bight and Dogger Bank before he led his battlecruisers into action at Jutland. Despite having his force mauled, he was acclaimed as a hero. He subsequently rose to command the Grand Fleet, and was promoted to First Sea Lord after the war. He was noted for the rakish angle with which he wore his cap, and his quote at Jutland, that "there's something wrong with our bloody ships." *AK*

Belgian Air Forces

The Belgian Air Force had origins similar to those of the RFC and when the country was partially occupied by the Germans in 1914, Belgian squadrons pulled back into France. Using mainly Maurice Farmans in the early days, the

Belgians operated alongside their French and British allies pending delivery of Voisin biplanes. Reorganized in 1915 as the Aviation Militaire with Nieuport fighters, a Belgian pilot of No. 1 Squadron made the country's first enemy aircraft claim, on April 17, 1915. Flying Sopwith 1½ Strutters, Hanriots, and Spads, Belgian fighter pilots took part in the Flanders campaign, after which new units were formed. Sopwith Camels later equipped the three Belgian fighter squadrons, pilots of which included Le Chavalier Willy Coppens de Houthulst, who scored thirty-six victories. *JS*

Belgian Army

Belgium, one of Europe's smallest major powers, was supposedly a neutral country, one whose security was guaranteed by international agreement. Although this proved mistaken in 1914, the prewar political situation had worked against the expansion and modernization of the Belgian Army, despite the suggestions of the country's ruler, King Albert I. However, the monarch did push through some reforms. In 1912 a reluctant government agreed to limited compulsory service—fifteen months in the infantry —but there were numerous exemptions. In 1913, as these reforms were being introduced, the Belgian Army also began a process of modernizing its training program and equipment, but war intervened before any great progress had been made. In 1914 the country's armed forces comprised three main elements. The regular army, the 3,000-strong horse-mounted Gendarmerie, and the

Garde Civique, the latter a type of home guard numbering on paper some 90,000 men but probably less than half the figure in reality. The fully mobilized regular army consisted of six infantry divisions, each of 22,000 men, a cavalry division of 5,000, and two independent infantry brigades—a total of around 158,000 troops. Many of these were equipped with outdated weapons, and there were major shortages of machine guns and modern artillery. Given the small size of this force and the overwhelming numerical superiority of their potential enemies, the Belgians had created a number of great fortresses along their frontier and around certain key cities to delay an invading force, but these were quickly neutralized by German heavy artillery in 1914. Their capture and the loss of the garrisons, coupled with the mauling the field forces received as they retreated to the line of the Yser River in Flanders, left the army with a total strength of just 32,000 men. Policies were rapidly introduced to effectively rebuild and expand this token force. Almost as soon as most of Belgium had been occupied, the army introduced measures to increase its strength. Many men who had fled the country as refugees volunteered for service, and on March 1, 1915, universal conscription for Belgians aged between eighteen and twenty-five living in the unoccupied part of the country, Britain, and France was introduced. From July 1916 this was extended to include all Belgians aged between eighteen and forty based in any Allied or neutral

Below: Belgian native troops returning to the coast after a German attack, Ndanda, East Africa, January 1918. *Chrysalis Photo Library*

Right: Belleau Woods, France. *National Archives via Chrysalis Photo Library*

Below Right: Men of the AEF's 2nd Battalion, 6th Marines (Major T. C. Holcomb commanding) resting after the Battle of Belleau Wood. *Collection of Bill Yenne*

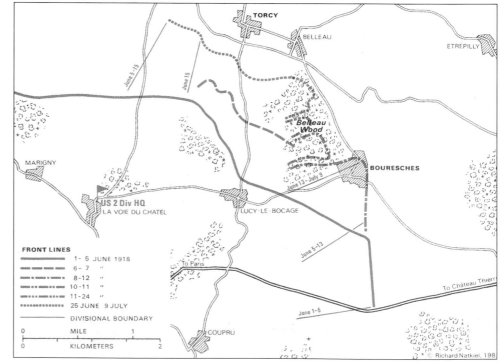

country. With these measures in place, the army gradually reached and maintained a strength of around 170,000 men. Much of their equipment was provided by the British and French. Given its small size the army could only play a limited role on the Western Front. However, joint offensive operations with Belgium's allies were also limited in scope for much of the war, in part because Albert was reluctant to bring down further destruction on his increasingly destitute country. This policy was reversed in 1918, and in the final days of the war Albert was made commander of the largely Belgian Flanders Army Group. Around 270,000 Belgians saw active service between 1914 and 1918—some 14,000 were killed and 43,000 wounded before the armistice. *IW*

Belgian Coast, Liberation of the

The liberation of the Belgian coast formed part of the "Hundred Days" offensives that led to the Armistice of November 11. It began on September 28, 1918, as Allied forces pushed east from their positions at Ypres, and on September 29 Admiral Schröder was advised to consider evacuating the coast. Retreat began on October 15, 1918, as

the Allies moved forward, and the Belgian ports of Ostend, Zeebrugge, and Brugge suffered heavy damages before the Allied advance halted at the Dutch border. King Albert made his state reentry into Bruges on October 25, and his country's coast was finally free. *MC*

Belleau Wood, Battle of

Belleau Wood is memorable as the point at which the Allies began to take the AEF seriously as an effective fighting force,

and the Germans found the U.S. troops to be a force to be reckoned with. It was also the first major battle of World War I in which U.S. troops experienced heavy casualties. It was also a battle in which the U.S. Marine Corps acquitted itself especially well. The Battle of Belleau Wood took place between June 1 and June 26, 1918, on the Aisne-Marne Sector of the Western Front, in a thick forest northwest of the French town of Chateau-Thierry near the Marne River. The involved AEF units—under the

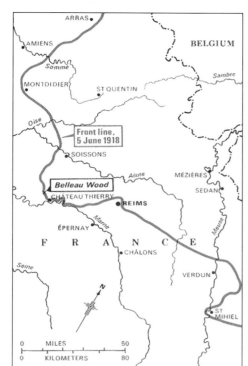

FRONT LINES
- 1- 5 JUNE 1918
- 6 - 7 "
- 8-12 "
- 10-11 "
- 11-24 "
- 25 JUNE 9 JULY
- DIVISIONAL BOUNDARY

© Richard Natkiel, 198

command of the XXI Corps of the French Sixth Army—included elements attached to the 2nd and 3rd Divisions. The former included the 4th (U.S. Marine Corps) Brigade and the 2nd Engineers (U.S. Army). The 3rd Division contribution to the action would be the U.S. Army's 7th Infantry Regiment. Opposing them were the 461st Regiment of the German 237th Division and elements of the 10th Division. These were reinforced by elements of the German 28th, 87th, and 197th Divisions. The battle began with the Marines of the 2nd Division holding a position near the village of Lucy-le-Bocage coming under attack by the German 237th Division, which occupied Belleau Wood. On June 4, the U.S. troops turned back a major German assault that would have brought the enemy within fifty miles of Paris. This was an important moment for the defenders, who were ordered to go over to the offensive the following day. On June 5, the 2nd Division was ordered to recapture Belleau Wood. This action was undertaken with the assumption that the wood was lightly held. On the contrary; the Germans had heavily fortified the entire Belleau Wood, and the assault by the 4th Marine Brigade failed. On June 6, the Marines made a little headway, but paid dearly in terms of casualties suffered. The strategic Hill 142 was taken, and a German counterattack was turned, but at a cost of 1,087 casualties, the greatest one-day total in U.S. Marine Corps history to that date. An attempt by the Marines on June 8 to exploit their momentum failed to gain any ground, but another assault was launched on June 10, this time with heavy artillery support. By the end of the day on June 11, the U.S. forces controlled most of Belleau Wood, but at a tremendous cost. An attempt to capture the remainder of the wood was launched the following day. The Germans struck back on June 13, using poison gas to support their drive, thus inflicting heavy casualties. On June 14, the Germans were stopped near Bouresches, as the 23rd Infantry came into the line to support the Marines. Two days later, the 7th Infantry was added to back a renewed assault spearheaded by the Marines. This would take place on June 18–19, and would fail to gain ground. On June 21, the 7th Division launched a battalion-scale attack that was heavily cut up by German artillery and machine guns. The Marines tried again on June 23, but took heavy casualties and made little headway

Above: The Kaiser and General von Below, 1916. *Chrysalis Photo Library*

Opposite, Below Left and Right: The Battle of Belleau Wood. *Richard Natkiel*

against stiff German resistance. On June 25, supported by heavy reinforcements of French artillery to reduce the woods, the AEF launched its final assault. Despite determined resistance, the Americans had secured Belleau Wood by the end of the day on June 26. *BY*

Below, Otto von (1857–1944)

Below was commander of I Reserve Corps on the Eastern Front, serving at Gumbinnen and the first Battle of the Masurian Lakes. In November 1918 he became commander of the Eighth Army, Serving at the Second Battle of the Masurian Lakes. In May 1915 he became commander of the Niemen Army and, in October 1916, moved to the Balkan Front, where he commanded the German forces during the Monastir Offensive. In April 1917, he was transferred to the Western Front, assuming command of the Sixth Army at Lille, before moving in September 1917 to the Italian Front, where his Fourteenth Army played an important role at Caporetto. He returned to the Western Front in February 1918, commanding the Seventeenth Army during the Kaiserschlacht Offensive against Arras. In October 1918 he became commander of the First Army during its retreat from Rheims. *MS*

Benedict XV, Pope (1854–1922)

Born Giacomo Della Chiesa, the future Pope Benedict XV came from a noble Italian family. Ordained at twenty-four, he rose through the Catholic hierarchy, becoming a bishop in 1900, Archbishop of Bologna in 1907, and a cardinal in 1914. Later, on September 3, 1914, he succeeded Pius X to the throne of St. Peter. Opposed to war, he made strong efforts to bring peace and also organized

considerable war relief, although his efforts were hampered by the domestic political situation in Italy. *MS*

Bernstorff, Johann Count von (1862–1939)

German ambassador to the United States from 1908, Bernstorff had a close friendship with many of the most important U.S. politicians of the period. He was undoubtedly influential in the maintenance of United States' neutrality until the German policy of submarine warfare gradually eroded his position. After the United States entered the war, Bernstorff became ambassador to Turkey, before retiring in late 1918. After a further career as a deputy in the Reichstag, he died in 1939. *MS*

Berthelot, Henri (1863–1931)

The French general Henri Berthelot was assistant chief of staff in August 1914, ably assisting Joffre during the important battles that led to the Marne. In December 1916, after Joffre was replaced, Berthelot was seconded to the Romanian army, assisting it during the defense of the Arges. Returning to the Western Front in 1918 as commander of the Fifth Army, he served at the Second Battle of the Marne, before again being sent to Romania in October 1918. *MS*

Beseler, Hans von (1850–1921)

Although retired in 1910, Beseler returned to the army in August 1914. He served as a corps commander during the

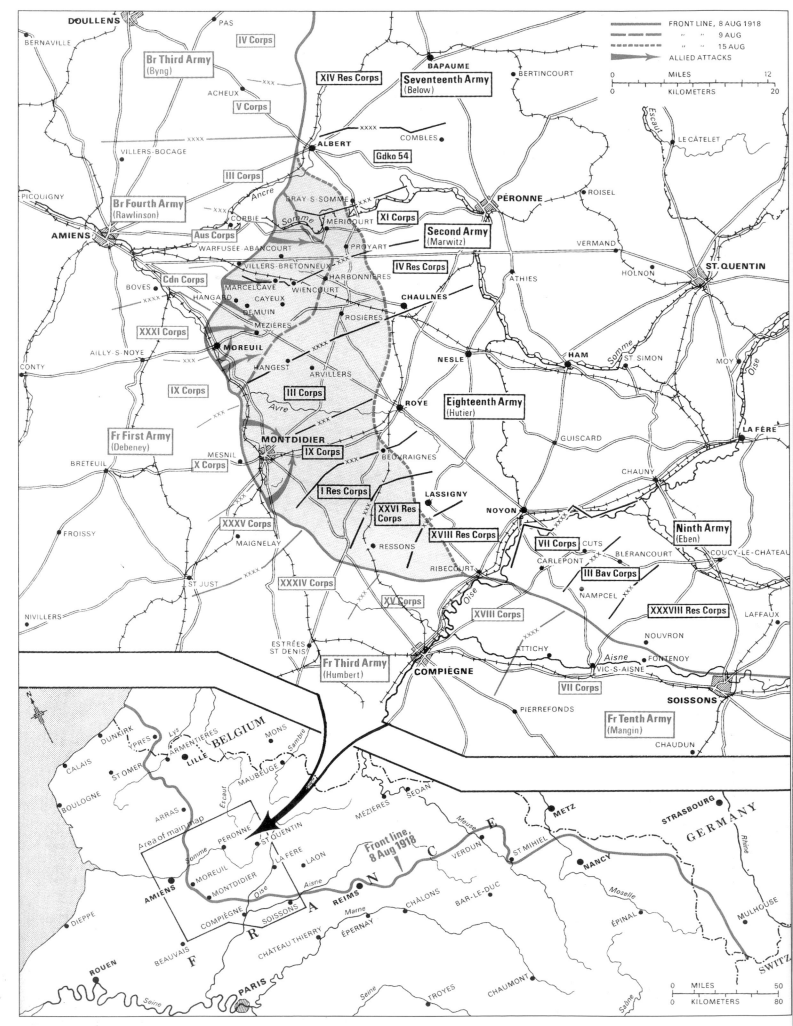

invasion of Belgium, capturing Antwerp in October 1914 and serving at the Battle of the Yser. In the spring of 1915 he was transferred to the Eastern Front, serving with the Ninth Army during the Gorlice-Tarnów Offensive. With the success of the Triple Offensive in the summer of 1915, Beseler was appointed military governor of Russian Poland, territory captured during the campaign. His period of command saw him increasingly perceived as pro-Polish and he resigned in late November 1918. *MS*

Bethmann Hollweg, Theobald von (1856–1921)

The German statesman Theobald von Bethmann Hollweg was born in Hohenfinow, Brandenburg. A lawyer by profession, he served both Prussian and German governments, reaching the position of Imperial Chancellor in 1909. Although fearful of the results that war would cause, his position was such that he played a pivotal role in the onset of war in August 1914. In 1917, he was forced from office as a result of his belief in the necessity for a negotiated peace. *MS*

Birdwood, Sir William Riddell (1865–1951)

Born in India, where his father was a senior official with the government in Bombay, Birdwood pursued a military career, passing through Sandhurst. In 1914 he was appointed commander of the forces arriving in Egypt from Australia and New Zealand prior to the ill-fated Dardanelles campaign. He drew up the plans for the invasion of the Gallipoli peninsula. With the withdrawal of the forces from Gallipoli, he then led the Australian and New Zealand forces on the Western Front in 1916 and 1917, serving at both the Somme and Ypres. At the cessation of hostilities he returned to India, where he took command of the Northern Army prior to his appointment as commander-in-chief of the Indian Army in 1925. He retired from active service in 1930. *MS*

"Black Day of the German Army"

Von Ludendorff coined this phrase in response to the joint British and French attack near Amiens on August 8, 1918. Following the failed German offensives of the spring and early summer the strategic offensive was taken up by the Allied forces, and on the 8th the British Fourth Army under Rawlinson and the French First Army under Debeney attacked on a fourteen-mile front to the south of the Somme. Surprise was absolute, and the British and French forces advanced with minimal opposition until they reached the shattered ground of the Somme battles of 1916. What shocked von Ludendorff in particular was the willingness of German troops to surrender; over 21,000 prisoners were taken between August 8 and 12. *MC*

Black Sea, Operations in the

In 1914 the Russians maintained a powerful Black Seas Fleet of five predreadnought battleships and two cruisers, while other vessels were under construction in Nikolaev. The principal Russian naval base was at Sevastopol, on the Crimean peninsula. The German battlecruiser *Goeben* and the cruiser *Breslau* augmented the Turkish fleet of two predreadnought battleships and two cruisers. Both German vessels were involved in a brief naval clash off Cape Sarych on the eastern Crimean coast in November 1914, and although both sides scored hits on the enemy, the Russians avoided any further encounters with the *Goeben*. During 1915 two Russian dreadnoughts entered service, altering the naval balance in the Black Sea. From January 1916 the *Goeben* stayed in port, effectively surrendering the sea to the Russians, allowing the Russian transport of troops and supplies by sea to support land offensives in the Caucasus. Although Bulgaria joined the Central Powers in 1915, the Romanians sided with the Allies, and no strategic advantage was provided to either side. Although submarine activity took place, no significant surface naval clashes occurred until the collapse of Russia in 1917, at which point most of the naval bases fell into Turko-German hands. *AK*

Bliss, Tasker Howard (1853–1930)

The Chief of Staff of the U.S. Army at the time of the American entry into World War I, General Tasker Bliss was a career military officer, and an 1875 graduate of the U.S. Military Academy at West Point. Born in Lewisburg, Pennsylvania, he served under General James H. Wilson in the Puerto Rico campaign of the Spanish-American War in 1898. After that war, he served as collector of customs in Cuba, and in 1902 he negotiated the treaty of reciprocity between Cuba and the United States. After serving in the Philippines and in several stateside posts, Bliss was appointed as U.S. Army chief of staff in 1917. As such, he undertook and oversaw the Herculean task of mobilization of U.S. Army forces for World War I. Later in 1917 President Wilson appointed him to the Allied Supreme War Council. In 1919, he served as a delegate at the Paris Peace Conference, where he urged the admission of Germany and the Soviet Union to the League of Nations, as well as postwar disarmament. *BY*

Boelcke, Oswald (1891–1916)

One of Germany's crack fighter pilots, Oswald Boelcke devised a tactical code that made him the true "father of the German fighter force." Taking command of the first Albatros D fighters at the front on September 17, 1916, Boelcke's score rose to twenty-one during his service with Jasta 2. He died in a flying accident on October 28, 1916, when his Albatros collided with another aircraft in the formation. His score was then forty. *JS*

Opposite: "Black Day of the German Army."
Richard Natkiel

Below: Captain Oswald Boelcke.
Chrysalis Photo Library

Bolsheviks

Russian revolutionary Communist party, led by Vladimir Ilich Lenin, that seized power in the aftermath of the revolutions of 1917. It took the name *Bolshevik*, meaning "majority," following a split with the more cautious reformist Menshavik "minority" at a congress in London in 1903. It opposed Russian participation in World War I, boosting support in the aftermath of the March 1917 revolution, and was able to seize power in October/November following the collapse of the provisional government. Renamed the Communist Party, the Bolsheviks made peace with the Germans at Brest-Litovsk, and ultimately secured victory in the Russian Civil War that followed. *DC*

Bombing raids

Aerial bombing was almost totally unknown in 1914 and there were few suitable aircraft or bombs for them to carry. But the more aeronautically advanced nations on both sides soon turned to developing both tactical and strategic bombers. Russia led the field with her giant Sikorsky Ilya Mouromets, their crews having trained on the equally impressive Bolshoi Bal'Tisky. German factories concentrated on long-range bombers such as the Friedrichshafen GIII, the four-engined Zeppelin-Staaken RVI, and the Gotha GV; although these aircraft proved more effective than Zeppelins they were too few in number to alter the outcome of the war. In Italy, Caproni's famous Ca46 appeared in 1915, while Britain's Handley Page V/1500 and Vickers Vimy were advanced designs to equip a strategic force. Such did not exist anywhere in 1914, and for two years bombing raids were generally restricted to tactical operations over the army front lines by single and twin-engined aircraft. Things changed in 1917 when the Germans introduced their four-engined types. Bombing Paris and London from the summer of that year, they caused considerable damage and no little panic among the civilian population. World War I bombs ranged from the British 20lb Hales to the heaviest used, the German

Right: Air raid damage to London.
Chrysalis Photo Library

2,205-pounder. British bombs proliferated in weight to the point where in May 1917 some standardization was necessary. It was achieved with about ten types remaining in use. *JS*

Boroevic von Bojna, Svetozar (1856–1920)

Boroevic von Bojna was one of the most influential Croat commanders of the war. Initially commanding the VI Corps under General Dankl in Galicia, then commanded the Third Army through the Battle of Komarow and the Carpathian Campaign until after the Gorlice-Tarnów Offensive he was transferred to the Southern Front in mid-1915. Commanding the Fifth Army, he was to triumph at Caporetto in late 1917, for which he was promoted field marshal in January 1918. His opposition to the

Above: Handley Page night bomber.
Chrysalis Photo Library

Piave Offensive in the spring of 1918 was overruled and his forces were beaten. With the defeat of the Austro-Hungarian forces and the failure of Karl I to retake the throne, he retired. *MS*

Botha, Louis (1862–1919)

One of a number of erstwhile Boer leaders who subsequently served the British Empire, Louis Botha was born at Greytown, Natal. He succeeded, as a member of the Transvaal Volkjsraad, Piet Joubert as commander-in-chief of the Boer forces in 1900. Following the end of the Second Boer War, he entered politics, becoming the Prime Minister of Transvaal in 1907 and the Prime

70

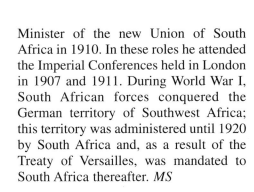

Minister of the new Union of South Africa in 1910. In these roles he attended the Imperial Conferences held in London in 1907 and 1911. During World War I, South African forces conquered the German territory of Southwest Africa; this territory was administered until 1920 by South Africa and, as a result of the Treaty of Versailles, was mandated to South Africa thereafter. *MS*

Bratianu, Ion (1864–1927)

Prime Minister of Romania in 1914, Bratianu was a liberal with pro-Allied sympathies who managed to keep Romania out of the war until it joined the Allied forces in August 1916. He remained Prime Minister until December 1917, when an armistice with the Central Powers was signed, although he continued to have influence. On November 10, 1918, Romania reentered the war, and in the following month Bratianu again became Prime Minister, leading the Romania delegation to the postwar peace conference. *MS*

Brest-Litovsk, Treaty of

Peace treaty between Russia and the Central Powers signed following the collapse of the Russian Army in the aftermath of the revolutions of 1917. The severity of the terms offered initially prompted the Russian delegation led by Leon Trotsky to delay discussions, but a renewal of hostilities by the Central Powers quickly obliged the Russian leadership to concede to even more drastic conditions. Russia ceded Finland, Poland, Estonia, Livonia, Kurland, Lithuania, the Ukraine, and Bessarabia, as well as Ardahan, Kars, and Bat'umi to Turkey. The treaty was annulled in November 1918 following the Allied victory. *DC*

Briand, Aristide (1862–1932)

Briand was one of the most significant French politicians of his era, being Prime Minister for almost six years (on eleven different occasions) between 1909 and 1929, including the critical period of October 1915 to March 1917. From 1894, he was allied with a group of socialists led by Jean Jaurès, a group which founded the paper *L'Humanité* in 1904. However, Briand was to be expelled from the party in 1906 when he accepted the post of Minister of Public Instruction and Worship in a Radical Coalition government. In 1909 he became Prime Minister for the first time, but fell out with the left by his use of military reservists to break a railway strike in 1910. In the 1920s, as a strong exponent of the League of Nations, he was an influential voice in French foreign policy and was awarded, with Gustav Stresemann, the Nobel Peace Prize in 1926 for his efforts at Franco-German reconciliation. *MS*

British air forces

British military aviation was reorganized as the Royal Flying Corps (RFC) on May 13, 1912, with a component Military and Naval Wing and an establishment of 179 aircraft. Although its actual combat strength in 1914 was modest at 113 machines, RFC air operations expanded steadily, weathering such disasters as the loss of 782 aircraft during the Battle of the Somme between July to November 1916. Then desperately short of effective fighters, the RFC turned to France and requested the Spad VII pending quantity deliveries of the Sopwith Pup. At the

same time there was a need to replace the BE12, a makeshift fighter which was a dismal failure in that role. No. 19 Squadron eagerly took to the excellent French fighter. Another disaster in "Bloody April" 1917 saw 140 RFC aircraft destroyed in the first two weeks of combat, but the line was held and the Battle of Cambrai in November was a long-awaited turning point when 289 British aircraft were available for army support sorties. These ground attacks significantly broadened the use of air-power and proved decisive in spring 1918, during Germany's final offensive which so nearly succeeded in capturing Amiens and Hazebrouck to sever the BEF's railway supply lifeline. Strafing RFC/RAF fighters inflicted such heavy casualties on German troops that the

Left: Bristol Fighters over France, June 2, 1918. *Chrysalis Photo Library*

Below Left: Sopwith F1 Camel. *Chrysalis Photo Library*

Right: Cockpit of an SE5a. *Chrysalis Photo Library*

Below: SE5a of No. 111 Squadron in Palestine 1917–18. *Chrysalis Photo Library*

WORLD WAR I: A VISUAL ENCYCLOPEDIA

offensive was neutralized, the British Army rallied, and retreat was turned into an unstoppable advance. A lengthening list of RFC pilots who became multiple aces was led by "Billy" Bishop with seventy-two victories, Mick Mannock (sixty-eight), Thomas McCudden (fifty-seven), and Ray Collishaw, who was credited with sixty-two. At a time when the country needed some positive news to offset the slaughter in the trenches, the exploits of these and numerous other pilots made them the popular heroes of the day. By the armistice the unique nature of air operations had been recognized by the formation of the Royal Air Force as a separate entity divorced from the army and navy. By November 1918 the RAF had a strength of 188 squadrons and 3,300 first line aircraft. That coveted independence had not been won without enormous cost—35,973 aircraft had been lost in combat to all causes by November 1918. The Royal Naval Air Service (RNAS)—formed as a flying branch of the Royal Navy in July 1914 —remained a smaller but effective force equipped with both airplanes and airships. Using Short 184 seaplanes, RNAS pilots carried out several spectacular raids, including those on the Zeppelin sheds at Düsseldorf and Köln in September 1914. This type of attack was repeated on November 21, when Avro biplanes hit the Zeppelins based at Friedrichshafen. A raid on Cuxhaven took place the following month, and there was low-key activity against Turkish forces during the Dardanelles

Far Left, Top: Handley Page V/1500 prototype.
Chrysalis Photo Library

Far Left, Bottom: RE8 of No. 52 Squadron, RFC, August 6, 1917. Based at Bray-Dunon, this unit was tasked with the interception of raiders flying toward England.
Chrysalis Photo Library

Left: Sopwith Triplanes, probably of No. 1 Naval Squadron. Note the white fin identifying the flight commander's aircraft.
Chrysalis Photo Library

Below: Bristol Fighter of No. 22 Squadron, RFC, seen near Agincourt, July 1918. Note the improvised top mounting for a Lewis gun.
Chrysalis Photo Library

campaign. The RNAS made the first aerial torpedo attack in history on August 12, 1915, and claimed to have sunk a Turkish freighter. Working in the region alongside RFC units for the first time, naval aviators attacked Kut, which later fell to the Turks, but in September 1918 the destruction of enemy forces at Wadi el Far'a was achieved entirely by aircraft. Squadrons transferred to Italy to help Britain's ally remained for the duration and the war in Palestine also demanded an increasing RFC presence to contain the Turks. Naval aircraft were also effective against Zeppelin raids on England, the first being destroyed on June 7, 1915. With the creation of the RAF in April 1918, the RNAS was absorbed into the single service. *JS*

Above Right: Army BE2c.
Chrysalis Photo Library

Right: Bristol Scouts of No. 85 Squadron over St. Omer aerodrome, June 21, 1918.
Chrysalis Photo Library

Opposite: Remarkable photograph of a Sopwith Camel looping. *Chrysalis Photo Library*

Below: BE2cs of No. 13 Squadron at Gosport waiting to start for France, October 12, 1915.
Chrysalis Photo Library

British aircraft

With military aviation in its infancy, Britain was not alone in being unable to deploy very effective aircraft when war broke out in Europe in August 1914. Equipped with slow and vulnerable two-seater biplanes such as the BE2a and RE8, the RFC carried out the vital task of aerial surveillance and made some largely ineffectual attacks in the battle area and behind enemy lines. From ad hoc beginnings with makeshift equipment and tactics largely dictated by localized conditions on the battlefield, the RFC gradually built up the necessary experience to conduct useful reconnaissance operations. The paradox of slow aircraft that made for a better camera platform while being very vulnerable to enemy fighter attack was difficult to overcome; the answer was an escort of fighters which had to be able to beat off the enemy if the two-seaters were to be protected. Few aircraft could be spared for bombing sorties, which were not undertaken on any scale until the spring of 1915. Carrying 99lb of bombs, the two-seaters laid the foundations for British tactical bombing. Not that all BE2s were docile, on the night of September 2–3, 1916, a BE2c single-seater flown by Lieutenant William Leefe Robinson of No. 39 Squadron destroyed the SL11, the first German airship to fall over England. Robinson was awarded the Victoria Cross. Reconnaissance remained the cornerstone of air operations and represented the most intensive activity by crews of the two-seat pushers. Attempting to save development costs by adapting this outdated configuration into a fighter, the authorities gave the front-line squadrons the FE2b armed with two machine guns, and the DH2 with one. Remaining vulnerable, they were hardly able to adequately protect the "eyes of the army," and British industry eventually responded with several excellent, more conventional fighters. They were sorely needed, for the RFC's early fighters suffered high losses in combat, particularly against Fokker monoplanes armed with synchronized machine guns. Although they took time to reach the front, the Royal Aircraft Factory's SE5/5a series, the Sopwith Company's Pup and Camel, and the Bristol F2B, redressed the situation. The Camel was highly maneuverable, a superb dogfighter even against Germany's best. Bristol changed the belief that a successful fighter had to have only a single seat: the "Brisfit" with its two back-to-back crew members enjoying a very successful career. Credited with the original triplane design to see action on the Western Front, the single-gunned Sopwith was one of the few departures from the tried and tested biplane. Germany's copy of the sturdy British Triplane was probably the best-known testimonial to its flying qualities. In common with other combatants Britain did explore the futuristic monoplane but none were operational during the war. Air fighting over the Western Front ranged from small-scale sorties, invariably to protect reconnaissance aircraft and shoot up enemy observation balloons, to large-scale dogfights if the enemy was encountered in force. Air superiority was won and lost periodically over ground positions that remained static for much of the war. The RFC continued to expand, however, and with the very high rate that the airplanes of 1914–18 could be produced, there was rarely a time when Britain's strength in the air was seriously challenged, although losses were relatively high at certain periods. Home defense took on a more critical urgency, particularly after the German air raids on London began on June 13, 1917. Two fighter squadrons were withdrawn from France to counter this increasing menace. These and additional home defense units succeeded in making daylight incursions over the UK too costly, and the Germans had abandoned them by September. Night attacks continued but these were also contained and all operations against London had ceased by May 1918. To better prosecute her own strategic air war against Germany, Britain assembled a force of heavy bombers with range enough to reach the German capital. As a nucleus of the Independent Air Force formed on June 5, 1918, three squadrons were equipped with the Handley Page O/400 and V/1500 to operate against Germany from French airfields. Carrying out raids on cities such as Köln and Frankfurt, the O/400s were by October 1918 being armed with 1,650-pounders, the largest British bombs of the war, the ultimate aim being to drop them on Berlin. But in the event the armistice was signed before such an epoch-making raid could take place. Bombs were hung on every convenient aircraft for tactical raids during periods of great danger, such as to counter the German push in the spring of 1918. Doing nothing for the performance

of otherwise excellent fighter airplanes such as the Bristol Fighter, some of the bombs did hit their targets but ground strafing probably caused greater material and psychological damage. The RNAS widely deployed seaplanes such as the workhorse Sopwith Baby in all war theaters, from the North Sea to Palestine. Antisubmarine patrols by this small aircraft contributed greatly to the defeat of the Germany's U-boats. Innovation was made tangible in the form of the Fairey F17 Campania, the first aircraft designed to be based on a sea-going carrier. More ambitious long-range operations were planned for the American-designed Felixstowe F2A, which from November 1917 conducted numerous effective ASW patrols. Aerial torpedo operations against ships matured during World War I, the first RNAS drop being made with a Whitehead torpedo on July 28, 1914. The Short 184, universally known as the "225" after its Sunbeam engine horsepower, commenced torpedo operations during the Dardanelles campaign in 1915. Although the chance to attack with this "traditional" naval weapon were comparatively rare, there were successes such as that in August when a Turkish steamer and a tug were destroyed by 225s in the Sea of Marmara. *JS*

British Army

Unlike its European counterparts in 1914 the British Army was an all-volunteer force, one primarily designed for home defense and the protection of the country's far-flung empire. As Britain relied on its navy and did not employ conscription, the army was considerably smaller than those of many other states, but its units contained some of the best-trained and most experienced soldiers in the world. The infantrymen had normally enlisted for seven years in the regular army and five in the reserve forces, although individuals could reenlist in the regulars for a further seven years. Supporting these full-time professionals was the special reserve, a force created from what had previously been the militia, and the Territorial Army. This body had been established in 1908 and comprised volunteers who were expected to attend an annual training camp as well as regular sessions in their local drill halls. Although officially earmarked for home defense, members of the Territorial Army could volunteer for service overseas—and the vast majority did. In August 1914 the country's land forces were split between 247,000 regulars of which half were based overseas and the

remainder, six infantry and one cavalry divisions, was stationed on home soil but ready to serve in Europe under the name of the British Expeditionary Force (BEF). The reserve force available numbered 224,000, while the Territorial Army added a further 269,000 men to the total. The nature of the British Army changed due to demands of war, not least because of the virtually destruction of the BEF in France between August and December 1914. The two key changes were the vast increase in manpower and the switch from an all-volunteer force to a mass conscript army. In the first weeks and months, men rushed to enlist, many caught up in an wave of war enthusiasm. For example, the war minister, Lord Kitchener, was able to create six new

Below Left: British troops pass through a French village on their way to the front, Battle of Loos, September 1915. *Chrysalis Photo Library*

Left: The "Kitchener Blue" uniform as worn by men of C Battery, Royal Field Artillery. They are in camp at Aldershot, Hampshire in December 1914. *Chrysalis Photo Library*

Below: British troops receiving dinner rations from field kitchens near the Ancre, October 1916. *Chrysalis Photo Library*

divides by the end of August, and by March 1915 the minister's so-called "New Armies" consisted of twenty-seven divisions. However, by June the flow of volunteers had dropped significantly and the government began to move toward compulsory service. In July the National Registration Act called for potential servicemen aged from eighteen to forty-one, while in October the scheme named after the Earl of Derby, the director of recruitment, asked potential recruits identified by the National Registration Act to agree to volunteer if asked to do so, although married men were to be called last. This mild measure of coercion brought in around 350,000 men, a far lower figure than required. Consequently, the Military Service Act passed into law in January 1916. This conscription legislation made all single men between eighteen and forty-one liable to call up and was extended to married men in May. An additional act in April 1918 extended the upper age limit to fifty-one. Figures show that the number of volunteers up to February 1916, some 2.6 million, compared favorably with the 2.3 million men conscripted between then and the end of the war. When the BEF arrived in France in 1914,

Left: 2nd Battalion Argyll & Sutherland Highlanders in the Bois Grenier Sector, June 1915. As well as their Glengarry headgear they wear Government issue fur jackets. *Chrysalis Photo Library*

Below Left: The 1st Lancashire Fusiliers being addressed by their divisional commander, General de Lisle, before the Battle of the Somme, June 29, 1916. *Chrysalis Photo Library*

Right: Men of the 15th Highland Division march back to rest headed by their pipers after taking Martinpuich, off the Albert Road, September 15, 1916. *Chrysalis Photo Library*

Below: B Company, 1st Battalion Scots Guards, in "Big Willie" trench, October 1916. *Chrysalis Photo Library*

it was not equipped for the trench warfare that soon developed. Its tactics, reflecting experience in recent colonial campaigns, were based on high-volume and accurate rifle fire, rapid maneuver, and artillery support from light field pieces. Cavalry was still considered a decisive weapon. Thus, when trench warfare broke out, the BEF lacked appropriate weapons, chiefly machine guns, grenades, mortars, and heavy artillery. These inadequacies were matched by many other shortages. There were two main reasons for the difficulties First, the vast expansion of the country's armed forces created all types of shortages, from uniforms to rifles, that manufacturers struggled to fill. Second, the ongoing war, which many had expected to last no more than a few months, was calling for unforeseen volumes of war materials on a daily basis. These problems were highlighted in mid-1915, when a lack of shells almost brought British operations to a standstill and caused a public scandal that contributed to the removal of the BEF's commander, Field Marshal John French. French's replacement, Field Marshal Douglas Haig, benefited from reforms, such as the encouragement of women into munitions factories, that boosted industrial output but supply always remained an issue. The ebb and flow of the war also brought significant changes in the burden borne by the BEF. In 1914 and 1915, its small size meant that it was essentially an adjunct to the

WORLD WAR I: A VISUAL ENCYCLOPEDIA

BRITISH ARMY

French Army, albeit an important one. Matters began to change in 1916 for two main reasons. First, the French had already suffered horrendous casualties and the Battle of Verdun was further draining the country of its manpower reserves. Second, the vastly expanded BEF was holding a growing part of the Western Front and had the resources to launch its own major offensives. Evidence of this first came with the Battle of the Somme, which marked the fully deployment of the New Armies, and reached its greatest expression in 1917. Mutinies in the French Army crippled its offensive capabilities and the British, for a time, shouldered the responsibility for aggressive activity on the Western Front, not least in the Third Battle of Ypres (Passchendaele). British losses in these battles were on a previously unknown scale, but the BEF was not ravaged by unrest, although the enthusiasm of previous years was replaced by a simple determination to get the job done. Other outcome of the fighting in these years was the transformation of conscripts into hardened professionals and the molding of the BEF into a truly efficient fighting machine. Perhaps the greatest expression of this was found in the artillery, which was highly regarded for its skill. The British Army's overseas commitments were also greater than any other combatant. Aside from the Western Front, significant forces, often backed by troops from the wider empire, served in Africa, the Balkans, Italy, Mesopotamia, and Palestine, as well maintaining the internal security of the empire. The extent of the British Army's involvement in the war is reflected in its casualty list—some 662,000 killed and 1.65 million wounded. *IW*

Top Right: Arrival of the BEF in France: troops on the Le Havre quay, August 16, 1914. *Chrysalis Photo Library*

Center Right: Instructions being given to a group of British soldiers. Note Lee Enfield rifles and variety of headgear. *Collection of George Forty*

Right: British "Female" (ie armed with machine guns) heavy tanks of C Company. *Collection of George Forty*

British Empire, Part played by in the war

Very little fighting actually took place in British Imperial possessions, although there was some minor skirmishing in East Africa with troops from neighboring German colonies. Far more significant were the troops that major colonies sent to fight alongside the British in Europe. Australia and New Zealand, Canada, and to a lesser extent South Africa and India all supplied significant numbers of soldiers. Australian and New Zealand (ANZAC) troops saw their finest hour in the doomed offensive against the Turks at Gallipoli. New Zealand had 8,566 troops serving on the peninsular yet recorded 14,720 casualties including wounded men who returned to action two or more times. Two-thirds of all the Australians who went to the Great War were injured or killed, many thousands of them falling at Gallipoli. Today all Australians still observe a day of remembrance for the fallen of Gallipoli on April 25. Over 600,000 Canadians enlisted in the Canadian Expeditionary Force, serving alongside the British and the French in their own sections of the trenches. Among the offensives in which they played an important part was the Second Battle of Passchendaele in which four divisions of the Canadian Corps lost 15,634 men killed or wounded. Indians also saw action and heavy casualties on the Western Front, but by the end of 1915 British generals considered Indian troops to be unsuited to trench war and the two infantry division were transferred to Mesopotamia. *DC*

Below: **4th Australian Division troops in respirators near Ypres, September 27, 1917.** *Chrysalis Photo Library*

Brooke, Rupert Chawner (1887–1915)

One of the famed poets of World War I, Rupert Brook was educated at Rugby School and King's College Cambridge. When he was twenty-two he moved to Grantchester, near Cambridge, which became a haven for him and fellow writers. In the years before World War I he traveled widely—to Germany, Tahiti, and the USA—and his first volume of poetry was published in 1911. Commissioned into the Royal Navy as sub-lieutenant, he was to die of septicemia on the island of Skyros *en route* to the Dardanelles in 1915. Many of his poems were published posthumously and, in his poem *The Soldier*, written in 1914, he perhaps penned some of the most famous lines of all the World War I poets:

If I should die, think only this of me:
*That there's some corner of a foreign
    field*
That is for ever England.
MS

Brusilov, Alexei (1856–1926)

One of the leading commanders of the Russian Army during World War I, Brusilov was born in Tflis (Tbilisi) in Georgia. He served in the war against Turkey in 1877. He was the Russian commander during the invasion of Galicia in 1914 and during the subsequent campaign in the Carpathians. In 1916, he commanded the Southwestern Army Group in its Brusilov Offensive against the Austrians, which was partially successful. In 1917 he became chief of staff, but his plans for a second Brusilov Offensive were thwarted by the revolution at home and by mutiny by his troops in the period leading up to the Bolshevik Revolution of October of that year. He continued to serve in the Russian Army after the revolution, leading it against the Poles in 1920. MS

Brusilov Offensive, 1916

Named after its chief architect and commander of the Southwest Army Group, General Alexei Brusilov, this offensive was the most effective Russian attack on the Eastern Front of the entire war. It was in part Russia's response to calls from its allies to relieve some of the pressure they were under due to the ongoing Battle of Verdun on the Western Front

and fighting in the Asiago sector of the Italian Front. Brusilov determined to attack simultaneously on a broad front from the Pripet Marshes to the Romanian frontier with four armies. Facing him were a roughly equal number of Austro-Hungarian troops with a stiffening of German forces. Russian preparations were thorough and carried out in great secrecy, and when the storm broke on June 4, the advance made considerable early progress. With the exception of the South Army, which contained some German troops, the Austro-Hungarian forces collapsed. Fearing disaster, German reinforcements were transferred from the Western Front and elsewhere on the Eastern Front, and Austro-Hungarian units were moved from Italy. A German-led counterattack in the north on June 20 limited further Russian gains there, but

in the south Brusilov's forces were able to advance to the Carpathians in July and August. However, this marked the high point of the offensive. Starved of reinforcements and supplies, the Russian advance stalled. Each side reported casualties of around one million men. The offensive had profound consequences for both the Central Powers and Russia. First, although successful, the scale of losses tore the heart out of the Russian Army and spread demoralization. Second, it highlighted the military weakness of Austria-Hungary. Henceforth, Germany effectively ran the empire's military affairs and had to release troops from other fronts to prevent its collapse. Finally, the early successes of the Russian attack encourage Romania to declare war on the Central Powers on August 27. *IW*

Bucharest, Treaty of

Peace treaty between Romania and the Central Powers signed May 7, 1918. Reflecting the disastrous defeats suffered by Romanian forces in 1917, it imposed extremely harsh terms, including the transfer of large tracts of territory to Bulgaria and Austria-Hungary. The Central Powers were entitled to requisition supplies of oil and grain that proved a vital addition to their dwindling resources. On November 9, 1918, Romania reentered the war and the Treaty of Bucharest was annulled at Versailles. Its territorial losses were reversed and new regions gained, resulting an almost doubling of national area. *DC*

Bulgarian Army

Bulgaria's decision to join the Central Powers in late 1915 greatly boosted their manpower in the Balkans. The army had a peacetime strength of some 85,000 but this figure reached 500,000 on full mobilization as most Bulgarians aged between twenty and forty-six had to undergo some military service. Equipment was a mixture of old and new, but the army had a significant shortage of heavy artillery. As Bulgaria had a small industrial base, it relied on Germany to supply large quantities of equipment, but at the price of having its army's planning directed from Berlin. The army recorded some 260,000 casualties, including 100,000 killed, during campaigns in Romania, Salonika, and Serbia. *IW*

Bullard, Robert Lee (1861–1947)

As an American military commander in World War I, General Robert Lee Bullard initially commanded the U.S. Army's 1st Division, and he ultimately commanded the Second Army of the AEF. In May 1918, as U.S. troops were preparing for battle, Bullard's 1st Division took over the Somme River Sector, then occupied by the French First Army. Until October 1918, the AEF consisted of the U.S. First Army, but on October 12 the size of the force had grown so much that AEF commander, General John J. Pershing, created a second numbered army. The First Army would be under the command of General Hunter Liggett, and General Bullard would command the newly created Second Army. Bullard's Second Army then assumed the task of a new major offensive east of the Meuse River and southeast of Verdun near the St. Mihiel salient. The objective would be the city of Metz. The Second Army's first and only offensive was launched on November 7 and terminated four days later by the Armistice. The Alabama-born Bullard has often been depicted in revisionist histories as having been a racist for having once remarked that African-American troops under his command were "hopelessly inferior." *BY*

Bülow, Karl von (1846–1921)

Von Bülow was approaching seventy when given command of the German Second Army for the invasion of Belgium. For a short period, between August 9 and August 17, he also controlled three other armies in order to coordinate the invasion better, but this arrangement did not work well. It was his strategic shortcomings at the First Battle of the Marne in September 1914—where he retreated having been refused the backing of the First Army—that was a major contribution to the German defeat. Despite this, he retained command and was promoted field marshal in January 1915. He retired, after a heart attack in March 1915. *MS*

Byng, Sir Julian Hedworth George (1862–1935)

Byng was the younger son of one of the most famous of British military families (his grandfather had served at Waterloo). Prior to World War I he served with the 10th Hussars and then commanded a cavalry regiment during the Second Boer War. After service in Egypt, he was recalled to Britain and sent to France in 1914, succeeding Allenby as commander of the Cavalry Corps. In 1915 he was sent to Gallipoli, where he commanded the withdrawal from Suvla, before returning to the Western Front to take command of the Canadian Corps. Under his command the Canadians took Vimy Ridge in April 1917. He then succeeded Allenby again, this time to command the Third Army, which, under his command, launched the Cambrai tank attack of November 1917 and was also heavily involved in the final British offensive of the war. He was created the first Viscount Byng of Vimy in 1919, served as Commissioner of the Metropolitan Police 1928-31, and was later promoted field marshal. *MS*

Opposite: The Brusilov Offensive of 1916. *Richard Natkiel*

Left: Major General Robert E. Lee Bullard with staff officers. Front row, left to right: Major General Bullard; Brigadier General Stuart Heintzelman; Second row: Lieutenant Colonel G. W. Wilson; Lieutenant Colonel F. M. Thompson; Colonel David L. Stone; Colonel W. N. Haskell; Back Row; Lieutenant Colonel G. P. Tyner; Captain Shirey; Lieutenant Colonel O. Hope. *Collection of Bill Yenne*

CADORNA, LUIGI

October/November 1917 and, after the Rapallo Conference of November 5, he was replaced by Diaz. His military career was effectively over, although he was partially rehabilitated when promoted field marshal by Mussolini in 1924, four years before his death. *MS*

Cambrai, Battle of

Following the intense disappointment that the Third Battle of Ypres (Passchendaele) had become, Field Marshal Haig was unusually receptive to new ideas and tactics and responded positively to the suggestion of an attack at Cambrai by Third Army, commanded by Julian Byng. The plan outlined a sweep that would encircle and capture Cambrai. Novelties included in the plan for attack included the use of airpower to prevent the German's reinforcing their troops by rail; the use of previously registered targets by the artillery, so as not to give away the attack by a heavy preliminary barrage; and the massed use of tanks supported by artillery. The attack was launched in the morning of November 20.

Cadorna, Luigi (1850–1928)

Appointed chief of staff to the Italian Army in July 1914, having turned it down earlier, Cadorna used the period of Italian neutrality to strengthen its northern defenses. Tactically suspect, his eleven campaigns on the Isonzo, between June 1915 and September 1917, resulted in high casualties for little reward. His limited gains were more than offset by the success of the Central Powers' Caporetto Offensive in

Opposite, Top: British Mk. II ditched in a trench, Cambrai, November 20, 1917.
Chrysalis Photo Library

Opposite, Below Left and Right: The Battle of Cambrai, November 20, 1917. *Richard Natkiel*

Right: Men of the 11th Leicester Regiment in a captured trench, Ribecourt, November 20–30, 1917. *Chrysalis Photo Library*

The attack opened with an intensive barrage on the Hindenburg Line and key points to the rear, which caught the Germans by surprise. This was followed by a creeping barrage that covered the advance of tanks and infantry. After ten hours the attack had managed to break through to a distance of five miles beyond the German front line, an unprecedented advance at this point in the war, and one that had the church bells in celebrating a victory. However, the attack had failed to capture the key position of Bourlon Wood, which took another five days to capture, and the offensive was closed down on November 26. On November 30 the Germans counterattacked and by December 3 they had managed to recover almost all the ground lost in the initial offensive and this battle ended with honors even. *MC*

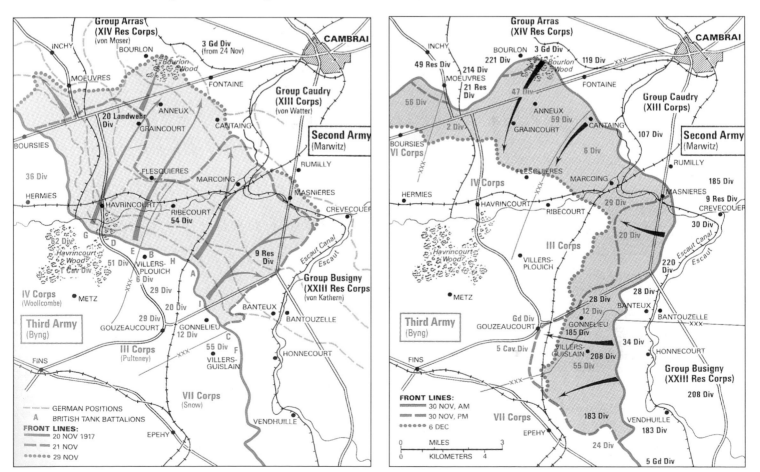

Cameroon, Operations in

Early Allied attempts to invade the German colony of Cameroon were rebuffed and it was not until September 27, 1914, that a British-led amphibious invasion under General Charles Dobell secured the port of Duala and with it the county's coastal region. The Germans retreated into the inhospitable interior, forcing a number of Allied invasion columns, Dobell's and others from neighboring Allied colonies, to converge against them. Dobell's troops advanced inland, making for the new German headquarters at Yaunde, which fell on January 1, 1916. However, the bulk of the German defenders conducted a skillful retreat to the neighboring Spanish Guinea and were interned. The remaining German resistance was finally overcome in late February. *IW*

Canadian forces

At the outbreak of war Canada's forces were tiny, just 13,000 troops, but a call for volunteers in early August 1914 led to the creation of the Canadian Expeditionary Force. By September 1915. two divisions were serving on the Western Front in the Canadian Corps, and a total of five were raised in total. Around 600,000 joined up during the war and something like forty percent served overseas. Of these some 210,000 became casualties, including 56,000 dead. The Canadians gained a reputation as an elite force and fought with distinction at Vimy Ridge in 1917 and Amiens in 1918. Canada also provided naval personnel, some 8,000 men serving in its own and the British navies. *IW*

Right: Canadian ration party carrying food to a forward area, Lievin, September 25, 1917. *Chrysalis Photo Library*

Below: Some 13,000 Canadians served in the RFC; here's one in a Sopwith Camel. *Chrysalis Photo Library*

Bottom: Canadian 20th Battalion soldier reading the *Daily Record* near La Coulotte, February 19, 1918. *Chrysalis Photo Library*

Caporetto Offensive, 1917

In August 1917, the Italians launched the Eleventh Battle of the Isonzo and came close to breaking through the Austro-Hungarian defenses. The recently appointed Austro-Hungarian chief of staff, General Artur Arz von Straussenburg, called on Germany's military leadership to provide troops for a counter-offensive to stabilize the situation. Germany's Third Supreme Command was headed by Field Marshal Paul von Hindenburg and General Erich von Ludendorff, who since July 1916 had effective operational control of Austro-Hungarian war planning, and they rejected Arz von Straussenburg's suggestion of an attack in the Trentino and determined to strike along the Isonzo. The operation, which was initially to have limited objectives, was to be spearheaded by German troops transferred from the Eastern Front. These six divisions were backed by nine Austro-Hungarian divisions and together they formed the Fourteenth Army under General Otto von Below. When the German-led attack began on October 24, it took place on a narrow sector of the front held by General Luigi Capello's Italian Second Army. Aided by their local superiority, the poor Italian defenses, a thick mist, and a brief but ferocious artillery barrage, the German assault troops rapidly cut though the Second Army in the direction of Caporetto. Although supporting Austro-Hungarian attacks to the north and south made little headway, Italian attempts to plug the gap around Caporetto over the following days failed. The chief of staff, General Luigi Cadorna, ordered a wholesale withdraw to the line of the Tagliamento River to prevent his forces south of the breakthrough from being surrounded. The Italians did not defend the Tagliamento line for long, despite the growing exhaustion of the German forces and the inability of the Austro-Hungarian supply system to cope with the demands placed upon it in mountainous terrain. Cadorna ordered a further withdrawal, this time to the Piave River, which was reached by November 10. The Italians had been pushed back to within twenty miles of Venice, and the scale of their defeat had widespread consequences. First, Cadorna was dismissed and replaced by General Armando Diaz. Second, the Italian government fell and the new leader, Vittorio Orlando, sought urgent talks with his Allied counterparts. The subsequent meeting was held at Rapallo and two critical decisions were made— British and French troops would be immediately sent to the Italian Front, and the Allies would establish a Supreme War Council. This was initially established to oversee ongoing operations in Italy but would develop much wider powers to coordinate Allied efforts on all fronts. While the discussions at Rapallo continued, the Austro-Hungarians attempted to break through the Piave River by launching two armies southward from the Trentino against the Italian left flank on November 6. However, the Austro-Hungarians proved unequal to the task and had been repulsed by the 18th. The arrival of five British and six French divisions in Italy further helped to stabilize the position along the Piave River in early December. Winter weather, mounting supply problems, and the withdrawal of German units to the Western Front brought the fighting to an end during the last days of the month. *IW*

Carpathians, Operations in the, 1915

The Austro-Hungarians had abandoned much of their province of Galicia to the Russians during 1914 and withdrawn to the line of the Carpathian Mountains. The chaotic situation had only been stabilized by the arrival of German troops. However, the fortress of Przemysl held out in the lost lands and its liberation became a national crusade. Consequently, the chief of staff, Field Marshal Franz Conrad von Hötzendorf, planned an offensive to relieve the fortress in January 1915. He was not deterred by the fact that it was to take place in the depths of a terrible winter for which his forces were ill-equipped and which caused the flow of supplies to be haphazard. Unsurprisingly, the offensive rapidly ran into difficulties. The Third Army, led by Field Marshal Svetozar Boroevic von Bojna, acting in a diversionary role, was blocked in the northwest, although Russian attacks were halted after desperate fighting. Better news came from the south, where elements of General Karl von Pflanzer Baltin's army group were able to capture Czernowitz on February 17. However, this again was a diversionary advance and the main advance in the center toward Przemysl floundered in the passes through the Carpathians. By March the Austro-Hungarians had effectively abandoned all hope of saving Przemysl and the fortress surrendered on the 22nd. A series of Russian counterattacks through the Carpathians were held during April but at high cost to both sides. Austria-Hungary reported 800,000 casualties since January, a staggering seventy-five percent due to the harsh winter climate, and there were worrying signs of severe demoralization that would force Germany to shoulder the burden of operations on the Eastern Front in the future. *IW*

Carson, Sir Edward Henry
(1854–1935)

Born in Dublin, Carson, a lawyer by training, was to become one of the most controversial politicians of his age. First entering parliament, as Member for Dublin University, in 1892, he held the seat until 1918 and then, until 1921, represented the seat of the Duncairn division of Belfast. Under the Conservative government of 1900 to 1905, he was solicitor general, having been knighted in 1900. However, it was during the Liberal administration after 1905 and its policy of attempting Irish Home Rule, that his controversial pro-Unionist position became fully developed. He was at the forefront of Protestant opposition to Home Rule, establishing in 1911 the Ulster Unionist Council, which anticipated the separation of the predominantly Protestant north from the rest of Ireland, and in the following year raised a volunteer army of some 80,000 to defend the Union. With the creation of the coalition government in 1915, Carson became again Attorney General for a short period, but was one of the leading conspirators in the plot to unseat Asquith in 1916. With Lloyd George now established as Prime Minister, Carson returned to the cabinet. After the war, Carson returned to the law, becoming a lord of appeal in 1921—for which he became a life peer—until 1929. *MS*

Casualties, Overall

It is difficult to be precise as to the casualties caused by World War I, not least because many countries kept imprecise or misleading records. However, estimates suggest there some 9.8 million soldiers were killed and at least twenty million wounded in some way between 1914 and 1918. It must also be remembered that many survivors of the fighting never regained full fitness and would

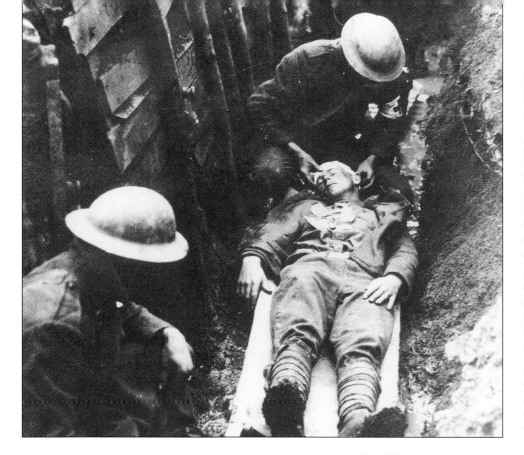

later succumb to their wounds. Psychological damage and the lingering affects of wounds carried off many after 1918. However, military deaths tell only part of the story as civilians also suffered to an unparalleled extent during the conflict. Again figures are conjectural. Something like two million ordinary Russians died, along with 500,000 Germans, due to the Allied blockade. 600,000 Armenians died in what many consider to have been a campaign of genocide waged by the Turks. On a smaller scale, aerial bombing and very long-range artillery added to the final total. On top of these figures are the seventy million people worldwide who died during the influenza pandemic in 1918–19. Not all of these deaths can be linked to the conflict, but World War I intensified the overall impact as many were already weakened and, therefore, more susceptible to infection. *IW*

Above: A U.S. Marine receives first aid, March 22, 1918. *National Archives via Chrysalis Photo Library*

Right: Grim reading: the "Roll of Honour" published in the British newspaper *The Sphere* of April 7, 1917. *Chrysalis Photo Library*

Below: German dead outside Beaumont Hamel, November 1916. *Chrysalis Photo Library*

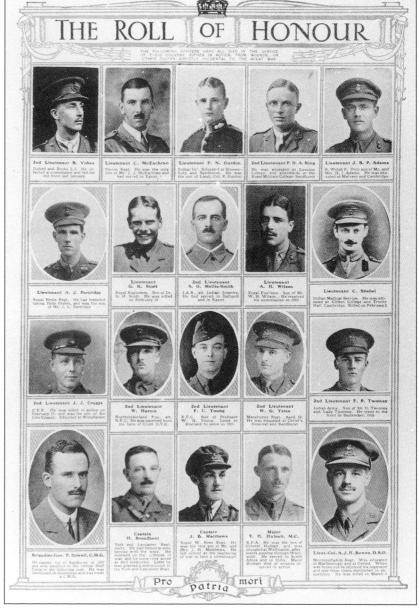

Caucasia, Operations in, 1914–16

The campaign in Caucasia, the border region between Turkey and Russia, began with a Turkish push into the Russian Caucasus led by Enver Pasha, the country's war minister. This proved a disaster, not least due to the appalling winter weather and Enver's incompetence, and the Turks were thrown back at the Battle of Sarikamish between December 29 and January 3, 1915. Russian forces pushed tentatively into Turkish Armenia, where the local Christians had risen against their Muslim rulers with Russian backing. On April 20 the Armenians rebels took Van and proclaimed their independence. This provoked the Turks to take draconian measures. In what became known as the Armenian Massacres, some 1.5 million Armenians died during a campaign of violence, starvation, and ill treatment. In July Enver ordered another Turkish attack in Caucasia, but the new Russian commander, General Nikolai Yudenich, halted this at the Battle of Malazgirt in mid-July, and the front line stabilized for the remainder of the year. At the beginning of 1916, the Russian forces in the theater launched a series of offensives. In the center the fortress of Erzerum was captured on February 16 and then Yudenich switched the focus of his attacks to the coast of the Black Sea. Trebizond fell in April, whereupon the advance in the center was resumed, with the Russians winning a major victory at Erzincan in late July. This marked the high point of Russian operations in Turkish Caucasia, but the revolutions of 1917 made it impossible to capitalize on these successes, and Turkish forces reconquered much of the territory in the spring of 1918. *IW*

Causes of the war

The assassination of the Hapsburg Archduke Ferdinand in Sarajevo on June 28, 1914, set in motion a confrontation between Austria and Serbia from which neither side was prepared to back down; allies were drawn in on both sides, armies mobilized, and war spread rapidly

Opposite: The power blocs of Europe, 1914. *Chrysalis Photo*

Right: Sarajevo, June 28, 1914, the world is still at peace. Archduke Franz Ferdinand and his wife Sophie, Duchess of Hohenberg, are about to get into their car where they will be assassinated by Serb Gavrilo Princip. *Chrysalis Photo Library*

Above: Arrest of the assassin Gavrilo Princip, June 28, 1914. *Chrysalis Photo Library*

across Europe. Yet behind this immediate set of events lay wider reasons and conditions that allowed an essentially local dispute to spiral into a worldwide conflict of unprecedented scale. Chief among these was the intense nationalism that had developed in Europe during the nineteenth century with the establishment of the ideal of the nation state as the embodiment of each people's destiny. This not only left a number of peoples, prominent among them the Serbs, without satisfactory states of their own focusing unrest within larger political units, particularly the outmoded Austro-Hungarian Empire. More widely, nationalism was the impetus behind the rivalry of major powers, expressed in economic and military competition that was to culminate in war. The inflexibility of military planning and the system of wider alliances ensured that, when the moment of conflict arrived, a wider war was almost unavoidable. Nationalism resulted in both regional tensions in areas such as the Balkans, where the new aspirations for national self-determination were unsatisfied, and in a greatly increased rivalry between the leading nations of Europe. One expression of this rivalry was in imperial expansion, where serious clashes between France, Britain, and Germany over the division of Africa were only narrowly averted. The continued rapid growth of industrial economies, which had begun with the Industrial Revolution in Great Britain in the late eighteenth century, was seen as vital to national survival. This heightened sense of rivalry and of constant danger from potentially hostile neighbors inevitably found expression in military preparations. With the exception of Great Britain, all the European powers maintained very large standing armies,

which they kept manned through the use of conscript soldiers. Major fortifications were built along likely routes of enemy attack. The logistics of mobilization, of utilizing the newly important railways in particular, to move large bodies of soldiers rapidly into position for attack and defense and to keep them supplied and supported thereafter, were a constant preoccupation of military leaders. Elaborate but highly inflexible plans of mobilization were developed. The German high command became committed to a plan of rapid mobilization that was intended to enable a quick victory over France before turning to face their other enemy Russia, who could mobilize in large numbers only slowly due to poor communications and the vast distances involved. Diplomacy focused not on reducing the risks or causes of war, but on cementing the continent into two

blocks of alliances, the Triple Alliance of Germany, Austria-Hungary, and Italy, confronting the rival block of France, Great Britain, and Russia. The danger was that mobilizing for war compelled rival powers to respond or risk immediate disaster—a German mobilization against Russia in aid of its ally Austria had, in terms of the military and political logic of the day, to be checked by the mobilization of France, after which German strategy dictated a rapid move to actual combat. Yet the year 1913 held out illusions of peace. In August the Treaty of Bucharest ended the second Balkan War, and September brought the Treaty of Constantinople. To some it appeared that the opportunity for German aggression might have passed. In Britain the Irish Home Rule question seemed more likely to cause violence than Europe. Yet, just as Bismarck had predicted, it was

some "damned foolish thing in the Balkans" which struck the spark that led to war. On June 28, 1914, Archduke Franz Ferdinand and his wife were driving through Sarajevo when Gavrilo Princip attacked their car: the heir apparent to the throne of Austria-Hungary was assassinated. Within three weeks Austria was claiming that this was not the work of a small group of extremists, but a plot engineered by the Serbian government. On July 23 a protest and ultimatum was sent to Serbia. Of the ten demands made by Austria, Serbia acceded to seven, and asked for international arbitration. Having ascertained that it had German support, the Austrian government rejected this response. The next day The German ambassadors delivered notes to the Entente powers setting forth the view that the dispute should be "localized" in the Balkans.

CENTRAL POWERS, 1914
NEUTRAL COUNTRIES LATER ALIGNED WITH CENTRAL POWERS
ALLIES, 1914
NEUTRAL COUNTRIES LATER ALIGNED WITH ALLIES
ALLIED WITH CENTRAL POWERS, DECLARED NEUTRALITY AT OUTBREAK OF WAR, THEN JOINED ALLIES
COUNTRIES REMAINING NEUTRAL

© Richard Natkiel, 1982

WORLD WAR I: A VISUAL ENCYCLOPEDIA

93

The Russian government stated that it "could not remain indifferent," and began the preliminary phase of mobilization on July 25. From Britain Lord Grey proposed a four-power conference to avert conflict, but Austria declared war on Serbia on July 28. The next day Austrian batteries were shelling Belgrade. Momentary hesitation followed as Germany and Russia hoped that the other would climb down, or order full mobilization first, thus sacrificing the moral high ground. In the event Russia was too far over the precipice, and issued the order on July 30, even as Austria made the same announcement. Germany and France followed suit with mobilization announced in Paris and Berlin on August 1. The declarations of war which followed have been aptly described as a chain reaction. For while the Kaiser assumed it might be possible to fight only in the east, Moltke was at pains to point out that in the event of a major war there was only one option, the Schlieffen Plan. Thus it was that the bulk of the German armies moved west with the intention of knocking France out of the war before Russia's numbers could be brought to bear. Germany declared war on Russia on

August 1 and on France on August 3. France would respond with alacrity, her Plan 17 dictating that Germany should be invaded as quickly as possible in the event of war. Having made demands for free passage German troops crossed the Belgian frontier on August 4. This was in accordance with the predetermined timetable for a heavy and wide right hook around Paris. Yet it was this maneuver which turned likely British support for France into a certainty. For while Britain had attempted to maintain the peace, she had guaranteed Belgian neutrality: furthermore, German domination of the Channel was unacceptable. Britain declared war on August 4. Though Italy remained temporarily aloof, and Austria's declaration of war with Russia did not materialize until August 6, the war was already a world war. *SB/DC*

Cavalry

Mounted troops had been a battle-winning weapon through much of the nineteenth century. At the outbreak of war there was still a plethora of types including the French cuirassiers, chasseurs, and dragoons; the German Ulans

and Hussars; the Russian Cossacks and the British Household cavalry to name but a few. Cavalry skirmishing was a characteristic feature of the first campaigns on all fronts. Yet it had already been realized that the role of cavalry was changing, for while horsemen were ideal scouts, the magazine rifle, machine gun, and barbed wire now made them extremely vulnerable during the charge. As transport the horse was still useful, particularly in broken country over short to medium range, but no match for railways. Where they could be properly used, as in more open theaters in less developed countries, cavalry could still make breakthroughs or useful maneuvers. This was demonstrated by British cavalry in Egypt and Mesopotamia, and in Palestine under General Allenby. Where they were misused the result was

Above: Arrival of the French president in Petrograd, July 1914. *Chrysalis Photo Library*

Above Right: German cavalry during the occupation of Warsaw, August 5, 1915. *Chrysalis Photo Library*

Right: The Queen's Bays on the march during the Battle of Flers-Courcelette, September 18, 1916. *Chrysalis Photo Library*

CAVALRY

Right: Serbian cavalry cross a river in a wintry landscape. *Chrysalis Photo Library*

Below: British cavalry riding through Arras, April 11, 1917. *Chrysalis Photo Library*

Bottom: The 1st Hertfordshire Yeomanry, with the Bikanir Camel Corps in the rear, on a reconnaissance in force during the Egyptian Campaign, February 14, 1915. *Chrysalis Photo Library*

frustration or disaster. Cavalry waited in vain to exploit breakthroughs in the west, and by the end of 1917 the British and French had lost over 600,000 horses of all types killed, missing, and destroyed. About this time many cavalry regiments, already fighting on foot, were permanently unhorsed. The Germans used several divisions of dismounted cavalry; the British 74th Division was entirely composed of dismounted Yeomanry. *SB*

Cavell, Edith Louisa (1865–1915)

Few casualties of World War I were to have as dramatic an impact on British public opinion at the time as the nurse Edith Cavell, who was executed by the Germans in 1915. Born in the Norfolk village of Swardeston, she qualified as a nurse in 1895, before becoming the first matron of the Berkendael Medical Institution in Brussels, Belgium, in 1907. The hospital became a Red Cross center during the war, and it was while she was based at the hospital that she was arrested in August 1915. Accused of assisting more than 200 Allied soldiers to escape to the neutral Netherlands—a charge that she never denied—she was tried by a court martial and condemned to death. *MS*

Central Powers' command structure

As Emperor of Germany and King of Prussia, Kaiser Wilhelm II was both head of state and titular head of the German armed forces. Practical military control was operated by the Chief of the General Staff, originally Helmuth von Moltke, but from late 1915 the incumbent was Erich von Falkenhayn, who also served as Prussian War Minister. Following Verdun, von Falkenhayn was replaced by Paul von Hindenburg, who worked in close cooperation with his Quartermaster General Erich von Ludendorff. The German chancellors of the period were Bethmann Hollweg until 1917, followed by von Hertling, and finally in the last month of war, Prince Max of Baden. By 1918 the General Staff had expanded to include directors of railways, signals, mechanical transport, survey, medical services, and antiaircraft guns; generals of air forces and foot artillery; an intendant general of the field army; and an inspector of gas regiments. Separate command headquarters were maintained for the Eastern and Western Fronts, and individual armies had an Armee Oberkommando. Though the existence of individual states within the German Empire caused minor complexities, the position was worse in the dual monarchy of Franz Joseph's Austria-Hungary. The Hungarians maintained a separate prime minister and defense minister, and there were significant Romanian, German, Slovak, Croat, and Serb minorities. At the outbreak of war the Austrian war minister was Alexander von Krobatin: chief of staff to the "*Kaiserlich und Königlich*" (Imperial and Royal) army was Conrad von Hützendorf. *SB*

Champagne Offensive, First (1914)

Following the stabilization of the Western Front after the "Race to the Sea," Joffre, the French commander-in-chief, was determined to launch an offensive that would win the war and drive the invader from the sacred soil of France. He resolved to launch a major attack extending along the whole line from Nieuport to Verdun, throughout the Artois and Champagne regions. The main force of the attack was to be launched along the front from Rheims to Verdun with an attack on the German Third Army at the base of the Sayon Salient. The offensive was launched on December 10 near Perthes in eastern Champagne. French initial gains were minimal. The Germans had strongly fortified their entrenched positions and the advancing French forces were cut down by well placed machine guns. The Allied commanders had yet to realize that this was a war in which those holding the defensive had an undisputed advantage. Fighting continued throughout the winter until March, with a short break in mid-February to reorganize. The attack had made very limited gains across the front, far from the grand breakthrough predicted by Joffre. The cost to the French was huge: over 90,000 had become casualties during the course of the campaign. *MC*

Below: German field gun firing during the Champagne Offensive. *Chrysalis Photo Library*

Champagne Offensive, Second (1915)

Following the failure of the First Champagne Offensive, in early 1915 Joffre resolved to try again. His losses had been made good by the arrival of more colonial divisions, while the British were starting to receive the first of their New Army divisions. Over Haig's objections that he had neither the trained infantry divisions nor the shells, Joffre resolved to launch a combined assault around Artois and Champagne in September 1915. On September 25, following a four-day artillery barrage, twenty French divisions attacked on a front twenty miles wide against the German Third Army. The attackers of Pétain's Second Army and Langle de Cary's Fourth Army made some impressive immediate gains and by the end of the 26th they had reached the German second line. However, this was to be the extent of their success and the attack bogged down. When the offensive was finally called off on October 31 the French had lost over 140,000 men and the German second position had not been breached. *MC*

Channel Ports, Defense of (1914)

The Channel ports were vital to the survival of the Allied effort throughout the early days of the war. The BEF was almost entirely reliant upon cross-Channel shipping for its supplies and reinforcements. It was therefore vital to the Allied war effort that these ports were kept free from the enemy. The German General staff realized this position and, following the Battle of the Aisne, both sides sought to exploit each other's open flanks in a series of maneuvers that came to be known as the "Race to the Sea." This culminated in the First Battle of Ypres, where the British line held and the Western Front stabilized. *MC*

Charleroi, Battle of

With the German advance through Belgium, the French Fifth Army was the only major formation that opposed the full might of the Schlieffen Plan. Joffre's original dispositions held that the Fifth Army should join with the Third and Fourth Armies in an invasion of Germany through the Ardennes. This assumed, however, that the Germans had not already outflanked this position and driven through Belgium to the north.

Lanrezac was deeply worried about this possibility, though Joffre discounted it altogether, though he did allow Lanrezac to extend his flank northwest to the Sambre on August 12. The battle comprised a major action fought between the French Fifth Army, advancing north to the River Sambre, and the German Second and Third Armies, moving southwest through Belgium. On August 20 Joffre finally agreed that Lanrezac could concentrate his forces further north, authorizing him to attack across the Sambre. However, on August 21 it was elements of von Bülow's Second Army that attacked across the Sambre forming a number of bridgeheads around Charleroi. Despite repeated French counterattacks the vastly superior German numbers told, and the French Fifth Army was forced back. At this point the German Third Army also managed to cross the Meuse and the French were in grave danger of being completely cut off. On August 23 Lanrezac ordered a general withdrawal, thus ending the battle. *MC*

Chinese Forces

China's chaotic domestic politics prevented any direct military involvement in the conflict, despite its declaration of war on the side of the Allies in August 1917.

Nevertheless, a number of military missions were sent to the Western Front on fact-finding and observer duties; while some medical staff supported the British. More important to the Allied war effort was the extensive use of Chinese labor behind the lines. This was on a massive scale. Estimates suggest that around 200,000 Chinese were supporting the British, French, and U.S. military efforts on the Western Front by 1918, while a further 175,000 worked in a similar capacity in East Africa and Mesopotamia. *IW*

Churchill, Winston Leonard Spencer (1874–1965)

It is very easy, in the light of his later pivotal role as Britain's leader in World War II, to forget how controversial a figure Churchill was prior to 1940. He was commissioned in 1895 into the 4th Queen's Own Hussars and saw military service in Cuba, Malakand, and at the Battle of Omdurman in 1898 before becoming a journalist reporting on the Second Boer War. Although the Boers captured him he escaped (with a £25

Below: Chinese laborers at Boulogne, August 12, 1917. *Chrysalis Photo Library*

Above: Winston Churchill, as Secretary of State for War, watching the march past of 47th Division in the Grande Place at Lille, October 28, 1918. *Chrysalis Photo Library*

reward on his head) and entered parliament as the MP for Oldham in 1900 as a Conservative. However, in one of his several shifts of political allegiance, he crossed the house to join the Liberal Party in 1904. He first became a cabinet minister in 1908, as President of the Board of Trade, before becoming Home Secretary in 1910 and First Lord of the Admiralty the following year. It was as First Lord that he strengthened the Royal Navy significantly, correctly anticipating the future war with Germany. He retained the position until the catastrophic failure at Gallipoli, for which he was made scapegoat. After his loss of ministerial power, he served briefly as a colonel on the Western Front before returning to government as Minister of Munitions in 1917 and was then, from 1919 until 1921 (but out of favor and excluded from the cabinet), Secretary for War and Air. In 1919 he broke with the Liberals and was not reelected to the House of Commons again until 1924 when he stood for the Conservative Party. He served as Chancellor of the Exchequer between 1924 and 1929, but was then out of power until the outbreak of World War II when he returned as First Lord of the Admiralty. These "wilderness years" saw him attack the policy toward greater

independence in India and also appeasement of Nazi Germany. In May 1940 he succeeded Neville Chamberlain as Prime Minister and guided Britain until defeated in the 1945 general election. He returned as Prime Minister between 1951 and 1955, being knighted in 1953. *MS*

Clemenceau, Georges Eugène Benjamin (1841–1929)

Clemenceau studied medicine before entering politics. A radical, he was elected mayor of Montmartre in 1870 and, the following year, was elected to the National Assembly, but was to resign his seat in protest over the government's policies over the Paris Commune. He reentered the National Assembly in 1876 but again lost his seat, in 1893, as a result of a scandal. However, his popularity was restored as a result of his campaign for Alfred Dreyfus, a Jewish officer in the French Army who was accused of spying on behalf of the Germans in a celebrated case in the mid-1890s, and he was elected a senator in 1903. He first held ministerial office, as Minister for Home Affairs, in March 1906, and became Prime Minister in October the same year. He served two terms as French PM—1906–09 and 1917–20. During the first three years of the war he was an ardent critic of French military

incompetence and defeatism. When he returned to power in 1917 he was a crucial figure in holding the country together after the military reverses of that year and of the following spring. As French PM he oversaw the postwar peace conference, although his desire to see any treaty guarantee French security was to be thwarted. He was perceived, domestically, to have been too soft on the Germans and he fell from power in January 1920. His belief that a revitalized Germany would prove a threat was to be correct, although he didn't live to see his prophecies fulfilled. *MS*

Codes and codebreaking

Cryptography was already centuries old in 1914, yet the war offered many new opportunities both for long-range transmission of intelligence, and for interception of wireless telegraphy and telephones. Following the work of Auguste Kerckhoffs, author of *La Cryptographie Militaire*, it was the French who made significant initial progress, establishing the Bureau de

Below: From left to right: Clemenceau, unknown, Foch, Weygand (back to camera). *Chrysalis Photo Library*

Chiffre before the outbreak of hostilities. They later erected six direction-finding stations, and were among the first to realize that Morse code operatives could be identified by their individual "fist." The Germans established their own specialized cryptanalytic bureau, the "*Abhorchdienst*," in 1916. An early British contribution to electronic espionage was the dredging up and severing of Germany's transatlantic cables, forcing enemy messages to be transmitted by less secure routes. One of the most important episodes came in 1917 when the Zimmerman telegram was intercepted by the British Admiralty's cypher bureau. Deciphered by the Reverend Montgomery and former publisher Nigel de Grey, this revealed both a plot with Mexico and impending unrestricted submarine warfare. These revelations were a factor in bringing America into the war. In mid-1918 French code breaker Georges Painvin succeeded in cracking the German "ADFGVX" cypher, thus helping to parry an assault in the Compiègne. At the end of the war it was Major Joseph Mauborgne, head of U.S. Army cryptographic research, who

introduced single-use random keys. This made codes significantly more difficult to break as it removed all obvious patterns from messages. *SB*

Colonial troops

Particularly for the Allies the colonies represented a huge pool of potential manpower. Even in 1914 the French maintained a colonial army corps of three divisions in France with a headquarters in Paris. The Armée d'Afrique raised to garrison the North African possessions included both Frenchmen serving in the Zouaves and Chasseurs d'Afrique, and native troops in the Tirailleurs and Spahis. Other French colonial formations included regiments of Europeans and Senegalese in Morocco, native Moroccan regiments, and independent battalions in other states. All of these fought in the front lines: Indochinese and Chinese tended to serve as laborers and support troops. The particularly cosmopolitan attitude of the French to non-Europeans serving in combat would come as a particular surprise to the Americans whose black

troops were more strictly segregated. Britain's colonies also made a significant contribution. The most important group was the more than a million Indians who left the subcontinent to serve in other theaters. The end of the war found two whole corps of Indian troops in Mesopotamia, with significant numbers in Egypt and Palestine. In Africa there were battalions of the King's African Rifles. Additionally there were numerous labor companies and battalions: the bulk of these were Chinese, but others included West Indians, Mauritians, Fijians, Egyptians, "Cape Colored" South Africans, and a handful of Maltese. *SB*

Communications

Though technology had improved considerably during the nineteenth century,

Right: Battle of Mahiwa during the East African campaign: the Kashmir Mountain Battery in action October 19, 1917. *Chrysalis Photo Library*

Below: The 3rd Battalion, Nigerian Brigade, advancing toward Rufiji during the East African campaign. *Chrysalis Photo Library*

with inventions such as the telegraph and telephone, inadequate communications were a significant factor in hampering breakthroughs for much of the war. Local successes were difficult to exploit as the relaying of information and the sending of reserves was usually slow. Field telephones were the best communication available in 1914, but had the serious disadvantage that they required landlines. They were best suited to static conditions, but bombardments led to severed wires. Other methods of 1914 included flag, heliograph, and lamp signaling, but all had drawbacks, needing either clear visibility or bright sunshine. Carrier pigeons could operate over greater distances, but only worked in one direction and were prone to gas or interception. Nevertheless pigeons were widely used, and even carried inside tanks. Runners and couriers were similarly vulnerable, and slow across devastated terrain, though motorcycles made a significant contribution behind the lines. Considerable advances were made in the early part of the war with the use of simple pyrotechnic signals which were especially useful at night. Flares

Left: A wiring party at work. Note Very lights in the distance; Cambrai, January 12, 1917.
Chrysalis Photo Library

WORLD WAR I: A VISUAL ENCYCLOPEDIA

from "Very" or "light" pistols could alert artillery to fire or ceasefire, or inform of the presence of enemy or friendly troops. Rifle grenades were also used to project firework signals, and in the British instance these were sometimes arranged so as to give changing colors to convey more complex meanings. Wireless telegraphy was doubtless the key to the future, but wireless sets of the time were large and delicate and no effective man-portable wireless system would be introduced. Nevertheless, by the end of the war the British were experimenting with "wireless tanks" which could potentially have revolutionized battlefield communication. The German signal service—or *Nachrichtenwesen*—was comprehensively reorganized in 1917 to take account of new developments. Establishments of this period included a signaling detachment—or *Truppen-Nachrichtenabteilung*—comprising about 140 men, for each regiment. This provided the manpower for field telephone and lamp signal sections and handlers for the pigeons and messenger dogs. Use was also made of "message projectors" and mortar "message shells," which literally shot dispatches over the battlefield. Another important element of the German system were the "Arendt" detachments attached to each army. The duty of these was to provide a listening service which would monitor both German and enemy communication. The communication of information on the state of the war to the general public was also extremely strictly controlled, and heavily censored both by the military and also by the Press itself. *SB*

Right: The Bureau de la Presse, Bourse, Paris. French, British, American, Belgian, and Serbian censors at work. *National Archives via Chrysalis Photo Library*

Below: Testing telephone lines. The low poles are just high enough to form an air line, October 23, 1917. *Chrysalis Photo Library*

Conscientious objectors

Pacifists who, for moral or religious reasons, refused to fight in the military and campaigned for better treatment of those with similar views were called "Conscientious objectors." In the early stages of the war, enrolment in the British Army was voluntary, but by 1916 heavy losses on the Western Front required the introduction of conscription enforced by the Military Service Act. Some objectors were willing to serve in noncombat roles, with about 7,000 acting as cooks, laborers, medical orderlies, stretcher-bearers and ambulance drivers. Many medical workers and stretcher-bearers in the front line demonstrated great bravery, and casualty rates among them were high. Absolute conscientious objectors rejected any participation in the war and endured considerable persecution and vilification as a result. Two leading absolutists, Fenner Brockway and Clifford Allen, formed the No-Conscription Fellowship to encourage others to resist the draft and oppose punishment for objectors. Most were drafted and then court-martialed when they refused to obey orders. By the end of the War 8,608 such men had appeared before military tribunals. Over half were sent to do other work of importance such as farming, but seventeen were sentenced to death (later commuted), 142 to life imprisonment, and sixty-four others to terms of twenty-five years or more. Prison conditions were severe and sixty-nine of them died in custody. American objectors were exempt from combat service and only some 450 who refused to cooperate with the draft system were sent to federal prisons. Around 4,000 others were allocated tasks ranging from medical work to manual labor in military camps. Organizations opposed to conscription included the American Friends Service Committee and the National Civil Liberties Bureau, which later became the American Civil Liberties Union. *DC*

Constantine I, King (1863–1923)

King Constantine I of Greece was born in Athens and succeeded to the throne in 1913 on the death of King George. He had had limited military success prior to his accession—defeat in the Turkish War of 1897 but victory in the Balkans War on 1912–13—and favored neutrality, as Kaiser Wilhelm II's brother-in-law, during World War I. Allied pressure and the government of Eleutherios Venizelos forced him to abdicate in favor of his son Alexander in 1917, but he regained the throne in 1920 following a plebiscite. This restoration was, however, short-lived as a rebellion by the military in 1922 forced him once again to abdicate, this time in favor of his son George. Constantine died the following year. *MS*

Convoys

While German U-boat attacks began as early as August 1914, the peak of U-boat activity was in 1917, when the United States entered the war. The losses of Allied merchant ships were mounting, particularly in the coastal waters of the Western Approaches to the British Isles, in the Mediterranean Sea, and along the Atlantic seaboard of Canada and New England. In April alone, 373 Allied ships were lost, with a total displacement of

Below: HMS *Monmouth* was sunk at the Battle of Coronel. *Chrysalis Photo Library*

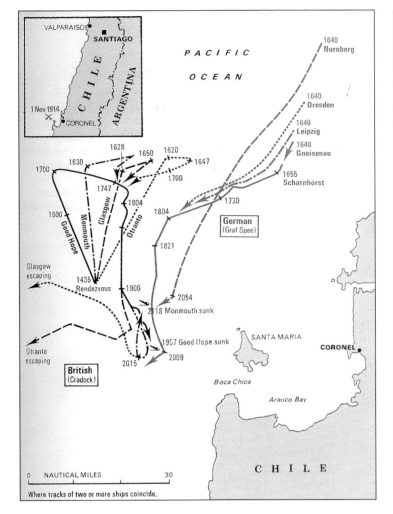

over 500,000 tons. This crisis forced the British Admiralty to institute a convoy system. The first convoy sailed from Gibraltar to Britain on May 10, 1917. Screened by destroyers and armed merchantmen, every ship reached port safely. This success led to the first trans-Atlantic convoy, which sailed from Norfolk, Virginia on May 24, bound for Britain. Only one ship in the formation was torpedoed. The number and size of convoys grew throughout the remainder of the war, and in general losses due to U-boat attacks fell proportionately. By the last months of the war, over a thousand merchant ships were sailing as part of one of dozens of convoys at any particular moment, and the convoy system was dubbed an unqualified success by the Admiralty. *AK*

Coronel, Battle of

At the start of the war, the German East Asia Squadron under Count Maximilian von Spee was in the Pacific Ocean. His force consisted of two armored cruisers (*Scharnhorst* and *Gneisenau*) and three light (protected) cruisers (*Dresden, Leipzig,* and *Nürnberg*). His squadron made landfall off the coast of Chile in

Above: Admiral Sir Christopher Craddock, commander of the British ships at Coronel.
Chrysalis Photo Library

Above Left: The Battle of Coronel.
Richard Natkiel

October 1914, then sailed south. A British force was sent to intercept them, commanded by Admiral Christopher Craddock. The British force consisted of two old armored cruisers (*Good Hope* and *Monmouth*), the light cruiser *Glasgow*, and the armed ocean liner *Otranto*. The two forces met in the late afternoon of November 1, 1914, with the British ship silhouetted by the setting sun. The seas were rough, making it difficult for the larger British ships to fire their hull-mounted sponson guns, while the light made it difficult to spot the German ships. Around 4:30pm the two forces opened fire, but finding themselves outgunned, the British squadron reversed course to the south. Just before 8pm the *Good Hope* sank after being ripped apart by an explosion, taking Craddock down with her. The badly damaged *Monmouth* foundered just over an hour later, but the remaining two British ships escaped the disaster. *AK*

Cost of the war

World War I resulted massive loss of life as outlined in **Casualties, Overall**. Yet death was only one type of cost, as the war would also have far-reaching social and economic implications. The Empires of Austria, Germany, and Russia all collapsed, and all suffered to a greater or lesser extent from civil war or unrest. Ultimately the Austrian Empire was split up. Large parts of Eastern Germany were lost to Poland and smaller parts of the West occupied, or reoccupied, by France. After hostilities it was calculated that Europe owed America $10 billion, yet Germany's interim reparations were set at just $5 billion, a figure which in any case was wildly beyond her ability to pay. Britain's total expenditure was £8,742,000,000, and, with the cost of

Right and Below: In its most basic form, the cost of the war to many people was their livelihood, their towns, their churches, and their homes. These two photographs show images of Ypres in 1916. *Chrysalis Photo Library*

the Commonwealth War Graves Commission and munitions disposal taken into account, she is still paying to this day. The cost to the Central Powers is difficult to estimate, but has recently been calculated at 1.37 trillion marks. On the micro scale the cost is more meaningful but equally stark. By 1918 starvation had begun in Berlin, where the number of prostitutes had doubled and clothing cost ten times what it had in peacetime. In Vienna food riots occurred as early as 1915. In Britain, where privation was less severe, food was rationed, income tax rose from 9d to 1s 3d, tax on tea and beer almost doubled, as did the prices of flour and sugar. *SB*

Creel, George (1876–1953)

The administrator of the quasi-governmental Committee on Public Information (CPI), George Creel was a promoter and propagandist who created the public relations machine that helped to build a high level of support in the United States for the country's participation in World War I. Born in Lafayette County, Missouri, Creel worked as a reporter for the *Kansas City World* in the 1890s before starting his own newspaper, the *Kansas City Independent*, in 1899. In 1909, he went to work for the *Denver Post*, but moved across town to the *Rocky Mountain News* in 1911. When the United States declared war on Germany in April 1917, the country was still deeply divided. A strong pacifist element still opposed United States' involvement, and the Wilson Administration needed to rally support for the effort. Wilson created the CPI and handpicked Creel, a fellow Democrat, to run it. Creel energetically threw himself into the task, designing a slick and sophisticated advertising and public relations campaign and organizing a team of 18,000 public speakers. These speechmakers, known as the "four-minute men," were sent out to give speeches throughout the nation in support of United States' involvement. Reportedly, there were 755,190 speeches given to 314 million Americans. Most memorable was the CPI's Division of Pictorial Publicity, which employed such famous illustrators as Charles Dana Gibson and N. C. Wyeth to create poster artwork. Probably the most famous was James Montgomery

Flagg's portrait of a finger-pointing Uncle Sam (see page 312), who declared "I Want You . . . for the U.S. Army!" While the Committee on Public Information was set up as a committee, it reportedly met as such just once. Creel ran the CPI as his private fiefdom, and, while he was very successful in doing his job during the war, he came in for strong criticism after it. The CPI, which might have been of continuing use to Wilson during his ill-fated attempt to sell the United States on the League of Nations, was disbanded. Creel later ran unsuccessfully for governor of California. *BY*

Creeping barrage

The idea of artillery fire which lifted from target to target ahead of attacking troops was conceived as early as 1915, but its development was hampered by poor communications, lack of suitable shells and fuses, and inflexible infantry tactics. By the latter part of 1916 however, barrages which crept forward so many yards per minute had become a common feature of battle,, and fire plans of increasing sophistication were used. No longer did batteries hammer away for days before each attack, spoiling every possibility of surprise, but there was an increasing use of shorter and more intelligent bombardments. What the Germans called the fire "waltz" was particularly feared: barrages which crept over a position, paused, allowed defenders to emerge, and then "walked" back. *SB*

Cruisers

Cruisers—as a distinct ship type—date from the 1880s, but have their origins in the frigates of the age of sail. These vessels combined the roles of commerce raider and protector with that of scouting. By 1885, armored protection was provided to the cruiser's deck (unlike the belt armor on larger ships), and the term "protected cruiser" came into being. Protected cruisers were considered somewhat obsolete by 1914, and rarely saw active service during the war. Instead, they were frequently used in colonial waters, or as escorts. While these protected cruisers were designed for traditional roles, a different design evolved, better armed and armored but having less speed and endurance. In 1899 the first of six British "Cressy" class cruisers appeared, protected by a light armored belt. These successful warships were followed by the increasingly powerful "Monmouth" class (ten ships), "Drake" class (four ships), and "Devonshire" class (six ships). Although not officially dubbed "armored cruisers," these "belted cruisers" were a compromise between armored and protected cruisers. In 1904 the Royal Navy introduced the first of nine true armored cruisers, with a main armor of three to six inches, a powerful main battery of 9.2-inch guns and a secondary battery of either six-inch or 7.2-inch guns. They were designed for use away from the main battle fleets, and their poor performance at the Battle of Jutland reflects their use in the wrong role, rather than poor design. The Germans also employed armored cruisers, and the "Scharnhorst" class were used effectively as powerful cruisers, until they met the even more powerful battlecruiser design. Around 1903, a series of light cruisers entered service, an improved version of the protected cruiser. Speed was emphasized at the expense of armament and protection. Designed as "the eyes of the fleet," these light cruisers were used extensively by both the British and the Germans (as well as most other navies), and typically, although gun size was restricted to six inches or less, most light cruisers could attain speeds of twenty-five knots or more. Light cruisers commissioned before 1912 displaced less than 3,600 tons (such as the British "Active" class or the German "Bremen" class), but later light cruisers (like the British "Weymouth" class or the German

Above Left: The German cruiser *Dresden*, here flying the White Flag at Juan Fernandez. *Chrysalis Photo Library*

Left: The wreck of the British light cruiser *Arethusa*. *Chrysalis Photo Library*

Above: The German cruisers *Nürnberg* and *Emden*. *Chrysalis Photo Library*

"Breslau" class) were larger displacing 4–6,000 tons, and carried a more powerful armament. These were designed for an new cruiser role; screening the main battle fleet from enemy destroyers and torpedo boats. *AK*

Ctesiphon, Battle of

By November 1915 the British advance in Mesopotamia along the Tigris River in the direction of Baghdad had run into extensive Turkish defenses running through the site of the ancient city of Ctesiphon. The British commander, General Charles Townshend, attempted to break through the Turkish positions on November 22 with his small force. The

attack was only partly successful, with both sides suffering heavy casualties, and Townshend ordered a withdrawal to Kut on the 25th. Harassed by the Turks under Nur-ud-Din, the British had reached the town by early December and dug-in to await the arrival of reinforcements. The pursuing Turks placed Kut under siege. *IW*

Czech forces

Although nominally members of the Austro-Hungarian Empire, many Czechs desired the creation of an independent homeland. Consequently, many found themselves fighting against the empire. Some Czech units of the Austro-Hungarian Army simply deserted wholesale, usually to the Russians or Italians, while other Czechs formed units serving with the French, particularly after some of their leaders advocated incorporating the Czech-dominated province of Slovakia into Russia in 1915. Czech forces tended to adopted the uniforms and equipment of their host country, although the troops wore insignia

indicating their origin. The largest and most renowned of these units was the Czech Legion, which operated in Russia during World War I and in the subsequent civil war. *IW*

Czech Legion

The most famous of the three Czech legions initially fought as part of the Russian Army. It was formed in late 1917 when Czech nationalist leader Tomas Masaryk convinced the Bolsheviks to create a unit from Czech prisoners, former members of the Austro-Hungarian Army, under distant French control. At the end of the war, the Legion, some 100,000 strong, was ordered by the French to leave the Eastern Front for Vladivostok prior to withdrawal. Relations between the Bolsheviks and Czech Legion broke down during the journey through Siberia, and fighting broke out. During the Russian Civil War, the legion fought with anti-Bolshevik forces along the Trans-Siberian Railroad until its evacuation was completed in 1920. *IW*

D'ANNUNZIO, GABRIELE

Above Right: Naval operations in the Dardanelles, 1915. *Chrysalis Photo Library*

D'Annunzio, Gabriele (1863–1938)

One of the most important Italian literary figures of his age, D'Annunzio initially worked as a journalist in Rome. His first poems were published when he was sixteen; in the 1890s, he wrote a trilogy of novels with Nietzsche, before being elected to the Italian parliament in 1897. As a result of his affair with the actress Eleanora Dusa, he turned his attention to the writing of plays. An ardent nationalist, he was a firm advocate of Italian involvement in World War I. Indeed, he was to lose an eye in 1916 while on active service as a pilot—he served as a soldier, sailor, and airman during the war! In September 1919 he seized the city of Fiume, a port on the northern Adriatic which was disputed between Italy and Yugoslavia, and he ruled until ejected by the Italian government the following year. A supporter of Mussolini, d'Annunzio died in 1938. *MS*

Dallolio, Alfredo (1853–1952)

An Italian soldier and politician, Dallolio was appointed under-secretary of state for munitions in July 1915—being promoted to secretary of state in June 1915—with the task of preparing Italian industry for war. Taking control of more than 2,000 factories, production increased dramatically, although military reverses, in particular the Caporetto Offensive, led him to resign in May 1918. Dallolio was also to be Mussolini's commissioner for war production between 1935 and 1939. *MS*

Danilov, Yuri (1866–1937)

Born in 1866, Danilov was one of Sukhomlinov's main assistants prior to 1914, drafting the famous Plan 19 in 1910. His plan envisaged Germany fighting a war on two fronts, but leaving the Eastern Front less well defended while concentrating action against France, thereby allowing Russian forces to invade East Prussia. In 1914 Danilov became deputy chief of staff at Stavka, but found himself unable to exercise power to prevent the various military disasters. Sacked when Nicholas II assumed control of Stavka in September 1915, Danilov then served as a corps commander and briefly, in 1917, commanded the Fifth Army, before going into exile in France. *MS*

Dardanelles, Attack on the

In early 1915 the Allies devised a plan to attack the Gallipoli Peninsula, in an attempt to force a passage through to the Black Sea, and knock Turkey out of the war. From November 1914 on, a combined British and French fleet bombarded the Turkish forts guarding the Dardanelles, the channel linking the Aegean and Black seas. The First Sea Lord, Winston Churchill, was the leading advocate of the assault, and gathered a force of fourteen Allied battleships (most of them being obsolete predreadnought warships) under Admiral John de Roebeck. A major bombardment in mid-February 1915 was followed by an attempt to force a passage through the Dardanelles on March 18. In broad daylight the Turkish shore batteries were presented with a perfect target. At 1:45pm the French battleship *Bouvet* exploded and sank, having hit a mine. Two hours later the battlecruiser *Inflexible* and the predreadnought battleship *Irresistible* also struck mines in the same field. While the battlecruiser limped to safety, another predreadnought battleship, *Ocean*, also struck a mine, and both battleships sank shortly after 6pm. Faced with the loss of three major warships and the crippling of a fourth, de Roebeck abandoned the attack. *AK*

De Castlenau, Noël (1851–1944)

De Castlenau was chief of staff to Joffre from 1911 until August 1914, when he took command of the Second Army. An arch-exponent of French Plan 17, which envisaged a swift French attack through Lorraine in the event of a German invasion, his beliefs were undermined by the trench warfare that dominated. After a period as commander of the French Central Army, he returned as Joffre's chief of staff in late 1915, where he was in charge of the defense at Verdun. He retired in December 1916 briefly, before taking command of the French Eastern Army Group in 1918. *MS*

Deflector Gear

Air combat took a significant step forward when a French Morane-Saulnier L monoplane fighter was fitted with blade deflector plates to enable a machine gun to be fired directly through the arc of the spinning propeller. Originated by Roland Garros, the steel

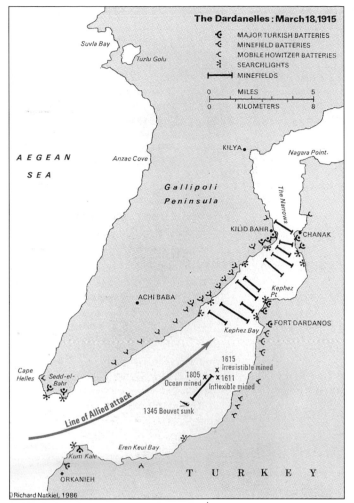

The Dardanelles: March 18, 1915

MAJOR TURKISH BATTERIES
MINEFIELD BATTERIES
MOBILE HOWITZER BATTERIES
SEARCHLIGHTS
MINEFIELDS

MILES 0 — 5
KILOMETERS 0 — 8

Suvla Bay
Tuzlu Golu
KILYA
Nagara Point.
AEGEAN SEA
Anzac Cove
Gallipoli Peninsula
The Narrows
KILID BAHR
CHANAK
ACHI BABA
Kephez Pt
Kephez Bay
FORT DARDANOS
1615 Irresistible mined
1805 Ocean mined
1611 Inflexible mined
1345 Bouvet sunk
Cape Helles
Sedd-el-Bahr
Line of Allied attack
Eren Keui Bay
Kum Kale
ORKANIEH
TURKEY
©Richard Natkiel, 1986

plates or wedges deflected bullets without damaging the blades, a primitive but effective method soon copied and improved upon by the Germans. *JS*

Derby, Lord (1865–1948)

Born Edward Stanley, the Conservative peer succeeded to his title in 1908. As an opponent of conscription, he was appointed Director of Recruitment by Prime Minister Asquith in October 1915 in order to try and find an alternative. His "Derby Scheme," however, was to prove inadequate, and was, therefore, abandoned in December of that year. In December 1916, he succeeded new Prime Minister Lloyd George as War Minister, but was increasingly marginalized and was replaced in April 1918. He would later serve as Ambassador to France. *MS*

Destroyers

The development of fast steam-powered torpedo boats inevitably led to the development of a ship type designed to counter the threat posed by these vessels. During the 1880s, some torpedo boats were converted, having their torpedoes removed and replaced with light, quick-firing guns, becoming "torpedo gunboats," designed to protect the fleet from enemy torpedo boats. By the 1890s, these were replaced by "torpedo-boat destroyers," improved versions of torpedo boats, combining the characteristics of the earlier torpedo gunboats but having a larger displacement, and more powerful engines. In the Royal Navy, the Class "A" torpedo-boat destroyers (shortened to destroyers during the 1900s) were introduced in 1894–95. They displaced under 310 tons, and carried six small guns. Subsequent classes were progressively larger and better armed, while being fitted with more powerful engines, capable of speeds of 25–30 knots. As an example, the "L" class of twenty-four destroyers displaced 1,112 tons and carried three four-inch guns as well as two pairs of twenty-one-inch torpedo tubes. All but two of these "L" class vessels were in service at the outbreak of war. German prewar destroyers were typically smaller, displacing less than 650 tons, but they were faster, achieving speeds in excess of thirty knots. As destroyers came to carry torpedoes, the role between torpedo boat and torpedo-boat destroyer became blurred. Effectively, by 1916, while the Germans still called their light forces "torpedo-boat" flotillas, they were really units of light destroyers. The tactics used by both fleets were the same, as destroyers were used to screen the main battle fleet from enemy torpedo boats, while retaining the ability to launch torpedo attacks against the enemy battle fleet themselves. During the war, most maritime powers continued to commission destroyers, and these continued the trend of increasing displacement and power of armament. As an example, the British "V" class

Below: HMS *Goshawk* and the 1st Destroyer Flotilla in line ahead, circa 1912.
Chrysalis Photo Library

destroyers commissioned in 1917–18 displaced 1,457 tons, carried four four-inch guns and two pairs of twenty-one-inch torpedo tubes, and could steam at thirty-four knots. By 1918 the U.S. Navy was employing over 200 flush-decked destroyers, displacing over 1,200 tons, and armed with four four-inch guns and no fewer than twelve twenty-one-inch torpedo tubes. Also, their role as escort vessels led to their eventual deployment as antisubmarine vessels, armed with depth charges and fitted with hydrophonic listening devices. Given their powerful torpedo armament, destroyers were some of the most deadly ships per ton of the era. *AK*

Diaz, Armando (1861–1928)

Diaz was a senior Italian officer before the country entered the war, being promoted to a divisional command in May 1915. One of the more successful commanders during the numerous campaigns on the Isonzo, he was promoted corps commander in mid-1917 and chief of staff after the defeat at Caporetto. Following his appointment, he organized the successful defense along the Piave but was reluctant to wage

an offensive war once other troops had been diverted to the Western Front until September 1918, when he launched his Vittorio Veneto Offensive, which resulted in victory over a weakened enemy. In 1922 he became Mussolini's War Minister, retiring (with promotion to field marshal) in 1924. *MS*

Djemal Pasha, Ahmed (1872–1922)

Born in Constantinople, Ahmed Djemal Pasha was a Turkish politician and soldier. An early member of the Young Turks movement, he rose rapidly, becoming minister of marine in the cabinet in 1913. Initially keen to avoid war with the Allies, he was eventually persuaded to back the Central Powers. He held a number of military commands during the war, including the military governorship of Syria, based in Damascus, from where he attempted to prevent growing Arab nationalism and also to threaten the Suez Canal. He returned to Constantinople after the fall of Jerusalem in December 1917 but retained power until the government collapsed in October 1918, when he and other Turkish leaders departed on a German ship. Remaining an influential figure after the war, he was to be assassinated in 1922. *MS*

Dogfights

One of many descriptive terms associated with air combat in World War I, "dogfight" passed into aviation lore. It referred to a skirmish between one or more enemy aircraft—usually single-seat fighters—but not necessarily with fatal consequences for either side, for many dogfights proved inconclusive. But it was in the dogfight that many aerial victories were scored, once the successful pilot(s) had out-maneuvered his opposite number, stayed out of trouble himself and avoided colliding with another machine—a very real possibility. Theoretically lasting as long as fuel remained in the tanks of the opposing aircraft, a dogfight was usually over in a matter of minutes. *JS*

Below: General Diaz with General Batington, OC British 23rd Division on the Italian Front.
Chrysalis Photo Library

Above Right: "Beware the Hun in the sun" —a striking lesson in dogfight tactics from British Air Technical Services, June 1918. *Chrysalis Photo Library*

Right: Another tactical diagram—in "Outmanoeuvred" the subject is attacking a two-seater. *Chrysalis Photo Library*

WORLD WAR I: A VISUAL ENCYCLOPEDIA

This diagram is the property of H.M.Govern... and is intended for Official use only.

INCORRECT METHOD.
THE NATURAL INCLINATION OF THE ATTACKER, IF INEXPERIENCED, IS TO TURN IN THE SAME DIRECTION AND FOLLOW.
THIS RESULTS IN GIVING THE ENEMY JUST THE OPPORTUNITY HE DESIRES.

2ND POSITION
SCOUT FOILS ENEMY'S ATTEMPT BY IMMEDIATE TURN IN OPPOSITE DIRECTION.

1ST POSITION
ATTACKING MACHINE DIRECTLY BEHIND & BELOW OPPONENT.

3RD POSITION
REGAINS FAVOURABLE ATTACKING POSITION BY TURNING TOWARDS ENEMY.

2ND POSITION
ENEMY MACHINE BANKING IN AN ATTEMPT TO BRING HIS GUN TO BEAR ON SCOUT.

1ST POSITION
ENEMY'S GUN UNABLE TO BEAR ON SCOUT.

3RD POSITION
ENEMY MACHINE COMING OFF HIS BANK AS MANOEUVRE HAS FAILED.

4TH POSITION
ATTACKING MACHINE AGAIN IN POSITION UNDER ENEMY'S TAIL.

4TH POSITION
ENEMY'S GUN AGAIN UNABLE TO BEAR ON SCOUT.

A HOSTILE TWO-SEATER WHEN ATTACKED FROM BEHIND AND BELOW ALMOST INVARIABLY TURNS WITH A VIEW TO BRINGING THE OBSERVER'S GUN TO BEAR ON THE ATTACKER.
THIS MANOEUVRE CAN BE EFFECTIVELY COUNTERED BY TURNING AT FIRST IN THE OPPOSITE DIRECTION AND THEN, TAKING ADVANTAGE OF SUPERIOR SPEED AND HANDINESS, TURNING AFTER THE ENEMY AND AGAIN COMING UNDER HIS TAIL.

This diagram is the property of H.M Government and is intended for Official use only.

WORLD WAR I: A VISUAL ENCYCLOPEDIA

Dogger Bank, Battle of

Under the command of Vize-Admiral Hipper, the German 1st and 2nd Scouting Groups left Wilhemshaven to raid the British coast. His force consisted of four battlecruisers (*Seydlitz, Moltke, Derfflinger*, and *Blücher*), and four light (protected) cruisers. British intelligence warned the Royal Navy, and while Admiral Jellicoe led the Grand Fleet south from Scapa Flow to intercept Hipper, Rear-Admiral Beatty, commanding a force of battlecruisers and light cruisers, sailed east from Rosyth in the Firth of Forth. Another cruiser squadron steamed northeast from Harwich. Beatty and Hipper's forces clashed off Dogger Bank on January 24, 1915. Beatty's force consisted of five battlecruisers (*Lion, Princess Royal, Tiger, New Zealand*, and *Indomitable*), and several light cruisers. The two sides opened fire at 7:15am, and Hipper turned his ships away, heading back toward Wilhemshaven. By 9:30am the two battlecruiser squadrons were steaming on parallel courses, exchanging salvoes. While three German battlecruisers concentrated their fire on Beatty's flagship *Lion*, British fire concentrated on the *Blücher*. The crippled *Blücher* fell behind her consorts, and at 12:13pm she rolled over and sank. The *Lion* herself was badly damaged, and while Beatty transferred his flag to the *Princess Royal*, the remaining German ships escaped. *AK*

Dreadnought

Designed by Admiral "Jackie" Fisher, the British battleship HMS *Dreadnought* never fired a shot in anger, yet her place in history is assured, representing a technological breakthrough in naval design. When she was commissioned in 1906 she was so advanced that she rendered all previous battleships obsolete, and gave her name to a new type of warship. Her biggest technological breakthrough was the fact that she carried a ten twelve-inch guns, mounted in five turrets. Where previous battleships had carried a variety of calibers, the *Dreadnought* boasted a homogenous broadside, making it devastatingly effective, particularly when this was coupled with its improved system of fire control. A secondary armament was used for defense against enemy light ships, while her armor was proof against the largest battleship guns then available. Even more impressive were her engines, powered by steam turbines, generating 23,000 horsepower, and giving the battleship a top speed of twenty-one knots. At 527ft long, with a beam of 82ft and a displacement of 17,900 tons, she was larger than any other battleship afloat, and it was felt she could hold her own against a fleet of earlier battleships, which were almost derisively dubbed "predreadnoughts." *AK*

Right: HMS *Dreadnought* as built.
Chrysalis Photo Library

Below: Battle of the Dogger Bank.
Richard Natkiel

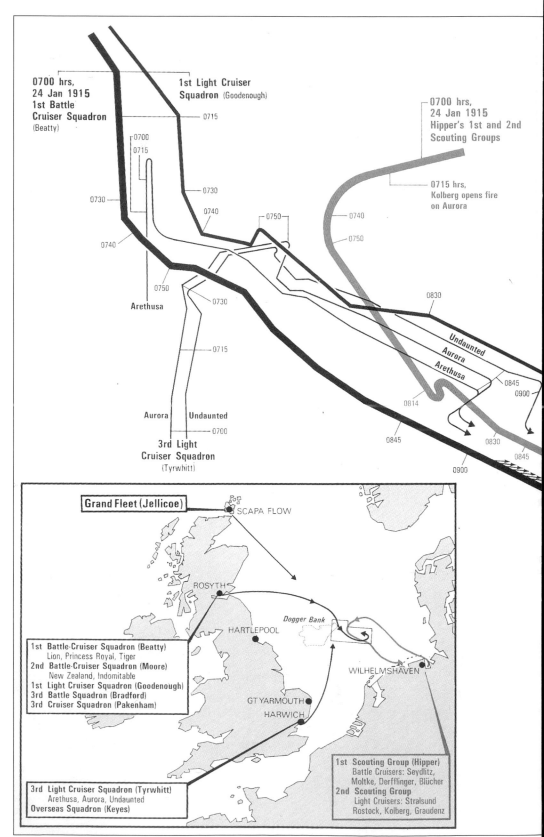

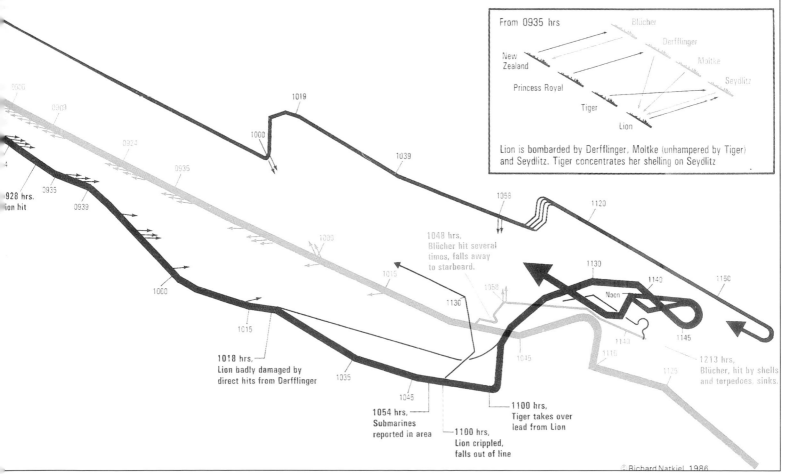

From 0935 hrs

Blücher
Derfflinger
Moltke
Seydlitz

New Zealand
Princess Royal
Tiger
Lion

Lion is bombarded by Derfflinger, Moltke (unhampered by Tiger) and Seydlitz. Tiger concentrates her shelling on Seydlitz

0900
0909
0924
0935
0939
1000
0928 hrs. ion hit
0935
0939
1000
1015
1000
1015
1019
1039
1000
1015
1058
1120
1048 hrs, Blücher hit several times, falls away to starboard.
1058
1130
1130
1140
1150
Noon
1145
1213 hrs, Blücher, hit by shells and torpedoes, sinks.
1110
1125
1045
1018 hrs, Lion badly damaged by direct hits from Derfflinger
1035
1045
1054 hrs, Submarines reported in area
1100 hrs, Lion crippled, falls out of line
1100 hrs, Tiger takes over lead from Lion

© Richard Natkiel, 1986

East Africa, Operations in

Allied attempts to capture German East Africa centered on a protracted and costly campaign to track down the small force under the command of General Paul von Lettow-Vorbeck. The German general scored some notably early successes, such as defeating an amphibious invasion at the Battle of Tanga in November 1914. Facing a build-up of Allied forces, Lettow-Vorbeck resorted to a highly successful guerrilla war that took his forces across much of East Africa, all the while chased by Allied forces. Despite losing more than thirty percent of his command in November 1917, the general fought on until November 25, 1918, when—having been informed of the recent armistice in Europe—he surrendered. *IW*

East Prussia, Russian offensive in (1914)

As its mobilization plans proved seemingly more efficient than many believed possible, Russia was able to support its allies on the Western Front by launching an invasion of the isolated German province of East Prussia on August 15, thereby opening the war on two fronts that Germany feared. Indeed, General Maximilian von Prittwitz's badly

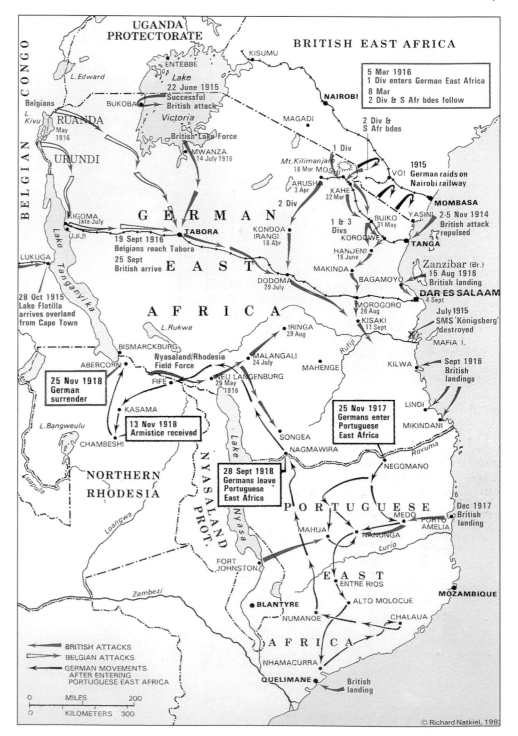

Right: The war in German East Africa.
Richard Natkiel

outnumbered German Eighth Army faced two threats. Along the province's eastern border with Russia was massed General Paul von Rennenkampf's First Army, while several days' march away along the southeast border lay the Second Army under General Alexander Samsonov. Rennenkampf attacked first with the aim of drawing von Prittwitz's forces toward him, thereby allowing Samsonov to push northward two days later to sever the German line of retreat. Initial events seemed to confirm von Prittwitz's gloomy predictions. A small German raid against Rennenkampf was brushed aside at Stallupönen just inside East Prussia on the 17th, while a more forceful counterattack was blocked by the Russians at Gumbinnen three days later. Von Prittwitz signaled a plan to abandon all of East Prussia and was promptly sacked, to be replaced by Generals Paul von Hindenburg and Erich von Ludendorff, who took charge on the 23rd. The new German commanders were of a higher caliber than their predecessors. They saw that the Russian forces were short of all types of supplies and equipment, particularly artillery, and that the inefficient Russian railroad network was unlikely to improve matters quickly. More importantly, it soon became apparent that the Russian invasion was poorly coordinated, with the two armies involved effectively isolated from each other by the Masurian Lakes. Matters were made worse for the Russians as Rennenkampf and Samsonov held each other in contempt and were barely on speaking terms, and the Germans made full use of intercepts of their uncoded radio transmissions. Hindenburg and Ludendorff opted to destroy the two Russian armies in turn, using East Prussia's efficient rail network to switch troops from one threatened front to the other, confident that Rennenkampf and Samsonov were effectively operating in isolation. Their plan proved a masterstroke. Samsonov's Second Army was virtually annihilated at the Battle of Tannenberg fought in late August, while Rennenkampf's First Army was badly mauled at the First Battle of the Masurian Lakes in early September. The two victories guaranteed the security of East Prussia. *IW*

Easter Rising

This was an armed rebellion by Irish nationalists in Dublin on Easter Monday, April 24, 1916, in an attempt to overthrow British rule. In September 1914, following the outbreak of World War I, the British had suspended the Home Rule Bill, which had granted a limited degree of local political autonomy to the Irish. This had prompted an upsurge of nationalism, strengthening organizations such as the radical Sinn Fein, the Citizen Army, and the Irish Volunteers. Leading members of these groups, such as Padhraic Pearse and the British Consul Sir Roger Casement, planned to strike a decisive blow against a weakened British occupation. At midday on April 24 Pearse led 2,000 men who took over the central Post Office (GPO) and other key Dublin buildings, proclaiming the independence of Ireland. Initially, they were able to take control of much of the city, but by the following afternoon British reinforcements had arrived and martial law was declared. Fierce street fighting followed, in which the rebels were gradually driven back. By April 29 only the GPO building still held out under heavy artillery fire. Pearse recognized the impossibility of escape and surrendered without conditions. The harsh treatment meted out to the captives broadened public support for the Free State movement that was to achieve Irish independence after the war ended. Pearse and other leaders were brought before a court martial and fifteen were executed by firing squad. Casement was convicted of treason and hanged; others received long prison sentences. The attitude of the Irish public, most of whom had been lukewarm toward rebellion, hardened immediately. *DC*

Below: A Sinn Fein prisoner being escorted to Dublin Castle after the Easter Rising.
Chrysalis Photo Library

Eastern Front, Operations by the Central Powers on the (1917)

The rapid collapse of the Kerensky Offensive in the first half of July and the successful German-led counterattack that ended in early August effectively signaled the demise of the Russian Army as an effective fighting force. Against a background of revolutionary turmoil, its soldiers were demoralized and mutinous, with many simply deserting. Yet in the Russian capital Petrograd, the Provisional Government, which had taken power during the February Revolution, gave no indication of withdrawing from the war, something that would have allowed German to greatly strengthen its forces on the Western Front. Consequently, an offensive was planned to bring Russia to the negotiating table. The German Eighth Army under General Oskar von Hutier was ordered to capture Riga, a strategy that would place

Petrograd, some 300 miles distant, under threat. Using a combination of surprise and new infiltration tactics, Hutier's offensive, which began on September 1, was wholly and rapidly successful. Riga fell on the 3rd, although the defending Russian Twelfth Army was able to retreat without severe losses. To reinforce the message to the Provisional Government, German amphibious forces carried out landings on Oesel, Moon, and Dagö Islands at the mouth of the Gulf of Riga, during mid-October. Fearing further attacks, the Provisional Government moved the capital from Petrograd to Moscow. This proved a fateful decision. On November 5 Bolshevik revolutionaries led by Vladimir Ilyich Lenin overthrew the Provisional Government and then

sought an end to Russian involvement in the conflict. They agreed an armistice with the Central Powers on December 15, 1917, allowing German troops to move west for the 1918 spring offensive. *IW*

Eastern Front, War on the

The three great powers on the Eastern Front in 1914, Austria-Hungary, Germany, and Russia, each had their own military plans at the outbreak of war. Austro-Hungarian strategists feared war on possibly two fronts. The generals believed any conflict might be against just Serbia in the south or, more likely, against both Serbia and Russia, the former's closest ally. Consequently, their forces were divided into three groups. Two were to be mobilized against Russia and Serbia, while the third was to act as a mobile reserve, ready to rush to where it was most needed, although the

Below: General von Hutier during the Battle of Riga. *Chrysalis Photo Library*

empire's lack of planning and poor rail network made any rapid movement of troops highly unlikely. Similarly, Germany faced the dilemma of a war on two possible fronts—against France and Russia. France was seen as the more immediate threat and was to be dealt with first by the greater part of the German Army launching a preemptive strike. Once victory had been achieved, the forces from the west would transfer to the Eastern Front, joining up with the small holding force stationed there, and then overwhelm Russia. Both of these strategies were based on the belief that full Russian mobilization would be slow. Russia's strategy, known as Plan 19, centered on the need to support its allies. If Austria-Hungary attacked Serbia, Russia would invade the latter's province of Galicia. If Germany attacked France first, Russian troops would invade German East Prussia to force the withdrawal of troops from the Western Front. In the event, Russian mobilization was faster than anyone expected, and both of its principal opponents faced the war on two fronts they had feared. Germany failed to deliver a swift knockout blow against France, and a series of Austro-Hungarian invasions of Serbia were easily repulsed. Russia put Plan 19 into operation by advancing into East Prussia. Although a minor victory was achieved at the Battle of Gumbinnen on August 20, the much smaller German force, chiefly the Ninth Army, inflicted two severe defeats on the Russians, first at the Battle of Tannenberg (August 26–30) and then at the First Battle of the Masurian Lakes in the second week of September. Russian forces suffered large losses and withdrew from East Prussia, although they regrouped along the line of the Niemen River and continued to pose an obvious threat. Russian plans to invade Galicia were preempted by an Austro-Hungarian offensive from Galicia into Russia, but this quickly stalled due to faulty planning and defeats, most notably at the Battle of Lemberg (August 23–September 12). The Austro-Hungarians retreated from Galicia pursued by the Russians, though the fortress of Przemysl held out, and took up positions along the line of the Carpathian Mountains during early October. The German Ninth Army rushed south from East Prussia to shore up the Austro-Hungarian line, heralding a pattern that became usual as the war progressed. Events now switched to the

Russian province of Poland, from where they planned a major drive into the German province of Silesia. However, the German reinforcements sent to Austria-Hungary struck first by launching a spoiling attack through southern Poland that delayed the anticipated Russian offensive. When it did take place in late October and early November, it was met by a German counterattack into northern Poland made possible by the rail transfer of the Ninth Army. The ensuing defeat at the Battle of Lodz (November 18–25) ended Russian attempts to invade Silesia and brought the 1914 campaign to a close. The next year, 1915, opened with Austro-Hungarian attempts to regain Galicia and relieve Przemysl, but the offensive, which took place in the depth of winter, ended disastrously. Przemysl surrendered on March 22. Germany again had to bail out its much-weakened ally. A victory had already been won at the Second (or Winter) Battle of the Masurian Lakes in the first half of February to ensure the security of East Prussia, but Germany's main effort lay against Poland. Russian attempts to advance cross the Carpathians during March and April in the aftermath of the mismanaged Austro-Hungarian offensive were blocked and then a major German-led attack into southern Poland was launched, directed between the towns of Gorlice and Tarnów, on May 2. The Gorlice-Tarnów Offensive proved hugely successful, forcing the Russians in southern Poland to withdraw and those in Galicia to follow in their wake. Przemysl was recaptured in June and Warsaw threatened. A second German drive toward the Polish capital, this time from the north, developed in mid-July. Facing possible encirclement in Poland that would leave his other forces open to flank attacks, the Russian chief of staff, Grand Duke Nicholas, ordered a wholesale fighting withdrawal along virtually the whole of the Eastern Front. Warsaw fell on August 5 and Poland was abandoned. The Russian Army survived this ordeal, although its confidence was fatally undermined by the loss of two million men during the year. In 1916 Germany concentrated its efforts on the Western Front by opening the Battle of Verdun, although it remained acutely aware of its need to shoulder the greater part of the Central Powers' effort on the Eastern Front due to Austria-Hungary's clear military weakness. Verdun opened in late

February and prompted the French to ask the Russians to launch an unexpected and unplanned offensive on the Eastern Front to draw troops away from the west. The subsequent Battle of Lake Naroch (March 18–26) cost the ill-prepared Russians some 100,000 casualties, and the German victory was won without the need to move troops from the Western Front. A second offensive to achieve a similar aim took place in June. Named after its commander, General Alexei Brusilov, the attack, which opened on June 4, made major initial gains against the faltering Austro-Hungarian forces in its path. However, German-led counterattacks during late July coupled with Brusilov's lack of reinforcements, large losses, and the troops' demoralization, stabilized the front, although the increasingly ineffective Russian advance continued into September. The Brusilov Offensive was the last successful Russian attack on the Eastern Front. Russia was gripped by revolutionary turmoil throughout 1917, and the Russian Army gradually disintegrated. Evidence of this came in July during the Kerensky Offensive, Russia's last attack on the Eastern Front. Despite early successes, counterattacks led by German forces blocked the Russian advances. What began as an orderly retreat soon turned into a rout, with ordinary Russian soldiers refusing to fight or obey orders. Germany now acted to force Russia's withdrawal from the war. In September the capture of Riga, close to the Russian capital, Petrograd, put pressure on the government. Meanwhile, Germany encouraged the activities of Russian radicals, such as the Bolsheviks, to overthrow the Provisional Government. In November the Bolsheviks took power and signed an armistice with Germany. Once the peace delegates met at Brest-Litovsk on December 23, the Germans grew to suspect that the Bolshevik representatives were delaying any agreement, and therefore ordered their troops to recommence operations. Facing little opposition, they captured huge swathes of Russian territory, not least the Ukraine, which was an important source of grain. This unanswerable pressure forced the Bolsheviks to sign the highly unfavorable Treaty of Brest-Litovsk on March 3, 1918. Much of the territory ceded by the Russians remained in German hands until Germany itself agreed armistice terms the following November. *IW*

Egyptian forces

Egypt was nominally part of the Turkish Empire but Britain's influence was so widespread, chiefly due to the latter's interests in the Suez Canal, that it declared the country a protectorate in December 1914. Although ordinary Egyptians and its small army were not asked to fight by the British, many did take part in the Allied war effort. Artillery personnel contributed to the defense of the Suez Canal, while other units operated in the Arabian and Libyan deserts. The greatest contribution came from the volunteer Egyptian Labor Corps. This 120,000-strong body played a vital logistical role in supporting the British-led forces campaigning in Palestine. *IW*

Emden, Cruise of the

When the war broke out, the German light cruiser *Emden*, commanded by Captain Karl von Müller, was based at Tsingtau. She left to cruise as a commerce raider against Allied shipping in the Pacific and Indian Oceans. Entering Indonesian waters in late August, she cruised up the coast of Sumatra before entering the Bay of Bengal. She sank several Allied vessels before appearing off Madras on September 22. The *Emden* bombarded the city and then escaped to Diego Garcia, where her keel was overhauled (October 5–15). Next, Müller headed north into the Arabian Sea before

Below: The sinking of the *Emden* by the Australian HMAS *Sydney* as seen in *The Daily Mirror*. *Chrysalis Photo Library*

steaming south and west across the Indian Ocean. He reappeared at Penang Island, off Malaya, catching the Russian cruiser *Zemchug* unawares. The *Zemchug* was duly sunk by torpedo. The *Emden* sank another thirteen merchantmen off Sumatra until Müller's luck ran out on November 9. While many of his crew were ashore destroying the wireless station on Cocos Island, the Australian cruiser *Sydney* caught up with her. After a brief engagement the *Emden* was beached and forced to surrender. Müller and a few survivors escaped in the yacht *Ayesha*, sailing to Arabia before returning through Turkey to Germany as heroes. *AK*

Engineering

Engineers were traditionally responsible for construction, demolition, and a variety of specialist tasks. During the war British Royal Engineers assumed responsibility for such diverse functions as camouflage dumps, tunneling, flamethrowers, gas, carrier pigeons, surveying, meteorology, printing, railway personnel, and concrete supply in addition to matters such as bridging, and signaling, for which no specialist service would appear until after 1918. By mid-1917 the strength of the Royal Engineers had reached about 300,000. The burden of basic construction tasks such as road and dugout building was so great that many "Pioneer" battalions were also formed, although these were drawn from the infantry rather than the Royal Engineers. The basic Royal Engineers unit at the front was the Field Company commanded by a major, with a total complement of six officers and 211

NCOs and men. Field companies could be either mounted or dismounted, and maintained a variety of trades and skills within their ranks. A dismounted company included forty carpenters, twenty bricklayers, fifteen blacksmiths, twelve masons, eight fitters and turners, eight plumbers and gas fitters, as well as coopers, electricians, saddlers, surveyors, tailors, wheelwrights, painters and plasterers. The basic equipment of the Field Company included not only the tools of the trades, and digging tools, but enough materials to build a bridge and 570lb of explosives. Additionally REs were trained and armed with rifles. French engineers included: field companies; fortress sections; searchlight, railway, and telegraph companies; plus cyclist and mountain engineer troops. In the German Army the engineers were three distinct branches: the "Ingenieur" Corps, the "Festungsbau" (fortress construction) Corps, and the "Pioneer" concerned with field and assault engineering. The pioneers also assumed responsibility for many of the mortars, tunneling, and gas. *SB*

Enver Pasha (1881–1922)

One of the leading Turkish politicians of his generation, Enver Pasha was a leader of the 1908 Young Turks rebellion which restored the 1876 constitution and deposed Sultan Abdulhamid II in 1909. Enver Pasha served as the Minister of War prior to the outbreak of World War I, his pro-German feelings leading him to negotiate a secret treaty with Germany. After the outbreak of war, Turkish forces invaded the Caucasus, an action that, while backed by Germany, severely weakened the Turkish defensive forces, making Allenby's assault through Palestine and Syria easier. Following the Turkish defeat, Enver Pasha fled, via Berlin, to Moscow, where he was encouraged by Lenin to head to central Asia in the hope of fostering rebellion in British India. In the event, Enver Pasha was to be killed in 1922 while leading an insurrection in Turkestan. *MS*

Erzberger, Matthias (1875–1921)

A controversial German politician, particularly when he advocated peace without annexation in 1917 and again the following year, Matthias Erzberger was born in Buttenhausen, Württemburg. A leading member of the Center Party, he

HOW WE SANK THE EMDEN: PHOTOGRAPHS

The Daily Mirror

CERTIFIED CIRCULATION LARGER THAN ANY ● OTHER DAILY NEWSPAPER IN THE WORLD

No. 3,482.   Registered at the G.P.O. as a Newspaper.   MONDAY, DECEMBER 21, 1914   One Halfpenny.

THE END OF THE EMDEN: THE LAST PHASE OF GERMANY'S MOST FAMOUS DESTROYER OF BRITISH COMMERCE.

was one of the German delegates at the peace conference after the Armistice and was also an advocate of German acceptance of the terms of the Treaty of Versailles. He achieved high political office after the war—as Vice-Premier and Finance Minister—in 1919 and undertook the nationalization of German railways and the reform of the domestic tax structure. He was forced to resign in 1921 as a result of a failed libel action and was assassinated in August that year in the Black Forest by members of the Organization Consul, one of a number of extremist groups that emerged in post-Versailles Germany. *MS*

Above Left: The 1st Engineers, 1st Division, AEF, on the march near Wirges.
Collection of Bill Yenne

Left: Company B, 303rd Engineers, 78th Division AEF rebuilding a bridge near Grandpre.
Collection of Bill Yenne

Below: Bridge over the Yser Canal north of Ypres, August 1917. *Chrysalis Photo Library*

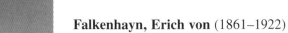

FALKENHAYN, ERICH VON

Falkenhayn, Erich von (1861–1922)

One of the leading German generals of World War I, von Falkenhayn replaced von Moltke as the Chief of the German General Staff in 1914. It was under his command that the German forces refused to retreat after the French victory at the first Battle of the Marne in 1914. However, his failure at the Battle of Verdun in 1916 led to von Hindenburg replacing him the following year. His military reputation was restored as a result of his successes on the Eastern Front, where he led the German forces into Romania when that country entered the war and into Lithuania, as well as in Palestine. *MS*

Falklands, Battle of

Following victory at Coronel, von Spee led his ships around Cape Horn in a bid to escape into the Atlantic. The Royal Navy dispatched a powerful force to intercept him, and by early December this squadron had gathered off Port Stanley. Commanded by Vice-Admiral Doveton Sturdee, the British squadron consisted of two light battlecruisers (*Invincible* and *Inflexible*), two armored cruisers (*Kent* and *Cornwall*), the light cruiser (*Carnarvon*), and the predread-nought battleship *Canopus*. Late in the morning of December 8, 1914, the five German cruisers approached Port Stanley, and the British squadron steamed out to meet them, the *Canopus* opening fire soon after 11am. Realizing the danger, von Spee ordered his ships to retreat to the south. A high-speed stern chase developed, where the superior speed and gunnery of the battlecruisers proved decisive. Von Spee's flagship *Scharnhorst* sank at 4:17pm, followed at 6pm by the *Gneisenau*. The *Kent* pursued the *Nürnberg*, sinking her shortly before 7:30pm, and the *Leipzig* went down an hour later. Only the *Dresden* escaped the disaster, but three months later she was cornered off the Chilean coast and forced to scuttle herself. *AK*

Top Right: Taken from *Invincible*, this shows survivors from *Gneisenau* in the water. HMS *Inflexible* is in the background.
Chrysalis Photo Library

Far Right, Top: The Battle of the Falklands.
Richard Natkiel

Below Right: The British light cruiser *Carnarvon*.
Chrysalis Photo Library

Bottom Right: The German cruiser *Nürnberg*.
Chrysalis Photo Library

Right: General von Falkenhayn and staff conversing with a Turkish officer, Palestine Front. *Chrysalis Photo Library*

Fayolle, Marie (1852–1928)

The French artillery officer Marie Fayolle had already retired before being recalled in 1914. Promotion followed and in February 1916 he took over command of the Sixth Army. He was transferred to the First Army in 1917 and then assumed command of Army Group Center when Pétain became commander-in-chief. In November 1917 he became commander of French forces in Italy returning to the Western Front in March 1918 as commander of the Reserve Army Group. This army was involved in the French defense against the Kaiserschlacht and Aisne offensives and at the Second Battle of the Marne in July 1918. *MS*

Feisal Ibn Hussein (1885–1933)

Feisal was one of the leaders of the Arab Revolt. His father, Hussein Ibn Ali, was the founder of the movement, and Feisal acted on his father's behalf in attempting to encourage support for the revolt against Turkey. Returning to Hedjaz, he led the attack on Medina in June 1916, meeting with T. E. Lawrence (of Arabia) in October of that year when British support was provided. He retained a prominent role through the remainder of the war and attended the postwar peace conference. A short period of rule in Syria, where he proclaimed himself king, came to an end in June 1920, but he was to become king of Iraq in 1921 following nomination by the British (who held the League of Nations' mandate over the territory). He ruled until his death. *MS*

Ferdinand I, King (1861–1950)

In the late nineteenth century, Turkish power over the Balkans gradually diminished and a number of states emerged or expanded at this time. One of these was Bulgaria. Born in Vienna, Ferdinand was the youngest son of Augustus I of Saxe-Coburg and Princess Clementine of Orléans. He was initially called Prince of Bulgaria—from 1887 until 1911—and was to become then the country's first king, having declared the country independent of Turkish rule in 1908. He sought to maintain a balanced policy between the competing alliances, but in 1915 decided to side with Germany and invaded Serbia. The Bulgarian army was severely defeated in Salonika in 1918 and Ferdinand was forced to abdicate.

His son, Boris III, assumed the throne. Ferdinand retired to Coburg, where he died. *MS*

Festubert, Battle of

Forming part of Joffre's Artois Offensive in the spring of 1915, the Battle of Festubert against German positions in the Ypres Salient took place on May 15, 1915, by two divisions of the BEF (mainly Indian forces). The assault made good initial progress and the Germans retreated to a line directly in front of the village of Festubert. A further assault upon these lines, by Canadian troops, was begun on May 18, but was unsuccessful due to severe German artillery fire. Renewed attacks between May 20–24 resulted in the capture of the village itself. The attack was ended on May 27, with the British having suffered some 16,000 casualties. *MC*

Fisher, John Arbuthnot "Jackie" (1841–1920)

One of the most influential naval personalities of the period, "Jackie" Fisher first served in the Crimean War, and subsequently specialized in the improvement of naval gunnery. He was appointed First Sea Lord in 1904, and almost single-handedly masterminded the development of HMS *Dreadnought*, the first truly modern battleship. He also strove to improve naval gunnery, and was an advocate of the big gun. Although he retired in 1910, he returned to duty at the outbreak of war, but resigned over his criticism of Churchill following the Dardanelles Campaign of 1915. *AK*

Above: German flamethrowers in use against a British Mk. IV tank. *Chrysalis Photo Library*

Flamethrowers

Though fire has been part of war for millennia, the first practical, portable, modern flamethrower was designed in the first decade of the twentieth century, and patented by Berliner Richard Fiedler in 1910. Tactical application of the weapon was worked out by Landwehr Captain Reddemann, and it was first used in action at Malancourt near Verdun on February 26, 1915. Immediately after this the formation of a *Flammenwerfer* company was ordered. Eventually Germany would have over 3,000 flamethrower troops organized as three battalions of the Guard Reserve Engineer Regiment, with twelve combat companies, plus a training company and a testing company. During the war these troops would execute a total of 653 flame attacks. The basic principle of fuel oil, squirted under nitrogen pressure, then ignited, remained the same for all the German flamethrowers. In addition to large static projectors the main types used were the *Kleif* (a contraction of *klein Flammenwerfer*—small flamethrower) Models 1912 and 1916; and the ring-shaped Wix Model 1917. By 1918 Wix equipments were organized into forty-four-man sections, each with ten flamethrowers. Allied use of flame weapons was more limited. Even so the French developed the Hersent-type

Left and Center Left: German flamethrowers in action, 1917. *Chrysalis Photo Library*

Below Left: Albatros DIIIs of Jasta II; Richthofen's all-red aircraft is second from the front. *Chrysalis Photo Library*

flamethrower, and British also made use of static projectors, most notably on fourteen occasions on the Somme. Trials were also made of Morris and Lawrence backpack models, and also of the use of flame projectiles from Livens projectors. *SB*

Flying Circus

A term common among RFC pilots who met German fighters in combat and likened their tactics to an aerial circus, partly because they were so brightly decorated compared to their own drab machines. Circus came to be a self-explanatory description for any large formation of enemy machines and was qualified by the name of the pilot who led it. Enemy pilots' fame (or notoriety) spread quickly into the opposing camp: thus von Richthofen became synonymous with his Flying Circus, at least in Allied eyes. This was Jagdgeschwader 1, formed on July 26, 1917, and comprising Jastas 4, 6, 10, and 11 which received its first Fokker Dr 1s that August. *JS*

Foch, Ferdinand (1851–1929)

Born in Tarbes, Foch joined the French Army in 1870, at the time of the Franco-Prussian War. Following service with the artillery in the 1880s, he served for ten years as a lecturer or commandant at the École de Guerre (School of War). Promotion followed: he was a divisional commander in 1911, a corps commander in 1912, commander of the French Ninth Army at the First Battle of the Marne in September 1914, and commander of an army group on the Somme in July 1916. Following a brief retirement, he returned as chief of staff to Pétain, the French commander-in-chief, in May 1917. He was appointed overall commander of the Allied armies on the Western Front in April 1918, and commanded these forces in both the successful second Battle of the Marne on July 15, 1918, and the August offensive. Following work at the Paris peace conference, Foch again

WORLD WAR I: A VISUAL ENCYCLOPEDIA

retired (having disagreed with Clemenceau about the Treaty of Versailles, believing that it failed to give adequate protection to France). *MS*

Forts

By the latter part of the nineteenth century forts were being designed in which artillery and trenches were combined with low-lying earthworks. Concrete was coming into use, and forts were laid out so as to provide overlapping fields of fire. Fortresses were developed both for land borders, and for naval bases, such as Marseilles, Kronstadt, and Portsmouth. The Eastern Frontier of France was protected by fortresses at Verdun, Toul, Epinal, and Belfort—all designated first class—and by intermediate second class works. Yet forts did not fit comfortably into the French military plans which were primarily offensive, and fixed defenses were often neglected. Even so certain forts had significant impact on the progress of the war. At Liège and Namur the works of engineer Henri Brialmont, which had been superimposed over existing defenses, caused a short but significant delay to the German invasion of 1914. In the east the great fortress city of Przemysl was a focus of fighting in 1914 and 1915. The rings of forts at Verdun became a death trap for both sides and Verdun gained a propaganda value far beyond its strategic importance. *SB*

Franchet d'Espérey, Louis Félix Marie (1856–1942)

Born in Algeria (then a French colony), d'Espérey was one of the most successful of French commanders during World War I. He was Commanding General of the French Fifth Army at the Battle of the Marne in 1914. In 1918 he was appointed by Clemenceau to be commander-in-chief of forces in the Balkans. As such, he defeated the Bulgarian forces in Salonika, forcing the defeated army to retreat. He reached Budapest before the Armistice brought a cessation of hostilities. If the Armistice had not occurred then, it is likely that his advance would have continued through Austria and into Germany from the ill-defended south. He became a Marshal of France in 1920. Despite his right-wing sympathies, he did not back Pétain and the Vichy government after the fall of France in 1940, shortly before his death. *MS*

Franz Ferdinand, Archduke (1863–1914)

There are many tragic figures in history and Archduke Franz Ferdinand, heir to the Hapsburg Empire, and his wife Sophie are two of them. Ruthlessly murdered by Gavrilo Princip, a Serbian nationalist, in Sarajevo on June 28, 1914, it was the consequences of these murders that led to the outbreak of World War I as the great prewar alliances came to act. (See page 92.) Franz Ferdinand was born at Graz, but was only to become the heir presumptive to the throne of Austria-Hungary (held by his uncle Franz Josef), in 1896 when Franz Josef's son Rudolph committed suicide. *MS*

Franz Josef I, Kaiser (1830–1916)

Franz Josef succeeded to the throne of the Hapsburg empire in 1848 on the abdication of his uncle Ferdinand. During his long reign of sixty-eight years, Franz Josef was to witness the radical alteration of his realm, including the creation of the kingdom of Hungary in 1867, but was resistant throughout his life to the democratization that had affected many other states in Europe. His long reign was also marked by a number of personal tragedies, including the suicide of his son Rudolph at Mayerling, the assassination of his wife Elizabeth at Geneva in 1898, and the killing of his nephew, Archduke Franz Ferdinand, and his wife at Sarajevo in 1914. It was his invasion of Serbia in 1914 that resulted in the outbreak of World War I, but he had already shown considerable territorial ambition in the early years of the twentieth century through his annexation of Bosnia-Herzegovina in 1908. As emperor of the Austro-Hungarian empire, Franz Josef ruled over much of central Europe and the Balkans. Following his death in 1916, he was succeeded by his great-nephew Charles, who was more reformist by inclination. Unfortunately, the wartime conditions precluded meaningful change, and the empire disintegrated, although Charles never formally abdicated. *MS*

French air forces

One of the most powerful air arms to deploy on the Western Front, the French Aéronautique Militaire had just 138 aircraft, nearly 100 less than Germany, at the start of hostilities in August 1914. This may have masked the fact that France appreciated the military potential of aircraft more readily than some other nations and had taken steps to establish flight training schools before the war. By 1912 there were three Groupes d'Aéronautique including ten aircraft sections as well as balloon and dirigible companies. The *escadrille* or squadron became the basic flying unit, with an establishment of six aircraft, their pilots, mechanics, and other ground staff. Armament trials, conducted with an eye to Germany's airship-building program, included a requirement for a two-seat "dirigible destroyer" as well as machines tailored to tactical bombing and PR. On the outbreak of war France had twenty-three escadrilles equipped with a mix of Farmans, Blériots, Deperdussins, Voisins, Breguets, Caudrons, REPs, and Nieuports. The build-up was rapid and there were thirty-four escadrilles in existence by October. Having achieved an early coup by detecting von Kluck's army making for the Marne and thereby thwarting it by a timely warning, the Aviation Militaire concentrated on PR in the first months of war. Bomber units were formed as such in September 1914 and steadily built-up. The need to take the war to enemy became acute in 1915 and types such as the Voisin 5, Farman F40, and Caudron G4 paved the way for the Voisin 8, Breguet BRM5 and 14B2, and the Caudron R11. These types appeared in 1916–17 and remained in service until war's end. By the time Germany's fighting scouts appeared in force over the front lines the following summer, French aircraft had bombed targets in Germany and developed radio for air-to-ground communications. Formed into *escadrilles de chasse*, machines such as the Morane-Saulnier Bullet monoplane gave way to the Spad SVII and SXIII, and various models of Nieuport including the 17, 27, and 11C-1 Bébé. Taking on the German fighter circuses during "Bloody April" 1917, French pilots wrested air superiority from the enemy and never again relinquished it. A 600-aircraft-strong Division Aérienne was formed in May 1918 to undertake large-scale escorted bombing raids, and by the time of the final German offensive in July, French aircraft (and her production capacity) were more than capable of breaking this last effort on the enemy's part. With many battle honors to its name, the French air arm had, since the first aerial

126

Right: Hanriot HD1s of Lafayette Escadrille.
Chrysalis Photo Library

Below: Aircrew were extremely exposed in World War I aircraft. Open to the elements, flying without parachutes, it must have been extremely difficult to operate a ring-mounted machine gun.
Chrysalis Photo Library

victory on October 15, 1914, when a Voisin dispatched an Aviatik, accumulated a roll of ace pilots. At the head was Réné Fonck with seventy-five victories, second only to von Richthofen in terms of the highest scores on the Western Front. Others included Georges Gunemyer (fifty-three) and Charles Nugasser with forty-five. By the end of the war France had eighty-three fighter escadrilles with a total of 1,392 aircraft based on the Western Front and others based overseas. France had also supplied several Allied nations with many first-line aircraft types, including the United States, Russia, Italy, and Belgium. The French aero industry had responded admirably with technical advances, particularly in developing aerial cameras and radio communications. *JS*

French aircraft

Having taken an early world lead in the construction of airplanes, France had considerable prewar aviation experience thanks to the design expertise of such pioneers as Maurice and Henri Farman, Louis Blériot, and Gabriel Voisin. France built on this technical lead, one that was exploited and funded by licensing agreements with other countries. Manufacturers recognized the future potential of the monoplane over the traditional biplane and with fighters such as the Morane Saulnier H, L, and N, France had demonstrated typical foresight. But World War I was not to see monoplanes oust the biplane—it was one

Left: French antiaircraft gun in action, Salonika, March 1917. *Chrysalis Photo Library*

breaking the air superiority won by Germany over the trenches. The Aéronautique Militaire grew rapidly thanks to energetic fighter production (running to 5,600 examples in the case of the Spad VII). Continuing development brought about several aircraft that, in common with some of their contemporaries built by other nations, failed to find so much favor with pilots. On the French side these included the Hanriot HD1 and the parasol-winged Morane Saulnier A1. As regards bombers, Breguet produced the BR14B2 in 1917 and the little-known Paul Schmitt 7 appeared during the year. Both were two-seaters and the former was destined to see wider service, although France was not to build many types specifically intended for a bombing role. For reconnaissance the well-liked and powerful Dorand AR.1 appeared in 1917, this two-seater also being intended to undertake a secondary, training, role. The Salmson 2 was another late-war newcomer that quickly found favor, so much so that twenty-four units were equipped with it during 1918 and 3,200 examples were completed. Equally at home in a day bombing and ground-attack role, the aircraft also saw service with U.S. air forces. In addition, the Caudron Frères company built the three-seat R11, which also entered service in 1918. France's air arm grew to be the largest in the world by 1918 with 4,511 aircraft in front-line service; wartime production totaled 67,987 machines. *JS*

French Army

The humiliation suffered by the French at the hands of Prussia during the Franco-Prussian War (1870–71) brought about wholesale reforms within the French Army in terms of its war strategies, tactics, and organization. One chief concern was that Germany's already larger population was growing at a faster rate than that of France, a situation that would allow the highly militarized country to field a much larger army than France's in any future war. The French countered this by tightening their conscription regulations. In 1905, for example, the authorities removed several exemptions. Henceforth, all eligible males between twenty and forty-five

of history's ironies that early monoplanes were replaced by biplanes rather than the other way around. Types such as the AG4, the last of the Breguet biplanes (with armor-plated pilot protection), a handful of Deperdussin TTs, and the REP N (also a monoplane) were phased out as more combat-worthy aircraft were developed. By concentrating on a relatively small number of sound designs France became a cornerstone of Allied aircraft production. In 1915 the Nieuport 12 appeared. It was given a dual fighter-reconnaissance role with either one or two crew as necessary. Thereafter the

company concentrated almost exclusively on single-seat fighters. The Nieuport 11 "Bébé," the 17, and 28 were variations on this theme, the last named introducing twin guns, similar armament being fitted to the Nieuport 27 and the Nieuport-Delage 29. Examples of these types remained in service until the war's end. They were joined in 1916 by the first of the Spad (*Société Anonyme Pour l'Aviation et ses Derives*) fighters, the robust SVII. An earlier venture into this field was the A2, followed by the SXI and SXIII—among the finest fighters of the war. They were more than capable of were required to serve with the regular army for two years, eleven with the army reserve, and then progress to the territorial army for the remainder of their service. The 1905 act was modified in 1913 in an attempt to match German military expansion. This saw the increase of the two-year period with the regular army by twelve months, volunteers permitted to enlist from eighteen, and offered financial inducements to those above forty-five who wished to serve for a maximum of fifteen further years. By 1914 these various reforms had created a regular army of some 825,000 men (a figure including some 50,000 colonial troops) and a vast pool of reservists. Of the latter, some 2.9 million had been mobilized by mid-August and a further 2.7 million had been called up by late June 1915. Such figures, which included a large number of reservists too old or badly trained for front-line service, were not matched during the remainder of the conflict. By 1918 the total number of men mobilized had reached 8.3 million, of which some 500,000 were drawn from the country's many colonial possessions. The Franco-Prussian War had also produced a radical shift in France's military doctrines. First, all planning was directed toward ensuring victory in a future war with Germany. At the center of these plans was the recapture of the former French provinces of Alsace and Lorraine. By 1914, this was embodied in Plan 17, which envisioned major offensives into both provinces. This had been developed by General Ferdinand Foch and accept by the army's commander-in-chief, General Joseph Joffre, in 1913. Tactical doctrines had been developed to match this aggressive strategy, embodied in the term *offense à l'outrance* (offense to the utmost). Based on the supposed spirit and élan of French troops, this stated that the psychological impact of infantry and cavalry attacks, backed by massed fire from highly mobile field guns, would sweep away any enemy irrespective of the firepower they could bring to bear on the attacking French units. Consequently, the bulk of the army's training and equipment was directed to launching such attacks. Troops were dressed in brightly colored uniforms to

Right: French Chauchat 8mm light machine gunner of Tenth Army in the Somme area, August 25, 1916. Note ammunition drums.
Chrysalis Photo Library

Above: French Renault of 1915 armed with a 37mm autocannon.
Collection of George Forty

Left: A company of Annamites, French colonial marine infantry from Cochin, China, Salonika, May 1916.
Chrysalis Photo Library

Above Right: French Schneider CA1, armed with a 75mm gun. 400 of these were built, each carrying a crew of seven.
Collection of George Forty

Right: French FT17: an excellent light tank, 1,800 were built and served with French, British, and United States' tank units.
Collection of George Forty

inculcate them with a suitably martial spirit. Defensive weapons, such as machine guns, were neglected, and artillery units were equipped with the mobile, rapid-firing 75mm field gun that could keep pace with fast-moving infantry and cavalry units, but was not suitable for demolishing fortifications. In 1914, the French had some 4,000 field guns as against just 389 heavy guns. The shortcomings of French military doctrines were exposed in 1914, when a brief period of mobile warfare gave way

to trench warfare. Between August and December 1914 the French suffered some 995,000 casualties, something in the region of three times the comparative figure for each of the remaining war years. Although the attachment to offense remained undimmed for much of the war as the German occupation of French territory was seen as an affront to national pride, the scale of losses in 1914 brought about several changes. Gaudy uniforms were abandoned for a more subdued color known as horizon blue,

steel helmets were introduced, and there was a greater provision of machine guns—from around 2,000 in 1914 to more than 60,000 in 1918—and other weapons appropriate to trench warfare. Equally, there were moves to introduce a greater proportion of heavy artillery weapons. The shortfall was initially plugged by a number of often-obsolete weapons taken out of storage or moved from fortresses, but more modern types slowly became available. The importance of artillery was reflected in

Right: The French St. Chamond heavy tank had a crew of nine, a 75mm gun in the nose and four machine guns; 400 were built. *Collection of George Forty*

Below Right: Corps Expeditionaire d'Orient: a French field kitchen near Turkish lines in Salonika. *Chrysalis Photo Library*

Opposite, Top: The Battle of Sharon in the Middle East involved French troops of the 4th Regiment Chasseurs d'Afrique. *Chrysalis Photo Library*

Opposite, Bottom: French troops on the Aisne, 1914. *Chrysalis Photo Library*

the number of men serving in such units, from 395,000 in 1914 to around 600,000 in 1918. The French also founded their own tank corps and greatly increased the size of their air force. The outcome of these changes, coupled with the smaller pool of replacements, led to a drop in the number of troops serving in infantry units from some 1.5 million in early summer 1915 to 850,000 at the opening of 1918. The French continued to launch large-scale offensives in 1915 and had to fight desperately during 1916's Battle of Verdun. The crisis came in 1917, when the Nivelle Offensive in April brought about huge French losses for no appreciable gains. At the end of the month mutinies broke out among the dispirited troops that lasted until June, with fifty-four divisions being affected. The new commander-in-chief, Marshal Henri Philippe Pétain, successfully quelled the outbreaks by executing a few ringleaders and improving the troops' terms of service. The events of 1917 had a long-term impact on the French Army's role in the war. It did make one last major counterattack, in the spring of 1918, but large-scale offensives were avoided. These were left to the British and United States during the final stages of the war on the Western Front. Although the greater part of the French Army's strength was deployed on the Western Front, it did have several commitments elsewhere. Troops, often local forces, were stationed to protect France's colonies, such as Indochina (32,000), Madagascar (3,000), and North Africa (75,000). More directly involved in the conflict were the large forces sent to Salonika, the corps that took part in the Gallipoli campaign, and the handful of divisions that were transferred to the Italian Front. France's forces suffered some of the highest casualty rates of the war. A total of 4.2 million casualties, including 1.5 million dead, were reported between 1914 and 1918. *IW*

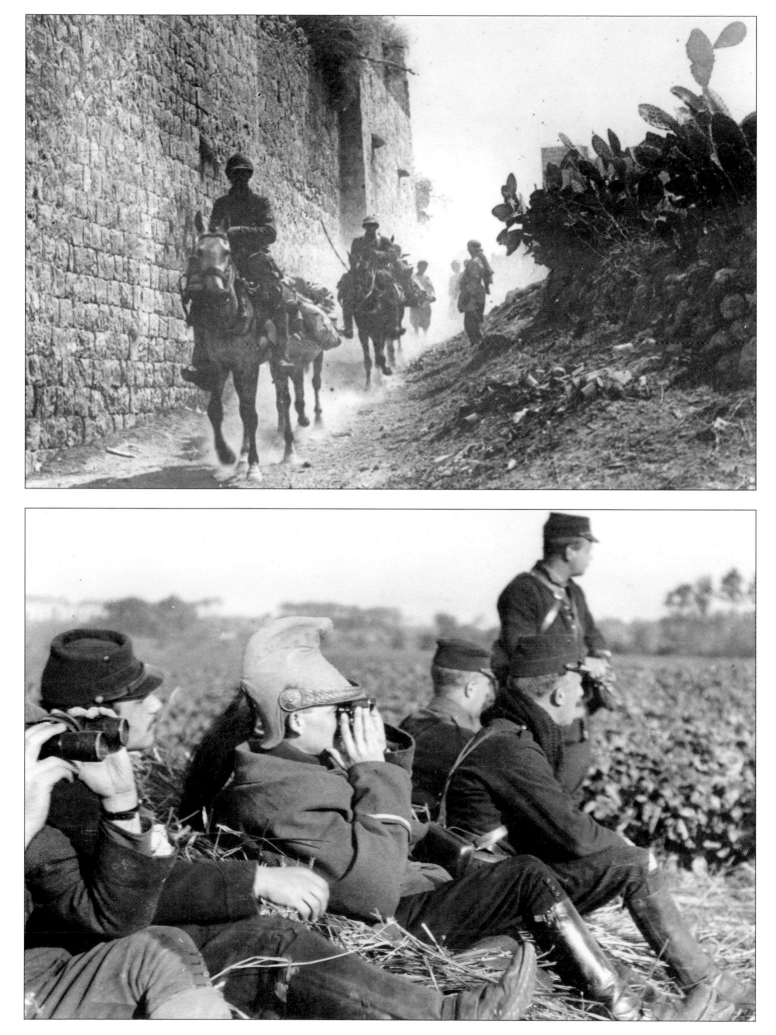

Opposite, Top: French 220mm at the Marne. *Chrysalis Photo Library*

Opposite, Bottom: French officers, Gallipoli. *Chrysalis Photo Library*

Left: 155mm gun in action during the Artois Offensive, May 1915. *Chrysalis Photo Library*

Below: Loading a 400mm railroad gun, Somme-sous-Marne, April 4, 1916. *Chrysalis Photo Library*

FRENCH ARMY

Right: A French machine gun position in Fort Douaumont. *Chrysalis Photo Library*

Below: Battle of the Lys. French cavalryman passing through Hesdin, April 14, 1918. *Chrysalis Photo Library*

Right: General Sir John French.
Chrysalis Photo Library

French Navy

In the decades leading up to the war, the French continually changed their minds regarding a naval policy. While one school advocated the creation of a powerful battlefleet, another favored the use of light forces, particularly torpedo boats. After a period of relative stagnation, the *Dreadnought* "leveled the playing field," and under the guidance of the Minister of Marine, Admiral de Lapeyrè, the French laid the foundations of a dreadnought fleet. When the war began seven French dreadnoughts were in service, and augmented the fleet of twenty-one predreadnoughts and nineteen armored cruisers, plus lighter vessels. The French was divided between the Atlantic Fleet (based in Cherbourg and Brest), the Mediterranean Fleet (based at Toulon) and units deployed overseas, the majority of which were in the East Indies. Although the fleet was divided into regional squadrons, the bulk of the French fleet was deployed in the Mediterranean Sea, as the British Grand Fleet was more than capable of screening the German fleet. The French performed well during the Gallipoli campaign, and were responsible for the transport of the defeated Serbian army from Albania to the relative safety of Corfu, and the support of Allied landings in northern Greece. *AK*

French, Sir John Denton Pinkstone
(1852–1925)

Although now regarded as one of Britain's foremost soldiers, French, who was born in Kent, initially joined the Royal Navy (in 1866) before transferring to the army eight years later. He served in the Sudanese campaign of 1884–85 and in the Second Boer War (1899–1901), where he was a cavalry commander, before acting as Chief of the Imperial General Staff between 1911 and 1914 (being promoted to the rank of field marshal in 1913). On the outbreak of World War I he was appointed commander of the BEF, until he was replaced by Haig, becoming commander-in-chief of

home forces in 1915. Between 1918 and 1921 he held the virtually impossible position of Lord Lieutenant of Ireland at the time of the Angle-Irish War. In 1922 he was ennobled as the first Earl of Ypres and was to die three years later. *MS*

Fuller, John (1878–1966)

A noted military theorist and author, Fuller was born in Chichester (West Sussex) and was to serve both in the Second Boer War (1899–1902) and in World War I, where he developed the theory of coordinated offensive action based around the use of armor and aircraft. This was the theory of *Blitzkrieg* that was to be so effectively adopted by the German forces of World War II. His theories were developed in a number of books that appeared from the early 1920s onward. Fuller retired from the army in 1933 and was to die, at the grand old age of eighty-eight, in 1966. *MS*

Right: Colonel J. F. C. Fuller.
Chrysalis Photo Library

Galicia, Operations in, 1914

The Austro-Hungarian province of Galicia bordered Russia and was the springboard for an Austro-Hungarian offensive against the latter in the opening weeks of the war. Overall command rested with the empire's chief of staff, Field Marshal Franz Conrad von Hötzendorf, and involved four widely separated armies advancing on a 200-mile front. Opposition was provided by the four armies of the Russian Southwestern Army Group commanded by General Nikolai Ivanov, who was under orders to advance into Galicia and had actually advanced some of his forces just inside Austro-Hungarian territory when Conrad von Hötzendorf's offensive finally began. Early engagements, chiefly at the Battle of Krasnik (August 23–24) in which the Russian Fourth Army was just able to halt the pursuing Austro-Hungarian First Army, and Zamosc-Komarów (August 26–September 1), in which the Russian Fifth Army narrowly avoided encirclement by the Austro-Hungarian Fourth Army, were portrayed as significant victories in Austria-Hungary. However, this proved an illusion. The Austro-Hungarian forces were spread too thinly, badly organized, poorly supplied, and indifferently commanded. The Russians struck back farther to the east, pushing toward the Austro-Hungarian fortress of Lemberg in Galicia. A series of battles now developed around the fortress, collectively known as the Battle of Lemberg. At the Zlota Lipa River (August 26–28), Gnila Lipa (August 29–30), and Rava Ruska (September 4–10) the fighting was confused and not wholly decisive. However, having suffered 400,000 casualties since August, Conrad

Above: Captured Russian trenches and barbed wire defenses following the battles in East Galicia, July 24, 1917. *Chrysalis Photo Library*

appealed for German support to stem these reverses. It was not forthcoming and he ordered a wholesale retreat beyond the Carpathian Mountains on the 11th. Most of Galicia was abandoned, with only the fortress of Przemysl remaining in Austro-Hungarian hands behind Russian lines. German help would be needed to regain the lost ground. *IW*

Galliéni, Joseph Simon (1849–1916)

One of the critical French military figures in the early years of World War I, Galliéni served with the French Army during the Franco-Prussian War of 1870–71 and in several campaigns overseas. He served the French state in a number of colonial posts, including that of Governor-General of Madagascar, from 1897 until 1905. His pivotal role in World War I came as the Military Commander of Paris in 1914. Under his auspices, the defenses of Paris were strengthened, and it was under his command, on September 5, 1914, that the French Army defeated the Germans at the First Battle of the Marne, thereby preventing the Germans from capturing Paris and emulating their success of the Franco-Prussian War. *MS*

Gallipoli, 1915–16

By late 1914 some senior Allied figures believed the Western Front was a stalemate and that the situation was unlikely to change in the foreseeable future. Perhaps, they argued, Germany's war

Above: Destroyer HMS *Laforey* following a hospital ship into the crowded anchorage at Mudros just before the Gallipoli Campaign, 1915.
Chrysalis Photo Library

Left: British officers of the 42nd East Lancashire Division question Turkish officers during the Third Battle of Krithia, June 4, 1915.
Chrysalis Photo Library

Below Left: Turkish shells bursting near SS *River Clyde* on "V" Beach, Gallipoli.
Chrysalis Photo Library

effort could be undermined with fewer casualties by striking at one of the other Central Powers. Austria-Hungary was a possibility, but a decisive blow against Turkey offered additional strategic benefits. By knocking it out of the war, the previously blocked supply route to Russia by way of the Turkish-controlled Dardanelles could be opened. The plan was bold and controversial, but seemed to offer a real opportunity for a much-needed victory. It was given the go-ahead, but those opposed to it fought a stubborn rearguard action that saw the entire operation starved of all types of military resources. An Anglo-French naval task force was initially ordered to break through the Dardanelles. The first attempts in late February 1915 failed and those that followed in March were eventually called off, although the Turks were by then acutely short of ammunition for their shore batteries. By this stage, it had been agreed to used ground troops to capture the Gallipoli Peninsula on the north side of the Dardanelles and from there strike at Constantinople, the Turkish capital. The forces first assembled for the landings comprised British,

French, and ANZAC (Australian and New Zealand) troops, most of whom landed on a number of beaches around Cape Helles, the southern tip of the peninsula, on April 25. However, their advance up the peninsula was soon blocked, chiefly in the fighting around the village of Krithia between April and June. To break the deadlock at Helles, the local commander, General Ian Hamilton, ordered an amphibious assault behind the Turkish lines at Suvla Bay to the north. The landing commenced on August 6 but the failure to push inland against initially light Turkish opposition led to the beachhead being contained within a few days. Vicious trench warfare broke out everywhere. Hamilton was sacked on October 15 and his successor, General Charles Munro, successfully argued for total evacuation. Suvla was abandoned in late December 19–20 and Helles in early January 1916. The Allies had suffered some 250,000 casualties and the Turks probably an equal, if not greater, number. *IW*

Right: The landings on the Gallipoli Peninsula. *Richard Natkiel*

Top: Mudros—British hospital ship *Britannic*, **sister ship to the** *Titanic*, **and the British battleship** *Lord Nelson*. *Britannic* **would sink after hitting a mine.** *Chrysalis Photo Library*

Opposite, Top: 2nd Royal Naval Brigade, RN Division, practicing an attack from a trench on the island of Imbros, June 1915. *Chrysalis Photo Library*

Opposite, Bottom: The main landings were at Helles on the southern tip of the Gallipoli Peninsula. This is a view of V beach taken from SS *River Clyde*. *Chrysalis Photo Library*

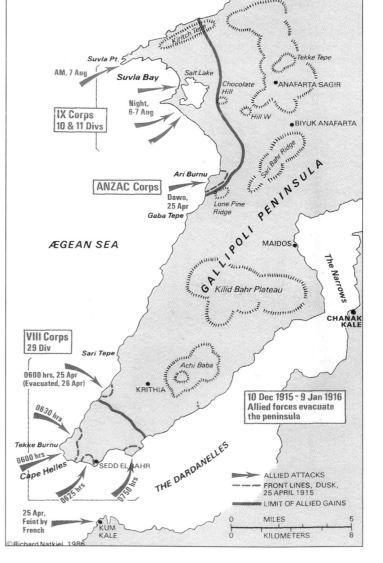

Gallwitz, Max von (1852–1937)

A Prussian artillery officer, Gallwitz initially served on the Western Front in 1914 before being transferred to join Hindenburg's Ninth Army on the Eastern Front. He commanded Army Group Gallwitz—later the Twelfth Army— during the Triple Offensive of July 1915, before being transferred to the Balkans in command of the Eleventh Army's invasion of Serbia. In March 1916, back on the Western Front, he saw service at Verdun and on the Somme, where he commanded the German defenses, and at Ypres, with the Fifth Army, in 1917. After Ypres, Army Group Gallwitz was stationed at Verdun, where it faced various Allied offensives in the last months of the war. He left the army in December 1918 and, for a short period in the early 1920s, sat in the Reichstag. *MS*

Garros, Roland

Frenchman Roland Garros won a lasting place in the history of aviation as the pilot who presented the Germans with the details of his own propeller inter- rupter gear that made air combat so much more deadly. Garros himself was captured by the Germans on April 19, 1915, and they lost little time in fitting a similar device to their own Fokker Eindecker fighters. Garros himself was killed on October 5, 1918, while flying a Spad. *JS*

Gas

Though there had been various experi- ments before, and during, the war, the first full-scale use of gas was made by the Germans near Ypres on April 22, 1915. Chlorine gas was released from the cylinders of 35th Pioneer Regiment

Above Right: Gas sentry of the 4th Seaforth Highlanders, 51st Division, at Wancourt, October 23, 1917. Note Strombos horn. *Chrysalis Photo Library*

Right: Bombardment of Béthune, April 1918. French and British military policemen on patrol in gasmasks, May 20, 1918. *Chrysalis Photo Library*

Far Right, Top: 2nd Argyll & Sutherland Highlanders, 19th Brigade, Bois Grenier Sector, June 1915. These are some of the first gasmasks; respirators were first issued to the battalion on May 3, 1915. *Chrysalis Photo Library*

Far Right, Bottom: Gas sentry ringing an alarm near Fleurbaix, June 1916. *Chrysalis Photo Library*

Above: John Singer Sargent's classic *Gassed*, of the dressing station at Le Bac du Sud on the Arras road, August 1918. *Chrysalis Photo Library*

Above: Gas projector emplacement. *Chrysalis Photo Library*

Right: It wasn't just the men that needed gasmasks if artillery pieces were to move forward. *Chrysalis Photo Library*

Above: The AEF's 130th Field Artillery, Battery "A," firing under gas attack, Varennesen Argonne, March 10, 1918. *Collection of Bill Yenne*

Above Right: A soldier of the 40th Division at Camp Kearny in San Diego, California, uses his gasmask while peeling onions. *Collection of Bill Yenne*

Right: Soldier laughing during gas drill, November 5, 1918. *National Archives via Chrysalis Photo Library*

causing panic among French Colonial troops, and casualties in 1st Canadian Division who stood their ground preventing full-scale rout. Much propaganda capital was made on the Allied side regarding this new terror weapon, but most nations now put their minds to the development of both new gases, and defenses against gas. Phosgene, which was both more deadly and less obvious, made its appearance at the end of 1915. Chlorine and phosgene mixed together was known as "White Star" gas, and particularly effective as the chlorine added weight making the cloud slower to dissipate. Mustard, or "Yellow Cross" gas, which was actually Dichlorodiethyl Sulfide, was first used by the Germans in 1917. This was especially noxious as it was a blistering agent, attacking not only the respiratory system and eyes, as with most gases, but the whole surface of the body. Delivery methods also improved with the use of not only cylinders but shells and special mortars like the British "Livens Projector." Contrary to popular belief, gas was not a major cause of death, and the majority who were gassed returned to active duty. Yet gas did have a significant impact, putting large numbers of men temporarily out of action, causing panic in raw troops, and forcing nations to devote significant resources to gas defense. Some men gassed would survive as invalids until the late twentieth century. *SB*

Gaza, Battles of

The British forces advancing across the Sinai Peninsula into Palestine made three attempts to break through the Turkish defenses that stretched across the coastal plain from Gaza to Beersheba during 1917. The First Battle of Gaza was fought on March 26 and, despite initial successes, the British attack ended in confusion, which allowed the Turks under German General Friedrich Kress von Kressenstein, to hold their positions. The second battle, fought on April 17–19, was badly handled by the British and their frontal assault on Gaza was repulsed. The Third Battle of Gaza (October 27–November 7) involved a successful flank attack inland around Beersheba, which forced the Turks to abandon their positions to escape encirclement. *IW*

Geddes, Sir Eric (1875–1937)

A professional railwayman, Eric Geddes served in the Ministry of Supply where he came to the attention of Lloyd George. From the ministry, he moved to take command of the BEF transport section before becoming Inspector General of Transport (with an honorary rank of major general). He then transferred to the Royal Navy (with the honorary rank of vice-admiral) in May 1917. In July 1917 he became Navy Minister in the War Cabinet—a seat in the House of Commons followed at a subsequent by-election—although his relations with First Sea Lord, Lord Jellicoe, were not harmonious, given their differing views over the role of convoys. Geddes lasted less than a year in the Admiralty, but retained his seat in the War Cabinet until December 1918. *MS*

George V, King (1865–1936)

George was the second son of King Edward VII and, therefore, the grandson of Queen Victoria, like his German counterpart Kaiser Wilhelm II. As Edward's second son, he was not initially heir to the throne and, from 1877 until 1892, he pursued a career in the Royal Navy; he retained his love of naval matters until his death in 1936. It was only on the death of his elder brother, the Duke of Clarence, in 1892, that he became second in line to the throne. The following year he married Princess Mary of Teck. He became Prince of Wales in 1901 and succeeded his father as King-Emperor in 1910. George was very much a constitutional monarch, involving himself in politics only when advised to do so, and during his reign there were a number of significant constitutional changes and crises. These included the Parliament Act of 1912, which defined the powers of the unelected House of Lords; the creation of the Irish Free State in 1922; the Statute of Westminster in 1931, which defined the Dominion status and the relationship between Britain and its Empire; and the Government of India Act of 1935. He was a popular monarch—as reflected by the great celebrations on the occasion of his Silver Jubilee in 1935—and one who took his imperial role seriously: he was the only British monarch to visit the Indian Empire while on the throne. It was George V who inaugurated the now annual Christmas Day broadcasts by the ruling monarch. *MS*

Above Left: Inspection by HM King George V of 29th Division prior to its departure for Gallipoli, March 12, 1915. *Chrysalis Photo Library*

Left: HM King George V inspecting U.S. troops with General Pershing, August 6, 1918. *Chrysalis Photo Library*

German air forces

Greatly aided in its early war aims by the products of Dutch designer Anthony Fokker, the German Air Service was potentially the strongest in Europe in terms of quality on the outbreak of war. This status translated to just 232 effective combat aircraft in August 1914, but the inventory included some of the world's first military monoplanes. One of these, a Taube, dropped two 4lb bombs near Paris on August 13 in the first long-range bombing by a German aircraft. Progressive introduction of Fokker EI, EII, and EIII monoplanes helped maintain air superiority over the Western Front until late in 1915 when Allied types began to pose a real threat. The steady expansion of Germany's aero industry and a flow of personnel to man units in the west, in the east, and in

Above: A captured German Rumpler, 1917. *U.S. Air Force via Chrysalis Photo Library*

Left: Halberstadt DIII with pilot and ground-crew. *Chrysalis Photo Library*

Macedonia meant that improved aircraft continued to be supplied, and first-line strength was maintained. Tactics improved with the formation of circuses equipped initially with the Fokker DIII and Halberstadt DII, fine fighters that outclassed those of the enemy. By April 1916 the Air Service was at its wartime peak and the qualitative edge was maintained with improved fighters. In common with the British, they were obliged to mount many fighter patrols primarily to protect their reconnaissance aircraft but in the main these latter were numerous and capable. Gradual Allied superiority, particularly in terms of several excellent new French and British fighters being issued to first-line squadrons, caused a general rethinking of air strategy. Within the general ebb and flow of air fighting, the lack of lasting success over the Western Front led to a major reorganization of the Air Service in February 1916 but henceforth the bulk of Germany's air effort would be defensive rather than offensive. In 1917 a new "CL" class of aircraft, following the previous "C" class of observation types, were the Halberstadt, Hannover, and Junkers two-seaters. These light observation types were armed with machine guns for both pilot and observer and were formed into *Schlachstaffeln* or trench-fighting groups. Using radio links to work in conjunction with the ground-force commanders and carrying grenades and small bombs, the ground-attack units were used successfully in such actions as that against British forces at Cambrai in November 1917. Such success could not be guaranteed with aircraft that in some instances could be quite unreliable due to engine and structural failure. Almost in the nick of time Fokker gave the Air Service its best fighter of the war although even substantial numbers of DVIIs could not finally turn the Allied tide when the last German ground offensive failed. The other German air force was the German Naval Air Service, which had been active from the first days of the war when frequent attacks were mounted on targets in Belgium, on the coast of England, and out into the Baltic. Using Brandenburg and Friedrichshafen floatplanes, the force was steadily expanded to meet war commitments. Supporting the commerce raider *Wolf* operating in the Indian Ocean, a single German seaplane contributed to several sinkings by spotting enemy shipping and giving early warning of the presence of Allied naval vessels. *JS*

Right: Albatros DIX single-seat fighter.
Chrysalis Photo Library

Below: Albatros DV biplane, 1917.
Chrysalis Photo Library

German aircraft

With aircraft that were qualitatively excellent and more numerous than the Allies when war broke out, Germany fully expected to maintain control of the skies over the battlefield. In this they were often successful and able to take a grim toll of Allied machines, particularly as more inexperienced Allied pilots were introduced. But even German industry, exemplified by the energetic Fokker works, could not outperform the combined industrial might of the Allies, and soon both qualitatively and quantitatively, there was more of a challenge. To maintain some freedom of action the skies over the battlefields had to be cleared of Allied reconnaissance aircraft and when in 1915 these encountered the Fokker EI/III Eindecker, there was widespread alarm. With its single synchronized gun, the Germans appeared to have a terrible

Left: Maintenance on an Albatros CV, 1916.
Chrysalis Photo Library

Below: Fokker Triplanes being wheeled back to their sheds after a patrol, March 1918.
Chrysalis Photo Library

aerial weapon, against which there was little defense. But remedial action from the enemy saw Germany began to lose its quality edge, particularly in fighters. A copy of a British triplane led to the Fokker Dr 1, a renowned design when it functioned well but there were numerous engine failures which reduced its effectiveness and cut production to 320 examples. When in September 1916 the first Albatros DI appeared at the front, followed by the DII, aerial supremacy was regained for a short time. The succeeding DIII, DV, and DVa were soon matched by the Camel, the SE5, and the Spad. When the latest Albatros types also began to experience technical failures, the Idflieg (*Inspektion der Fliegertruppen*) had to introduce drastic new measures. Thus the fighter units were reorganized into Jastas and subsequently *Jagdgeschwadern*, initially operating the Pfalz DIII and Fokker Dr I. Neither type was a complete answer to the improved Allied fighters but the strafing and ground-attack work by the CL aircraft had some adverse effect on Allied ground troops. Clearly the Air Service needed a much-improved fighter if air superiority were to be won back and maintained. That call was answered in 1916 by the redoubtable Anthony Fokker, who had been somewhat in the background since the success of his

earlier products in the hands of German pilots. In the meantime he had been investigating a new fighter with cantilever wings. After winning the fighter competition held at Adlershof on January 21, 1918, Fokker began producing the superlative DVII, delivering 775 examples to the front-line Jastas by November 1. An outstanding aircraft, the Fokker DVII could hold its own against any Allied fighter. It was highly maneuverable, pilots delighting in literally hanging the aircraft on its propeller while its opponents were fighting a stall. But despite equipping forty-eight Jastas, there were simply too few DVIIs to overwhelm the enemy, boosted since 1917 by American manpower; the attrition of past years had also resulted in the loss of too many experienced German and Austrian pilots for a weakened training organization to replace them quickly enough. As the foremost builder of rigid airships, Germany's long-range bombing of enemy targets hinged on the designs of Count von Zeppelin. Powered by up to six engines these airships gained a short-lived psychological advantage. Various designs were used throughout the conflict, culminating in the "X" class of 1918. Able to carry 8,000lb of bombs, only the L70, one of three completed,

attacked Britain on August 5, 1918, and was promptly shot down in flames. On a much more modest scale were the C category of armed reconnaissance aircraft which included the products of the Aviatik, Rumpler, Ago, Lloyd, and LVG factories. Two-seaters had become an integral part of the air inventory and Germany added to these 1915 models half a dozen Albatros variants plus the DFW CV and the AEG CIV. In succeeding months. Austrian output by Hansa-Brandenburg and Lohner swelled the inventory still further, and with armament and excellent cameras available, these types enabled reconnaissance sorties of up to four hours' duration to be flown with a degree of safety not apparent at the start of the war. Germany introduced more two-seaters into service than other nations and at the end of the conflict the Austrians had additionally produced the UFAG and the Phoenix to meet the C category, these being joined by the German Halberstadt CV and the Hannover CLIIIa. In terms of heavy bombers the German aircraft of 1917–18 were as advanced as current design practice could make them, favorably comparable with those of the enemy. Once again, the Air Service had more of them in inventory than any other

combatant power. "Heavy" in 1918 terms included the twin-engined AEG GIV which weighed slightly less than 8,000lb and was powered by Mercedes liquid-cooled engines. At the other end of the scale was the mighty Zeppelin-Staaken RVI and subsequent models. With four engines the RVI spanned just over 138 feet, weighed 25,269lb, had a crew of seven and an endurance of up to eight hours. Long-range air attacks by the Kampfgeschwadern on Britain and France with examples of these R—*Riesenflugzeug*—(giant aircraft) and the smaller twin-engined Gotha V and Friedrichshafen GIII achieved results superior to those of the Zeppelins, but Allied defenses and operational accidents continued to take a steady toll. In this field—as in others—German production barely kept pace with losses in both men and machines. Having kept abreast of developments in naval aircraft—universally float-equipped for operations from water during World War I —Germany produced a number of excellent designs. These included the sleek single-seat Rumpler 6B1 fighter floatplane and the Hansa-Brandenburg CC which had a boat hull fuselage with a pusher engine mounted on struts. The same manufacturer produced the KDW,

Far Left: Albatros DV. *Chrysalis Photo Library*

Above: Albatros CV, January 1917.
Chrysalis Photo Library

Left: A squadron of Albatros DVA scouts.
Chrysalis Photo Library

Below Left: German airfield.
Chrysalis Photo Library

a more angular design with twin floats. The Hansa-Brandenburg W12, designed by Ernst Heinkel, had a distinctive upswept rear fuselage. A two-seat biplane with a single rear gun, the W12 was intended to be self-defending and garnered considerable respect from its opponents. It was joined by the mono-plane W19, a sturdy design with a very broad-chord wing to support the twin floats. *JS*

German Army

Germany was the most militarized state in the world at the outbreak of World War I, chiefly due to the widespread belief that the empire should adhere to the concept of a nation in arms based on universal short-term conscription followed by prolonged service in the reserves. For many sectors of German society military service was seen as an honor, not least because of the all-pervading influence of the army in the country's political and national life. Consequently, the German Army had a peacetime strength of some 700,000 men but could be expanded to 3.8 million within a matter of days once full mobilization had been ordered. At the heart of this force was a large body of well-trained and experienced officers and NCOs. Conscription was on the basis of regulations made into law in 1895. Between ages seventeen and twenty recruits to the infantry served in the *Landsturm*, a form of home guard. Between twenty and twenty-seven, they spent two years in the regular army and five in the first-line reserve. Next they progressed through the two classes of the

Landwehr between the ages of twenty-seven and thirty-nine. Finally, they returned to the *Landsturm*, where they remained to the age of forty-five. However, Germany's population was rising so rapidly before World War I that only around fifty percent of those liable actually joined the regular army; the remainder either served with the *Landsturm* or the Ersatz Reserve, which was a body created for men with slight disabilities or personal circumstances that precluded the normal type of conscription. After twelve years in the Ersatz Reserve, recruits transferred to the *Landsturm*. In terms of the recruits' origins, there was a distinct bias toward those with a background in the countryside or from small rural towns, as these men were considered to be hardier and more adaptable than their urban counterparts. Control and direction of this vast reservoir of manpower ultimately rested with the German emperor, Wilhelm II, but effective control lay with the army's chief of staff, who operated through the general staff, which was the heart of the military machine. This highly ompetent body controlled all of the army's activities, from planning and

supply to strategy. Like much of the regular army, officers attached to the general staff were members of the land-owning aristocratic class. It was the general staff that codified the nation's war strategy, the Schlieffen Plan, and created the railroad-dominated plans for mobilization that almost produced victory in 1914. The German Army had an advantage over its rivals in terms of its equipment, partly due to the demands of the Schlieffen Plan, which recognized that any attack into a neighbor's territory might be delayed by frontier fortresses. Consequently, weapons were developed to neutralize such targets as quickly as possible. Among these were heavy artillery pieces, such as the 420mm howitzer known as *Dicke Berta* (Big Bertha), grenades, flamethrowers, and mortars. All of these were to prove invaluable for trench warfare. Standard infantry equipment was also of the modern type, and the provision of machine guns was well above that of Germany's rivals. Due to its training, leadership at all levels, and equipment, the German Army was undoubtedly the best conscript force in the world in 1914, and it remained a formidable opponent until

Far Left: Bombers following the stormtroops in Champagne, 1918.
Chrysalis Photo Library

Above: German soldiers in Bucharest.
Chrysalis Photo Library

Left: German prisoners being brought in, Battle of Albert, August 21, 1918.
Chrysalis Photo Library

the last months of the war. However, its overall effectiveness did show a fall as the war progressed. Evidence of this came in 1916. On the Western Front, the Battles of Verdun and the Somme produced huge German casualties, not least among the highly motivated officers and NCOs that formed the backbone of the prewar army—these proved difficult to replace. Due to these and subsequent losses, Germany's reserves of manpower were placed under mounting strain. For example, those who should have been called for service in 1919, if the war had continued, were actually inducted in 1917. Paralleling this was a change in recruitment patterns. Men were increasingly drawn from urban and industrial areas; there was a general belief among senior officers that such recruits were less reliable and, most worryingly, had what were considered radical and destabilizing political opinions. Also many had witnessed at first hand the hunger and misery brought to the home front, particularly in the cities, by the tightening Allied naval blockade that the German naval forces could not counter. The blockade also placed greater strains on the industries that supported the army. While every

Opposite, Top: German troops advance in 1914.
Chrysalis Photo Library

Opposite, Bottom: German communication trench near Rheims. This provides a good view of the personal equipment of the German infantryman.
Chrysalis Photo Library

Above: The German occupation of Brussels, August 26, 1914. The rapid advances of the early months of the war showed the skills of the German infantryman.
Chrysalis Photo Library

Left: German troops storming out of their defensive trenches.
Chrysalis Photo Library

effort was made to supply those in the front line with food and equipment, the technical edge enjoyed in the early war years was eroded. For example, Germany never developed a tank force of any size and the air force was more and more outnumbered by those of the Allies. Equally, military control of the economy proved disastrous. At a higher level, there were also fundamental problems in the general staff's direction of the war. Some of these were partly self-inflicted, while others came about because of the weaknesses of Germany's allies, chiefly Austria-Hungary. The Schlieffen Plan, which was supposed to avoid a war on two fronts, effective failed with defeat at the First Battle of the Marne in September 1914. It was overly ambitious in its initial form but subsequent tamperings made success even more uncertain. Thus Germany had to face a two-fronted war from the Marne until the collapse of Russia in 1917. Second, after the Marne failure, German strategy faced the dilemma of where to win the war—the Eastern or Western Front—and emphasis regularly switched between the two. However, one fundamental fact could not be ignored— the whole German Army could not be in two places at once, nor could it afford

to denude one or other front of truly significant forces as the Allies proved quite adept at launching simultaneous offensives on both. This division of effort was magnified by the military weakness of Austria-Hungary, which necessitated the deployment of German troops away from the Western and Eastern Fronts on a regular basis to prevent its defeat. Germany's last chance of victory came in the spring in 1918. Units moved from the Eastern Front and elite groups of stormtroopers almost brought victory, but at a cost of the army's last reserves of manpower and its best troops. Defeat followed within a few months, although elements of the army fought to the last. The army's casualty list for the entire war reflected its dominant position within the armed forces of the Central Powers—1.75 million dead. *IW*

Left and Right: These photographs show a good range of German Army uniforms and equipment. The photo at right is of German infantry on pre-war maneuvers. That at bottom left is a group picture of the men of the Punt Battery with a 38cm gun, May 1918. *Chrysalis Photo Library*

German invasion of Belgium 1914

Following the pattern laid down by the Schlieffen Plan the German armies started their route westward on Saturday August 1, 1914, moving through Luxembourg toward the Belgian frontier. On August 3 Germany declared war on France and on the 4th Belgium. The German Army entered Belgium on August 4 and met unexpected resistance. The first target of the Germans was the fortified city of Liège, which was duly invested on the 6th by von Bülow's Second Army. Von Kluck's First Army had pushed on to the right, bypassing Antwerp and taking Brussels on August 21. To the south the German Third, Fourth, and Fifth Armies were arrayed in line to wheel into France while the Sixth and Seventh Armies remained on the defensive in Lorraine, ready to receive any French counter-thrust. It was, however, the First and Second Armies that were the key to a swift German victory. Having subdued Liège on the 12th von Bülow moved on, crossing the Sambre and driving off the French Fifth Army on the 23rd. Meanwhile von Kluck's First Army had experienced a sharp encounter with the BEF on the 23rd, driving them back and beating them again at Le Cateau on the 26th. Here von Kluck diverged from the original plan, turning southeast to support von Bülow and hit the French Fifth Army in the flank. This meant that he passed to the east of Paris rather than enveloping it from the west. The stage was now set for a French counterattack from the "Mass of Maneuver" gathering to the east of Paris. *MC*

Right: The French blew bridges to stem the onslaught. This is over the Oise. *Chrysalis Photo Library*

Below Right: J Battery, RHA, in open positions in 1914. *Chrysalis Photo Library*

Below: The German invasion. *Richard Natkiel*

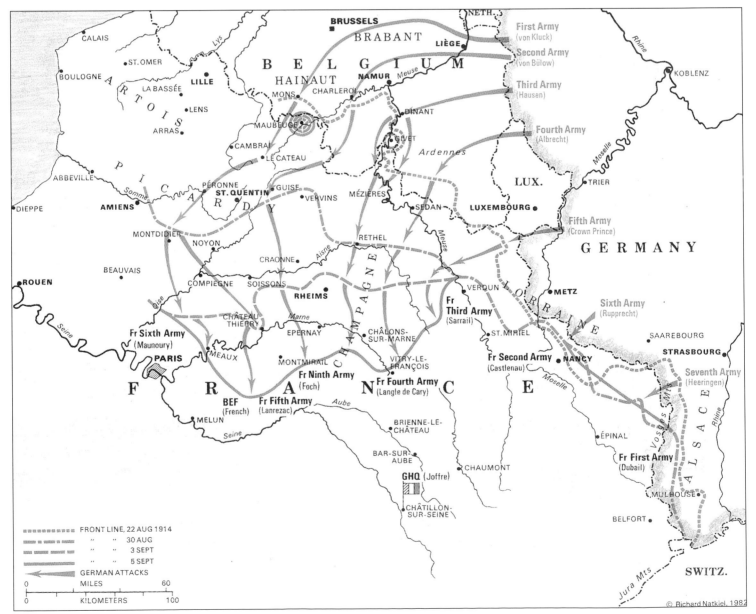

German Navy

Under the guidance of Admiral Tirpitz, the Imperial German Navy had become the second largest naval power in the world. It was quick to follow Britain's lead in the race to build dreadnoughts, and saw the German fleet as a deterrent to British aggression. Tirpitz initiated a naval expansion which accelerated over the next sixteen years. By August 1914 the German fleet consisted of seventeen dreadnoughts and two more entered service during the war. A fleet of five (later seven) battlecruisers and a powerful fleet of cruisers and lighter warships supported the main battlefleet. This force, the High Seas Fleet, was based at Wilhelmshaven, on the North Sea. At the outbreak of war the Germans also maintained several light units overseas; these became commerce raiders, achieving considerable success before they were tracked down and destroyed. Apart from the occasional sortie by the High Seas Fleet—such as those which led to the engagements at Dogger Bank (1915) and Jutland (1916)—the Germans avoided risking their fleet, and instead they increasingly relied on U-boats to defeat the British. The ultimate failure of both the battlefleet and the U-boat campaign were significant contributory factors in Germany's defeat. *AK*

Above: The German fleet.
Chrysalis Photo Library

Below: The British may have had the best navy in the world in 1914, but they lost a lot of ships to German gunnery during the war. This is the wreck of HMS *Invincible* taken from HMS *Benbow*. Torpedo boat destroyer *Badger* is approaching to pick up the six on board who survived the explosion that sank her at Jutland in 1916. *Chrysalis Photo Library*

Above Right: The German cruiser *Scharnhorst*, 1907. *Chrysalis Photo Library*

Below Right: The German cruiser *Blücher*, 1910. *Chrysalis Photo Library*

Previous Page: A closeup of the battleship *Schlesien. Chrysalis Photo Library*

Above: The flagship *Preussen;* **behind it SMS** *Pommern, Hessen, Lothringen, Hannover,* **and** *Schlesien. Chrysalis Photo Library*

Left: German naval landing party preparing to leave Direction Island, November 10, 1914. *Chrysalis Photo Library*

German Eastern Front offensives of 1915

By spring 1915 the German high command was laying plans to deliver a crippling blow to Russia on the Eastern Front. The Russian Army had been hit hard during the previous winter's fighting and was acutely short of supplies, particularly ammunition. Also, Austria-Hungary's commander-in-chief, Field Marshal Franz Conrad von Hötzendorf, argued that his own forces urgently required German help in holding the Russian armies massed along the Carpathian Mountains in Galicia. Field Marshal Paul von Hindenburg and General Erich von Ludendorff decided to accede to Conrad's request. Their aim was to attack through Galicia, between the towns of Gorlice and Tarnów, and then drive north between the Bug and Vistula Rivers. This, they believed, would allow them to encircle the Russian forces operating in Poland to the north. Although the Austro-Hungarian Third and Fourth Armies were available for the offensive, it was to be led by the newly formed Eleventh Army under General August von Mackensen, which comprised German forces withdrawn from the Western Front but also included a sprinkling of Austro-Hungarian troops. The Austro-Hungarian Fourth Army, holding the line to the north of the Eleventh Army, was placed under von Mackensen's control, and more than 900 artillery pieces were made available for the opening barrage. The opposing Russian forces, which held a 100-mile front, consisted of the understrength Third Army led by General Radko Dmitriev. Dmitriev's forces were outnumbered by four to one and faced an artillery force eight times stronger than their own. The offensive began on May 2 and was heralded by a four-hour artillery bombardment that took the Russians by surprise. Resistance crumbled rapidly in the face of the follow-on infantry assaults and the Germans were able to capture the three lines of Russian trenches by the following day. By the 4th, the breakthrough was total. The Russian Third Army had been smashed, along with reinforcements rushed to the front. The Central Powers captured 120,000 prisoners and close to 100,000 Russians had been killed or wounded. In appreciation of the scale of the victory von Mackensen was promoted to field marshal. The breakthrough at Gorlice-Tarnów precipitated a wholesale Russian withdrawal from much of Galicia, allowing Austro-Hungarian and German troops to recapture the key fortress of Przemysl and the provincial capital of Lemberg in June. The Russian withdrawal, which never quite turned into a rout, also allowed the attackers to occupy much of southern Poland, thereby creating a deep salient in the line around Warsaw. The salient offered the further opportunity to encircle several Russian armies. Thus, while von Mackensen continued his drive from the south in the direction of Brest-Litovsk, a newly activated German Army, the Twelfth under General Max von Gallwitz, struck in the north on July 13 with the intention of capturing Warsaw. Fearing encirclement the Russian chief of staff, Grand Duke Nicholas, ordered a wholesale withdrawal that left the Germans in control of the greater part of central Poland by late August but saved the Russian Army from destruction. Warsaw, itself, had fallen on the 5th and Brest-Litovsk followed suit on the 26th. Further German encircling operations took place in the north over the following weeks. The Grodno salient was eradicated in the first week of September; that around Vilna thereafter. Subsequent attacks on the flanks, by the Germans against Riga in the north and by the Austro-Hungarians against Tarnopol in the south, gained little and the fighting subsided. After several months of combat the Central Powers had captured huge swathes of territory but failed to destroy the Russian Army completely. Their attacks had also engineered one significant event in the

Russian high command. Grand Duke Nicholas, whose skillful withdrawals had preserved the Russian Army, was effectively demoted in early September, and in a move that was to have profound consequences, Tsar Nicholas II took personal command of his empire's armed forces. *IW*

German raiders, Operations of

In August 1914, the German naval base at Tsingtau in China was the home port for the East Asia Squadron commanded by Count Maximilian von Spee. His force included two armored cruisers (*Scharnhorst* and *Gneisenau*) and four light cruisers (*Emden*, *Nürnberg*, *Leipzig*, and *Dresden*). Together with the light cruisers *Karlsruhe* in the Caribbean and *Königsberg* off East Africa, these forces were deployed to protect German overseas interests and colonies. In the event of war, it was considered extremely unlikely that any of them would be able to return to Germany, so they were given orders to act as commerce raiders until they were destroyed. When war broke out the *Leipzig* was off San Francisco, but rendezvoused with von Spee's fleet off Easter Island, as did the *Dresden*, which had been cruising in the Atlantic. The *Emden* was given orders to operate independently, and wreaked havoc in the Indian Ocean until she was destroyed on November 9. Almost a month later, von

Spee's squadron was destroyed during the Battle of the Falklands (December 8), and only the *Dresden* escaped. She was finally cornered in the Juan Fernandez Islands, and her crew scuttled her on March 14, 1915. The *Karlsruhe* spent two months attacking Allied shipping off Brazil before steaming northward toward Barbados. On November 4, 1914, she blew up 200 miles north of Trinidad. The cause was never fully explained. The *Königsberg* was in German East Africa when the war began. She sank the old British cruiser *Pegasus* off Zanzibar before hiding up the Rufiji River. She was duly located and blockaded, so her commander sent several guns and crew ashore to support German land operations. The last of the German raiders was finally destroyed by British warships on July 11, 1915. *AK*

Giolitti, Giovanni (1842–1928)

Giolitti was one of the most important politicians in Italy during the years following the country's unification and into the twentieth century. He first entered parliament in 1882 and achieved his first ministerial position seven years later. He was first to serve as Prime Minister in the period between May 1892 and November 1893, when he was forced to resign over a financial scandal involving the Bank of Rome. He next served as Prime Minister, after a brief

period in exile, between October 1903 and March 1905 and again between May 1906 and December 1909. He was next in power between 1911 and March 1914, during which time the country annexed Tripoli and went to war with Turkey, resulting in Italy's acquisition of Libya, Rhodes, and the Dodecanese. However, the high cost of the war and the resulting high taxation led to a general strike and to him being forced from office. Giolitti was one of the strongest supporters of Italian neutrality at the start of the war—despite the alliances with Austria-Hungary and Germany that he had helped to create—and was to serve as Prime Minister for a fifth and final time between June 1920 and June 1921. During this last administration, he was unable to deal with the postwar chaos and the rise of Mussolini's fascists to power. *MS*

Goeben, Flight of the

When the war broke out, the German battlecruiser *Goeben* and the accompanying light cruiser *Breslau* were in the Western Mediterranean. After bombarding French ports in Algeria, the two

Right: The flight of the *Breslau* and *Goeben*. *Richard Natkiel*

Below: The *Goeben*. *Chrysalis Photo Library*

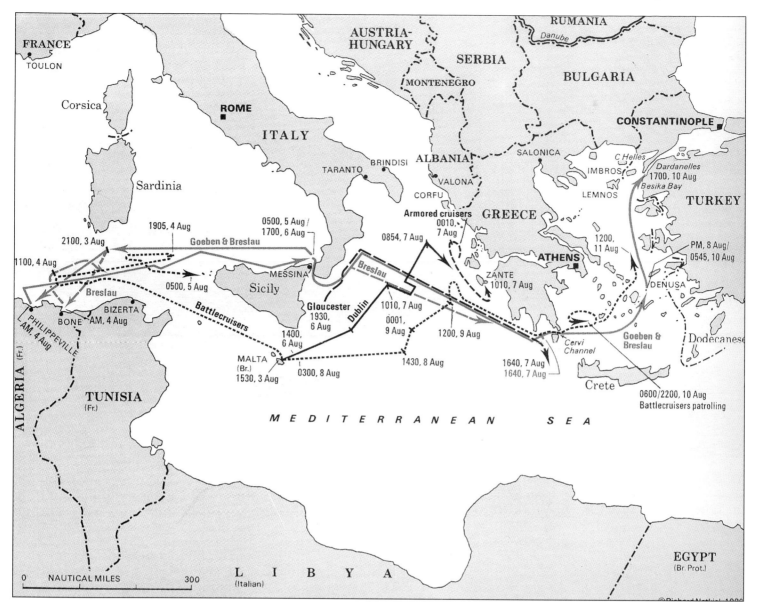

warships were forced to flee from the British ships sent to stop them. They evaded three British battlecruisers by sailing north past Sicily, before passing south through the Straits of Messina during August 5–6. Once more they slipped through the British cruiser screen sent to block their progress, but as they sailed east they were shadowed by British cruisers. By August 7 the *Goeben* was off the southern tip of Greece, and the British ook up blocking positions in the southern Aegean Sea. By heading east around them, the *Goeben* and her consort circled round the British, reaching the Aegean island of Denusa on August 8. The pursuit continued, but by this time the Germans were too far ahead of their pursuers to be stopped. They passed through the Dardanelles, reaching the Turkish port of Constantinople on August 11. Their arrival helped persuade Turkey to join the Central Powers, and the two warships continued to operate in the Black Sea until the end of the war. *AK*

Goering, Hermann (1893–1946)

Hermann Wilhelm Goering had obtained three victories by the time he joined Jasta 7 in 1916. He was wounded while flying with Jasta 5 later that year and was with Jasta 26 between February and May 1917. Goering shot down four more enemy aircraft before becoming CO of Jasta 27 in May 1917, during which command his score rose to twenty-one. Receiving the "Blue Max" in May 1918 he became Rittmeister of JG1 on July 8 and obtained his twenty-second and last victory on July 18. *JS*

Right: Hermann Goering in 1918 as CO of the Richthofen squadron. *Chrysalis Photo Library*

Goltz, Colmar Baron von der
(1843–1916)

Goltz served with the Prussian Army—reaching the rank of major—until 1883. He then spent thirteen years helping to train the Turkish Army. Returning in 1896 as a lieutenant general, he was promoted field marshal in 1911. Although an opponent of the Schlieffen Plan, he was to spend a brief period as military governor of Belgium, before being transferred to Turkey in December 1914. His time in Turkey was, however, not harmonious, although he was in nominal control of the Sixth Army in Mesopotamia in October when it successfully defended Ctesiphon and defeated Townshend at Kut. Goltz died in April 1916, possibly the victim of poison. *MS*

Gompers, Samuel (1850–1924)

A British-born American labor leader, Samuel Gompers is credited with having helped to keep organized labor in line with the American war effort throughout World War I. Gompers emigrated to the United States at age thirteen and went to work in a cigar factory. He became a union man at age fourteen and a union local president at age twenty-four. In 1881, he helped to found the Federation of Organized Trades and Labor Unions, which became the American Federation of Labor (AF of L) in 1886. Gompers became the first president of the AF of L, a post that he would hold for most of the remainder of his life. As perhaps the leading spokesman for the labor movement, he was called upon in 1917 to head the War Committee on Labor, and to serve as a member of the Advisory Commission to the Council of National Defense. In these roles, he assured the United States that the unions would do their part to support the American war effort. *BY*

Gough, Sir Hubert de la Poer
(1870–1963)

Born in County Waterford, Ireland, de la Poer was commissioned in 1889 and served with the British Army in the Boer War, where he led the relief of Ladysmith despite orders to the contrary. In 1911 he was appointed commander of the 3rd Cavalry Brigade in Ireland; however, he and fifty-seven fellow officers refused to act against Carson's Ulster Volunteers when the government sought to impose Home Rule. Their action led to the failure of the policy and to a belief among Irish nationalists that democratic methods to achieve home rule were doomed to failure. Despite this overt act of mutiny, de la Poer was to achieve rapid promotion during World War I and by 1917 had achieved command of the Fifth Army prior to the Third Battle of Ypres. His failure at this battle, combined with his weak defense against the German advance in early 1918, led to him being made a scapegoat. Between 1919 and 1922 he led a military mission to the Baltic; this was again a failure. *MS*

Grand Fleet

In late July, as war loomed, Admiral Callaghan led the Royal Navy's Home Fleet to its wartime station at Scapa Flow, in the Orkney Islands. On August 4, as Britain declared war on Germany, the command was handed to Vice-Admiral Sir John Jellicoe, and the name of the British armada changed to the "Grand Fleet." Jellicoe raised his flag in the dreadnought *Iron Duke*. When the war began the fleet consisted of twenty dreadnought battleships, and two more were added soon after, bringing the British superiority in dreadnoughts to eight over the fourteen German warships. German lack of numbers was partially offset by her fleet of twenty pre-dreadnought battleships, so Jellicoe

Above: Units of the Grand Fleet passing through the North Sea. *Chrysalis Photo Library*

received reinforcements of eight British predreadnoughts of the "King Edward" class. He also boasted a superiority in battlecruisers (five to Germany's four). The new battlecruiser *Tiger* joined the fleet in November 1914, and following the defeat of the German East Asia Squadron, the three remaining battlecruisers rejoined the Grand Fleet, while other powerful vessels were added to the fleet as the war progressed. By May 1916 the Grand Fleet consisted of three "Battle Squadrons" (1st, 2nd, and 4th, containing a total of twenty-five dreadnought battleships), another battle squadron (the 3rd) consisted of eight predreadnoughts. A small group of light cruisers was attached to the main battlefleet as scouts, while Jellicoe's main force was further supported by the 3rd Battlecruiser Squadron's three battlecruisers. The entire force was screened by three large destroyer flotillas The semi-independent Battlecruiser Fleet commanded by Vice-Admiral Beatty operated from Rosyth in the Firth of Forth, where it was better placed to intercept German "hit-and-run" raids on the British eastern coast. His force consisted of the 1st and 2nd Battlecruiser Squadrons, with five battlecruisers, and the 5th Battlecruiser Squadron with four "Queen Elizabeth" class fast battleships. Attached to Beatty's main force were three squadrons of light cruisers and three destroyer flotillas. The Grand Fleet was the most powerful single instrument of war in the world, and its loss would be a devastating blow to Britain. It was also a source of immense national pride, a symbol of British naval might and moral supremacy. As such, its use in battle had to be outweighed by the risk of its loss, so Jellicoe's responsibility was immense. When Jellicoe was promoted after the Battle of Jutland (1916), Beatty took over command of the Grand Fleet. *AK*

Graves, William Sidney (1865–1940)

A career military officer, General William Graves commanded the U.S. Army force that occupied the Russian city of Vladivostok in the wake of the 1917 Russian Revolution. Born in Mount Calm, Texas, Graves was a member of the Class of 1889 at the U.S. Military Academy at West Point. He served with the 7th and 6th Infantry Regiments in the western United States during the latter part of the Indian Wars. In 1899, as a captain, he was given the first of two tours of duty in the Philippine Insurrection. In 1909, Graves was assigned to duty with the General Staff in Washington, where he served until World War I. In July 1918, he was promoted to major general and given command of the 8th Infantry Division. However, a month later, he was relieved of that post in order to undertake a secret mission under direct orders of Secretary of War Newton Baker. The assignment was command of a U.S. Expeditionary Force consisting of 10,000 men, including two infantry regiments. The mission was to protect Allied military supplies that were in depots along the Trans-Siberian Railway, to render whatever aid possible to the Czech Legion stranded in Siberia, and to discourage the Japanese from occupying Russian territory during the confusion that followed the Russian Revolution. Graves' force arrived in Siberia in August 1918, and remained until April 1920. He had been ordered not to engage the Bolshevik factions, and he successfully resisted pressure from some Allied diplomats to do so. After the American withdrawal from Russia, Graves briefly commanded of Fort McKinley in Philippines, and then commanded the 1st Infantry Brigade and the 1st Infantry Division through 1925. He served as commander of VI Corps Area, Chicago through 1926 and the Panama Canal Division through 1928, when he retired from the U.S. Army. *BY*

Below: Major General William S. Graves (Commanding General Allied Expeditionary Force, Siberia) is seen here (seated, center) with his staff in Vladivostok on November 23, 1918. *Collection of Bill Yenne*

Greece, War in

For much of the war Greece was destabilized by political infighting, with various pro-Allied, pro-Central Powers, or neutral factions vying for control of the country's affairs. The pro-Allied group eventually gained the upper hand and declared war on the Central Powers in June 1917. Despite its ambiguous position prior to mid-1917, Greece had been effectively forced to accept the presence of large Allied forces on its soil since October 1915. These had remained largely inactive apart from a successful but limited counterattack against Bulgarian and German forces following the Battle of Florina in August 1916. By 1917 the Allied troops stationed in Salonika totaled some 500,000 men, but these troops had mostly remained inactive, not least because many were suffering from malaria. Two small-scale offensives, the Battles of Lake Prespa and the Vardar River, were launched in March and May respectively, but achieved little. Matters began to change at the end of the year with the appointment of a new Allied commander, France's General Marie-Louis Guillaumat, who reorganized the forces under his command and established a better working relationship with the other local commanders than his predecessor. Guillaumat was recalled to France in June 1918 but his replacement, General Louis Franchet d'Esperey, was able to capitalize on his work. A second offensive along the Vardar River opened in mid-September and the largely Bulgarian forces faced by the Allies quickly collapsed. The subsequent Allied advance, although slowed by shortages, had reached the borders of the Austro-Hungarian Empire by the end of the war. Nevertheless, many believed that the diversion of Allied resources to Greece was a strategic mistake and that they would have been better employed on the Western Front. *IW*

Greek Army

The Greek Army had divided loyalties until the country sided with the Allies in June 1917. Those that would eventually form the nucleus of the forces fighting with the Allies consisted of the 60,000-strong Army of National Defense, which had been established by the pro-Allied politician Eleutherios Venizelos in late 1916. Much of this force's equipment

Above: An artillery team taking a bank, Struma Front, November 1916. *Chrysalis Photo Library*

was outmoded and its was largely reequipped by the Allies. Following a period of recruitment the Greek Army was able to field some 250,000 men and these played a role in the Allied advance through the Balkans from Salonika from September 1918. Greek casualties totaled 100,000 men with 15,000 fatalities. *IW*

Grey, Sir Edward (1862–1833)

Born into a traditionally Liberal political family, Grey was Liberal Member of Parliament for Berwick-on-Tweed for thirty-one years between 1885 and 1916, when he was created Viscount Grey of Falladon (having become a baronet in 1882). His first ministerial office was in 1885, but it was as British Foreign Secretary from December 1905 until May 1916 that he oversaw the development of British foreign policy in the build-up to war. In particular, he worked on the rapprochement with Russia—traditionally seen by Britain as a threat to the Indian Empire through Afghanistan—in the Anglo-Russian Entente of 1907, and stronger links to France and Belgium. An opponent of war, he nonetheless believed that Britain should fulfil its obligations once Belgium had been invaded. His comment at the time still resonates: "The lamps are going out all over Europe; we shall not see them lit again in our lifetime." He continued to be active in politics after the war and was a strong supporter of the League of Nations. *MS*

Gröner, Wilhelm (1867–1939)

Gröner was a colonel in August 1914, when he was in charge of German field railways. In June 1915 he was promoted major general and he added control of food supply to his existing remit over railways in May 1916. Later in 1916 he took charge of the Supreme War Bureau, the body established to maximize production as part of the Hindenburg Program. In August 1917 he became a divisional commander on the Western Front, moving to the Eastern Front in February 1918, as chief of staff to Army Group Eindhorn. On October 29, 1918, he returned to Berlin as Deputy Army Chief of Staff, and played a pivotal role in the build-up to the Armistice, the abdication of Wilhelm II, and the creation of the postwar Ebert government. He retired from the army in September 1919 before pursuing a new career in politics. *MS*

Guerrilla warfare

Guerrilla warfare was in its infancy in 1914 though major powers already had experience of irregular combat in the colonies. Nevertheless incidents occurred in Belgium as early as August 1914 in which German troops were, or claimed to be, fired upon by "franc-tireurs." The reaction to what von Kluck called this "extremely aggressive guerrilla warfare," was reprisals. These tended to backfire, presenting the Allies with easy propaganda victories. *SB*

Guillaumat, Marie (1863–1940)

A French general, Guillaumat was a divisional commander in August 1914. In December 1916 he replaced Nivelle as commander of the Second Army at Verdun, masterminding the French offensive in August 1917. Transferred to the Balkans, he took charge at Salonika in December 1917 before being recalled to Paris in June 1918. He took command of the Fifth Army during its advance through the Ardennes during the last weeks of the war. *MS*

Guise St. Quentin, Battle of

The Battle of Guise St. Quentin was one of the many encounters that took place during the Battle of the Frontiers of late August 1914. The retreating French Fifth Army under Lanrezac had fallen back to Guise when it was ordered to attack St. Quentin in order to relieve the pressure on the British at Mons and allow for a French regrouping around Paris. The attack was mounted on August 29 and 30 and proved to be little more than a delaying action as superior German numbers immediately threatened Fifth Army's

flanks. On the 30th Lanrezac broke off the action and withdrew, having caused considerable German casualties and disrupted the timetable of their advance. *MC*

Gumbinnen, Battle of

On August 20, 1914, less than a week after Russian forces had crossed into East Prussia, the local German commander, General Maximilian von Prittwitz, unleashed his outnumbered Eighth Army against General Paul von Rennenkampf's Russian First Army. His aim was to crush von Rennenkampf and then turn south to deal with a further invasion force, the Russian Second Army under General Alexander Samsonov. Three corps were earmarked for the assault but only General Hermann von Francois' I Corps was initially in a position to do so due to the chaotic state of the local roads. Although his forces made some headway against the Russian right flank, ill-coordinated attacks by the other two corps, chiefly due to Francois' impetuousness, made little headway. Indeed, heavy Russian artillery fire forced the commander of the German XVII Corps in the center, General August von Mackensen, to retreat, which in turn precipitated the withdrawal of General Otto von Below's I Reserve Corps to the south. To von Prittwitz, these events seemed to herald a successful Russian offensive deep into East

Prussia, one he believed he could not halt. He panicked and ordered his subordinates in the Eighth Army to fall back on the Vistula River, a move that would have effectively abandoned the province to the invaders. The order was, in fact, ignored by the corps commanders and von Prittwitz was removed from command of the Eighth Army. His replacement was General Paul von Hindenburg who quickly recognized weaknesses in the Russian invasion plan and, along with General Erich von Ludendorff, moved swiftly to develop a strategy to thwart the invaders that would lead to a great victory at the Battle of Tannenberg. *IW*

Gunboats

In the nineteenth century, European colonial powers developed gunboats to protect the security of their overseas dominions. These small, but maneuverable and reasonably well-armed, warships dispensed "gunboat diplomacy" across the globe. By 1914, small scout cruisers and miniature monitors augmented traditional colonial gunboats on overseas naval stations. Although most European powers as well as the United States and Japan employed these vessels, the British had the most extensive empire at the time, and the most gunboats. Monitor gunboats cornered and destroyed the German cruiser *Königsberg* in East Africa, while smaller gunboats were towed across Africa for use in Lake Tanganyika against German forces in the region. The British also made extensive use of gunboats in Mesopotamia, and even used them to support British operations against the Bolsheviks in northern Russia after the war. The term was also applied to motor launches and motor gunboats used as coastal vessels in the English Channel and the Adriatic Sea, and these vessels were eventually adapted to carry torpedoes, creating the motor torpedo boat (MTB). Italian vessels of this type were particularly successful in operations against the Austrian navy, while British motor gunboats were crucial to the effectiveness of the Dover Blockade. *AK*

Left: British six-inch howitzer in action in the Balkans, December 1916.
Chrysalis Photo Library

H

HAIG, SIR DOUGLAS

Haig, Sir Douglas (1861–1928)

Haig was one of the more controversial figures in British military history, given that he was faced by a war of attrition, with massive losses particularly in the Somme and Ypres campaigns of 1916 and 1917. Born in Edinburgh and educated at Oxford and Sandhurst, Haig, as a cavalry officer, saw service in Egypt, South Africa, and India before being appointed General Officer Commanding Aldershot. In August 1914 he commanded the British I Corps of the BEF (seeing service at Ypres), before succeeding French as British commander-in-chief in December 1915. Criticized at the time, Haig's position was undermined by the deterioration of French forces and by lack of support from Lloyd George. Haig, however, retained command, being backed by the chief of staff, Robertson, and, under the overall command of Foch, led the final decisive offensive in August 1918. He was created the First Earl of Bemersyde in 1919 and, in postwar years, undertook great work in the care of ex-servicemen, including helping to create the Royal British Legion. *MS*

Top Right: The British commander-in-chief, Field Marshal Sir Douglas Haig, 1918.
Chrysalis Photo Library

Right: Haig congratulating Canadian troops after their victory at Amiens, August 11, 1918.
Chrysalis Photo Library

Haldane, Richard Burdon
(1856–1928)

Born in Edinburgh and a lawyer by training, Haldane was a prominent Liberal politician who did much to overhaul the British Army prior to the outbreak of World War I. He first entered parliament in 1879 and was Secretary of State for War between 1905 and 1912. While at the War Office he oversaw the reform of the army, the creation of the Territorial Army (Britain's army reserves) and drew up the plans for Britain's deployment in the event of a European war. In 1912, having been ennobled as the first Viscount Haldane, he became Lord Chancellor, a post he held until 1915. He was again Lord Chancellor in 1924, having switched party allegiance to Labor. *MS*

Hamilton, Sir Ian Standish Monteith
(1847–1947)

Regarded by the Germans as perhaps the most experienced soldier in the world, Hamilton was born on Corfu, Greece. He saw service, having been commissioned in 1872, in Afghanistan, Egypt, Burma, and in both Boer Wars. He was Inspector General of Overseas Forces between

Right: The German "potato masher" hand grenade. *Chrysalis Photo Library*

Below: General Sir Ian Hamilton and Lieutenant Colonel Doughty-Wylie on *Arcadian*, **Mudros.** *Chrysalis Photo Library*

1910 and 1914 and, in 1915, was appointed to command the ill-fated Gallipoli expedition. He was removed from this command in October 1915 and between 1918 and 1920 served a Lieutenant of the Tower of London. After World War I he advocated closer ties with Germany, indeed met with Hitler in 1938. *MS*

Hand grenades

In the fast flowing wars of the nineteenth century hand grenades had but little part, and despite experience of sieges in the American Civil and Russo-Japanese wars, few grenades were available on the eve of the Great War. Most of those that

were available were black powder ball types such as the German 1913 and French 1914 models. It was only in 1914 that it was realized how vital the bomb would be in trench warfare. While industry struggled to devise and manufacture suitable patterns, soldiers of both sides were thrown back on their own ingenuity, producing explosive-filled tins and crude racquets to propel them. "Emergency Patterns" from the home factories helped in early 1915, but it was only later that year that really reliable models appeared in quantity. The famous German "potato masher," more properly known as the 1915 model stick grenade, featured a pull cord and five and a half-second delay fuse. The British Mills Bomb was

Left: Australian troops practice throwing "ersatz" bombs (see page 33). *Chrysalis Photo Library*

Center Left: German hand grenade thrower, May 1917. *Chrysalis Photo Library*

Bottom Left: U.S. troops practice hand-grenade throwing. *National Archives via Chrysalis Photo Library*

Bottom Right: The Battle of Heligoland Bight. *Richard Natkiel*

particularly effective, and had fearsome fragmentation. It was also supplied to Belgium and other Allies. Rifle-projected grenades were similarly improved and became a useful support weapon in infantry attacks. *SB*

Handguns

Despite being short-range weapons, prone to accident, handguns were manufactured in quantity and filled a distinct combat niche. They were carried by officers, and as a secondary weapon by specialists such as tank crew and machine gunners. They also played a useful role in raids and trench fighting where compactness and swiftness of operation were at a premium. In the U.S. Army it has been calculated that one handgun was supplied for every 3.5 soldiers. Handgun theorists were divided between the merits of traditional revolvers and semi-automatic pistols. Revolvers were robust, reasonably idiot-proof, and had the advantage that they would continue to function after a misfire. Semiautomatics were generally swifter, both to shoot and load, and were usually capable of more shots before reloading. Arguably the most famous pistol of the war was the P08 Luger semiautomatic adopted by the German Army in 1908. Inspired by the toggle lock mechanisms of Hugo Borchardt, Georg Luger's elegantly designed pistol combined an ergonomic grip with an easy-to-change eight-round box magazine. It fired the 9mm Parabellum cartridge: an excellent choice, powerful enough to be a highly practical combat round, while small enough for even relatively inexperienced shots to control. The Luger was also produced in a *lange* or long-barreled version, which, with the aid of a shoulder stock and thirty-two-round drum magazine, could be used as a species of semiautomatic carbine. Though Luger pistols equipped the regulars by 1914, rapid expansion of the army meant that the Germans had to use many other handguns. Prominent among these were the semiautomatic

C96 Mauser "broom handle," produced first in 7.63mm and later in 9mm; Mauser self-loaders Models 1910 and 1914; and obsolete "Reichs Commission" revolvers some of which dated back to 1879. Very highly regarded was the American .45-inch, Model 1911 semiautomatic. Developed from the similar Colt Military Model of 1905, the new pistol was ruggedly built, used the excellent J.M. Browning mechanism, and featured a seven-round box magazine. The .45-inch ACP round was notable for both stopping power and accuracy. Though the Model 1911 was used extensively by the U.S., and by the British in small numbers, the Americans also manufactured many other handguns. These included various models of Smith and Wesson revolver and the Colt New Service revolver. Though they fielded automatics on a limited basis Britain, France, and Russia were mainly reliant on revolvers. The British used several different models of Webley with an emphatic .455-inch round, originally designed to be capable of stopping a charging tribesman. These were supplemented by various American handguns, and by the so-called "Old Pattern" revolver imported from Spain. The French issue was the Modèle d'Ordonnance 1892 a solid-frame, six-shot weapon, firing an 8mm round. The Russian revolver was the 1895 model Nagant, a gun most remarkable for its gas seal system. *SB*

Heligoland Bight, Battle of

Following a series of German raids on the English coast, the British planned to launch a reprisal raid against Heligoland Bight, the approaches to the German base at Wilhemshaven. A series of attacks by British submarines would lure German cruisers and destroyers out into the Bight, where they could be ambushed by a force of British battlecruisers, cruisers, and destroyers commanded by Vice-Admiral Beatty. This took place on August 28, 1914, and initially German forces got the worst of the engagement, but the German light cruisers *Frauenlob* and *Stettin* arrived around 8:00am, and crippled the British light cruiser *Arethusa*. A confused fight followed in poor visibility, as both sides brought in reinforcements, and the Germans tried to extricate their torpedo boat units from the battle. The German light cruiser *Mainz* was sunk by a torpedo from a destroyer, and when the British battlecruisers arrived, the Germans began a full-scale retreat to the southeast. Before the end of the engagement around 2:00pm, both sides had lost another cruiser each, the British *Ariadne* and the German *Köln*. The confused skirmish was a clear British victory, and subsequently the Germans were reluctant to risk losses through any further unplanned, ad-hoc operations. *AK*

Helles, Landings at

The Allied Gallipoli Offensive opened on April 25, 1915, with a series of

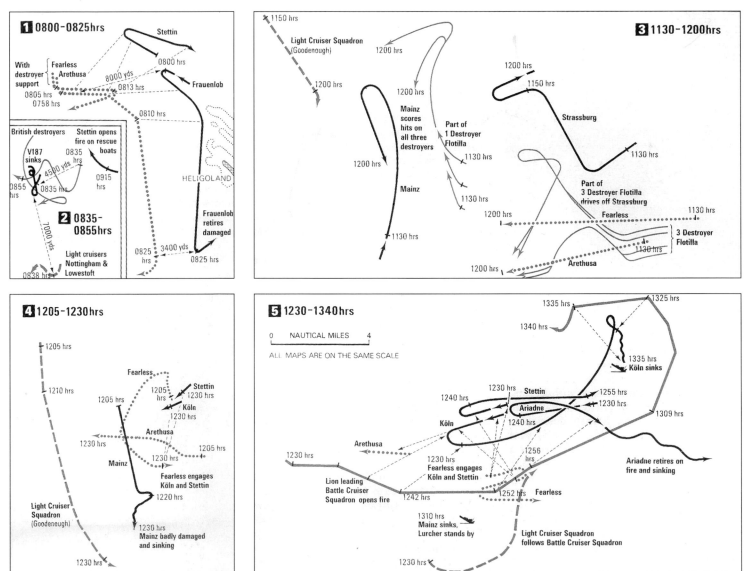

WORLD WAR I: A VISUAL ENCYCLOPEDIA

amphibious landings at Cape Helles at the southern tip of the peninsula. The local commander, Britain's General Ian Hamilton, opted to land the bulk of his multinational force at Cape Helles itself but ANZAC (Australian and New Zealand) troops were to disembark ten miles to the north at Gaba Tepe. The attack was opened by diversionary landings at Bulair far to the north and at Kum Kale across the Dardanelles from Cape Helles. At Helles itself there were five invasion beaches, code-named S, V, W, X, and Y. The troops committed to S and Y beaches, on the south and north coasts of the peninsula, were little more that diversionary forces. Their landings were relatively unopposed, but an attempted push inland from Y beach was rebuffed. Matters were rather different at V, W, and X, although just 1,000 Turkish troops were present. At X beach, the invaders landed without suffering a single casualty; at W beach a handful of Turks inflicted 533 casualties and caused severe dislocation before withdrawing; while at V beach the British ran into intense fire that caused 1,200 casualties among the first assault wave. Throughout the rest of the 25th the Allies attempted to unite their various beach-heads at Helles, rather

than push on to their first objective, a line running across the peninsula through the village of Krithia. Meanwhile, the landings at Gaba Tepe were going ahead, although not at the spot, Z beach, envisaged. The ANZACs landed slightly to the north at Ari Burna and had to fight hard to gain a foothold. The Turkish response grew steadily during the 25th and 26th. They forced the evacuation of Y beach and attacked the French at Kum Kale with sufficient determination to prompt a later withdrawal. As reserves moved down to the invasion front, the Turks established a new defensive line that ran through Krithia, leaving the Allies effectively bottled up on their invasion beaches. *IW*

Helmets

Trench warfare gave rise to a disproportionate number of serious head wounds, many of them caused by relatively small, low-velocity fragments. It was quickly realized that a good proportion of these might be avoided by the provision of protective headgear. One of the first to be adopted was the French *Calotte*, a simple steel skullcap, which could be worn under the cap. Later in 1915 the French

Left: Laying a 9.2-inch howitzer, September 1917. The gunners are wearing the Brodie-designed helmet. *Chrysalis Photo Library*

Below: German *Stahlhelm*. *Chrysalis Photo Library*

Right: Northumberland Fusiliers wearing German helmets and gasmasks captured at St. Eloi, March 27, 1916. *Chrysalis Photo Library*

Below Right: The AEF's 167th Infantry engaged at Seringes; they are wearing the British-style helmet. *Collection of Bill Yenne*

Quartermaster General Adrian introduced a multipiece construction helmet, which was issued to all French troops and became known as the "Adrian Model 1915." Similar helmets would be used by the Italians, Belgians, Romanians, and Russians. The shallow bowl-shaped steel helmet worn by the British was patented by John L. Brodie in August 1915 and began to arrive at the front a month later. This design was also taken up by the Americans in 1917. (See page 202.) The distinctive German steel helmet, or *Stahlhelm*, was used experimentally at the end of 1915, and officially adopted as the Model 1916. Its shape was inspired by medieval precedents, and by the desire to achieve all-round protection. The distinctive side lugs were intended to accommodate a special reinforcing plate which was only issued in small quantities. *SB*

High Seas Fleet

The creation of the German High Seas Fleet (*Hochseeflotte*) dates from 1907, when the Imperial German Navy adopted the title for its main battlefleet, based at Wilhemshaven, on the Jade Estuary. This powerful German fleet was rendered obsolete by the *Dreadnought*, so for the next seven years the Germans poured resources into a naval arms race with Britain, in an attempt to create a dreadnought fleet. Although unable to match the Royal Navy in numbers, it developed a qualitative advantage, as ship for ship the German warships were better protected, and employed more effective fire-control and damage-control techniques, making them more effective. By the outbreak of war the High Seas Fleet consisted of seventeen dreadnought battleships (organized into the 1st and 3rd Battle Squadrons. The 2nd Battle Squadron was formed from six predreadnought battleships in an attempt to make the numbers. This fleet was supported by a battlecruiser force of the five battlecruisers of the 1st Scouting Group, two light cruiser groups (squadrons), and seven small destroyer flotillas. Unlike the British, the Germans had few expectations, and adopted a strategy based around their ability to cause unacceptable casualties on the British fleet, and therefore forcing peace on favorable terms. It was hoped that the fleet could be used to lure small portions of the British Grand Fleet into battle, where they could be isolated and destroyed. This stratagem was thwarted by the British refusal to maintain a close blockade, and by the German reverses at Heligoland Bight (1914) and Dogger Bank (1915). When Vice-Admiral Scheer took over command of the fleet after Dogger Bank, he devised a plan to lure the Grand Fleet out, then entice it over a series of newly-laid minefields. The resulting operation led to the Battle of Jutland (1916), where although the

Above Right: The scuttling of the High Seas Fleet. *Richard Natkiel*

Right: Surrender of the German fleet. British airship *NS8* flies over the ships, November 21, 1918. *Chrysalis Photo Library*

Far Right, Top: British light cruiser *Cardiff* leading the German battlecruisers into the Firth of Forth. *Chrysalis Photo Library*

Far Right, Bottom: Scuttled battleship *Bayern* sinking at Scapa Flow, June 21, 1919. *Chrysalis Photo Library*

German fleet performed well, only superior tactical organization avoided its destruction by superior numbers of British ships. After Jutland the High Seas Fleet remained in port until, in November 1918 when the war was clearly lost, German sailors discovered plans were being made for a final suicide sortie. They mutinied and the resulting revolution led to the German call for an armistice and ended the war. On November 21, 1918, fourteen German capital ships and numerous smaller warships were escorted from Wilhemshaven to Scapa Flow, where they were interned, pending the outcome of peace negotiations. Fears that the fleet might be seized and used against Germany prompted the officers of the fleet to plan a mass scuttling. On June 21, 1919, the warships of the High Seas Fleet simultaneously scuttled themselves, and the British were only able to save the battleship *Baden*, as the remainder sank at their moorings. Most of the sunken ships were subsequently salvaged and sold as scrap, but several wrecks still remain in Scapa Flow, where they provide an attraction for divers. The squalid end to this symbol of German pride influenced the decision to create a new German battlefleet in the 1930s. *AK*

Hindenburg, Paul von Beneckendorf und von (1847–1934)

Born in Posen, in 1847, Hindenburg belonged to the Prussian elite Junker class and a career in the army was inevitable. After cadet schools at Wahlstatt and Berlin, he saw service in 1866 at the Battle of Königgrätz and also during the Franco-Prussian War of 1870–71 during the period of German unification. He was promoted to the rank of general in 1903 before retiring in 1911. Recalled in 1914, he oversaw, with von Ludendorff, as commander of the Eighth Army, the victories on the Eastern Front at Tannenberg and the Masurian Lakes. He continued to have success in the east in 1915, most notably the Gorlice-Tarnów Offensive, and as other German leaders lost credibility, he became chief of the general staff in August 1916. It was at this time that he developed the Hindenburg Program for the direction of German industry to maximize war production. However, his policies—particularly unrestricted submarine warfare—contributed to the entry of the United States into the war

Above: Von Hindenburg with Ludendorff. *Chrysalis Photo Library*

Right: Admiral Hipper. *Chrysalis Photo Library*

and weakened the Germans on the Western Front through the ill-considered offensives of March and April 1918. In the summer of 1918 he was forced to allow German forces to retreat to the defensive Hindenburg Line. Although von Ludendorff left office, von Hindenburg retained power during the crucial period of the armistice. In 1925 he became President of the German Republic and it was during his period of rule, which lasted until his death in 1934, that Adolf Hitler became Chancellor. *MS*

Hipper, Franz von (1863–1932)

Hipper joined the torpedo boat force in 1893, before serving in battleships and on the royal yacht. He commanded destroyers and cruisers before being given command of a German torpedo-boat flotilla. He was promoted to captain in 1907, and attained flag rank in 1912. He distinguished himself during the hit-and-run raids in the North Sea in 1914, and in June 1915 he was given command of the German battlecruiser squadron, and although he was defeated at Dogger Bank (1915), he retained control of this command. During Jutland (1916) he proved himself a capable and enterprising commander. *AK*

Hoffmann, Maximilian (1869–1927)

Based on the Eastern Front, Hoffmann was one of the officers who planned the successful German strategy in the east. Serving with the Eighth Army, he developed the plan which led to the victory at Tannenberg and, as von Ludendorff's deputy for two years, continued to develop strategy. He became Prince Leopold's chief of staff in August 1916 when von Hindenburg became chief of the general staff and was effectively in charge of strategy in the east thereafter. It was Hoffmann who undermined the Kerensky government in Petrograd by arranging for Lenin to be smuggled back to Russia. Hoffmann also helped to negotiate the treaty of Brest-Litovsk in March 1918, which resulted in the cessation of hostilities between the Central Powers and Russia. *MS*

Home Front (Europe)

The wars of the nineteenth century had often had only a limited effect on civilian life in areas away from the immediate theater of conflict. World War I was dramatically different. The unprecedented scale of the war and the vast number of casualties on both sides drew in all aspects of life in the countries involved. Organization and efficient control on the home front became a vital part of the war

Below: Return from the front—a German post-card. *Chrysalis Photo Library*

effort for the first time. Since such huge numbers of men were directly involved in the fighting, women became key to much of the organizational effort at home. War brought its hardships, not least the grief suffered by countless families informed of husbands, brothers, or sons killed, missing, or wounded at the front. Toward the end of the war in 1918 the influenza epidemic brought large-scale fatalities to the home front also. Among the key organizational challenges posed on the home front were recruitment, the supply of labor to industry and agriculture, the supply of food, the finance of the war effort, and the maintenance of morale. Recruitment in Britain was encouraged by the efforts of the War Propaganda Bureau and by pressure from women, most notably

Above: Bomb damage, Rugby Terrace, West Hartlepool, after bombardment by German warships on December 16, 1915. *Chrysalis Photo Library*

Right: "Wild scenes took place at the Brotherhood Chapel . . . when a pacifists' meeting was broken up." *Chrysalis Photo Library*

Far Right: The howitzer shop in the Coventry Ordnance Works. *Chrysalis Photo Library*

Above: Food lines in England—note "England Expects Economy." *Chrysalis Photo Library*

Left: German women working in a munitions factory, 1917. *Chrysalis Photo Library*

through the Order of the White Feather. Posters urged women not to date men who were not in uniform. Despite opposition from service leaders, women themselves were recruited to military support roles through the women's auxiliary branches of the three services, releasing men for front-line positions. In the U.S. War Department, opposition blocked similar recruitment into the army, but the U.S. Navy and Marine Corps enlisted 13,000 women. Factories drew on female labor both for domestic and military output. In Britain alone there were 950,000 women, known as "Munitionettes," employed in the armaments industry by 1918, many of them working in dangerous conditions for low wages. The German U-boat blockade had a serious impact on food supplies to the United Kingdom, making it vital that the output of domestic agriculture was maintained. The Women's Land Army helped direct over 250,000 young women to work as farm laborers replacing men serving at the front. Rationing of sugar was introduced in January 1918, and of butcher's meat shortly after, helping to guarantee a regular supply, allowing calorie intake to

WORLD WAR I: A VISUAL ENCYCLOPEDIA

187

Above: War kitchens for civilian use.
Chrysalis Photo Library

Left: Girls making up soldiers' grocery rations.
Chrysalis Photo Library

Below: Joining up Austrian style, Vienna.
Chrysalis Photo Library

be maintained at close to prewar levels. In both Britain and America efforts were made to encourage back yard cultivation and more efficient home economics. Financing the war without inflationary consequences required the sale of War Loans in Great Britain and of Liberty Bonds in America. Patriotic campaigns were organized in a successful attempt to boost subscriptions through posters and innumerable local meetings and sales drives. Through organizations such as the Red Cross and the British Voluntary Aid Detachments (VADs) thousands of women provided the backbone of the medical support services, including many doctors, nurses, ambulance drivers, etc, essential for caring for the wounded both in the front lines and at home. *DC*

Home Front (United States)

The changes to American society that came about because of World War I were more extensive than any changes to the United States wrought by an outside source since the Revolutionary War. Thanks to the efforts of George Creel's quasi-governmental Committee on Public Information, patriotism was stirred and a sense of unity of purpose was instilled in the populace. The country became more "American." People of Central European heritage, especially German and Austrian, buried their ethnicity and anglicized their names. The federal government reached out and touched people in their homes. A newly formed Federal Food Administration urged families to observe "meatless Mondays" and "wheatless Wednesdays" to conserve food for overseas shipment. The government regulated sales of coal and gasoline and nationalized the railroads via the U.S. Railroad

Left: Mrs. Mina C. van Winkle of Newark, New Jersey, is seen here in the uniform of the U.S. Food Administration. She was president of Woman's Political Union of New Jersey for eight years and in 1918, she headed the Lecture Bureau of the Food Administration. *Hulton Getty*

Below: Private T. P. Loughlin of the 69th Regiment, New York National Guard, bids farewell to his wife and child, 1917. *Collection of Bill Yenne*

HOME FRONT (UNITED STATES)

Administration (USRA) that saw President Wilson appointing William McAdoo, the Secretary of the Treasury, as Director General of Railroads. As would occur again during World War II, there was a dramatic disruption in American society brought about by enormous shifts in the job market and the labor supply. This brought about significant internal migrations on the American home front. Notably, a demand for labor shortages in the Northern steel mills, munitions plants, and stockyards brought thousands of African Americans from the South, establishing large black communities in such metropolitan areas as

Above Right: Mrs. Hattye Gaillard, Instructor at School No. 26, Indianapolis, Indiana, making preserves, circa 1917. *Collection of Bill Yenne*

Right: Patriotic old women making flags under the watchful eye of their flagmaking instructor, Rose Radin. The women were Americans who had been born in Hungary, Galicia, Russia, Germany, and Romania. *Collection of Bill Yenne*

Below: People are seen here tacking up U.S. Food Administration posters at Mobile, Alabama in 1918. *Collection of Bill Yenne*

supplies. As the war drew to a close, House became a de facto Secretary of State, working with Woodrow Wilson to draft the Fourteen Points of the peace plan, and in 1919, serving as a member of the United States' delegation to the Paris Peace Conference. *BY*

Hughes, William Morris (1862–1952)

The prominent Australian politician, William Hughes, who was Prime Minister between 1915 and 1922, was born in London in 1862 and lived in Wales for a period before emigrating to Australia in 1884. His first elected position was in the Legislative Assembly of New South Wales in 1894 and seven years later was elected to the federal House of Representatives. He first held a ministerial portfolio in 1904. He succeeded Andrew Fisher as Prime Minister in 1915 and was a staunch supporter of the Allied war effort. At Versailles, he obtained Australian control over the erstwhile German colony of New Guinea. Hughes continued in parliament until his death in 1952, and again held ministerial office for a period during World War II. *MS*

Hussein Ibn Ali, Sherif (1856–1931)

The founder of the modern Hashemite dynasty that continues to rule in Jordan, Hussein Ibn Ali was born in Constantinople. As Emir of Mecca from 1908 until 1916, he initially supported Turkey and Germany, but was persuaded to join the Allied cause by Lawrence of Arabia. He became the first king of Hedjaz in 1916. However, his position was weakened by his failure to support the Mandate regimes imposed by the Allies in 1919 and, following his defeat by Ibn Saud (the founder of the modern Saudia Arabia), he was forced to abdicate. Exiled to Cyprus, he died in 1931. *MS*

Detroit, New York, Philadelphia, and Chicago. With this, came racial tensions that boiled over into civil unrest. Also brought into the job market was an especially large number of well-educated women. Previously, uneducated— especially immigrant—women had done menial work in factories, but now women were working in higher paid clerical jobs as well as in responsible positions in industry and transportation. Women also volunteered for the war effort and sold war bonds. It was to be these women who would be responsible for the final push toward achieving the long-sought goal of universal suffrage. The 19th Amendment to the Constitution, granting women the right to vote, was ratified by the states in 1920. *BY*

House, Edward Mandell (1858–1938)

An independently wealthy rancher, "Colonel" Edward House was active in Texas politics for many years and an important advisor to governors and other politicians. The Cornell-educated House helped Woodrow Wilson win Texas during his 1912 presidential campaign and became a close consultant to the president after the election. When World War I began in Europe in 1914, House became Wilson's personal envoy to the European capitals, charged with trying to work out a negotiated settlement. House spent two years on the project, but failed. When the United States entered the war in 1917, House used his contacts in London and Paris in order to coordinate the organization of manpower and

Immelmann, Max

Max Immelmann, Germany's first air ace, gained his first victory on August 1, 1915, and six more by the end of the year. Known as the "Eagle of Lille" he was awarded the Pour le Merite on January 12, 1916. Immelmann's score had risen to seventeen when he was killed in combat on June 18, 1916. His knack of making a turn at the top of a zoom climb to reengage the enemy brought the term "Immelmann turn" into aviation lore. *JS*

India, War in

India lay at the heart of the British Empire, a vast source of manpower and materials. Some sixty percent of its territory was ruled directly by Britain, while the remainder consisted of some 700 states that had their own hereditary rulers assisted by British colonial officials. However, by no means all native Indians wished to be ruled by Britain and the British feared that local nationalists, either with or without German help, might take advantage of their embroilment in the war to take direct action to further the cause of independence. To counter any perceived threat the British did introduce legislation, such as the Defense of India Act in 1915. In reality, India remained remarkably stable during the war, a situation that allowed the administration to

Below: Oberleutnant Max Immelmann.
Chrysalis Photo Library

maintain order with fewer resources that expected. The nationalists generally held back from using force and German attempts at support were limited in scope and often badly handled. A scheme to provide arms for Bengali nationalists in 1915, for example, was wholly unsuccessful and the British moved swiftly to deal with the movement. German and Turkish efforts to foment unrest in Afghanistan, a state bordering India that had long preoccupied the British, also came to naught, although there were two short-lived and localized uprisings in 1915 and 1917. Wider support in India for the British is perhaps best expressed by the 1.3 million locals who served in the British-officered Indian Army, which fought in Palestine, Mesopotamia, and Africa, as well as on the Western Front. *IW*

Indian Army

The Indian Army consisted of British units, roughly twenty-five percent of its total strength in 1914, and British-officered local forces, which were mainly raised from among the Punjabi and Gurkha communities. At the outbreak of the war, it had a strength of around 155,000 troops, but this figure had risen to around 600,000 by late 1918. Although primarily established to defend British interests in India, the greater part of the army saw considerable overseas service, including East Africa, Gallipoli, Mesopotamia, Palestine, and

Below: March past of the 47th Division in the Grand Place, Lille, October 28, 1918.
Chrysalis Photo Library

the Western Front. A total of 1.3 million Indians fought during the conflict, of which 72,000 men were killed. *IW*

Infantry equipment (Europe)

By 1914 the foot soldier had obtained primacy on the European battlefield. By dint of numbers, the deadliness of the magazine rifle, and ability to occupy and hold ground, he was indispensable. As German regulations observed, infantry in tandem with artillery "batters the enemy" and breaks his resistance, "It carries the brunt of combat and makes the greatest sacrifices." Most divisions of most armies were infantry divisions in which the bulk of the troops were infantry organized in battalions supported by cavalry, artillery, and other arms. In

the German Army a three-battalion regiment normally formed a brigade. Each battalion of 1,076 officers and men was made up of four companies, and each regiment had an extra company with six machine guns. French infantry battalions had 1,030 officers and men. Though the infantry battalion was a universal concept, companies were now commonly accepted as a viable tactical unit. Many armies maintained historic distinctions between guards, "line" infantry, and "light" infantry, and although certain troops—such as the German *Jäger*—prided themselves on their skirmishing and sharpshooting skills, the majority of troops were equipped, and fought, in similar ways. So it was that, although the British Guardsman, Rifleman, and Fusilier appeared very different on the prewar parade ground, all used SMLE rifles, and wore khaki Service Dress on the battlefield. Despite minor differences occasioned by shortages, Territorials and New Army formations would also adopt, as near as possible, the same uniform and equipment. The standard British infantry equipment was the Pattern 1908 webbing, comprising waist belt, braces, cartridge carriers, main pack, haversack, carriers for water bottle, bayonet and entrenching tool. When fully stowed with ammunition, rifle, spare clothing, rations, great coat, mess tin, and sundries, the soldier's load was 61lb in full marching order. Fortunately the main pack was sometimes put in transport on long moves, and seldom carried in the attack. French infantry equipment was marginally lighter at 54lb, but included fewer cartridges. German equipment weighed 55lb, and, although based around a somewhat oldfashioned 1895 model pack and leather belts, also featured a neat shelter-half system which would allow two men to put up a small tent. Despite differences in detail, infantry tactics had many international similarities. Marches were conducted in columns, British march speed was ninety-eight yards per minute, or three miles per hour, including short halts. When the formation was within range of the enemy, lines were adopted allowing as many rifles to be brought to bear as possible. Quite how dense the lines

Left: **Soldiers washing in the Ancre, November 1916.** *Chrysalis Photo Library*

controversial and considered by some to be far too costly to implement fully. The decision to carry out the reforms on a truncated basis were, in fact, not agreed until 1910. However, Italy found itself over stretched during its war with Turkey in North Africa during 1911, and the conflict further delayed the adoption of the modernization program. Among the reforms that were pushed through was the decision to make all male citizens liable for successive service in three classes between the ages of twenty and thirty-nine. In reality, there were widespread exemptions and the peacetime army was usually undermanned, not least in trained officers. Estimates suggest that due to financial constraints as few as twenty-five percent of potential recruits actually received any military training

and it was not uncommon to find units that were just ten percent of their authorized strength. To make matters worse the army virtually ceased to exist in winter as the induction of new recruits was supposed to take place in November but was usually deferred until the following March. There were some attempts to rectify these deficiencies between the outbreak of war in 1914 and Italy's entry in May 1915, chiefly due to the actions of its chief of staff, General Luigi Cadorna. Efforts concentrated on improving the mobilization procedures, which had proved inadequate during the war with Turkey. The army grew from a theoretical peacetime strength of around 290,000 men to a fully mobilized total of 555,000 troops in May 1915, with the available units being split between the twenty-five infantry and six cavalry divisions that formed four field armies. In reality, the army was not prepared for war, despite Cadorna's intervention. Its troops were generally undertrained (with the exception of certain elite units such

as the Alpini and Bersaglieri) and its units were woefully short of officers. Equipment was a mixed bag, but there were a number of acute deficiencies in key areas. Only 700 machine guns were available and there were just 120 heavy artillery pieces in service, although most were obsolete. Nor could Italian industry manufacture the ammunition in the quantities needed—the country's supply system was wholly inadequate. Italy had little hope of addressing its shortages of equipment without outside help and this became all the more pressing after its devastating defeat at the Battle of Caporetto in late 1917, when it had to abandon much of its heavy equipment, including some 3,000 artillery pieces. Britain and France sent both troops and even greater quantities of supplies to Italy after Caporetto as the Italian Army had to be virtually rebuilt. Everything—from uniforms to all types of artillery—was made available in great quantities, thereby allowing a newly reconstituted force to launch the successful Battle of

Below: Italian Bersaglieri (mountain troops), July 1915. *Chrysalis Photo Library*

Vittorio Veneto against Austria-Hungary in October 1918. *IW*

Italian Navy

The Italians maintained a small but efficient navy, and by the time Italy entered the war in May 1915 its fleet comprised five dreadnoughts, eighteen relatively modern pre-dreadnoughts, sixteen cruisers, and a large fleet of torpedo boats. The Italian Navy took over much of the responsibility for containing the Austro-Hungarian Fleet in the Adriatic Sea, and joined the campaign against German submarines in the Mediterranean. Although the Italians never fought any large-scale naval engagements, they Italians made extensive use of small torpedo boats and submarines, and Italian torpedoes accounted for the loss of two Austrian dreadnoughts.

Italy, War in

Although Italy was a member of the Triple Alliance with Austria-Hungary and Germany, it did not meet its obligations under the treaty and and did not go to war with them in 1914. The Italian government argued that the two other members were waging aggressive war and, therefore, Italy was not obliged to follow their lead under the terms of the alliance. However, there was an another

reason for Italy's decision. Many Italians lived beyond Italy's borders, particularly in the Trentino and Trieste regions, both of which were under Austro-Hungarian control. Support for the movement to incorporate these two areas into Italy proper, known as irredentism, was popular. There was little enthusiasm for siding with Austria-Hungary, since many saw the empire as an oppressor of Italian people. Thus Italy remained neutral in 1914, but also became the focus of British and French attempts to win it over to their cause. They succeeded by backing any Italian takeover of the Trentino and Trieste, agreeing to the expansion of its influence in North Africa, and guaranteeing economic and military aid. Italy declared war on Austria-Hungary on May 23, 1915, although a war declaration against Germany was delayed until August 28, 1916. Italy's military efforts centered on two regions in the north of the country that bordered Austro-Hungarian territory—the Trentino in the north and along the line of the Isonzo River to the northeast. Despite being ill-prepared for war, the Italians concentrated their efforts in the northeast in a series of Isonzo Offensives. Four attacks were launched in 1915, and established a pattern that was to be repeated—heavy losses for little gain. Five further offensives were launched the following year,

Above: Italian destroyer Giuseppe Carlo.
Chrysalis Photo Library

one in March and the remainder between August and November. The lull between late spring and early summer was caused by the first Austro-Hungarian attack on Italy. The Asiago Offensive (also known as the Trentino Offensive) made initial gains but rapidly petered out due to supply difficulties and the transfer of Austro-Hungarian troops to the Eastern Front to combat Russia's Brusilov Offensive. Italy launched two further attacks on the Isonzo in 1917, during May and June, and during August and September. The latter placed excessive strain on the Austro-Hungarians, who demanded and received German reinforcements to shore up the front. The arrival of German units heralded a transformation of the static and stalemated Italian Front. In October, they spearheaded the Twelfth Battle of the Isonzo (better known as the Battle of Caporetto). Their stunning breakthrough drove the Italians back dozens of miles to the Piave River, and British and French units had to be sent from the Western Front to help stabilize the situation. Caporetto was the highwater mark of the Central Powers' efforts on the Italian Front. The German troops were subsequently withdrawn to the Western Front and the increasingly

ineffective Austro-Hungarians fought on alone through 1918. In June, they launched their last offensive of the war. The Battle of the Piave River achieved nothing but did confirm that the Austro-Hungarian forces were at the point of collapse. The Italian riposte, which did not come until late October, was the final engagement on the Italian Front. Bolstered by French and British troops, the Italians launched the Battle of Vittorio Veneto, which recaptured much of the ground lost during Caporetto and was instrumental in Austria-Hungary's decision to seek an armistice, which came into operation on November 4. *IW*

Above: Working party of 1st Battalion, South Staffordshire Regiment digging trenches in Italy. *Chrysalis Photo Library*

Right: Traffic on the bridge over the Tagliamento near Venice. *Chrysalis Photo Library*

Above: Italian prisoners.
Chrysalis Photo Library

Left: Italian Front: a gas shell halts traffic in spite of gasmasks. *Chrysalis Photo Library*

Above Right: German advance in November 1917. *Chrysalis Photo Library*

Right: Heavy artillery in the Piave Valley. *Chrysalis Photo Library*

Above and Left: War in Italy.
Chrysalis Photo Library

Izzet Pasha, Ahmed (1864–1937)

A Turkish politician and soldier, Ahmed Izzet Pasha was a supporter of the Young Turk movement and served as War Minister until January 1914, when he was replaced by Enver Pasha. In April 1916, after a period when his role was limited to criticism of the government's policy, he became commander of the Second Army. However, the failure of his Caucasian offensive resulted in his loss of the command. In October 1918 he became Grand Vizier at the head of a cabinet tasked with negotiating an armistice, which he achieved at Mudros on October 30. His government fell on November 11, although he remained active in postwar politics. *MS*

WORLD WAR I: A VISUAL ENCYCLOPEDIA

213

Japanese Navy

A decade before the outbreak of war, the Imperial Japanese Navy inflicted a crushing victory over the Russian Fleet at the Battle of Tsushima (1905), the climactic naval battle of the Russo-Japanese War (1904–05). As a result, her fleet was widely regarded as one of the most proficient and experienced navies in the world. Although the Japanese embraced the challenge of producing dreadnoughts, their approach towards design differed from other navies. When Japan entered the war in August 1914 its fleet consisted of seven dreadnoughts and two semi-dreadnoughts. The latter were built before the *Dreadnought* was launched, but were designed along similar principles, although they lacked the powerful single-sized armament, as they mixed ten-inch and twelve-inch guns in the same broadside. In addition, the Japanese launched a further three dreadnoughts during the war (one each in 1915, 1916, and 1917). The Japanese were also quick to adopt the concept of the battlecruiser, eight entered service before the war, including the highly successful "Kongo" class. Many of these battleships and battlecruisers and cruisers were subsequently modernized, and saw service in World War II. The older pre-dreadnought fleet that performed so well at Tsushima was relegated to coastal defense and bombardment missions.

Above: **Admiral Jellicoe.** *Chrysalis Photo Library*

Jellicoe, John Rushworth (1859–1935)

John Jellicoe first distinguished himself during the bombardment of Alexandria in 1882, and was present during the infamous collision of the battleships *Victoria* and *Camperdown* eleven years later. He led a naval shore contingent during the Boxer Rebellion in China where he was seriously wounded. After recuperating, he was appointed Director of Naval Ordnance (1905), where he worked with Admiral Fisher to design new guns and improve gunnery standards. In August 1914 he was given command of the Grand Fleet, on Fisher's recommendation. Dubbed by Churchill

Below: **The British-built Japanese destroyer** *Shirakumo* **in 1914.** *Chrysalis Photo Library*

strategic victory, he was removed from active command by being promoted to First Sea Lord, then given less responsible diplomatic assignments. *AK*

Jerusalem, Fall of

British General Edmund Allenby's success over the Turks at the Third Battle of Gaza in late October and early November 1917 allowed him to push deeper into Palestine along the coast in pursuit of the retreating Turkish Eighth Army. After defeating the Eighth Army at the Battle of Junction City (November 13–14), he switched the focus of his attack inland toward Jerusalem, which was being defended by the Turkish Seventh Army. The first British attack to the north of the city was held by the Turks, whose counterattack on November 27 was only just defeated. However, a second advance, this time from the west and south, pushed the Turks back to the gates of Jerusalem on December 7–8. The following day, as the Turks retreated northward to avoid encirclement, Jerusalem surrendered. *IW*

Joffre, Joseph Jacques Césaire
(1852–1931)

Although born into a relatively poor family as the eldest of eleven children at Rivesaltes and entering the army in 1870, Joffre rose through the engineers and through success in France's colonial wars to reach the position of chief of staff of the French Army in 1911. As commander, he draw up the strategy known as Plan XVII that envisaged a

Above: General Allenby's official entry into Jerusalem, December 11, 1917.
Chrysalis Photo Library

Right: General Joffre, President Poincaré, HM King George V, and Sir Douglas Haig in August 1916. *Chrysalis Photo Library*

as "the only man on either side who could have lost the war in an afternoon," Jellicoe was criticized for his overly cautious handling of the British fleet, but he was well aware that Churchill's remark was an accurate observation of his responsibility. During the Battle of Jutland (1916), he seemed preoccupied with the preservation of his Grand Fleet rather than the destruction of the German Navy, and consequently he was criticized for his lack of aggression. Although his disappointing performance resulted in a

rapid French attack through Alsace Lorraine in the event of war with Germany. This plan proved disastrous, but Joffre's skill as a commander showed as he realized that this was the case and then used his forces successfully against the Germans in the First Battle of the Marne. He was promoted to commander-in-chief, but was forced to resign in 1916 after the failure at Verdun. In 1917 he became president of the Allied War Council, having been made a Marshal of France. *MS*

Jutland, Battle of

The British Grand Fleet commanded by Admiral Jellicoe had been trying to lure the German High Seas Fleet of Admiral Scheer into battle for almost two years, but the Germans had managed to avoid fighting a pitched battle. The German strategy was to lure a portion of the British fleet into battle and destroy it. Scheer planned to use Hipper's battle-cruisers to draw Beatty's British battle-cruisers into action, and so lure Beatty toward the High Seas Fleet. British intelligence discovered the plan, and Admiral

Jellicoe set sail from Scapa Flow to intercept. Beatty also steamed to intercept the Germans, planning to rendezvous with Jellicoe off Jutland Bank. The German fleet sailed soon after midnight on May 31, 1916, and fourteen hours later the first contact between the two fleets was made at 2:15pm. At 3:48pm the battlecruiser squadrons opened fire on each other, and while Hipper's ships turned south to lure Beatty toward the German battleships, the British raced south to cut off Hipper's retreat. British gunnery proved less effective than that of the German battle-cruisers, at shortly after 4pm the battlecruiser *Indefatigable* was hit by a salvo from the *Von der Tann* which blew her apart. Twenty minutes later the *Queen Mary* was hit by a salvo from the *Derfflinger*, blowing her up as well. A squadron of four British fast battleships managed to catch up with Beatty, and at 4:08pm they opened fire, hitting the *Seydlitz*. At 4:40pm Beatty sighted the High Seas Fleet, twelve nautical miles to the southeast. He ordered his ships to run to the north, and the combined German fleet gave chase. Scheer's plan had

failed, and now his fleet was heading into the kind of trap he had planned to spring on Beatty. Around 5:15pm, Beatty's ships were joined by three more battlecruisers, sent ahead of Jellicoe's Grand Fleet, which was approaching from the northwest, and Beatty's reinforced squadron attacked the German battlecruisers, damaging Hipper's flagship *Lützow*. This skirmishing continued for another ninety minutes, until around 7pm the battlecruiser *Invincible* was hit and blew up. By this stage Jellicoe had deployed his battleships into a long line, and Scheer's ships were heading directly toward it, in line astern. In effect, while only the leading German ship could fire her bow guns at the British, all of the British battleships

Opposite, Above and Below: A sequence of maps (see also page 218) showing the Battle of Jutland. *Richard Natkiel*

Right: The German dreadnought *Köln* showing damage from a British shell hit at Jutland. *Chrysalis Photo Library*

Below: The largest British ship at Jutland: the battlecruiser *Tiger* armed with eight 13.5-inch guns. *Chrysalis Photo Library*

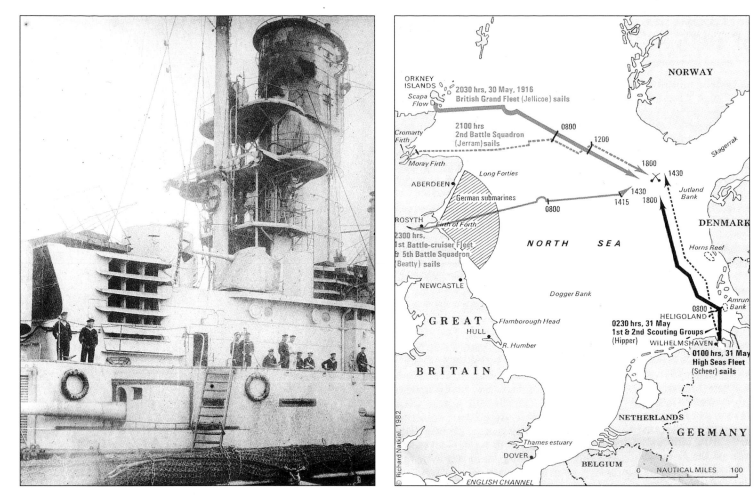

could fire on the German ships. Jellicoe had crossed the T of the High Seas Fleet, achieving the ideal tactical advantage in naval gunnery. At 7:18pm, Scheer ordered his fleet to execute the "battle turnaway," a simultaneous 180-degree alteration of course, which only the Germans had ever practiced. This saved the German fleet from destruction, and within minutes it was steaming south to safety. To screen the maneuver, German destroyers laid a smokescreen, and then launched a torpedo attack on Jellicoe's battleships, forcing them to turn away to the northeast to evade. Simultaneously, Hipper led his damaged battlecruisers in a "death ride" toward the Grand Fleet in support of the destroyers. Hipper's ships

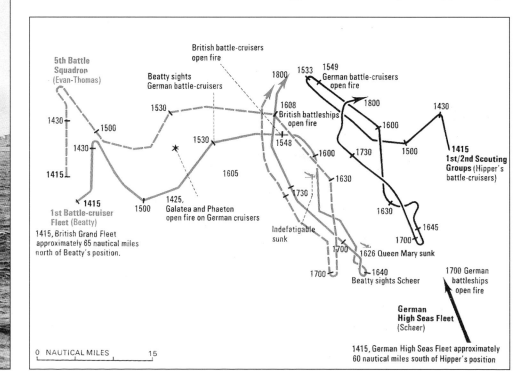

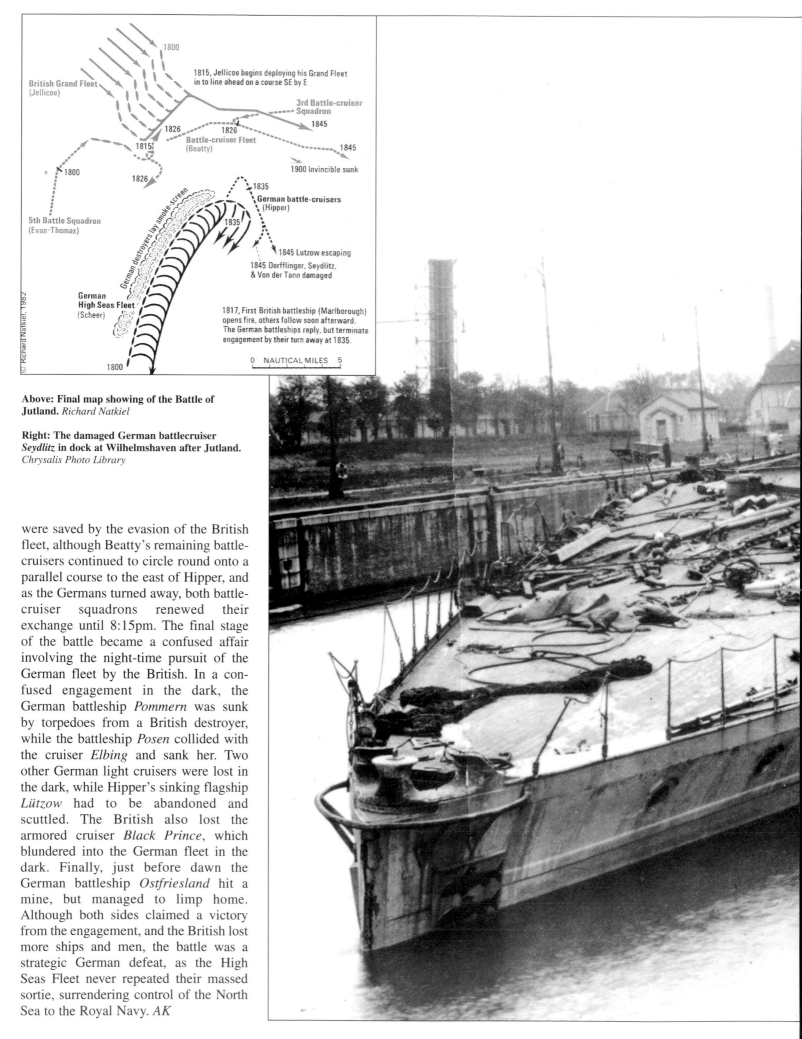

1800

1815, Jellicoe begins deploying his Grand Fleet in to line ahead on a course SE by E

British Grand Fleet (Jellicoe)

3rd Battle-cruiser Squadron

1826 1826 1845

1815

Battle-cruiser Fleet (Beatty)

1845

1800 1826

1900 Invincible sunk

5th Battle Squadron (Evan-Thomas)

1835

German battle-cruisers (Hipper)

1835

1845 Lutzow escaping

1845 Derfflinger, Seydlitz, & Von der Tann damaged

German destroyers lay smoke-screen

German High Seas Fleet (Scheer)

1817, First British battleship (Marlborough) opens fire, others follow soon afterward. The German battleships reply, but terminate engagement by their turn away at 1835.

© Richard Natkiel, 1982

1800

0   NAUTICAL MILES   5

Above: Final map showing of the Battle of Jutland. *Richard Natkiel*

Right: The damaged German battlecruiser *Seydlitz* in dock at Wilhelmshaven after Jutland. *Chrysalis Photo Library*

were saved by the evasion of the British fleet, although Beatty's remaining battle-cruisers continued to circle round onto a parallel course to the east of Hipper, and as the Germans turned away, both battle-cruiser squadrons renewed their exchange until 8:15pm. The final stage of the battle became a confused affair involving the night-time pursuit of the German fleet by the British. In a confused engagement in the dark, the German battleship *Pommern* was sunk by torpedoes from a British destroyer, while the battleship *Posen* collided with the cruiser *Elbing* and sank her. Two other German light cruisers were lost in the dark, while Hipper's sinking flagship *Lützow* had to be abandoned and scuttled. The British also lost the armored cruiser *Black Prince*, which blundered into the German fleet in the dark. Finally, just before dawn the German battleship *Ostfriesland* hit a mine, but managed to limp home. Although both sides claimed a victory from the engagement, and the British lost more ships and men, the battle was a strategic German defeat, as the High Seas Fleet never repeated their massed sortie, surrendering control of the North Sea to the Royal Navy. *AK*

Above: German shells land close to the British ships during the Battle of Jutland. Certainly the German gunnery was better than the British during this battle. *Chrysalis Photo Library*

Left: After Jutland, the damage to British battlecruiser *Chester*. *Chrysalis Photo Library*

Right: Admiral W. E. Goodenough (left) was in command of the Light Cruiser Squadron at Jutland. *Chrysalis Photo Library*

Below: The German dreadnought *Kaiserin*. *Chrysalis Photo Library*

Above: Jutland: the British battlecruiser *Lion*, **Beattie's flagship, hit amidships on "Q" turret.**
Chrysalis Photo Library

Above Left: The first aircraft carrier to play a part in a major naval action: HMS *Engadine* **was with the battle-cruiser force in the North Sea and her aircraft provided the only aerial reconnaissance at the battle. Originally a cross-Channel ferrry she was taken over by the Royal Navy as a sea-plane carrier.**
Chrysalis Photo Library

Left: The German dreadnought *Kronprinz Wilhelm*. *Chrysalis Photo Library*

Above Left: Broadside from one of the German ships. *Chrysalis Photo Library*

Above: The British battle-cruiser *Indefatigable* **during the battle.** *Chrysalis Photo Library*

Left: The German battle-cruiser *Seydlitz* **limps home after Jutland.** *Chrysalis Photo Library*

Right: The *Queen Mary* **explodes, after being hit by shots from** *Derfflinger*. *Chrysalis Photo Library*

Karl I, Kaiser (1887–1922)

Following the assassination of Archduke Franz Ferdinand at Sarajevo, Karl became heir to the Austro-Hungarian throne. Originally a cavalry officer, he served as a liaison officer in Galicia and as a corps commander in Italy before succeeding to the throne on the death of Franz Josef on November 21, 1916. A weak monarch, Karl was influenced by his pro-Allied wife Princess Zita of Bourbon-Parma and his distrust of Germany. He sought, from 1917 onward, a separate peace, although his advances were spurned. As the war progressed, so too did Austrian dependence on Germany and Karl's efforts to maintain independence—e.g. the October Manifesto of 1918—were doomed. Initially he vacillated about abdication before fleeing to Switzerland in March 1919. He made a number of unsuccessful attempts to reclaim the throne prior to his death in 1922. *MS*

Kazakov, Alexander (1891–1919)

Staff-Captain Alexander A Kazakov became a pilot at the Sevastopol Flying School and scored his first two victories in February 1915. As a member of the crack XIX "Death or Glory" Corps, he had seventeen victories by the time of the Russian Revolution, whereupon he was sentenced to death by the Bolsheviks. Kazakov avoided this fate and scored one more aerial victory before apparently taking his own life on August 1, 1919, by diving a Sopwith Snipe into the ground. *JS*

Kemal (Atatürk), Mustapha (1880–1938)

Mustapha Kemal—he adopted the name "Kemal Atatürk" in 1935—was born in Salonika. The founder of the modern secular state of Turkey, he served with the Turkish Army and supported the pro-reformist movement, the Young Turks, in the first decade of the twentieth century before disagreeing with the movement's leader. As an officer in the Turkish Army he fought against Italy in Libya during the 1911 war and also served in the Balkans. During World War I he served as a general, helping to defeat the Allied Gallipoli expedition (for which he was awarded the title "Pasha") and also countered Allenby's actions in Sýria. After World War I he opposed the break-up of the Ottoman empire and fought on to prevent Greece seizing Smyrna; peace with Greece only came in September 1922. His nationalist movement progressed into revolution and on April 23, 1920, he set up a provisional government in Ankara. In November 1922 the monarchy (Sultanate) was abolished in Turkey, with a republic being formally established the following October. Kemal remained in power, effectively a dictator, until his death on November 10, 1938. *MS*

Kerensky, Alexander Fyodorovich (1881–1970)

Born the son of a high-school headmaster (one of whose pupils was later to be known as Lenin), Kerensky was trained as a lawyer, achieving considerable success in political trials prior to the first revolution of 1917. He also served in the Russian Parliament—the Duma—from 1912 as a socialist. After the first—March—revolution in 1917, Kerensky entered the government, first as War Minister (in May 1917) and later as Prime Minister (two months later). A wholehearted supporter of the war effort, he was thwarted in his efforts to wage a summer campaign by war weariness at home. With the Bolshevik Revolution in October 1917, he was forced from office. Although he tried to organize resistance to the revolution, his efforts proved fruitless and he was forced into exile. He died in New York. *MS*

Kerensky Offensive (1917)

The Russian Kerensky Offensive during the summer of 1917 took place against a background of revolutionary turmoil and continued demands by Russia's allies to relieve some of the military pressure they faced on the Western Front by drawing German forces eastward. In an ill-judged attempt to reunite the divided nation behind a populist cause, the leaders of the Provisional Government decided to launch an attack against the Austro-Hungarian and German forces holding Russian territory in defense of national liberty. The origins of the offensive lay with the Provisional Government's minister of war, Alexander Kerensky, but he, like many of his government colleagues, failed to comprehend the extent of the war-weariness of ordinary Russians. General Alexei Brusilov, since early July the new commander-in-chief

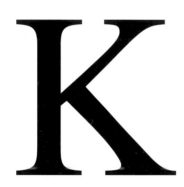

in part due to revolutionary fervor. Troops were refusing to advance or withdrawing without orders. Faced with these realities, Brusilov was forced to end the offensive on the 16th. Russian weaknesses were swiftly exploited by their opponents, chiefly the Germans, who had rushed six divisions from the Western Front to counterattack the fast-stalling Kerensky Offensive. Bothmer's strengthened South Army began its counteroffensive on the 19th. The initial focal point of the attack was the Russian right wing. A brief artillery bombardment opened the way and German forces were able to advance some ten miles meeting crumbling opposition on the first day. Subsequent advances followed a similar pattern and heralded the end of Brusilov's tenure as commander-in-chief. He was dismissed and replaced by Kornilov on August 1. When the end of the first week of August, the German-led counteroffensive had recaptured most of the territory in Galicia that had been lost to the Russians during 1916's Brusilov Offensive. For its part, the Russian Army had effectively ceased to exist as an organized fighting machine, a situation that would subsequently allow the transfer of many German divisions to the Western Front. *IW*

Khalil Pasha (1864–1923)

A Turkish military commander, Khalil Pasha commanded the Sixth Army in Mesopotamia and was also Military Governor in Baghdad. Initially defensive as a result of the British onslaught, victory at Ctesiphon (November 1915) and at Kut (1916) enabled him to pursue a more aggressive policy, although a planned offensive toward Persia in 1917 was thwarted by a renewed British onslaught that led ultimately to his defeat. *MS*

Kiel and Wilhelmshaven

The two principal naval bases of the German Navy were Kiel and Wilhelmshaven, although secondary bases were also maintained at Cuxhaven, Bremen and Emden for the stationing of light units or U-boats. Wilhemshaven on the Jade estuary provided a commodious harbor, and like Scapa Flow, the Jade Bay formed a safe haven, the fleet secure

in place of the recently dismissed General Mikhail Alexeev, was tasked with planning the offensive. Two armies, the Seventh and Eleventh, were earmarked for the opening attack, which was to be directed into Galicia with the intention of capturing the Austro-Hungarian province's capital, Lemberg. Opposing the Russians was the joint German and Austro-Hungarian South Army under a German commander, General Felix von Bothmer. The Kerensky Offensive was heralded by a three-day artillery bombardment and began on July 1, with the Russian Seventh Army attacking south of Lemberg. Initial progress was excellent with the Austro-Hungarians being caught by surprise and many prisoners captured. On the 2nd the Seventh Army continued its attacks and was joined by the Eleventh Army, which was directed

toward the junction between Bothmer's Austro-Hungarian and German forces. Again, considerable gains were made. Six days later the Russian Eighth Army commanded by General Lavrenti Kornilov entered the battle farther south and repeated the earlier successes. Attacking along a sixty-mile front his forces cut through the Austro-Hungarian forces around Stanislau on the 8th. Four days later, having advanced some twenty miles, the Eighth Army was within striking distance of the oilfields at Drohobicz. Although seemingly poised on the brink of success, the Kerensky Offensive was in fact fast running out of steam. The first waves of assault troops, Russia's best units, had suffered severe losses, and those behind them, the ones earmarked to exploit any breakthrough, were of generally inferior quality, often demoralized, and riddle with indiscipline

from attack behind screens of mines, coastal batteries, light patrol craft, and antisubmarine screens. It also formed the center of a network of directional wireless that provided German naval planners with information on British maritime activities. The base was chosen over the old base at Kiel as it provided better and faster access to the North Sea for the High Seas Fleet. It also permitted the fleet to reach Kiel if required, where it could pass through the Kiel Canal into the Baltic Sea. This move was never made, as the Russians posed no serious naval threat to Germany during the war. Wilhelmshaven was the base from which the High Seas Fleet ailed to give battle at Jutland (1916), and it was the scene of the mutiny which prevented any final naval confrontation in the North Sea in October 1918. *AK*

Kitchener of Khartoum and of Broome, Horatio Herbert, Earl
(1850–1916)

With a face familiar to contemporaries and to succeeding generations as a result of its appearance of the classic World War I recruiting poster urging Britons to join the army ("Your country needs you"), Kitchener was born in County

Below: Warships moored on the Kiel Canal.
Chrysalis Photo Library

Right: Kitchener at Anzac, November 13, 1915. With him is General Birdwood.
Chrysalis Photo Library

Kerry, Ireland. Following training at the Royal Military academy, Woolwich, he served with the Royal Engineers from 1871 in Palestine (1874–78), Cyprus, and the Sudan (1883–85). His victory over the Khalifa at Omdurman in 1898 reestablished Anglo-Egyptian control over the Sudan and resulted in him being created a baron in 1898 (he was raised to the rank of Viscount in 1902 and made an Earl in 1914). He acted as both chief of staff and commander-in-chief during the Second Boer War, successively bringing the war to a conclusion in 1902. From 1902 until 1909 he served as commander-in-chief in India before returning to Egypt in 1911, where he was agent (effectively the British ruler of the country) until 1914. On August 7 he was promoted to the rank of field marshal and made Minister of War in Asquith's Liberal government. Politically, however, he was naïve, not understanding the nature of cabinet government and he was also to disagree with a number of his senior officers. Kitchener was to drown on June 5, 1916, when the cruiser HMS *Hampshire* sank after being mined off the Orkney Islands. His death is commemorated by a memorial tower on the adjacent coastline. *MS*

Kornilov, Lavrenti Georgiyevich
(1870–1918)

A Cossack by birth, Kornilov was born in Western Siberia. Prior to World War I he gained both diplomatic and intelligence experience, and served as a divisional commander in the Tsarist forces during the war. He led the Russian

offensive against the Germans in June 1917 and, following its failure, then marched in August 1917 against the Kerensky-led government in Petrograd. This foolhardy escapade, however, was doomed to failure and he was forced to surrender his military command, but escaped before further retribution could be meted out. Following the Bolshevik revolution of October 1917, he led Cossack forces against the new regime, but was to be killed in action in 1918. *MS*

Kövess von Kövesshàza, Hermann, Baron (1854–1924)

An infantry general serving with the Hungarian army, Kövess had been due to retire, but was retained in 1914 to command XII Corps, serving on the Eastern Front in Galicia, the Carpathians and during the Gorlice-Tarnów Offensive. He then served as commander of the Third Army in the Balkans, capturing Belgrade in October 1915, and advancing through Montenegro and Albania in early 1916. He served then with the Third Army in Italy before being transferred to command the Seventh Army against the Russian Brusilov Offensive of October 1916. He continued with the Seventh Army into 1917, capturing Czernowitz in August of that year and being promoted to field marshal. In January 1918 he became commander of the combined Third and Seventh Armies, but this role was short-lived once the Treaty of Brest-Litovsk was signed. He became briefly the supreme commander of the Austro-Hungarian Army in November 1918, but this was a virtually meaningless position given the fact that the empire was disintegrating. *MS*

Krithia, Battles of

The village of Krithia, along with the nearby hill of Achi Baba, was the site of three unsuccessful attempts by the British and French to break through the Turkish defenses running across Helles, the southern tip of the Gallipoli Peninsula in 1915, following their amphibious landings on April 25. Orders for the assault were given by the operation's overall commander, Britain's General Ian Hamilton. The first battle began and ended on the 28th with the attackers making no gains, although counterattacks by the Turkish Fifth Army under German General Otto Liman von Sanders in early May were repulsed with

heavy casualties. Reinforcements allowed for a second attack on Krithia, which opened on the 6th. The fighting lasted until late on the 8th but with little ground being won, due to a shortage of artillery shells, poor planning, and a lack of coordination. Allied casualties reached 6,000 troops during the first two engagements. The exhausted Allies now regrouped, settling into the routine of trench warfare, and awaited the few reinforcements that were sent to them from Europe. By early June they were ready to tackle Krithia for the third time and opened the battle on the 4th with a barely effective artillery bombardment. Nevertheless, some early gains were made but these were lost to Turkish counterattacks in the afternoon. This fighting, in which a further 6,000 Allied troops became casualties, marked the end of Allied attacks on Krithia and the focus of their attentions switched to exploiting the tiny and isolated beach-head known as Anzac Cove, which lay to the north. *IW*

Krobatin, Alexander Baron von (1849–1933)

An Austrian soldier and politician, Krobatin was appointed War Minister in 1912 and, as such was a proponent of swift military retribution after the assassination of Archduke Franz Ferdinand in June 1914. His failure to harness the Austrian economy

effectively to war production led to his dismissal in March 1917 and his transfer to command the Tenth Army on the Italian Front. He was promoted field marshal for his part in the victory at Caporetto, but was less successful in the Piave Offensive of June 1918 and his army was ultimately to be defeated in the Vittorio Veneto Offensive of October/November 1918. *MS*

Kut, Siege of

After their defeat at the Battle of Ctesiphon in November 1915, the British forces in Mesopotamia under General Charles Townshend fell back on the town of Kut pursued by the Turks under Nur-ud-Din. By December 7, the town was under siege but Townshend was confident that he could hold out for at least two months until a relief column arrived. However, relief attempts were thwarted at the Battles of Sheikh Sa'ad and Hanna in January 1916, at Dujaila in March, and at the First Battle of Kut in April. Burdened with large number of sick and wounded, facing starvation, and with no hope of relief or resupply, Townshend surrendered unconditionally to the Turkish commander Khalil Pasha on April 30. *IW*

Below: Siege of Kut. *Chrysalis Photo Library*

L

La Bassée, Battle of

Part of the southern battlefield of the First Battle of Ypres, La Bassée saw action between October 10 and November 2, 1914. The first skirmishes came on October 12 as II Corps of the BEF, en route to relieve the French, were forced into retreat by two concealed German cavalry corps. A second British attempt at advance was repulsed by the newly formed Fourth Army, and after losing another mile of ground on October 21, Smith-Dorrien finally fell back into the reserve position that held for the next four years. Deadly British rifle fire held off the enemy at La Bassée until both armies turned their attention increasingly toward Ypres itself. *MS*

Lafayette Escadrille

Though the United States did not enter World War I until April 1917, and did not have its AEF Air Service fully operational until almost 1918, American pilots had been in combat over the Western Front almost from the beginning. Organized in April 1916, the Lafayette Escadrille was a contingent of American aviators who served as volunteer fighter pilots in the French Aviation Militaire (air force). The Lafayette Escadrille was named for the Marquis de Lafayette who brought a French Army to America in 1777 to aid the Americans in their War of Independence. Now the Americans were returning the favor. Though the Lafayette Escadrille pilots were not the only American airmen to serve with the Allies prior to April 1917, they were certainly the most colorful and the most storied. Originally called the Escadrille Americaine, the Lafayette Escadrille was formed at Luxeuil, France and subsequently operated from Bar-le-Duc, near Verdun. In 1918, the Lafayette Escadrille would be incorporated into the AEF Air Service as the 103rd Pursuit Squadron. The leading ace of the Lafayette Escadrille was Raoul Lufberry, who was born in France, but grew up in the United States. He served with the U.S. Army in the Philippines in 1908–10, and later met French demonstration pilot Marc Pourpe. Lufberry hired on as Pourpe's mechanic for a Far East tour, and when World War I started, the two men went to France to fly. Lufberry wanted to join the Aviation Militaire, but since he was an American, he had to join the Foreign Legion instead. Lufberry managed to transfer to the air force, completed pilot training and was assigned to Escadrille

Right: Lafayette Escadrille 1916: Sergeant R. Soubiran at Cachy. In 1918 Soubiran was transferred to the U.S. Air Service with the rank of captain. He would later command the 103rd Aero Squadron, formerly the Lafayette Escadrille.
Official U.S. Air Force photo via Chrysalis Photo Library

VB106 in October 1915. Meanwhile, the Lafayette Escadrille was being formed, and Lufberry transferred again. Lufberry scored his first aerial victory in July 1916 and became an ace in October. He remained with the Lafayette Escadrille until January 1918 before transferring again, this time to the newly-formed 95th Aero Squadron of the AEF Air Service. After a brief stint in the 95th, Lufberry became commander of the 94th Aero Squadron—the legendary "hat in the ring" squadron—which included Eddie Rickenbacker among its pilots. On May 19, 1918, with seventeen aerial victories to his credit, Raoul Lufberry suffered a cockpit fire during a patrol over the Western Front. He climbed out to escape the flames and fell to his death. *BY*

Right: Lafayette Escadrille 1916: Sergeant F. Prince, Jr. and his Nieuport Scout which is equipped with balloon-strafing rockets.
Official U.S. Air Force photo via Chrysalis Photo Library

Below: U.S. 11th Bombardment Squadron, 1918.
Official U.S. Air Force photo via Chrysalis Photo Library

Above: The Lafayette Escadrille at Ham, May 1917.
Official U.S. Air Force photo via Chrysalis Photo Library

Left: Some of the pilots of Escadrille No. 124 admiring their pet lions Whiskey and Soda: left to right, Sergeant Hall, Lieutenant Thaw, Adjutant Hill, Sergeant Marr, Sergeant Peterson, Lieutenant Lufbery, Sergeant Rockwell, Sergeant Bridgman, Lieutenant Manet (French).
Official U.S. Air Force photo via Chrysalis Photo Library

Above: Philip O. Parmales and M. S. Crissy in an early Wright machine.
Chrysalis Photo Library

Far Left: Lieutenant T. G. Ellyson, U.S. Naval Aviator No. 1.
Naval History photo via Chrysalis Photo Library

Left: Adjutant Raoul Lufbery.
Chrysalis Photo Library

Right: Lafayette Escadrille crew during the Battle of the Somme. *Chrysalis Photo Library*

Lanrezac, Charles (1852–1925)

One of France's foremost prewar strategists, Lanrezac commanded the Fifth Army in August 1914. Previously a supporter of the French Plan 17—the swift counterattack through Lorraine— his experiences convinced him that the plan would not succeed. The Fifth Army was transferred to the French-Belgian border, where he was ordered to attack the Germans at Charleroi. Lacking support and without the BEF, his outnumbered force was· defeated on August 21–23 and forced to retreat. Perceived as a failure, a view reinforced by a subsequent defeat at the Battle of Guise on August 29, 1914, he was forced out and replaced by d'Esperey. *MS*

Lansing, Robert (1864–1928)

The U.S. Secretary of State during all of World War I, Robert Lansing was one of the most qualified, yet underutilized persons ever to hold that position. Born in Watertown, New York, Lansing was a noted authority in the field of international law, and he founded the *American Journal of International Law* in 1907. In 1915, he succeeded the great William Jennings Bryan, who had served as Woodrow Wilson's Secretary of State from 1913 to 1915. Lansing had served under Bryan as counsel for the United States in several international disputes, and when Bryan resigned, Wilson appointed Lansing as Secretary of State. An advocate of the United States' participation in World War I on the side

Left: General Charles Lanrezac.
Chrysalis Photo Library

of the Allies, Lansing played little part in most of the diplomatic work that preceded the United States' declaration of war. Ironically, the eminently qualified Lansing was largely shut out of the foreign policy decision-making loop because Wilson preferred to use his personal envoy, Edward House, for most of the important work. It was similar to the relationship that President Richard Nixon had with Dr. Henry Kissinger during the Vietnam War a half century later. Kissinger would be Nixon's personal diplomatic point man, while Secretary of State William Rogers was merely a figurehead. If Wilson had shut Lansing out at the beginning of the war, Lansing turned the tables afterward. Lansing was the head of the U.S. commission to the Paris Peace Conference, but he disagreed with Wilson that the Covenant of the League of Nations was essential to the peace treaty. By this time, Wilson's health had limited his role in government, but he

held tenaciously to the reins of power. When he heard that Lansing had met with other cabinet members without Wilson's knowledge, the President asked for Lansing's resignation. In February 1920, he returned to private law practice. *BY*

Law, Andrew Bonar (1858–1923)

Born in New Brunswick, Canada, the son of a Scottish Presbyterian minister, Bonar Law was educated in Glasgow and worked as an iron merchant in the city before becoming a Conservative-Unionist MP in 1900. He lost his seat in the 1906 general election but was returned to parliament in a by-election in Dulwich shortly afterward. He succeeded Balfour as party leader in 1911 and, over the next few years, demonstrated his commitment to the Union with Ireland in strongly opposing the Liberal Home Rule legislation. With the creation of a coalition government in 1915, Bonar Law joined the cabinet as Colonial Secretary in 1915 and was promoted to Chancellor of the Exchequer

set upon by six German divisions, and these were soon joined by two more infantry divisions. Outnumbered by eight divisions to four, II Corps was struggling when Sordet's cavalry corps interceded. This intercession, combined with delaying actions fought by French Territorial divisions outside Cambrai and tactical errors on the part of the Germans, helped save II Corps from annihilation. Still, II Corps lost 8,000 men, thirty-eight guns and half of the divisional artillery in the day's fighting. *MC*

Le Prieur Rockets

Usually carried in batteries of four, Le Prieur rockets were the Allies' first operational air-to-air/ground missiles, intended primarily to destroy observation balloons. Installations varied, depending on the configuration of the carrier aircraft. They were attached to the outer interplane struts on the Nieuport 16c.1 scout and located mid-span in a framed, box-like structure on the wing of the Bristol F2B. No. 8 Naval Squadron, RNAS, used the rockets with some success on its Nieuports between late 1916 and October 1917. *JS*

(1916–18), before serving as Lord Privy Seal in 1919. He retired in March 1921, but returned briefly as Prime Minister in 1922 when the Conservatives broke with the coalition, thereby forcing Lloyd George to resign. Ill-health forced Bonar Law to resign after seven months. *MS*

Lawrence of Arabia (1888–1935)

Thomas Edward Lawrence, who had spent several years studying the archeology of the Middle East in his student days, was a key figure in the Arab Revolt against the Turkish Empire. In 1915 he had enlisted in the British Army and was sent to Cairo, where he served in the Arab Bureau. In 1916 Lawrence was dispatched to the Arabian Peninsula to discover the strength of Arab nationalism, and identified its most competent leader as Feisal Ibn Hussein. Later in the year, Lawrence returned to Arabia to liaise with Feisal and the two men forged a close working relationship. Lawrence's great strength was that he was able to smooth over any conflicts that arose between the sometimes divergent aims of the British military and the Arab nationalists. As the Arab Revolt grew, Lawrence played a major role in their guerrilla war against the Turks, which supported the British advance into Palestine from Egypt. This campaign had two main elements—hit-and-run raids on Turkish lines of communication and the

gradual reduction of their garrisons across the peninsula. Perhaps his most famous action was the capture of the port of Aqaba in July 1917, which paved the way for an Arab advance into Palestine. However, Lawrence became increasingly disenchanted with Britain's ambiguous stance on Arab nationalism, as well as being exhausted by the fighting, and he was allowed to resign in October 1918. *IW*

Le Cateau, Battle of

The Battle of Le Cateau took place on August 26, 1914, during the "Great Retreat" from Mons. The four divisions under General Smith-Dorrien that made up II Corps of the retreating BEF were

WORLD WAR I: A VISUAL ENCYCLOPEDIA

League of Nations

The League of Nations was an international body set up in the immediate aftermath of the World War I to promote the peaceful resolution of international disputes. A key provision of the treaty was that members were to pledge to come to the defense of any member that was attacked, a provision that its sponsor, the U.S. President Woodrow Wilson believed would deter any future wars. The U.S. Senate refused to accept this condition, and despite much debate and attempted compromise, America never joined the League. *DC*

Legacy of World War I

World War I claimed the lives of some ten million combatants (another thirty million were wounded), led to the collapse of four empires and the birth of seven new nations, and ushered in an era of economic and political instability throughout Europe. Military and civilian casualties on a previously unimaginable scale, the latter exacerbated by the devastating influenza epidemic, left population imbalances in many countries that took many years to resolve. The war accelerated the collapse of the ancient empires of the Austro-Hungarian Hapsburgs and the Ottoman Turks, along with the fall of the more recently established German and Russian empires. Among the political consequences of these events was the creation of new states in central Europe and the Baltic: Poland, Czechoslovakia, Yugoslavia, Latvia, Estonia, Lithuania, and Finland. Both the creation of these new nation states and the alterations to the borders of others such as France and Italy caused widespread dissatisfaction both among victors and vanquished. The economic impact of the war was severe. The major European victors were left with an estimated US$10 billion debt to the United States, vastly increased domestic debts, plus the huge costs of rehabilitating devastated areas and paying war pensions. Germany faced in addition the far greater burden of the huge reparations demanded by the Allies, while the confiscation of her coal producing provinces left little means to begin

Above Right and Right: One of the legacies of World War I: the rise of Hitler and Nazism had much to do with the political and economic settlements of 1918. *Chrysalis Photo Library*

WORLD WAR I: A VISUAL ENCYCLOPEDIA

making the payments. The inevitable economic collapse that followed was a key factor in increasing German hostility toward its rivals and in setting the stage for the rise to power of the National Socialists. More positively World War I lead to the creation of the League of Nations, the first global attempt to resolve international disputes by peaceful means. *DC*

Lenin—Ulyanov, Vladimir Ilyich
(1870–1924)

Better known as Lenin, Ulyanov was born at Simbirsk, where, ironically considering later events, he was to be taught by the father of Kerensky, whose regime Lenin deposed in October 1917. Trained as a lawyer, he soon became active in socialist politics, organizing the Union for the Liberation of the Working Class. This resulted in him being exiled—initially in Siberia (for three years) and then in the west. Spending time in both Switzerland and London, it was in the latter where the crucial congress establishing the Bolshevik wing of the Social Democratic Party as dominant. Lenin returned to Russia for the 1905 revolution, but its failure led him again to exile and he was to spend the period from

1907 until 1917 outside Russia. With the covert assistance of the Germans, Lenin made the train journey from Switzerland to Petrograd in April 1917 in order to attempt a further coup. This occurred in July 1917 and its failure forced Lenin once again abroad, this time to Finland. In October he returned to Petrograd and this time his coup was successful. Lenin became the head of the new Bolshevik government. Quickly he moved to seek peace with Germany, with an armistice followed by the Peace of Brest-Litovsk in March 1918. The early years of Bolshevik power were marked both by considerable reforms and by civil war. The effects of the latter were such that many of the economic reforms initially attempted proved short-lived. Lenin, having survived an assassination attempt, died on January 21, 1924. His body was mummified and placed on public display in a mausoleum in Red Square, outside the Kremlin in Moscow. *MS*

Leopold, Prince of Bavaria
(1846–1930)

Already retired when war broke out, Leopold of Bavaria returned to the German Army as commander of the

Ninth Army on the Eastern Front in April 1915. Under his command the army took part in the Triple Offensive of mid-1915, capturing Warsaw on August 4. Following this success, he was given command of the joint German-Austrian army, now known as Army Group Leopold, on the center of the front. When Hindenburg returned to Berlin, he became overall commander of the German and Austrian forces in the east, although General Hoffmann was largely responsible for the successful strategy prior to the Treaty of Brest-Litovsk, after which Leopold again retired. *MS*

Lettow-Vorbeck, Paul Emil von
(1870–1964)

Lettow-Vorbeck was the commander of the German forces in their East African colony of Tanganyika. After an initial incursion into Uganda, he was forced to retreat. Although his army was small—never numbering more than about

Below: General Count von Lettow-Vorbeck (second from right) German commander-in-chief in East Africa, circa 1913.
Chrysalis Photo Library

3,000—his successful campaign of near guerrilla activity against Allied forces proved an irritant to the British and ensured that Britain was forced to maintain a sizeable military force in East Africa. Although never actually defeated, Lettow-Vorbeck was forced gradually to withdraw, subsequently organizing raids into both Portuguese East Africa and Northern Rhodesia. He surrendered, after hearing of the Armistice, on November 25, 1918. *MS*

Liège, Siege of

Completed in 1892, the Belgian fortress of Liège was protected by twelve forts, 400 guns, 40,000 men, and a thirty-inch deep ditch. It was designed to withstand the 210mm gun, the highest caliber weapon of its day. Having refused the Kaiser's August 3 ultimatum demanding occupation of Belgium, King Albert placed General Gerard Leman in command at Liège. Leman found himself facing an invasion force of 320,000 led by General Otto von Emmich, in the first land battle of World War I. Liège held out against the new German seventeen-inch siege howitzers for eleven days, but on August 16 the inevitable German triumph came. *MC*

Liggett, Hunter (1857–1937)

The commander during World War I of the U.S. Army's 41st Division, General Hunter Liggett briefly commanded the First Army just before the Armistice and later commanded the Third Army during the postwar occupation of Germany. Born in Reading, Pennsylvania, he graduated from the U.S. Military Academy at West Point in 1879 and served in various posts, including Montana Territory, Dakota Territory, Texas and Florida. During the Spanish-American War of 1898, he was promoted to major and became adjutant general of volunteers for service in Cuba. The following year Liggett was sent to the Philippines with the 31st Infantry Volunteers. In 1909, Liggett was and was promoted to lieutenant colonel, and in 1910, he became president of the Army War College. The next year he took command of the 4th Brigade, 2nd Division at Texas City, Texas. He returned to the Philippines in 1916 in command of the Provisional Infantry Brigade and of Fort William McKinley. He served as commander of the Department of the Philippines from

Above: Walter Lippmann. *Collection of Bill Yenne*

April 1916 to April 1917 when he was named commander of the Western Department in San Francisco. In August 1917 he took command of the 41st Division at Camp Fremont in California and deployed with the unit to France. In January 1918, he served as I Corps commander for the battles of Cantigny and Belleau Wood, as well as in the defense and offensive operations of the second Marne campaign in July and August. Liggett received the Distinguished Service Medal "For exceptionally meritorious and distinguished services as commander of the First Army." In October 1918, General John J. Pershing divided the AEF assets between the First and Second Armies, giving Liggett, now a Lieutenant General, command of the First Army. He remained in this post until First Army inactivation in April 1919, when he moved to command the Third Army in occupation duty. Upon his return to the United States he commanded the IX Corps area headquartered in San Francisco. General Liggett retired in March 1921. Created before World War II, Fort Hunter Liggett, comprising 165,000 acres of Monterey County, California, was named for General Liggett. It is still used for maneuvers, live fire exercises and for training the Army Reserve. *BY*

Lippmann, Walter (1889–1974)

An columnist who became a long-time fixture on the American political scene, Walter Lippmann played an important

role in helping the Wilson Administration draft the Fourteen Points Peace Program. An associate editor of the *New Republic* magazine between 1914 and 1917, he left that job to become an assistant to Secretary of War Newton Baker. In 1921, after his work on the post-World War I peace conference, Lippmann returned to the world of journalism. He was on the staff of the *New York World* for a decade, serving as editor for the last two years. In 1931 he moved to the *New York Herald Tribune*, which would be his base for writing a popular syndicated column. In 1962, he moved again, this time to the *Washington Post*, where he continued his column for five years before going into partial retirement. A socialist during his college years at Harvard, Lippmann amended his political persuasion often. He supported Franklin D. Roosevelt's New Deal in the early years, but moved to the right in the late 1930s. After supporting the United States during World War II, he opposed both the Korean War and the Vietnam War. *BY*

Lloyd George, David (1863–1945)

Although widely (and correctly) perceived as Welsh, Lloyd George was actually born in Manchester—of Welsh parents. Following his father's death, in 1865 the family moved to North Wales where an uncle sponsored his education. Trained as a lawyer, he was first elected to Parliament as a Liberal in 1890. He served as President of the Board of Trade from 1905 until 1908 and from then until 1915 as Chancellor of the Exchequer. It was his budget of 1909–10 that led to the constitutional crisis and the eventual Parliament Act of 1911 that defined the power of the House of Lords to delay legislation passed by the elected chamber. Initially a pacifist—he had opposed the Boer War—he was a strong supporter of Belgian neutrality and, therefore, of Britain's role in World War I. In 1915 he became Minister of Munitions and the following year Minister of War. Later the same year he led the "coup" which ousted Asquith as Prime Minister, a position that Lloyd George then held until 1922. He represented Britain at the postwar peace conference and, in 1921, conceded the creation of the Irish Free State. This resulted in the break-up of the coalition government and Lloyd George's fall from power. He remained a member of the House of Commons until 1945 when he was created the first Early Lloyd-George of Dwyfor. He died shortly after his ennoblement. *MS*

Lodge, Henry Cabot (1850–1924)

One of the most powerful and influential Republican politicians in the United States at the time of World War I, Henry Cabot Lodge of Massachusetts served in the U.S. House of Representatives from 1887 to 1893, and in the U.S. Senate from 1893 to 1924. Born in Boston, he was a member of the bar, the editor of the *North American Review*, and a lecturer in American history at Harvard before entering politics. He was a biographer of his great-grandfather George Cabot (1877), of Alexander Hamilton (1882), of Daniel Webster (1883), and of George Washington (1889). He also edited a nine-volume edition of the works of Hamilton. In the Senate, he supported the Spanish-American War of 1898; the presidency of his friend, Theodore Roosevelt; and the gold standard. He was also a powerful opponent of Woodrow Wilson's peace plan and of the United States' entry into either the League of Nations or the World Court. Senator Lodge's son, Henry Cabot, Jr. (1902–85), occupied his father's seat in the U.S. Senate from 1937 to 1953 (except 1944–47). The younger Lodge was an occasional contender for the Republican presidential nomination, and

he was nominated in 1960 to run as the vice-presidential running mate to Richard Nixon during Nixon's first and failed attempt at being elected president. Lodge later served as U.S. Ambassador to South Vietnam. *BY*

Lodz, Battle of

This battle was the result of a German preemptive strike into Russian-controlled Poland launched by General August von Mackensen's Ninth Army in November 1914. Overall command of the operation rested with General Erich von Ludendorff, who correctly recognized that the recent Russian victory over Austro-Hungarian forces at Ivangorod in October would be used by them as a springboard for a major advance into the German province of Silesia, a key coal mining and industrial area. However, the Russian plans were delayed due to badly damaged railroads, which increased their already   acute supply problems. Von Mackensen's forces attacked southeast toward Lodz, a center of railroad communications, on November 11, destroying an isolated corps on the left of General Paul von Rennenkampf's Russian First Army in two days. Despite this pressure, the Russian high command ignored the growing threat and continued to prepare for the invasion of Silesia. As it did so, German troops crushed a second Russian corps, part of the Second Army, at the Battle of Kutno and opened the way to Lodz. Various Russian forces fell back on Lodz, arriving shortly before von Mackensen's forces on the 18th, and the plan to invade Silesia was discarded. For a week German units unsuccessfully attempted to take the town, despite being   outnumbered   two-to-one. Reinforcements from the Western Front failed to redress the imbalance, but the Russians defenders were finally forced to withdraw to a new line along the Bzura and Rawka Rivers west of Warsaw due   to   mounting   casualties   and dwindling supplies on December 6. German attempts to penetrate these positions were wound down from the 13th in the face of growing losses. German hopes of a decisive break-through to the Polish capital evaporated but Silesia had been saved from invasion. *MC*

Left: Henry Cabot Lodge.
Collection of Bill Yenne

London, Treaty of

Treaty negotiated in secret during April 1915 between the three major Allied powers and Italy, setting out the terms under which Italy would enter the war. It set out the extent to which any postwar settlement would award new territory to Italy and committed the Russians to position sufficient forces against Austria-Hungary to prevent the latter from concentrating its strength on the Italian front. *DC*

Loos, Battle of

The Battle of Loos, part of the wider Artois-Loos Offensive, began on September 25, 1915, with I and IV Corps of British First Army attacking between Loos and the La Bassée Canal, while II and III Corps provided diversionary attacks. On the first day IV Corps made significant gains, capturing the town of Loos itself, but problems of supply and a shortage of reserves ensured that these gains could not be consolidated and after a few days heavy fighting they were forced to retreat with heavy losses. The attack was renewed on October 13 but was equally unsuccessful and was called off due to bad weather and heavy casualties. *MC*

Lorraine, Invasion of (1914)

The French invasion of Lorraine formed one of the major objectives of the French prewar offensive strategy against Germany, Plan 17. The battle began on August 14, 1914, with the advance of the French First and Second Armies. The French First Army, under Dubail, was supposed to take Sarrebourg, east of Nancy, while De Castlenau's Second Army was to take Morhange. The German defenders, under Crown Prince Rupprecht, feigned a retreat before counterattacking heavily, driving the French Armies back to the prewar border by August 22. The Germans attacked again on August 24, but the French were prepared and minimal gains were made and the line stabilized. *MC*

Lowestoft, Hartlepool, and Yarmouth, Raids on

On November 3, 1914, German battle-cruisers commanded by Vice-Admiral Hipper initiated "hit-and-run" raiding against   the   English   east   coast,

bombarding Lowestoft and laying mines off the harbor before escaping out to sea. On December 16, 1914, a more intensive bombardment of Hartlepool by the battlecruisers *Moltke* and *Blücher* lasted forty-three minutes, and caused extensive damage. A covering force of four British destroyers, two obsolete cruisers, and a submarine were also engaged, forcing the scout cruiser *Patrol* to run herself aground to prevent sinking. A six-inch shore battery near Hartlepool Lighthouse scored eight hits on the *Blücher*. On April 25, 1916, Hipper's battlecruisers returned to Lowestoft, and bombarded the fishing town together with the nearby port of Yarmouth. A daring sortie by Vice-Admiral Tyrwhitt's Harwich Force of destroyers and light cruisers interrupted the leisurely bombardment of Yarmouth, and forced the German ships to withdraw. These engagements outraged the British public, and although the raids caused scores of civilian casualties, their psychological damage far outweighed any more tangible results. Though successful, these "hit-and-run" raids were called off after the Battle of Jutland (1916), due to the high risks involved for the German battlecruiser fleet. *AK*

Ludendorff, Erich von (1865–1937)

One of the most important German officers of World War I, Ludendorff was, like Hindenburg, born in Posen. By 1914 he had reached the rank of major general, having entered the army in 1882. He initially saw service on the Western Front, but was soon transferred to the east where, as Hindenburg's chief of staff, he helped achieve victory at Tannenberg and the Masurian Lakes. He remained close to Hindenburg until October 1918, having been appointed quartermaster-general in August 1916. It was Ludendorff that played a pivotal role in events in Russia in 1917; he assisted Lenin to return east and also formulated the strict terms of the Treaty of Brest-Litovsk. He was the mastermind behind the final German assault in the west in 1918, but faced by the victorious Allied offensive of July and August of that year, he lost heart. He advocated, in late September, that peace be sought and the following month fled in disguise to Sweden. In post-Versailles Germany he became linked to the nationalists, had a role in the Kapp Putsch of 1920 and was the nominal leader of Hitler's Beer Hall Putsch of 1923. However, following his failure to gain mass support as an NSDAP candidate in the 1925 presidential election, having been cleared of treason following the Beer Hall Putsch, he severed relations with Hitler. He became a pacifist in the years prior to his death, although never losing his hatred of Jews, freemasonry, and Jesuits. *MS*

Lusitania, Sinking of the

The barbarity of unrestricted U-boat warfare was most notably demonstrated when the *Lusitania* was sunk by a German U-boat, the *U-20*. Displacing 38,000 tons and capable of steaming at twenty-seven knots, she was the largest and fastest of the transatlantic liners, and had already completed five return trips, relying on her speed to avoid enemy submarines. *U-20* ambushed the liner off the southern tip of Ireland, sinking her with a single torpedo. 1,198 passengers were lost, including 128 Americans, an act which helped push America into the war on the Allied side. *AK*

Left: Hindenburg, Ludendorff, and Seeckt.
Chrysalis Photo Library

Right: A timely reminder and encouragement to enlist. *Chrysalis Photo Library*

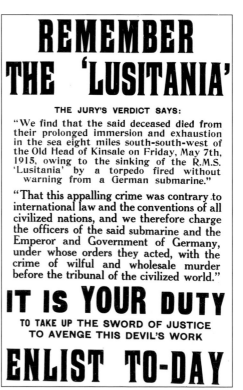

REMEMBER THE 'LUSITANIA'

THE JURY'S VERDICT SAYS:

"We find that the said deceased died from their prolonged immersion and exhaustion in the sea eight miles south-south-west of the Old Head of Kinsale on Friday, May 7th, 1915, owing to the sinking of the R.M.S. 'Lusitania' by a torpedo fired without warning from a German submarine."

"That this appalling crime was contrary to international law and the conventions of all civilized nations, and we therefore charge the officers of the said submarine and the Emperor and Government of Germany, under whose orders they acted, with the crime of wilful and wholesale murder before the tribunal of the civilized world."

IT IS YOUR DUTY
TO TAKE UP THE SWORD OF JUSTICE TO AVENGE THIS DEVIL'S WORK
ENLIST TO-DAY

MacDonald, James Ramsay
(1866–1937)

Britain's first Labor Prime Minister, Ramsay MacDonald was at Lossiemouth, Morayshire, in Scotland. Active in politics from a relatively young age, he joined the Independent Labor Party in 1894. He first gained elected office as a member of the London County Council in 1901 and at the 1906 General Election was elected to the House of Commons. He was leader of the Labor Party from 1911 until 1914 and again from 1922 until 1931. In 1922 he became Leader of the Opposition, a prelude to him becoming Prime Minister of a minority Labor government in January 1924. This was, however, to be a short-lived administration and it fell in November the same year. In 1929 he again became Prime Minister; however, this administration was rocked by the turmoil that occurred in financial markets and in the world economy as a result of the Wall Street Crash of that year. MacDonald's reaction to the crisis was the creation of a National coalition government, formed largely of Conservative ministers, which resulted in a split within the Labor Party and a feeling that MacDonald had betrayed the working class. MacDonald remained Prime Minister until 1935 when he was succeeded by Stanley Baldwin. MacDonald shortly after retiring from his final ministerial position, that of Lord President. *MS*

Machine guns

Repeating firearms worked by cranks or other mechanical systems have been known since the eighteenth century. Yet it was only with Hiram S. Maxim's patents of 1883 that reliable methods were devised of using the power of the cartridge to reload. Thus was born the true machine gun. Following demonstrations all over Europe it was now taken up with greater or lesser enthusiasm by all powers. In 1914 Maxim-inspired machine guns were in the majority, being fielded by the Germans, Russians, British, Serbians, Bulgarians, and Turks. Typical, and perhaps most significant, of these types was the German MG08. This was water-cooled, belt-fed, firing from 250-round fabric belts, and set atop a "sledge" mount. This clever device

Right: British machine gunners wearing gas-masks, 1916. *Chrysalis Photo Library*

Opposite, Top: A very posed photograph of a motor machine gun unit "firing at aeroplanes on the Western Front," circa 1915. *Chrysalis Photo Library*

Opposite, Bottom: Americans with captured German machine guns. *Collection of Bill Yenne*

provided a stable platform which could be raised or lowered, or carried like a stretcher by the crew: it was however very heavy. German organization was one machine gun company per regiment: these comprised six machine guns and 137 officers and men, with nine wagons and six small hand carts. This permitted the deployment of two guns per battalion, but since the machine gun proved murderously effective and there was a growing demand, by late 1916 every front-line battalion had a machine-gun company of six guns. The main competitor to the Maxim was the Hotchkiss, development of which had started about 1893. In 1914 Hotchkiss-type weapons were on issue to the French, Belgians, and Japanese. The most significant Hotchkiss type was the tripod-mounted French Hotchkiss Model 1914. This was air-cooled, and was fed by means of twenty-four or thirty-round metallic strips: though the mounting was lighter, the barrel assembly was roughly the same weight as that of the Maxim. Performance was also similar, though given the air cooling and strip feed the sustained fire capability was marginally inferior. Hotchkiss machine guns were also used, alongside other weapons, by

the AEF from 1917. The Maxim, Hotchkiss, and British Vickers, itself a refinement of the Maxim design, performed amazingly well and were one of the reasons that the front became so solidly locked. Yet none of them were particularly well adapted to offensive action as they required more than one man to bring them into action. This began to change with the introduction of light machine guns and automatic rifles, weapons which could be carried by one man, and set up in seconds, or

occasionally, be fired on the move. The LMG would help produce a revolution in small-unit infantry tactics. Star performer in this class was the Lewis gun. Originally designed by American Isaac Lewis, but further developed by the British, the Lewis was an air-cooled machine weapon with a drum magazine and a small bipod mounting. It allowed an infantry unit to carry its own fire support into the attack, moving at much the same speed as the riflemen. First used in combat in 1914 it became

available in significant numbers later in 1915, and by the end of that year was replacing the Vickers in the infantry battalions. The tripod-mounted guns were then grouped together to provide long-range fire in the companies of the Machine Gun Corps. Other light guns included the German MG08/15, and the excellent BAR—the Browning automatic rifle introduced by the Americans in the last months of the war. *SB*

Left: A Browning heavy machine gun team of the AEF's 80th Division. *Collection of Bill Yenne*

Below and Right: German machine gun teams. the most important German machine gun was the Maxim 08 7.92mm, water-cooled, belt-fed weapon that had a 600 round/minute rate of fire. *Chrysalis Photo Library*

Mackensen, August von (1849–1944)

Mackensen served as a corps commander with the Eighth Army on the Eastern Front before moving to the Ninth Army for its assault through Russian Poland. Leading the assault on Warsaw and Lodz, he became Ninth Army commander, replacing Hindenburg. In April 1915 he became commander of the Eleventh Army, with overall control of the Gorlice-Tarnów Offensive in May 1915, the success of which resulted in his promotion to field marshal. He was equally successful during the Triple Offensive of mid-1915 where his concentrated assault led to significant territorial gains. Transferred to the Balkans, his strategy again worked well in Serbia in September 1915 and as commander in Romania in late 1916. He commanded the occupying forces in Romania until the end of the war. *MS*

Below: Field Marshal von Mackensen inspecting troops in captured Bucharest, January 1917.
Chrysalis Photo Library

Mangin, Charles (1866–1925)

Nicknamed "Butcher" for his somewhat ruthless tactics, Mangin was one of France's most successful generals on the Western Front. At the Battle of Charleroi, in August 1914, he organized a successful counterattack at the Meuse and, at Verdun in 1916, he was promoted to command the Third Army in its counterattacks of October and December. He was commander of the Sixth Army during the Nivelle Offensive, leading it in the disastrous assault on the Aisne, after which he was removed from his command, not being active again until mid-1918 when he was appointed to command the Tenth Army. His successful side was restored when he led the counterattack during the second Battle of the Marne in July 1918. *MS*

Mannock, Edward

Interned in Turkey on the outbreak of war, blind in one eye, Edward "Mick" Mannock overcame his physical disability to emerge as the second

Left: Major Mannock, VC.
Chrysalis Photo Library

highest-scoring RFC ace of the war, officially with seventy-three victories. Irish-born Mannock was a deadly exponent of the Nieuport and SE5a until being killed by ground fire on July 26, 1918. His posthumous Victoria Cross was awarded in 1919 after representations were made by his former comrades; to many he was the unmatched "King of Fighter Aces." *JS*

Maps

Few factors were as significant to campaigns as accurate maps: in Britain the Ordnance Survey had been founded specifically for military purposes. Many of the German staff war games or *Kriegspiel* were based entirely on maps. Yet 1914 posed immediate cartographic problems. Much of France had been mapped only at the relatively small scale of 1:80,000, and the surveys were out of date. Furthermore French, Belgian, and British referencing and grid systems were different. The Royal Engineer Survey and Printing sections therefore had a vital task to perform. From October 1914 began the production of 1:20,000 and 1:40,000 maps, which were printed in Southampton and London. A new plane-table survey was commenced in January 1915, and not long after production of maps at a scale of 1:10,000 was undertaken. "Trench maps" with field works, either pencilled or printed on, were soon common, though surveyors often had to work in the front line. A dangerous hiccup in this progress was a series of maps produced in 1915 in which the enemy was always at the top of the chart, irrespective of the north orientation. Unsurprisingly these were quickly abandoned. Later, with the progress of aerial photography, it became possible to base map work on up to date photographs. With many bombardments now fired by map reference, accurate data became more, rather than less, important. *SB*

March, Peyton Conway (1864–1955)

A subordinate to General John J. Pershing early in World War I, General Peyton March was brought home from France in 1918 to occupy a newly enhanced post as Pershing's superior. Born in Easton, Pennsylvania, March

graduated from the U.S. Military Academy at West Point in 1888. After serving in a series of routine garrison posts from Washington, D.C. to California, Marsh attended the Artillery School at Fort Monroe. He commanded an artillery battery in the Philippines Campaign and in the capture of Manila during the Spanish-American War of 1898. He participated in numerous operations during the Philippine Insurrection and became a member of the War Department General Staff in 1903. He was a military observer to the Japanese Army during the Russo-Japanese War in 1904 and commanded the 8th Field Artillery on the Mexican Punitive Expedition of 1916. In June 1917, he was given command of the 1st Field Artillery Brigade of the AEF 1st Division and promoted to major general. As commanding officer of First Army artillery, March would serve as Pershing's top artillery man through March 1918, when Secretary of War Newton Baker brought him home to assume the job of U.S. Army chief of staff. This post, which had existed previously, was greatly elevated in stature and importance by Baker, who wanted to see a top commander with a great deal of power. With the four-star rank of general, the chief of staff took precedence over all officers of the U.S. Army. However, at the same time, General Pershing was serving as the four-star commander-in-chief of the AEF. Because Pershing had received his fourth star before March, he was technically the senior officer, but because March was

chief of staff, he outranked Pershing. There was a bit of a stand off, and the Secretary of War was usually the tie-breaker during disagreements. In the case of operational matters related directly to the AEF, Baker and March usually acceded to Pershing's point of view. Pershing's job was to win a war. March's job, as specified in the job description handed him by Secretary Baker, was to reorganize the U.S. Army General Staff specifically with respect to quartermaster, supply, and transportation problems that had been encountered in the early months of expansion for World War I. March served as chief of staff through June 1921, during which time he centralized control over supply, and created an Air Service, a Tank Corps, and a Chemical Warfare Service. He also supervised the demobilization. He was succeeded as chief of staff by General Pershing. The post of U.S. Army chief of staff continues to this day to be occupied by the highest-ranking officer in the U.S. Army. The only higher position in the U.S. chain of command is the post of Chairman of the Joint Chiefs of Staff. Created after World War II, this post rotates between four-star general officers from the various services. *BY*

Marne, First Battle of the (1914)

Fought from September 5–9, 1914, the First Battle of the Marne dashed German hopes of a fortieth-day victory. Although the Allies had been forced into a general retreat across the Western Front, with Sir John French planning the BEF's evacuation and the French planning a final defense of Paris, the battle lines on the Marne looked favorable for the Allies as the thirty divisions of the German First, Second, Third, Fourth, and Fifth Armies chased thirty-six retreating divisions over the river. The battle began badly for the French, with General von Gronau preempting Sixth Army's tactic of encirclement and staging an assault of his own before slipping away into the night. Sixth Army held its ground, however, and drew von Kluck's First Army away from the bulk of the fighting so that by September 9—the fortieth day—a thirty-five-mile rift had appeared between German First and Second Armies, into which Franchet d'Esperey's Fifth Army

Left: General Peyton C. March.
Collection of Bill Yenne

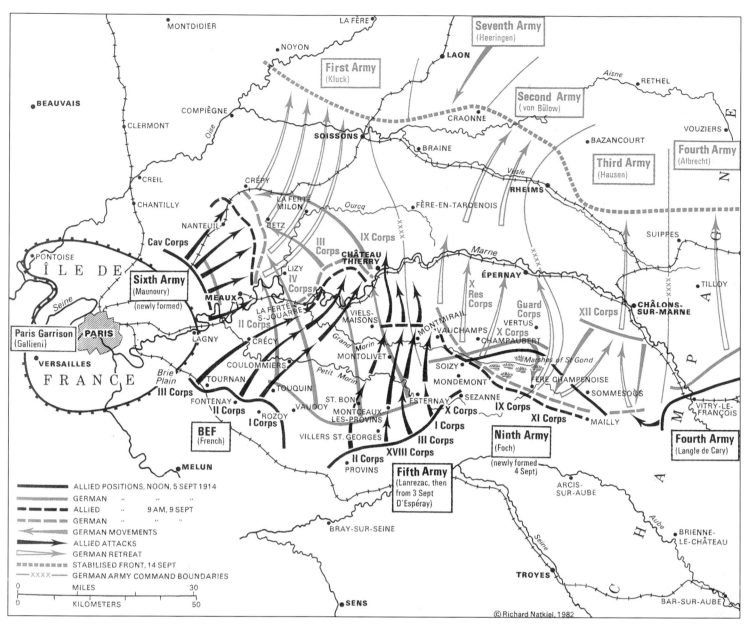

and the BEF were able to move. The First Battle of the Marne ended on September 9 when Lieutenant Colonel Richard Hetsch reached the much-debated conclusion that the German First, Second, and Third Armies' positions were untenable, and Moltke ordered a retreat to the Aisne. *MC*

Marne, Second Battle of the (1918)

Conceived as a diversionary tactic to draw Allied troops away from Flanders, the Second Battle of the Marne lasted from July 15 to August 5, 1918. Originally a German offensive, it ended as an Allied victory, setting in motion the German retreat that continued until the Armistice. On July 15, three and a half German armies attacked Gouraud's First Army, converging along a twenty-six-mile front only to be halted by 11am the same day. To the southwest, the German Seventh and Ninth Armies enjoyed more

success, smashing through the French Sixth Army under Degoutte to cross the Marne at Dormans. Their advantage was short-lived, and Seventh Army was repelled on July 17 by the French Ninth Army, supported by British, American, and Italian troops. As thirty-six Allied divisions halted a German offensive of fifty-two divisions strong, the tide began to turn. On July 18 the Allies launched the counterattack that eliminated the Marne salient, with French Tenth and Sixth Armies advancing five miles in the first day. Soissons was freed on August 2, and August 3 saw the Germans fall back to the Vesle and Aisne rivers at the base of the old salient. The counteroffensive ended on August 6, when the Allies could push no further. *MC*

Marwitz, Georg von der (1856–1929)

A German cavalry officer, Marwitz served on the Western Front in August 1914,

including the First Battle of the Marne and the campaign in Flanders, before being transferred to the east. He commanded a ski corps during the Carpathian campaign of early 1915. After helping to oppose the Brusilov Offensive, he returned west as commander of the Second Army in December 1916 and led the German counterattacks at the Battle of Cambrai. After nearly achieving a breakthrough during the Kaiserschlacht Offensive, he took command of the Fifth Army once the Second had been severely mauled in August during the Allied Amiens Offensive. *MS*

Masurian Lakes, First Battle of the

The battle was the second phase of the German plan to clear East Prussia of the Russian forces that had invaded their province in August 1914. Following the great victory at the Battle of Tannenberg, which had destroyed one of the two invading Russian armies, the new German command team of Field Marshal Paul von Hindenburg and General Erich von Ludendorff moved the German Eighth Army northward by rail. They added reinforcements from the Western Front and confronted General Paul von Rennenkampf's First Army, which by early September was strung out in East Prussia slowly advancing on Königsberg. The German commanders had seen a weakness in von Rennenkampf's position—most of his forces were concentrated in the north opposite Königsberg, while the southern sector around the Masurian Lakes was only lightly defended. This was in anticipation of the arrival of the newly activated Russian Tenth Army, which was to plug the gap. On September 7 the Eighth Army's I Corps attacked around the lakes and quickly broke through in the first stage of a strategy designed to encircle the Russian First Army. However, successive supporting attacks in the north made only limited progress and von Rennenkampf was able to extricate his forces from the 9th. Nevertheless, the battle cleared East Prussia of Russian forces, but the survivors had regrouped just over the border along the line of the Niemen River by the 20th. A series of German assaults to dislodge them failed and a Russian counterattack at the end of the month known as the Battle of the Nieman River forced the exhausted

Eighth Army to end its offensive. The Russians reported some 125,000 casualties, while German losses totaled 100,000 men. *IW*

Mata Hari (1876–1917)

Born Margaretha Gertruida Zelle at Leeuwarden in the Netherlands, the future dancer, who adopted the stage name Mata Hari, married a Scottish officer called MacLeod, who served in the Dutch army in 1895. After a decade of marriage she moved to France and became famous as a dancer and romantic figure, who was alleged to have had affairs with many men, including many of high rank in the government and military (without recognizing national boundaries). She was accused and found guilty of treason by spying for the Germans and executed in 1917. *PW*

Maubeuge, Siege of

Maubeuge, a major fort on the French northern border with Belgium, was cut off from the Allied forces following the retreat of the BEF and the French Fifth Army from August 23, 1914. From August 29, Maubeuge was under a state

Left: Map showing the course of the First Battle of the Marne. *Richard Natkiel*

Below: Patients and staff at the 1st Eastern General Hospital, 1916. *Chrysalis Photo Library*

of siege, and following the fall of its forts, General Fournier surrendered the town on September 8. *MC*

Maude, Sir F. Stanley (1864–1917)

Maude served on the Western Front until he was wounded after which he took command of the 13th Division at Gallipoli, moving with it to Mesopotamia in March 1916. In July 1916 Maude replaced Gorringe as commander of the Tigris Corps and took command of the front a month later. Reequipped and reinforced, Maude's army began to advance slowly, gaining victory at the Second Battle of Kut in February 1917 and capturing Baghdad the following month. His successes continued with the capture of Samarrah in April 1917, but he was die of cholera on November 18 the same year. *PW*

Medical care

With wounded outnumbering fatalities by a factor of about three to one, medical services were a vital component of all armies. British Army medical care was the responsibility of the Royal Army Medical Corps, from which a medical officer was allotted to each battalion. Together with battalion orderlies and stretcher bearers the MO provided the wounded man's first line of care. If the case was more than trivial the patient was transported first to the regimental

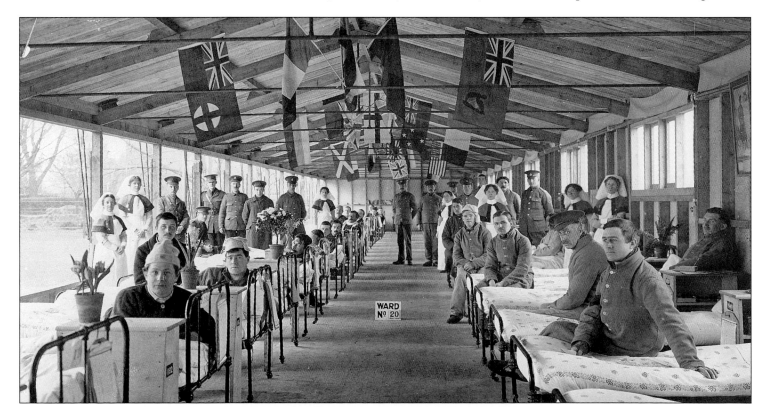

aid post; then the advanced dressing station, or main dressing station. Those requiring serious surgery passed on to the casualty clearing station. Base hospitals well behind the lines provided longer-term care, but those receiving a "Blighty One" would be taken to Britain, usually by hospital train and ship. Roughly 2.5 million casualties were returned to Britain from the various theaters of war. Nurses were provided by various bodies including not only the RAMC but also female Voluntary Aid Detachments and Queen Alexandra's Imperial Military Nursing Service. There were as many non-battle casualties as there were wounded from battle. According to British statistics, important causes of non-battle casualty included influenza (with over 350,000 hospital admissions), malaria, pneumonia, and dysentery. There were over 80,000 cases of trench foot and frost bite from 1916 to 1918, of which half were serious enough to lead to admission to a base hospital. Interestingly the incidence of venereal disease was slightly higher than that of trench foot. *SB*

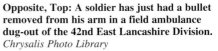

Opposite, Top: A soldier has just had a bullet removed from his arm in a field ambulance dug-out of the 42nd East Lancashire Division. *Chrysalis Photo Library*

Opposite, Bottom: A German prisoner having his wounded hand dressed in the VAD dressing station at Abbeville, while his escort looks on, June 27, 1917. *Chrysalis Photo Library*

Above: An ambulance wagon passing through Gully Ravine, Helles Front, Gallipoli. *Chrysalis Photo Library*

Left: Drivers of the American Ambulance Field Service. *Collection of Bill Yenne*

Below Left: Red Cross worker Mary Shannon Webster serving hot chocolate. *Collection of Bill Yenne*

Mediterranean, Operations in the

Strategically, the Allies enjoyed an overwhelming naval presence in the Mediterranean Sea, with a substantial British fleet supported by a large portion of the French Navy. The initial drama provided by the pursuit of the *Goeben* and *Breslau* in August 1914 was replaced by the tedium of maintaining a blockade on the Austrian and Turkish fleets. The Adriatic Sea was sealed by warships and an antisubmarine barrage at Otranto, while Allied naval operations in the Dardanelles to seal the Turks off from the Aegean were costly and ineffective. From mid-1915 on, German U-boats infiltrated the Mediterranean Sea, forcing the Allies to devote resources to the countering of this growing threat. Even the Japanese sent an antisubmarine force to Malta to assist in the fighting. U-boats laid minefields off the coasts of France, Italy, Tunisia, and Egypt, while merchant and naval vessels were attacked in increasing numbers. In 1917 alone, almost 900 Allied ships were sunk by U-boats in the region. Gradually, the introduction of convoys and better antisubmarine tactics turned the tide, and the U-boat threat receded. Although serious, it never prevented the movement of troops to the Balkans, or through the Suez Canal. *AK*

Memorials

World War I brought mass death and its accompanying heartbreak throughout Europe, America, and the British Empire on a scale not seen since the plagues of the Middle Ages. In the aftermath of the conflict there was great popular support for the establishment of local memorials to provide a focus for grief and commemoration. In the United Kingdom alone up to 60,000 memorials were erected, listing the war dead of virtually every community. Similar monuments can be found in many places in France, Italy, and the other combatant nations, while in churches and cathedrals across Germany solemn memorials mark their loss. Across much of the world wreaths are still laid annually to honor those fallen in the Great War. *DC*

Above and Right: Maps showing operations in Mesopotamia and the Middle East. *Richard Natkiel*

Below: Artillery train in Mesopotamia. *Chrysalis Photo Library*

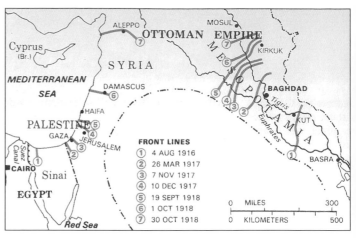

Mesopotamia (Iraq), Operations in

British operations against Turkish-controlled Mesopotamia began in late 1914 and culminated with the capture of Basra on November 23, which was to be used as a base for a future advance on Baghdad by mainly Indian Army forces under General John Nixon. Turkish attempts to test Basra's defenses were defeated at the Battles of Qurna in December 1914 and Ahwaz in early 1915. In May, Nixon ordered a small expeditionary force commanded by General Charles Townshend to move northward along the Tigris River. Townshend was able to capture the town of Kut in late September but his progress

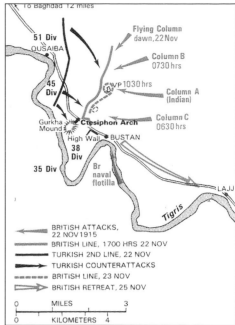

Map legend:
- BRITISH ATTACKS, 22 NOV 1915
- BRITISH LINE, 1700 HRS 22 NOV
- TURKISH 2ND LINE, 22 NOV
- TURKISH COUNTERATTACKS
- BRITISH LINE, 23 NOV
- BRITISH RETREAT, 25 NOV

MILES 0 — 3
KILOMETERS 0 — 4

Left: The gun battery on HMS *Sedgefly* at full recoil. *Chrysalis Photo Library*

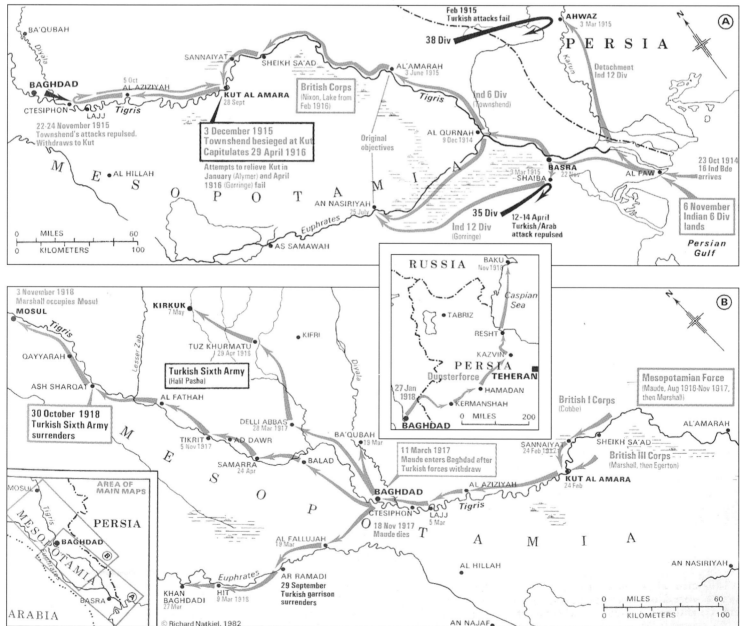

toward Baghdad was halted at the Battle of Ctesiphon (November 22–25). Townshend made a fighting withdrawal back to Kut but was besieged and forced to surrender on April 29, 1916. Following a period of reinforcement and reorganization, the new British commander in Mesopotamia, General Frederick Maude, relaunched the push along the Tigris from December 1916. Following the Second Battle of Kut, the town was finally recaptured on February 25, 1917, and Maude's forces were able to take Baghdad on March 11. Over the following months Maude launched various limited expeditions up the Tigris to Samarrah and the Euphrates to Ramadi to secure his recent gains but further major offensives were disrupted by his death from cholera in mid-November. British operations recommenced in early spring 1918, although on a more limited scale. A push along the Euphrates succeeded in capturing Khan Baghdadi in late March, while the main drive up the Tigris, which began at the end of the hot summer season, made steady progress in the face of crumbling Turkish resistance. Turkey agreed an armistice to begin on November 1 and British forces occupied Mosul the next day, signaling the end of the campaign. *IW*

Messines, Battle of

The Battle of Messines was carried out on June 7, 1917, by the British Second Army under General Herbert Plumer. after the detonation of nineteen massive underground mines underneath the German lines. Following the explosion nine divisions of infantry advanced under protection of a creeping artillery barrage and all initial objectives were taken within three hours. *MC*

Above: Captured Turkish gunners with the Lancashires. *Chrysalis Photo Library*

Right: Sappers digging a communication trench to Messines Ridge during the Battle of Messines, June 7, 1917. *Chrysalis Photo Library*

Below: An eighteen-pounder belonging to the 1st Cavalry Brigade in action at Bois de Ploegsteert during the Battle of Messines, October 19–20, 1914. *Chrysalis Photo Library*

WORLD WAR I: A VISUAL ENCYCLOPEDIA

Meuse-Argonne Campaign

The Meuse-Argonne Campaign had the distinction of being the both the last and the bloodiest campaign involving troops of the AEF. It was also the biggest operation and victory by U.S. troops in World War I. The fighting began with an American offensive on September 26, 1918, and ended with the Armistice on November 11, 1918. It occurred in the Verdun Sector of the Western Front, immediately north and northwest of the town of Verdun. The Meuse-Argonne Campaign pitted the U.S. First Army against roughly forty German divisions. The AEF troops were commanded directly by General John J. Pershing until October 16, on which date, he placed Lieutenant General Hunter Liggett in command of First Army. The bulk of the German units were from General Max Karl von Gallwitz's Fifth Army, commanded directly by General Georg von der Marwitz. The objective of the U.S. offensive was the capture of the railroad hub at Sedan which was the keystone of the rail network supporting the German armies in France and Flanders. It was believed that this would break the ability of the Germans to operate on the Western Front. The terrain was rugged, and it had been heavily fortified by the Germans during the four years that they had occupied the salient. During the week of September 29 through October 5, the bloodiest week of the war for the AEF, there were 6,589 U.S. battle deaths. The following two weeks, the second and third bloodiest of the war, saw 6,019 and 5,019 troops killed in action. The seven weeks beginning with September 29 and concluding with the Armistice on November 11 saw 27,840 battle deaths, more than half the overall total for the war. The number of U.S. troops on the wounded roster reached to nearly 100,000. The first of three phases of the operation began with a massive artillery barrage on September 25, followed by an attack the next day by ten American divisions comprising more than a quarter million troops. The units were I Corps, containing the 92nd, 77th, 28th, and 35th Divisions; V Corps, containing the 91st, 37th, and 79th Divisions; and III Corps, containing the 4th, 80th, and 33rd

Left: American artillery fire supports the Argonne advance. *Chrysalis Photo Library*

Divisions. They were aligned—pointing north—from the eastern edge of the Champagne region to the west bank of the Meuse River. The Germans were amazingly ill-prepared, but because of the 79th Division's failure to take Montfaucon until September 27, they had time to regroup. Through October 3, the offensive continued to fall behind schedule as the terrain and bad roads slowed the Americans and aided the Germans. Pershing pulled out several inexperienced divisions, added the 1st Division to I Corps, and rebuilt V Corps with the 32nd and 3rd Divisions. The renewed offensive on October 4 resulted in high casualties being traded for minimal gains, but the AEF slogged forward, and Alvin York's heroic action on October 8 would prove particularly inspiring. With French XVII Corps augmenting the three AEF corps, Pershing launched another offensive on the Allied right flank on October 9. For nearly two weeks, this battle would rage

Below: Men from the AEF's 308th Infantry in action with their rifle grenades in the Argonne sector near Abri du Crochet, October 31, 1918.
Chrysalis Photo Library

along the east bank of the Meuse. On October 13, the AEF successfully captured the city of Romagne, which would later be the site of the largest American military cemetery outside the United States. The second phase of the Meuse-Argonne Campaign would begin on October 16. By this time, Pershing had divided the AEF between his two numbered armies. Essentially, all of the units involved in the Meuse-Argonne Campaign remained in the First Army under General Hunter Liggett, while all the units not involved in the Meuse-Argonne Campaign were assigned to the new Second Army under General Robert Bullard. As his troops pushed their way through the German defenses over the next two weeks, Liggett's engineers undertook a massive road-building program to facilitate fast and smooth logistical support. While the First Army reached Grandpre at the northwestern corner of the Argonne region on the first day, the city would not be captured until October 23. Meanwhile, Cunel was captured on October 21, and the Bois de Forêt and Bois des Rappes fell on October 22. With the AEF First Army's 2nd and 36th Divisions as a spearhead, the French Fourth Army swung into

position on the First Army left flank on October 27, allowing for an Allied advance across a wide front. The final phase of the Meuse-Argonne Campaign began on November 1, with four corps assigned to Liggett's First Army. These were I Corps, with the 78th, 77th, and 80th Divisions; V Corps, with the 2nd and 89th Divisions; III Corps with the 90th and 5th Divisions; and the French XV Corps, containing the U.S. 79th, 26th, and 81st Divisions. A ten-mile First Army advance in three days took the German defenses by surprise and compelled them to withdraw. By November 5, the Americans were within striking distance of Sedan, but the French Fourth Army was allowed the honor of recapturing the city because of its having been the site of their defeat in 1870. Beginning on November 7, First Army units operating on both banks of the Meuse River continued advancing northward toward Montmedy, which was to be their next objective. However, on the morning of November 11, news of the Armistice arrived. With the exception of a few units that did not get the news until later in the day, the guns fell silent at 11am. The Meuse-Argonne Campaign and World War I were over. *BY*

Mexico, Part played in the war

When World War I began in Europe, Mexico was in the middle of a civil war. The Mexican Revolution that began in 1911 had toppled long-time dictator General Porfirio Diaz, but the country devolved into bloody anarchy with warlords such as Emiliano Zapata, Victoriano Huerta, Francisco "Pancho" Villa, and Venustiano Carranza, jockeying for power. By December 1914, one of Carranza's gang leaders, Alvaro Obregon, drove both Villa and Zapata out of Mexico City, and Carranza took a tenuous hold on the reins of power. He dominated most of the country for several years, but his rivals continued to harass him militarily. In 1916, Villa attacked the city of Columbus, New Mexico, murdering civilians and burning property. It would not be until the attacks of September 2001 that there would be a terrorist action against United States' territory that would exceed the magnitude of the Columbus debacle. Woodrow Wilson ordered General John J. Pershing to lead a punitive expedition south of the border to capture Villa in Mexico, but the bandit leader managed to elude capture and he continued to be a thorn in the side for Carranza. Meanwhile, an influx of German money into Carranza's pocket was turning Mexico into the most pro-German of Western Hemisphere governments. The British depended on the oilfields near Tampico in the Mexican state of Tamaulipas, and Carranza threatened to cut them off. The Zimmerman Telegram, in which Germany called on Carranza to go to war with the United States, was the low point in relations between the United States and Mexico. When the United States finally declared war on Germany, Carranza did little to disguise his dislike for his northern neighbor. He stopped short of officially taking sides, but issued a statement that Mexico would maintain "strict and rigorous neutrality." In 1920, the warlords Plutarco Calles, Alvaro Obregon, and Adolfo de la Huerta all revolted against Carranza, who was killed in their uprising. Obregon then became president of Mexico, and in 1922, Mexico joined the League of Nations. *BY*

Middle East, War in the

The war in the Middle East centered on a two-pronged campaign led by the British

Above: Pack transport on the march. Jebel Hamrin, 1917. *Chrysalis Photo Library*

against Palestine and Mesopotamia, but the theater also saw several attempts by both sides to foment unrest in areas that they considered to be under their opponent's jurisdiction. The first objective of the British was to protect two of their vital strategic interests—the Suez Canal and India. The canal was uncomfortably close to Turkish-controlled territory, while Turkish Mesopotamia bordered Persia, which was partly controlled by Britain and seen as a potential avenue of attack against British-controlled India. For much of the war, British operations were restricted by the local conditions and shortages of men and equipment. In the longer term the British hoped that their two widely dispersed forces would conduct roughly simultaneous converging advances northward—along the coastal plain of Palestine and up the flood plains of the Tigris and Euphrates Rivers—and finally link up somewhere in the Turkish heartland. Between late 1914 and early 1917, the British made little progress in either theater and suffered a number of defeats. In Mesopotamia, a push on Baghdad was halted at the Battle of Ctesiphon in November 1915 and the

British expedition was ultimately forced to surrender at Kut in April 1916. In Palestine, two British attempts to push out of the Sinai Peninsula and break into southern Palestine ended in defeat at the First and Second Battles of Gaza in March and April 1917. British fortunes improved somewhat from these low points. First, Baghdad was captured in March 1917 and the defenses of southern Palestine were penetrated at the Third Battle of Gaza in October–November. Gaza heralded the collapse of the Turkish forces in Palestine, Jerusalem fell on December 9 and the British pushed northward until the end of the war aided by Arabs operating on their desert flank, who had rebelled against the Turks in mid-1916. Progress in Mesopotamia was somewhat slower but the British had captured the city of Mosul by the Armistice. The original plans for the two forces to link up were never completed. Aside from these major campaigns, there were numerous outbreaks of unrest among the local peoples.

The British-sponsored Arab Revolt was the most successful, but the Central Powers also promoted uprisings. The most successful of these involved the Senussi, a loose coalition of tribes along the western Egyptian border and in Italian-controlled Tripolitania. The revolt began in December 1915 and was not finally quelled until August 1918. Some 100,000 British and Italian troops, as well as French colonial forces, had been involved in actions against the Senussi. Persia was also the scene of unrest. Effectively split in a northern zone under Russian control and a southern sector in which Britain held sway, it saw German-led attempts to provoke a local uprising. By 1916, Turkish forces had pushed the Russians out of much of the north, and the British were confined to a number of ports along the Persian Gulf due to a campaign of assassination. However, a mixed force of Persians and British troops under General Percy Sykes gradually restored order in the south and moved into northern Persia to fill the vacuum left by the collapse of the Russians following the revolutions in 1917. *IW*

Milne, George (1866–1948)

At the start of the BEF campaign, Milne was an artillery colonel. By late 1915, when he was transferred to the Balkans to command the 27th Division, he had been promoted to major general and had served as chief of staff to the Second Army. Although his force expanded considerably over the next two years, he was unable to escape from the control of the French commander-in-chief for the Balkans, Sarrail, and the limited actions he undertook, such as the attack on Lake Doiran in early 1917, were failures. With the collapse of the Ottoman Empire, Milne occupied Constantinople. *MS*

Milner of St. James's and Cape Town, Alfred First Viscount (1854–1925)

One of the leading British imperialists of the late nineteenth century, Milner was actually born in Bonn, Germany, the son of a university lecturer; his father was German (of British ancestry) and his mother British. Educated in Germany and Oxford, he was a journalist before joining the Civil Service. After service in Britain and Egypt, he went to South Africa as Governor of Cape Town and High Commissioner in 1897. He played a pivotal role in the Second Boer War and in the postwar reconstruction as Governor or Transvaal and Orange Free State from 1902 until he was forced to resign in 1906. He was created a Viscount in 1902. On his return to Britain, he became an active member of the House of Lords and, despite earlier policy disagreements, served in Lloyd George's cabinet as Secretary of War from 1916 until 1919, and as Colonial Secretary from 1919 until 1921. In early 1917 he visited Russia in order to bolster Russian resistance after the first revolution of that year. *MS*

Mines and mining (land)

Portable charges carried across No Man's Land were used experimentally as early as November 1914. Yet it was soon appreciated that it might be more effective to use the techniques of the medieval siege engineers, and dig under the opposing lines before planting explosives. Some of the first such mines were exploded by the Germans under the Indian Corps sector of Festubert in December 1914. French and British engineering units responded in kind. An

early pioneer of mining was Major J. Norton Griffiths who suggested raising a specific body of tunnelers and "clay kickers" who had experience working under British cities. His volunteers were at work by February 1915, and they and other diggers became the nucleus of the Royal Engineer tunneling companies. Later that year Army Mine Schools were formed. Mining proved especially hazardous not merely because of premature explosions, collapses, and carbon monoxide but because the enemy would use "camouflets" or counter mines, or even break into the underground galleries. Techniques developed to help deal with these problems included air pumps, breathing apparatus, stethoscopes and other listening equipment, and canaries in cages to detect noxious fumes. For the French and Germans one of the most active sectors was the Vauquois, where there were a hundred significant detonations in late 1915 and early 1916. That July the Somme battle was also commenced with the explosion of several large mines including the "Lochnagar" and "Y Sap." One of the most concerted mining operations was that carried out prior to the Battle of Messines in June 1917.

Here, on a frontage of several miles, British, Canadian, and Australian miners prepared nineteen mines, including the 95,600lb St. Eloi mine and the 91,000lb Spanbroekmolen mine. The result was described by one newspaper reporter as like the Last Judgment, with massive explosions tearing craters up to 400ft across. One mine which failed to go off was detonated by a thunderstorm in July 1955. *SB*

Mines (sea)

During the war, mines were divided into two main types. "Controlled"—used to guard harbor entrances or straits, such as the Dardanelles. In most cases these mines were fired electrically from the shore. More common were "independent" mines, which could be used both in shallow coastal waters or in deeper ocean waters. These mines were of various types—moored mines, seabed mines, drifting, creeping, and more technical oscillating mines. Most mines were of the moored type, designed to float just below the surface, tethered to a mooring drum which sat on the seabed. A hydrostatic device ensured the mine was deployed at its correct depth. The

Left: General Sir George Milne with General Mishiteh, January 1917. *Chrysalis Photo Library*

Right: An exploding mine at the school at Aubigny, May 12, 1916. *Chrysalis Photo Library*

Below Right: German minelaying submarine *UC5* at Temple Bar Pier. *Chrysalis Photo Library*

majority of mines were contact types, with horns protruding from the main buoyancy chamber. In sophisticated German mines, when the metal horn was bent by coming into contact with a passing ship, a glass phial inside it containing a bichromate solution was released, which made contact with zinc and carbon plates, creating a current and igniting the charge. Other devices, such as antenna mines, relied on electrical contacts for detonation, while Swedish-designed oscillating mines used hydrostatic valves for their ignition. Whatever the system, mines proved one of the most deadly weapons of the war. While controlled mines were laid in inshore defensive fields (known as observation minefields), they were operated by a controller on the shore, and formed part of a static defense network. More commonly, independent mines were laid in extensive fields, used both offensively and defensively. Although the majority of these used contact mines, other more sophisticated mine types were also employed. Over 250,000 mines were laid during the war, the majority by Britain (128,000), the United States (56,000), and Germany (43,000), and the bulk of these (190,000 mines in all) were deployed in the North Sea. Mine barrages between Dover and Calais and Orkney and Bergen (Norway), sealed off the North Sea and prevented any German move into the Atlantic Ocean. Further extensive minefields in the Mediterranean, Aegean, Adriatic, and Black Seas all influenced the course of the war. A new style of warfare developed, with minelayers and mine clearance vessels becoming vital parts of any fleet. Minefields could be laid by fast destroyers or even submarines, making it vital that channels were regularly swept through busy coastal. The use of minesweepers increased dramatically throughout the war, as did the sophistication of mine warfare and mine-hunting techniques. *AK*

WORLD WAR I: A VISUAL ENCYCLOPEDIA

Mitchell, William Lendrum "Billy"
(1879–1936)

The commander of the AEF Air Service during World War I, General William Lendrum "Billy" Mitchell was one of the twentieth century's greatest advocates of the potential of strategic air power to win wars. Billy Mitchell was born in France, but raised in Milwaukee, Wisconsin. He enlisted in the U.S. Army as a private and rose to the rank of brigadier general. He was part of the army's first generation of pilots and an early officer in the U.S. Army Signal Corps Aviation Section (which became the U.S. Army Air Service in May 1918). Mitchell served in the Philippines, Cuba, Alaska, and in the Mexican Punitive Expedition of 1916. He was assigned to the U.S. Army General Staff in 1913, and was named in 1917 to command the AEF Air Service as it went overseas to France. Upon his arrival in France, Mitchell flew with the French Aviation Militaire, became the first American officer to fly over the front, and organized the first all-American squadrons in the war. Mitchell was the first tactician to plan and execute massive air attacks behind enemy lines, a doctrine that was followed successfully by the U.S. Air Force from World War II to the Persian Gulf War. His air operations in support of the Meuse-Argonne Campaign in 1918 were on a scale that was unprecedented in the war up to that date. He had designed an even larger air offensive for the Spring Campaign of 1919, and was bringing larger and more potent bombers into his units. Of course, the war ended before these operations would have taken place. Instead, Mitchell commanded the Air Service of the army of occupation until 1920, when he became Chief of Training and Operations for the U.S. Army Air Service. He served as assistant to the Chief of the Air Service from 1921 to 1926. In 1921, Mitchell organized a series of demonstrations to show that aircraft were an effective weapon against battleships, which were then assumed to be the ultimate long-range defense of the United States. In July, Mitchell's bombers sank the captured German battleship *Ostfriesland* and two other warships, and in September, they sank the retired U.S. Navy battleship USS *Alabama*. The U.S. Navy was both embarrassed and enraged, and they demanded that the U.S. Army declare officially that battleships would always

Left: Portrait of General William Lendrum "Billy" Mitchell. *Collection of Bill Yenne*

be America's first line of defense. Mitchell did not go away quietly. He continued to speak out about the importance of air power, even when ordered not to. For this, he was court-martialed in 1926 and demoted. He died before his theories were proven during World War II. He was posthumously promoted in 1947 and is today thought of as a martyr to inter-service rivalry. *BY*

Moltke, Helmuth von (1848–1916)

Nephew of the German field marshal who organized the Prussian Army in the late nineteenth century and ensured the success of Bismarck's aggressive pursuit of German unification, Moltke became Chief of the General Staff of the German Army in 1906, a post which he held through until September 14, 1914. He masterminded the German invasion of Belgium and France, but his failure to capture Paris and his defeat at the Battle of the Marne, led to his replacement by Erich von Falkenhayn. *MS*

Monash, John (1865–1931)

Born in Australia, of German-Jewish parentage, Monash was trained as a civil engineer. From 1887 he held a commission in the Australian Citizen Force. He commanded the 4th Australian Brigade at Gallipoli. He was made a major general in June 1916 and given command of the 3rd Australian Division; the regiment was then being trained in Britain and so missed the Somme Offensive. The

Division reached the Western Front in November 1916 where it played a prominent role at Messines with Monash impressing Haig. He was further promoted in May 1918 when he took command of the Australian Corps as lieutenant general until the Australian Imperial Force was withdrawn in October 1918. Monash retired from the army in 1930, the year before his death. *MS*

Mons, Battle of

Fought on August 22–23, 1914, Mons was the first major encounter between the German Army and the BEF. The British reached the Mons-Condé canal on August 22, and following Lanrezac's defeat at Sambre they agreed to defend the position at Mons for twenty-four hours, holding off the fourteen divisions of von Kluck's First Army. The Boer War had taught the BEF the techniques of trench warfare, and by evening they were entrenched along a twenty-mile front, with II Corps under General Smith-Dorrien to the west and I Corps under General Douglas Haig to the east. Their marksmen also set up defensive positions in the nearby buildings. The fighting began at 06:00am on the 23rd. The BEF was outnumbered by six divisions to four, facing not only the might of the German First Army but also the weight of the Schlieffen plan. The British battalions together with the sixty-pounders of the 48th and 108th heavy batteries held their ground as the opposition mounted, wielding their rifles with deadly accuracy. That evening the BEF received orders to retreat. The Belgian and French armies were already falling back, and it was crucial that the BEF should stay in line with the Allies. So began the "Great Retreat" of 1914. *MS*

Mons, Retreat from

When the BEF began their retreat on August 24, 1914, the whole front was being withdrawn in accordance with new tactics from Joffre who decreed that the Allies would end their attacks and

Right: XIth Hussars at the end of the retreat from Mons. The cavalry had a day's rest at Gournay near Paris when they were bivouaced in the grounds of Madame Townsend's chateau at Champs. September 1914.
Chrysalis Photo Library

Above: British cavalry during the retreat from Mons, August/September 1914.
Chrysalis Photo Library

Left: British infantry and cyclists retiring through a village during the retreat from Mons. August/September 1914. *Chrysalis Photo Library*

assume the defensive until a suitable window for offensive could be found. In fourteen days of marching, the "Great Retreat" brought the French Army and the BEF to the outskirts of Paris, with every mile of retreat effectively strengthening the French lines of command and supplies. Although the Germans began the pursuit in high spirits in the wake of their recent victories, by the end of the march their lines of communication and supply had been stretched almost intolerably and fatigue and food shortage were becoming unbearable. The battles of the "Great Retreat" included that of Le Cateau, where eight German divisions took on the four divisions of British II Corps; Guise or St. Quentin, where Franchet d'Esperey made his name with the Fifth Army; and that of Nèry where the British 1st Cavalry Brigade and 50th Battery, Royal Horse Artillery, held off the German 4th Cavalry Division. Meanwhile, rifts were opening between the Allies, as Sir John French considered himself let down by Lanrezac while the French commander was scornful of the abilities of the BEF. *MC*

Moronvilliers, Battle of

On the second day of the Nivelle Offensive, April 17, 1917, the French Fourth Army under Anthoine launched an attack to the east of Rheims toward Moronvilliers. However, von Below's German First Army readily repelled the assault, which failed to progress beyond the German front line, and the French withdrew with heavy losses. *MC*

Mortars

Mortars, capable of shooting explosive projectiles at high angles, had been known as a siege weapon since about 1500 but there were few in the armies of 1914. The Germans took them most seriously, having designed and built a heavy pioneer *Minenwerfer* which was accepted in 1910. Trench warfare demonstrated how useful such weapons could be, and there was a scramble for the introduction of trench mortars. In late 1914 and early 1915 many weird and wonderful pieces were in use. These included converted pipes of various descriptions; German "earth" mortars, which were sheet steel projectiles launched from tubes in the ground; and "bomb engines" and catapults which relied on springs, arms, bows, and centrifugal force to throw missiles. Perhaps the most impressive catapult was the British "West Spring Gun" which had a throwing arm and battery of powerful springs. By late 1915 many more effective designs had appeared. The British introduced the fearsome two-inch model, better known as the "toffee apple" bomb thrower, which hurled a 50lb high explosive bomb 500 yards. The French deployed a 58mm model which shot finned "aerial torpedoes," and a super heavy 240mm weapon which was later used by other Allies as the 9.45-inch. The Germans not only developed heavier *Minenwerfer*, but small *Granatenwerfer*

Right: A well sandbagged position for a trench mortar. *Chrysalis Photo Library*

Far Right: U.S. troops with a Stokes trench mortar. This model had an 800-yard range. *Chrysalis Photo Library*

Above: British 9.45-inch trench mortar and its crew in an old German trench, March 1917.
Chrysalis Photo Library

for throwing small finned bombs popularly called "pigeons" or "pineapples." The ultimate trench mortar was the Stokes. Designed by Wilfred Stokes this was a relatively light and unimpressive looking tube with a prop which could be dismantled and carried across the battlefield. It was cheap, and quick to bring into action with a rapid rate of fire. After the war it would be widely copied. *SB*

Murdoch, Keith (1885–1952)

The Australian journalist Keith Murdoch was one of the few journalists permitted to be present at Gallipoli during the ill-fated campaign. Along with the British journalist Ellis Ashmead-Bartlett, Murdoch was to bring news of the discontent of the troops to politicians and to the public in both Britain and Australia, thereby resulting in the dismissal of General Sir Ian Hamilton and, ultimately, the withdrawal of Allied Forces from the peninsula. *PW*

Mussolini, Benito Amilcare Andrea (1883–1945)

The future fascist dictator of Italy was the son of a blacksmith and initially worked as a teacher and journalist. Prior to World War I, he had been a socialist, but split with the party over its support of wartime neutrality. Mussolini believed that support of the Allies would assist Italy to regain territory from the Austrians and he served in the Italian army during the war. In 1919 he founded the Fascist Movement and, after limited democratic success, led the March on Rome in 1922. Having destabilized the existing government, he was asked by the Italian King to form an administration (in October 1922) and became *Il Duce* (the leader) three years later when the totalitarian state started gradually to emerge. He led Italy to a number of overseas adventures, such as the invasion of Ethiopia in 1935, and allied the country with Germany prior to World War II. He was ultimately murdered in 1945 following the collapse of the Fascist regime in Italy. *PW*

Mutinies

Unsurprisingly, given the scope of the war and the scale of the casualties, most combatant nations suffered from mutiny

to a greater or lesser degree. In the British case the effects were limited, though small bands of deserters did cause some problems behind the lines. For the French, Austrians, Germans, and Russians mutinies were serious and sometimes catastrophic. Coinciding with the Nivelle Offensive a wave of French mutinies commenced on April 17, 1917. During that summer a total of 250 cases of collective indiscipline were recorded, mainly in the infantry, some of whom refused to return to the front line. About 23,000 were ultimately sentenced for various crimes. Fortunately Allied support and the intervention of French commander-in-chief Pétain prevented this outbreak from becoming terminal. French troops were granted more leave and better conditions, while the offensive burden was taken up by the British and Americans. In the Russian instance exhaustion, German success in Romania, and failure of the Kerensky Offensive in mid-1917, were followed by widespread mutinies leading to Bolshevik Revolution. In the Austro-Hungarian case a year later, exhaustion, influenza, and mutiny were factors which led to calls for the break up of the Empire into national states. Finally it was German naval mutiny on October 29, 1918, effectively finished the war. *SB*

274

Naval airpower

Before the war, most maritime powers had considered using some form of flying machine. The Wright Brothers offered their services to the British in 1907, but they were rejected. In the same year, Count Graf von Zeppelin was experimenting with airships, and two years later in 1909, when Blériot's monoplane flew across the English Channel, Zeppelin launched his first "Zeppelin" for the German Navy. Initial teething troubles were overcome and by 1914 the German Navy boasted a small Zeppelin fleet, which it used for reconnaissance. During the war naval airships would also conduct long-distance bombing raids on St. Petersburg and London, but their main naval role was to provide reconnaissance information for the fleet. The endurance of Zeppelins meant they could perform extended patrols over the North Sea, and could even reach Scapa Flow. Zeppelins also accompanied the High Seas Fleet when it sortied. While the U.S. Navy began experimenting with aircraft in 1911, the British were slow to introduce heavier-than-air machines, but seaplanes were employed from 1914, and even raided the German base at Cuxhaven. By 1917, a rudimentary aircraft carrier served as a base for an aircraft raid on a German Zeppelin base, demonstrating the growing effectiveness of naval airpower. *AK*

N

Above Right and Right: A Sopwith Pup was used for landing trials on British aircraft carrier HMS *Furious*. **Success would herald major changes to naval warfare.** *Chrysalis Photo Library*

Above: Sopwith Pup making a flight from "B" turret of HMS *Repulse*. October 1918. *Chrysalis Photo Library*

Left: The first attempts to provide aircraft with a "flying-off" deck were successful, but didn't allow the aircraft to return to the ship. (See page 12.) *Chrysalis Photo Library*

Below Left: Rumplerflugboot 100 Argus. *Chrysalis Photo Library*

Right: Plane sitting on the flight ramp of HMS *Tiger*. *Chrysalis Photo Library*

Above: German naval airship *L31*.
Chrysalis Photo Library

Left: A Zeppelin setting off on a reconnaissance flight over Oesle Isle. *Chrysalis Photo Library*

Naval airships

Although German Navy Zeppelins carried out the first air raids on the British Isles in 1915, the wartime deployment of airships by other nations was most commonly in the important, if less demanding, second-line roles associated with offshore patrol and anti-submarine warfare. The RNAS used two airships, the *Astra-Torres* and *Parseval*, to maintain twelve-hour patrols across the Channel for one month in 1914 while the BEF crossed into France. Italy's wartime "M" series was based on a pre-war design and used for night bombing, nineteen examples being built and powered by two 250hp Maybach engines similar to those used in many Zeppelins. From the two dirigibles in inventory in 1914 the Italian Navy had twenty-two by 1918. *JS*

Naval guns

During the naval engagements of the World War I, the big gun reigned supreme. The predreadnought battleships of the Spanish-American War (1898) or the Russo-Japanese War (1904–05) almost exclusively carried their main armament in two twin turrets, giving these vessels a main armament of four guns, usually with calibers of between ten and twelve inches. Secondary batteries of guns (often six-inch pieces) and tertiary batteries of lighter guns invited the closing of ranges to less than 5,000 yards, despite advances in naval ordnance which permitted guns to fire at ranges of over ten miles. The introduction of the British battleship *Dreadnought* changed the nature of naval warfare, as the design of the vessels centered around its employment of twelve twelve-inch guns, designed to fire coordinated broadsides at long range. She had virtually no secondary armament, as the intention was to destroy enemy ships before any six-inch guns could be brought to bear. Previously, the existence of guns of different calibers (such as the 9.2-inch and twelve-inch guns on the predreadnought battleship *Lord Nelson*) made the job of the gun controller extremely difficult. Shell splashes from one salvo obscured those of the other size of guns, making it extremely difficult to adjust the range and bearing to score long-range hits on an enemy vessel. The *Dreadnought* also carried her turrets so that a maximum of eight guns could fire in a single coordinated salvo, a devastating broadside which outclassed all existing warships and forced other nations to follow the British in the naval race to build dreadnoughts. Imitation was the sincerest form of flattery, as Germany ordered its first two dreadnoughts in 1907 and the United States followed suit in 1910. Two years later the U.S. Navy introduced dreadnoughts that carried fourteen-inch guns. The era of the big gun had arrived. The standard British gun size also increased, from twelve-inch guns firing 850lb shells to 13.5-inch guns which fired a shell weighing 1,400lb, then the fifteen-inch gun, which fired a 2,000lb shell over 35,000 yards. Improvements in rangefinders and gunnery control permitted the firing of these massive guns at these great ranges, but improved German optics gave the High Seas Fleet a decided edge in accuracy which offset the larger shells fired by the British. The World War I was the heyday of the big gun, before aircraft and submarines could reduce the effectiveness of these impressive battlewagons. *AK*

Above: German battlecruiser *Derfflinger* back home at Wilhelmshaven showing evidence of damage from shell fire, June 2, 1916. *Chrysalis Photo Library*

Left: HMS *Queen Elizabeth* taking on board twelve-inch ammunition. *Chrysalis Photo Library*

Right: To supplement coastal forces the Royal Navy made use of monitors to support land operations in the Middle East, Balkans, and Western Front. *Chrysalis Photo Library*

Above Right: British battlecruisers such as the *Queen Mary* were armed with eight 13.5-inch guns. *Chrysalis Photo Library*

Previous Page: British battle-ship HMS *Canada*. *Chrysalis Photo Library*

Naval strategy

Naval operations in the World War I revolved around the maintenance of seapower and control of the sea lanes. The Central Powers other than Germany possessed limited naval resources. While the Austro-Hungarian fleet could only be expected to operate as a coastal defense force in the Adriatic Sea, the Turkish Navy was too old and weak to undertake offensive action, although its support by the German warships *Goeben* and *Breslau* gave it a powerful modern squadron to employ. The naval might of the Central Powers lay in the Imperial German Navy. This fleet had two

separate elements, each of which would influence German planning. The first was its cruisers and other light forces deployed overseas. Given the numerical superiority of the Allied fleets, it was considered highly unlikely that these ships would be able to return to Germany. Instead, they were expected to act as commerce raiders, disrupting the merchant shipping of the Allied powers across the globe and tying down their naval forces for as long as possible before they were caught. Germany started the war with a tiny fleet of sea-going U-boats, but a huge boat-building effort was initiated in August 1914, and by early 1915 new U-boats were entering

service. This coincided with the loss of the last surface commerce raiders, and one form of attack against Allied surface shipping was replaced by another even more efficient method. As the war progressed, the number of U-boats increased, with a proportionate rise in the tonnage of shipping sunk. Following the introduction of unrestricted U-boat warfare in 1915, this strategic threat to Allied sea lanes continued to grow until 1917, when the introduction of the convoy system and the entrance of the United States into the war altered the course of the campaign. The second element to German Naval planning was the High Seas Fleet. It was never

envisaged that it would be able to defeat the British Grand Fleet in a single battle. Instead, it was hoped that a British close blockade of the German coast would lead to heavy losses by mines and torpedoes, bringing the fleets to something akin to parity in numbers. The British adoption of a distant blockade denied this opportunity to their enemy. Instead, the Germans were content to keep the High Seas Fleet intact, as a fleet in being, thus forcing the British to keep their fleet concentrated in the North Sea. The German policy of "hit-and-run" raiding was a means of underlining the potential danger posed by their fleet, and it provided opportunities for catching and

defeating isolated groups of British warships. The Battle of Jutland in May 1916 ended this "hit-and-run" strategy, as a German attempt to lure the Grand Fleet into a trap backfired, and it was the Germans who faced isolation, then destruction in detail. For the remainder of the war, the fleet in being approach meant the battleships never sailed far from their home, and the British retained control of the North Sea, and maintained their blockade. For Britain, this blockade was the key to victory, and the strategy of sealing off the North Sea, then maintaining a distant blockade of Germany proved a decisive factor in Allied victory. Although the British were denied a

decisive naval battle, British seapower proved triumphant through a less spectacular yet ultimately more devastating blockade of the Central Powers. While morale in the German U-boat service remained high despite increasing losses, the sailors of the High Seas Fleet were driven to mutiny, a rebellion which spread throughout Germany and forced an end to the war. *AK*

Left: Maps show the naval blockade of Germany and the protection of the Straits of Dover. *Richard Natkiel*

Below: In spite of its excellent gunnery skills, German strategists never envisaged that their fleet would be able to defeat the British in a single battle. *Chrysalis Photo Library*

Naval tactics

During the World War I, naval tactics almost exclusively involved the use of big guns in surface combat. The naval powers such as Britain, Germany and America decided that any naval battle would be won by the side which made best use of the decisive firepower of its dreadnought battlefleet. The majority of major warships were designed so that they could fire their full armament of large guns at the enemy in a broadside, so the linear warfare of the Napoleonic age was reinvented for use by guns with a range of over fifteen miles. Divisions of warships steamed in line formation, so that each ship could fire its guns without having its line of fire blocked by other ships in its formation. This tight grouping of ships also helped maintain control within the fleet, as wireless communications could be augmented by signal flags or lights. At Jutland (1916), the German High Seas Fleet sailed in a long line. The British fleet was too large to use a simple line ahead, and instead it steamed in parallel columns. When contact was made these turned simultaneously to form a battle line. The main battle line was screened by light cruisers (which were also used to transmit signals), and by destroyers, capable of launching torpedo attacks against an enemy line, or screening their own main battlefleet from attack by enemy torpedo boats or destroyers. During Jutland, the British also managed to cross the T of the German fleet, where only the lead German ship could fire on the enemy,

while the entire British line could fire on it. This prompted the Germans to retreat, and it can be argued that, although Jellicoe failed to defeat the Germans at Jutland, his sound grasp of naval tactics prevented a British defeat.

Neuilly, Treaty of

Treaty between the Allied Powers and Bulgaria, signed November 1919, after an armistice agreement in September in 1918. Under its terms Bulgaria agreed to pay reparations and accepted a limitation on its army to 20,000 men. It ceded part of Thrace to Greece and border regions to Yugoslavia. *DC*

Neuve Chapelle, Battle of

The Germans had attacked in the area of Neuve Chapelle in October 1914, driving the British line backward and creating a salient from which they could shell the British trenches on either side. Sir John French decided to try to snuff out this salient in the spring of 1915 and Haig's First British Army was tasked with carrying out the attack. At 7:30am on March 10 the British began their advance, supported by an artillery bombardment across the whole of the line. The initial progress was good; breaking through the front-line positions of Crown Prince Rupprecht's Sixth Army and capturing the village of Neuve Chapelle itself within a period of four hours. However, once the position was gained the British system of communications and supply broke down,

allowing the Germans to counterattack on March 12. Although the British managed to hold their ground, further advances in this area were impossible and the battle ground to a halt on March 13. The battle proved influential for both sides: the British felt that with a more concerted artillery effort they could have pushed on, while the Germans realized that their front lines were vulnerable and set about improving their second-line defenses along the whole front. *MC*

New Zealand forces

The core of the country's armed forces in 1914 was its Territorial Army, some 26,000 men, the bulk of whom were part-time volunteers. However, there was a rush of recruits to fight and the New Zealand Expeditionary Force was organized. For much of the war, its troops fought in the Australian and New Zealand Army Corps—ANZAC. The New Zealanders saw action at Gallipoli, in Palestine, and on the Western Front. Despite its small population, the country provided 100,000 men for overseas service and suffered a high rate of casualties—some 58,000 in total, with 17,000 dead. The New Zealand Navy was tiny, little more than a coastal defense force, although one battlecruiser, the *New Zealand*, served with the British Grand Fleet. *IW*

Nicholas II, Tsar (1868–1918)

The last Emperor of Russia was born in 1868, the son of Tsar Alexander III, and prior to his accession to the throne in 1894 traveled widely around the world. He married Princess Alexandra of Hesse-Darmstadt, a granddaughter of Queen Victoria, who was to become the dominant partner, particularly in her belief in the maintenance of autocracy when there were strong undercurrents of revolution and social change in the country. Regarded as a weak leader, Nicholas abroad sought alliances with Britain and France, while unsuccessfully (and disastrously) going to war with Japan in 1904–05. Failure in the war led to the first Russian revolution (of 1905) and Nicholas was forced to call the Duma (parliament). However, his failure to trust politicians meant that the necessary reforms were never carried out. He took command of the Russian forces against Germany and Austria during the war; this resulted in his absence from St. Petersburg and Moscow, and for growing hatred and distrust of his wife to increase. The pent-up pressure for radical reform led to the first of the 1917 revolutions; the success of the Bolshevik revolution later the same year led to his abdication. Hopes that the Russian royal family would be given sanctuary by the British proved ill-founded, and Nicholas, along with the rest of his family, was murdered at Yekaterinburg in 1918. *PW*

Nivelle, General Robert (1857–1924)

The French general Nivelle was born in Tulle to a British mother and French father. As a result of his parentage, he spoke fluent English, which was to prove

a useful tool when dealing with Lloyd George and other British politicians. His most notable success was at Verdun in 1916 when he captured Douaumont and other forts. This success led him briefly, in 1916–17, to become French commander-in-chief. Under his aegis, the Aisne (Nivelle) Offensive was planned and executed in April/May 1917. This plan envisaged the use of a mass attack across a wide front supported, for the first time, by tanks and preceded by a mass artillery barrage. Unfortunately, the Germans had gained access to the plans, strengthened their defenses, and routed the Allied attack. The failure of the assault led to mutiny among sixty-eight of the 112 French divisions and led to Nivelle's sacking on May 15, 1917, and his replacement by Pétain. He was subsequently sent to command French forces in North Africa. *MS*

Nivelle Offensive

Following his appointment as commander-in-chief in December 1916, replacing Joffre, General Robert Nivelle set about planning an offensive that he was sure would end the war. He decided on a vast offensive along the front between the Somme and the Oise by the French Northern Army Group (Fifth, Sixth and Tenth Armies), while the British would attack to the north around Arras. Despite considerable opposition and the German withdrawal to the Hindenburg Line, Nivelle ordered the main offensive to begin on April 16. The attack was a total disaster, with the French losing 40,000 casualties on the first day alone. The all-out assault continued until April 20, before being scaled back and finally ending on May 5. *MC*

Nixon, Sir John (1857–1921)

Nixon had been commissioned into the Indian Army before being sent to command British forces in Mesopotamia in April 1915. Nixon, under orders to advance on Baghdad, moved his army northward to Amara, Nasiriya, and Ctesiphon. However, these advances severely weakened British supply lines, leading to the failure to relieve Kut, where Townshend was forced to surrender. Nixon's failing health led him to be invalided back to India in early 1916. *MS*

No Man's Land

The area between opposing front lines. Though a common concept, No Man's Land could be infinitely variable in reality. In places, as on Vimy Ridge, it could be narrow enough for sentries to hear each other's conversation, or to lob grenades into the enemy line. In other sectors the distance could be hundreds of feet. *SB*

North Sea, Operations in

The decisive theater in the naval war was the North Sea, where only 300 miles of cold gray sea lay between Germany and the British Isles. The geographical limitations of the area dictated the course of the campaign. The German coast was protected by a string of islands and shoals, while the main naval base of Wilhelmshaven was screened by minefields extending as far as the island of Heligoland, an outpost in a defensive

Below: **Dramatic photo of the German battleship** *Blücher* **already keeled over on her side and about to sink; battle of Jutland, 1916.** *Chrysalis Photo Library*

chain protecting the Jade Bay, and the Elbe and Weser estuaries. The long coast of Denmark stretched north from the Elbe, ending at the Skagerrack, the sea entrance to the Baltic Sea. The British Coast also ran north for 600 miles, and beyond it lay the Orkneys and Shetlands. The anchorage of Scapa Flow in Orkney became the wartime base of the British Grand Fleet. Scapa was chosen as the traditional British bases in the English Channel had to pass through the constricted waters of the English Channel, where they could be attacked by mines, submarines and coastal batteries. Following German "hit-and-run" attacks against Lowestoft and Hartlepool in late 1914, the British battlecruiser fleet was deployed further south at Invergordon, then Rosyth, where they were better placed to intercept German raiders before they escaped. Naval operations were also influenced by the extensive use of offensive and defensive minefields used by both sides. The distant

blockade policy of the Allies effectively sealed off the exits of the North Sea to German shipping through the use of minefields off Orkney and a barrage off Dover. The British sought a decisive naval clash between the Grand Fleet and the High Seas Fleet that would decide the course of the naval war in a single climactic battle. Although the German Fleet was brought to battle at the Dogger Bank (1915), the Germans managed to avoid a decisive engagement, preferring to keep their fleet intact, ready for a battle on their own terms. The Battle of Jutland in May 1916 came about through a German attempt to lure the Grand Fleet into battle, where its forces could isolate and destroy portions of the larger British fleet. Instead, the British had the advantage of a better intelligence service, and were well aware of the German plan. The German commander, Admiral Scheer was lucky to extricate his own fleet from a trap, and the High Seas Fleet returned to Germany with only minor losses.

After Jutland the German fleet remained in port, and a final clash between the battlecruiser fleets off Heligoland resulted in another German retreat. The campaign was fought in order to place a blockade around Germany. In the four years of the war, the German staff realized that this blockade more than anything else led to the end of the war, through the rebellion of the German people. British seapower in the North Sea won the war through the attrition of enemy morale, and the German fleet was unable to break this stranglehold. *AK*

Northcliffe, Alfred, Lord (1865–1922)

Born Alfred Charles William Harmsworth in Ireland, the future first Viscount Northcliffe—he was raised to the peerage as a baron in 1905 and became a Viscount in 1917—was one of the most influential press barons in Britain. He was one of the pioneers of mass newspapers, initially working with his brother

Harold Sydney Harmsworth (the future Lord Rothermere). His newspaper empire included the *London Evening News*, *The Daily Mail* (launched in 1896), *The Daily Mirror* (founded in 1908) and *The Times*. He parted company with his brother in 1914 over their differing attitude to the war; Northcliffe was a strong believer in military action and his forthright views, including a vitriolic attack on Kitchener, made him unpopular in many areas. In 1917 he was sent to the United States on a publicity tour and, on his return, was made Director of Propaganda to Enemy Countries.

Below: The first, failed, British attempt to blockade the entrance to Ostend Harbor, April 22–23, 1918. *Chrysalis Photo Library*

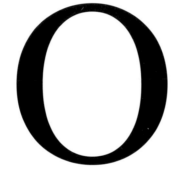

Orlando, Vittorio Emanuele
(1860–1952)

Born in Palermo, on Sicily, Orlando was initially trained as a lawyer and was Professor of Constitutional Law at Palermo University before entering the Italian parliament in 1897. Having served for a period as Minister of Education, he became Minister of Justice in 1916. During the catastrophic Italian defeat at the Battle of Caporetto (October 24, 1917–November 4, 1917), he became Prime Minister. He was to continued as Prime Minister until June 1919, and under his regime Italian morale improved and the country gained several military victories, including that at Vittorio Veneto in October 1918. Attending the postwar peace conference, his territorial ambitions led him to fall out with Woodrow Wilson and his failure to achieve the gains promised by the Treaty of London in 1918, led to his fall from power. Initially he was to support the Fascists, but broke with Mussolini in 1925. He remained in politics, and ran unsuccessfully for the Italian presidency in 1948, four years before his death. *MS*

Owen, Wilfred (1893–1918)

One of the famed generation of poets for whom World War I was a seminal (if not fatal) experience, Owen was born in Shropshire. Unlike many of the other wartime poets, Owen was not Oxbridge-educated and before the war had a career as a teacher both in Britain and in France, where he taught at the Berlitz School at Bordeaux. Following concussion while serving in the trenches, he met another of the wartime poets (Siegfried Sassoon) and, under his tutelage, improved his poetic skills, although only five poems were actually published during his life. Owen was killed in November 1918, a week before the Armistice. His most famous poems include *Anthem for Doomed Youth* and *Dulce et Decorum Est*. His verses, as these extracts from *Anthem for Doomed Youth* (1917) show, reveal the waste of war:

What passing-bells for those who die as cattle?
Only the monstrous anger of the guns.

The shrill, demented choirs of wailing shells;
And bugles calling for them from sad shires.
PW

Passchendaele
See Ypres, Third Battle of, on page 438.

Palestine, Operations in

Operations in the Palestine theater began with a Turkish push through the Sinai Peninsula to prize control of the Suez Canal away from the British in early 1915. This was repulsed between February 2 and 3 and the fighting in the region died down for the next eighteen months as troops from both sides were needed elsewhere. The British used the lull to push across the Suez Canal and create a new line in the peninsula from where an advance along the coast into Palestine could be launched. The Turks attempted to preempt any British strike from Sinai in August 1916, but were rebuffed with heavy casualties at the Battle of Romani on the 3rd. Following a victory at the Battle of Magruntein on January 8–9, 1917, the British advanced into Palestine to confront the Turks holding a defensive line stretching from Gaza on the coast to Beersheba inland. The first two attempts to break through the line were unsuccessful but a third push, directed by General Edmund Allenby, succeeded in late October and early November. His success split the two Turkish armies in Palestine, allowing him to capture Jerusalem on December 9. For much of 1918 Allenby's scope of

Right: Men of the 10th Australian Light Horse leaving the defensive line on the Suez Canal to destroy the supplies of water in the Wadi am Maksheih, June 10, 1916. *Chrysalis Photo Library*

Below and on Page 292: Maps of operations in Palestine and north Africa. *Richard Natkiel*

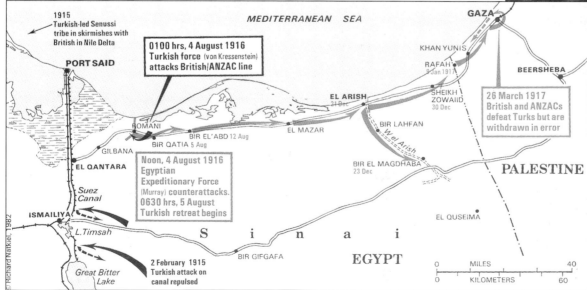

1915
Turkish-led Senussi tribe in skirmishes with British in Nile Delta

MEDITERRANEAN SEA

GAZA

PORT SAID

KHAN YUNIS

0100 hrs, 4 August 1916
Turkish force (von Kressenstein) attacks British/ANZAC line

RAFAH
9 Jan 1917

BEERSHEBA

EL ARISH
21 Dec

SHEIKH ZOWAIID
30 Dec

26 March 1917
British and ANZACs defeat Turks but are withdrawn in error

ROMANI

BIR EL'ABD 12 Aug

EL MAZAR

BIR LAHFAN

BIR QATIA 5 Aug

GILBANA

EL QANTARA

Wel Arish

BIR EL MAGDHABA
23 Dec

PALESTINE

Suez Canal

Noon, 4 August 1916
Egyptian Expeditionary Force (Murray) counterattacks.
0630 hrs, 5 August Turkish retreat begins

ISMAILIYA

EL QUSEIMA

L. Timsah

S i n a i

2 February 1915
Turkish attack on canal repulsed

BIR GIFGAFA

EGYPT

MILES   40

KILOMETERS   60

Great Bitter Lake

© Richard Natkiel, 1982

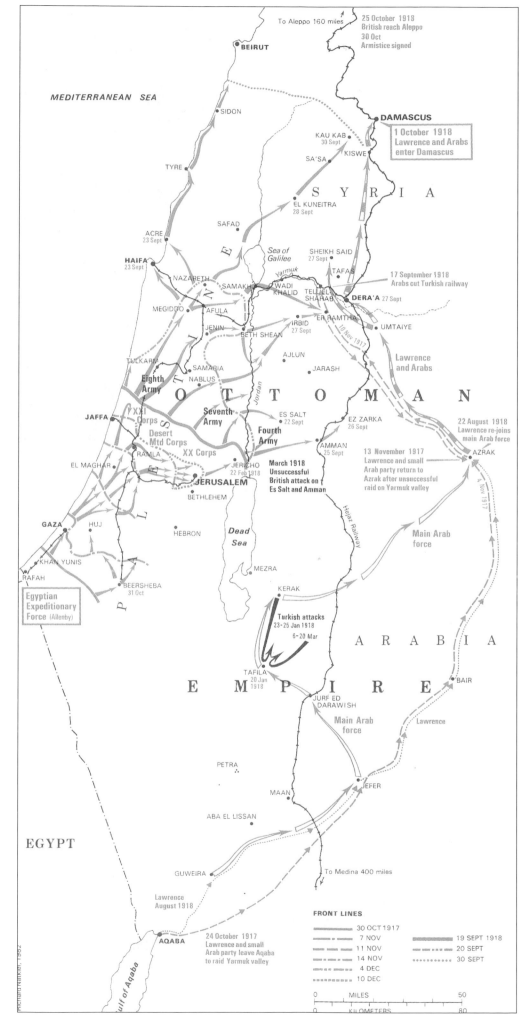

To Aleppo 160 miles

25 October 1918
British reach Aleppo

30 Oct
Armistice signed

BEIRUT

MEDITERRANEAN SEA

SIDON

DAMASCUS

KAU KAB
30 Sept

KISWE

1 October 1918
Lawrence and Arabs
enter Damascus

SA'SA

S Y R I A

TYRE

EL KUNEITRA
28 Sept

SAFAD

ACRE
23 Sept

Sea of
Galilee

SHEIKH SAID
27 Sept

HAIFA
23 Sept

NAZARETH

SAMAKH

Yarmuk

WADI
KHALID

TAFAS

17 September 1918
Arabs cut Turkish railway

MEGIDDO

AFULA

TELL EL
SHAHAB

DERA'A 27 Sept

JENIN

BETH SHEAN

IRBID
27 Sept

ER RAMTHA

UMTAIYE

TULKARM

SAMARIA

AJLUN

JARASH

Lawrence
and Arabs

NABLUS

**Eighth
Army**

O T T O M A N

JAFFA

XXI
Corps

**Seventh
Army**

Jordan

ES SALT
22 Sept

EZ ZARKA
26 Sept

22 August 1918
Lawrence re-joins
main Arab force

Desert
Mtd Corps

**Fourth
Army**

AMMAN
25 Sept

AZRAK

RAMLA

XX Corps

EL MAGHAR

JERICHO
22 Feb 1918

March 1918
Unsuccessful
British attack on
Es Salt and Amman

13 November 1917
Lawrence and small
Arab party return to
Azrak after unsuccessful
raid on Yarmuk valley

JERUSALEM

BETHLEHEM

GAZA

HUJ

HEBRON

Dead
Sea

**Main Arab
force**

Hejaz Railway

KHAN YUNIS

RAFAH

MEZRA

BEERSHEBA
31 Oct

KERAK

**Egyptian
Expeditionary
Force** (Allenby)

Turkish attacks
23-25 Jan 1918
6-20 Mar

A R A B I A

TAFILA
20 Jan
1918

E M P I R E

BAIR

JURF ED
DARAWISH

**Main Arab
force**

Lawrence

MAAN

JEFER

PETRA

ABA EL LISSAN

EGYPT

GUWEIRA

To Medina 400 miles

Lawrence
August 1918

FRONT LINES

AQABA

24 October 1917
Lawrence and small
Arab party leave Aqaba
to raid Yarmuk valley

	30 OCT 1917		19 SEPT 1918
	7 NOV		20 SEPT
	11 NOV		30 SEPT
	14 NOV		
	4 DEC		
	10 DEC		

Gulf of Aqaba

0   MILES   50
0   KILOMETERS   80

operations was limited as a large part of his force had been withdrawn to the Western Front, but in September he was able to resume operations. A major offensive was launched against the Turks on the 19th and the ensuing Battle of Megiddo smashed the Turkish armies operating in Palestine. Pursued by Allenby's mounted troops, harassed from the air and by Arab guerrillas operating on their flanks, the Turks collapsed in four days. Damascus was captured on October 1 and Beirut a day later. Aleppo was reached on the 25th and an armistice came into effect on the 30th. *IW*

Far Left: The end in Palestine, 1917–18. *Richard Natkiel*

Left: A railway raiding party of British and Arab soldiers. *Chrysalis Photo Library*

Below: The 4th Sussex Regiment marching through Bethlehem. The town was occupied by the 53rd Division on the night of December 8–9, 1917. *Chrysalis Photo Library*

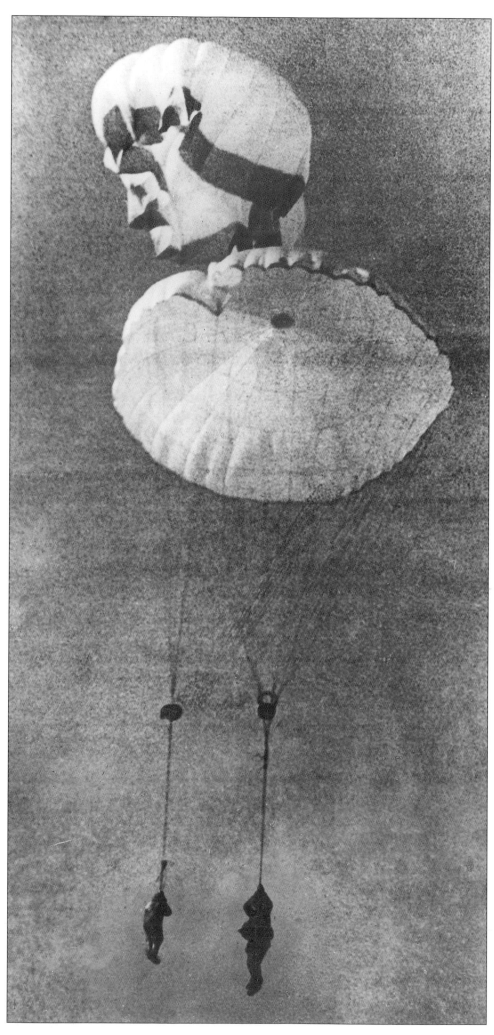

Pals' Battalions

Pals' Battalions grew out Britain's shortages of manpower following the virtual destruction of the regular army during the battles of 1914 on the Western Front. The war minister, Lord Kitchener, initiated a recruitment drive in the opening days of the war that capitalized on the public's enthusiasm and led to a flood of volunteers over the following months. These recruits formed a number of new divisions that were organized into what were termed Kitchener (K) or New Armies. In April 1915 K4, the Fourth New Army, was split between the existing new armies and K5, which contained the 37th to 42nd Divisions, was retitled the Fourth New Army and its divisions reclassified from 30th to 35th. A replacement Fifth New Army was raised containing the 36th to 41st Divisions. These two new armies contained the majority of the Pals' or Chums' Battalions. More so than most British units, these battalions contained recruits with close ties, usually through work or place of birth. For example, Glasgow raised three battalions, officially titled the 15th, 16th, and 17th Highland Light Infantry, but more commonly known as the Glasgow Tramways, Glasgow Boy's Brigade, and Glasgow Commercials respectively to reflect the background of their members. Pals' Battalions were heavily committed to the Battle of the Somme and many suffered severe casualties. The 11th Battalion, the East Lancashire Regiment, better known as the Accrington Pals, suffered more than most, reporting 585 casualties out of some 700 men present on the first day of the battle. Such a scale of loss had a devastating impact on the small Lancashire town and highlighted the key weakness of such localized recruitment. *IW*

Parachutes

Although the first parachute descent in Britain took place on May 9, 1914, and World War I balloon observers successfully used this form of life-preserver, it was slow to be accepted by governments for combat aviators. It was not until August 22, 1918, that Frigyes Hefty of

Left: Kite balloon observers descending by parachute. The further parachute has as yet only partly deployed. *Chrysalis Photo Library*

final actions involving the Sioux in 1890 and 1891. Pershing returned briefly to West Point as an instructor, and served in the Spanish-American War. Except for two years—including service as an observer in the Russo-Japanese War of 1905—he served in the Philippines from 1899 to 1913. It was here, during the insurrection, that he earned a stellar reputation for his defeat of the Islamic fundamentalist Moro terrorists on Mindanao. Promoted from captain to brigadier general in 1906, Pershing was clearly one of the U.S. Army's rising stars. In 1916, the Mexican bandit Francisco "Pancho" Villa attacked the city of Columbus, New Mexico, murdering civilians and burning property. Pershing was ordered to lead a punitive expedition south of the border to capture Villa in Mexico, but the bandit leader managed to elude capture. When the United States entered World War I in April 1917, Major General (two stars) Pershing was named to command the AEF in France. He was subsequently promoted to general (four stars) His organizational skills are credited for quickly turning hastily trained American troops into well-integrated combat units. He is also credited with being responsible for forming the AEF and its constituent divisions together as a

the 42nd Squadron, Austro-Hungarian Air Corps, bailed out of his burning Albatros DIII and landed safely that parachutes, previously looked upon as little more than a joke, were seen to be practical. The German Heinicke parachute (*Sitzolster*) was of the attached-type: as the airman bailed out, a 50lb break chord, long enough to clear the aircraft's tailplane, was pulled out of a bag that was worn strapped to a harness. Other German aviators owed their life to parachutes, yet no other country used them widely before the war ended. *JS*

Pershing, John Joseph "Blackjack" (1860–1948)

The commander-in-chief of the AEF in World War I, General John J. Pershing was born in Linn County, Missouri and graduated from the U.S. Military

Academy at West Point in 1886. He served as a cavalry officer during the late campaigns of the Indian Wars, especially in actions against the Apache leader Geronimo in the southwest and in the

Right: General John J. Pershing at his desk. *Collection of Bill Yenne*

cohesive combat unit, rather than having them serve as mere replacements for French and British units. Given the brevet rank of general of the armies during the war, Pershing was given this five-star rank permanently in 1919. This would give him the highest rank of anyone who had ever served in the U.S. Army. Between 1944 and 1950, nine U.S. military officers were given five-star rank, but Pershing still technically outranked them. In 1978, George Washington was given the posthumous rank of general of the armies of the United States, making him the highest ranking officer that has ever served, or will ever serve, in the U.S. armed services. To date, he is the only officer to outrank Pershing. In 1921, General of the Armies Pershing was made Chief of Staff of the U.S. Army, a post which he retained until his retirement in 1924. After hanging up his uniform, he was active with the American Battle Monuments Commission, and in 1937, he dedicated the Meuse-Argonne Monument on Montfaucon, France. In declining health, he spent the last eight years of his life—including the years of

World War II—at Walter Reed Hospital near Washington. He died in 1948 and is buried at Arlington with his men beneath a standard gravestone. General Pershing was the author of two books about World War I, *Final Report* (1919) and *My Experiences in the World War* (1931). *B*

Pétain, Henri-Philippe (1856–1951)

There are few more controversial figures in twentieth century French history than Marshal Pétain: World War I hero to excoriated leader of the puppet Vichy regime in World War II. Although to achieve high rank, Pétain's origins were, however, much more humble. He was born to a peasant family in the Pas-de-Calais, and entered the military college at St. Cyr in 1876. One of his military reports commented when he was a junior officer that, "If this officer rises above

the rank of major it will be a disaster for France." Despite this condemnation (which was ultimately remarkably prescient), Pétain was to rise through the ranks of the French Army, becoming a colonel in 1912 and a corps' commander two years later. He achieved prominence as the defender of Verdun in 1916 and, with the fall of Nivelle in May 1917, became commander-in-chief, although from April 1918 Marshal Foch held senior rank as commander-in-chief of the entire Allied army in France. Pétain's military career continued through the 1920s, culminating as Inspector-General of the Army in 1929. In 1934, as Minister of War, he entered politics within the cabinet of Doumergue. He became Ambassador to Spain in 1939 but was recalled to France to become Prime Minister on June 16, 1940, following the French defeat and the departure of Paul Reynaud. As Prime Minister he negotiated the Armistice with Germany and, for the next two years (until Germany occupied the rest of the country), acted as head of government of the Vichy regime. After 1942 he was effectively a puppet of the German occupiers. In 1945 he was tried for treason and sentenced to death; the sentence was, however, commuted to life imprisonment. *MS*

Peter I, King (1844–1921)

Born in Belgrade, the future King Peter I of Serbia lived in exile from 1858, when his father abdicated, until 1903, when the parliament of Serbia elected him king. During the period of his exile, he served with the French Army during the Franco-Prussian War of 1870–71. Forced into exile in Greece with his army in 1916, Peter returned as King of the Serbs, Croats, and Slovenes in 1918. Although Peter I was to reign until his death in 1921, his second son Alexander acted as regent due to ill health. *MS*

Pflanzer-Baltin, Karl von (1855–1925)

Pflanzer-Baltin was brought out of retirement in 1914 to command the Austro-Hungarian Seventh Army, he then led Army Group Pflanzer-Baltin in early 1915 during the Carpathian Campaign, taking Czernowitz on February 17. The Seventh Army was then involved in the defense against the Russians in the Bessarabian Campaign in late 1915, but was destroyed in June 1916 as a result of the Brusilov Offensive. Pflanzer-Baltin retained command of the remains, reinforced by German troops, before being transferred in take command on the Austro-Hungarian forces in Albania, where he surrendered on November 18, 1918. *MS*

Photo-reconnaissance

From the first RFC operational sortie by No. 3 Squadron on August 19, 1914, to the final weeks of the war, aerial reconnaissance took on an importance that surmounted all other uses of airplanes. No aerial activity was as useful to ground commanders than visual evidence of enemy activity on the other side. However, early PR operations were difficult; observers wearing heavy gloves invariably had to cope with freezing conditions to operate the cameras at all, but it was No. 3 Squadron that obtained the first aerial photographs of the war when five exposures were made from plates on September 15, 1914. It was soon obvious that the standard press camera with a bellows and a fabric focal plane shutter used on these early sorties was too unreliable and a new British

Below: General Pétain (center). *Chrysalis Photo Library*

camera with an eight-inch lens, made by Thornton-Packard, was first used on March 2, 1915. Hand operation was still difficult although some remarkable coverage was obtained from altitudes up to 10,000ft. Other RFC cameras preceded the late-war Williamson LB-type which used interchangeable lenses and panchromatic plates, enabling good results from 20,000ft using typically, an FE2b at the camera platform. Germany's reputation as a lens maker brought some excellent cameras into service such as the Flieger Kammer FIII, which along with others, used roll film rather than plates. *JS*

Left: An aerial photo taken during a gas attack.
Chrysalis Photo Library

Below: Aerial photo and annotated map of the area of Albert, July 13, 1918.
Chrysalis Photo Library

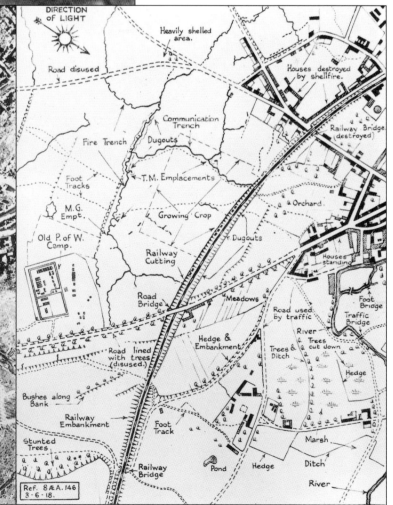

POINCARÉ, RAYMOND NICOLAS LANDRY

appointment of Clemenceau as Prime Minister in 1917. Poincaré again became Prime Minister in 1922 (until 1924), when he adopted a highly nationalistic agenda (including marching into the Ruhr in January 1923). He was to serve, for the last time as Prime Minister between July 1926 and July 1929, when he also served as finance minister to help deal with a financial crisis. *MS*

Polish forces

Lacking an independent homeland, Poles fought on both sides during the war depending on where they believed military service would best promote their nationalist cause. At the outbreak of war, the Austro-Hungarian Army contained three brigades of Polish troops, while the Russian Army formed its own Polish Legion in late 1914. However, as much of Poland was ruled by these two empires, the nationalists had little obvious chance of achieving their ambitions. A more useful bargaining counter was the Polish Army that fought as part of the French Army. Established in June 1917 under General Josef Haller, it reached a strength of some 80,000 men and became the core of independent Poland's army after World War I. *IW*

Ports, UK South Coast

The traditional Royal Navy ports of Portsmouth and Plymouth had served the country well in its wars with France, but were badly placed for a naval war with Germany. In order to attack the German battle fleet, if the Grand Fleet was based in its usual home ports it would have had to steam through the Straits of Dover, and would therefore be vulnerable to attack from coastal batteries, U-boats, and torpedo-boats. It was deemed safer to move the fleet to the anchorage of Scapa Flow in Orkney, where it was better placed to react to German sorties. Portsmouth and Plymouth were even abandoned by the light cruisers and destroyers of the fleet. Those light forces who were not attached to the Grand Fleet were based at Dover and Harwich, where they could cover coastal convoys, screen the English east coast, and deny enemy access to the English Channel. The Dover Patrol of destroyers and light craft was further supported by a series of minefields and submarine-nets. Instead, Portsmouth and Plymouth became major terminals and staging posts for convoys

and their escorts from May 1917, and provided dockyard facilities for damaged warships when required. *AK*

Portuguese Army

Portugal's military commitment to the fight against the Central Powers chiefly consisted of an expeditionary force that was deployed to the Western Front following the Central Powers' declarations of war on the country in March 1916. Formed in January 1917 the Portuguese Expeditionary Force, some 100,000 men at its peak, was trained in Britain and then moved to the Western Front in the middle of the year. However, its units performed badly during the German Lys Offensive in spring 1918 and were removed from the front line. Other Portuguese troops served in Africa. Casualties totaled 21,000 men, with more than 7,000 killed. *IW*

Potemkin

The crew of the Russian predreadnought battleship *Knaiaz Potemkin Tavritcheki* revolted in 1905, seizing the ship and prompting a mutiny in the Russian Fleet, an event celebrated in film by Sergei Eisenstein. She was renamed the *Pantelimon* and saw service in the Black Sea during the war. *AK*

Right: Portuguese sentry. Note signal rockets. *Chrysalis Photo Library*

Below: Men from the Portuguese Medical Corps pulling a light railroad trolley to take their field kits up to the line. Near Festubert, March 16, 1918. *Chrysalis Photo Library*

Above: Early morning scene before the asssault on Thiepval, September 15, 1916.
Chrysalis Photo Library

Preliminary bombardment

Military theory of 1914 suggested that artillery should fire in close support of attack. By 1915 the weight of fire had become considerable, including all natures of artillery. It was now thought that if enough shells were fired the enemy could be swept away. As Marshal Foch would put it, the "completeness of the artillery preparation is the measure of the success the infantry can obtain." By the time of the Battle of the Somme, bombardments could be a week long, but were still no guarantee of success. *SB*

Prisoners of war and prison camps

As a short war was predicted, no power made sufficient preparation for prisoners of war. Facilities were soon overwhelmed. In the initial campaign in East Prussia, Germany took 100,000 Russians: in Galicia 100,000 Austro-Hungarians were captured by the Russians, while 40,000 Russians were taken. Initially many POWs had to live in tented camps while they helped to build their own hutted prisons with watch towers and wire. At the end of 1914 the Germans were holding half a million captives of various nationalities, and by 1916 the figure had risen to about a million. A further influx of mainly British POWs came in 1918. Eventually the Germans would have 200 major prison camps divided into twenty-one districts each with its own commander. In addition there were many satellite camps, many of which were designed to provide prisoner labor to industry and agriculture. Within the camps the nationalities were usually segregated, and officers separated from other ranks. Though the situation was never as bad as in World War II, 118,000 died in German captivity, many of them Russians, and food shortages were acute, particularly in the final stages of the war. Nevertheless the standards of individual camps varied considerably; some were quite bearable, others, like Hülzminden, had reputations for brutality. The British took almost half a million prisoners during the war, the majority German but 119,000 Turkish, and a few thousand others. Of those captured by the British, over half were taken during 1918. About 9,000 died in British captivity, while official figures record about 1,500 escapees, the majority of which, surprisingly, were Bulgarians. Some of the POWs were released officially prior to the cessation of hostilities on medical grounds or to join the new Polish army; 311 men were returned to Denmark which was neutral. *SB*

Right: German prisoners examining their clothing at Acheux, July 4, 1916.
Chrysalis Photo Library

Above: Part of the camp living quarters at Stalag VIIA in Bavaria.
Chrysalis Photo Library

Above Right: A party of Germans surrendering to troops of the 45th Australian Battalion at Ascension Farm, near Le Verguier, September 1918.
Chrysalis Photo Library

Right: Exhausted British prisoners under escort.
Chrysalis Photo Library

Prohibition

Now regarded as one of the worst legislative disasters in United States' history, Prohibition was undertaken with respectable intentions and was described at the time as the "Noble Experiment." Under Prohibition, it became illegal to manufacture, transport, or sell alcoholic beverages—including beer and wine—in the United States. The move toward Prohibition had been gaining momentum in the late nineteenth century, due to the actions of various radical organizations, such as the notorious Anti-Saloon League, that were operating under the banner of the so-called "temperance movement." They demanded that government take a role in regulating personal interests. Some individual states had passed various forms of restrictive legislation during the nineteenth century, but by the early twentieth century, Prohibition became a national political issue. During World War I, it became associated with ethnic bigotry, as the Prohibitionists used anti-German sentiment against the owners of breweries, mainly in the upper Midwest, most of whom were German. The radicals also used the need to keep factory workers sober as an excuse to promote their agenda. The latter was to be the rationale for Britain adopting legislation requiring pubs to close at 11:00pm, a decree that would not be repealed after the war, and which would still be in force in the twenty-first century. In December 1917, bowing to Prohibitionist pressure, the U.S. Congress passed a constitutional amendment to prohibit the manufacture and sale of alcoholic beverages in the United States and submitted it to the states for ratification. Ratified as the Eighteenth Amendment, Prohibition became law in January 1920, enforced by the draconian Volstead Act of 1919. While forcing many family businesses—from the breweries of Wisconsin to the vineyards and wineries of California—out of business, the Eighteenth Amendment and Volstead Act served to unleash a wave of organized crime, the likes of which had never been seen. Throughout the 1920s, bootleggers and crime kings like Alphonse Capone virtually ruled many American cities. Finally, it would be Franklin D. Roosevelt who would end the national nightmare. Within a month of his inauguration in 1933, he signed emergency legislation legalizing beer,

and by December 1933, Congress and the states had ratified the Twenty-first Amendment to the Constitution, which completely repealed the Eighteenth Amendment. *BY*

Propaganda

Among the major European participants in World War I, propaganda efforts were focused primarily on encouraging voluntary recruitment into the armed forces and maintaining civilian morale. To a lesser degree they also aimed at under-

Above: Parliamentary Recruiting Committee poster No. 75. March 1915.
Chrysalis Photo Library

Right: Italian recruiting poster.
Chrysalis Photo Library

mining and counteracting the propaganda efforts of the enemy. A further effort, particularly for the British, was to bolster support among American public opinion in the hope of drawing the United States into the war on the Allied side. When America joined the war in 1917

Left: Men of the Hampshire Regiment estimating the destination of leaflets using the direction of the wind, length of burning fuze, and intervals between releasing the leaflets. The man is cutting a slit in the base of the neck of the balloon to allow gas to escape as it expands. Near Béthune, September 4, 1918.
Chrysalis Photo Library

President Woodrow Wilson created the Committee on Public Information (CPI) to direct propaganda efforts intended both to secure domestic support for the war effort and to promote American war aims. The United States had a large population of recent immigrants, among them some eight million German-Americans, whose support for the war could by no means be taken for granted. The CPI utilized advertising techniques and insights from psychology in the first organized attempt by a modern government to influence public opinion in favor of the war. Voluntary guidelines were introduced for the news media, policed by the CPI, which effectively censored much antigovernment information. The foreign language press that had served the many immigrant communities was decimated. The CPI formed divisions that operated via radio, newspapers, film-makers and academia, among other fields. Thousands of press releases ensured the media were filled with favorable reports. Hollywood needed little encouragement to churn out films with titles like "The Kaiser: the Beast of Berlin." Posters across the nation demonized the enemy and boosted the sale of liberty bonds. *DC*

Left: French recruiting poster.
Chrysalis Photo Library

Right: Australian recruiting poster.
Chrysalis Photo Library

Would you stand by while a bushfire raged

GET BUSY, and drive the Germans back!

THE WAR LEA

WORLD WAR I: A VISUAL ENCYCLOPEDIA

311

Above: James Montgomery Flagg's legendary 1917 poster of Uncle Sam, entitled "I Want You For The U.S. Army, Enlist Now."
Collection of Bill Yenne

Above Right: British recruitment poster.
Chrysalis Photo Library

Right: The British Navy was also after recruits.
Chrysalis Photo Library

Opposite: Australian recruitment poster.
Chrysalis Photo Library

Przemysl, Siege of

Sited on the San River, Przemysl was one of the key fortresses in the Austro-Hungarian province of Galicia, which lay along the border with the Russian Empire and was also a vital center of rail communications. Przemysl first came under siege during September 1914, when much of Galicia was abandoned by the Austro-Hungarian armies that had been forced to withdraw westward over the Carpathian Mountains following a succession of defeats at the hands of the Russians. Przemysl was under siege until October when relief forces were able to advance on the fortress following the withdrawal of the Russian besiegers—they had gone to take part in the forthcoming campaign in Poland directed toward the German province of Silesia. However, the respite was short-lived. Russian successes in Poland, notably at the Battle of Ivangorod fought in the second half of October, precipitated a second Austro-Hungarian withdrawal over the Carpathian Mountains. Przemysl and its 120,000-strong garrison was again left isolated and swiftly placed under siege by the Russian Eleventh Army. The Russians were ill-equipped to prosecute the siege, however. They

Above: Pictured after the war, a Vickers FB52 Gunbus. This was a cleaned-up version of the wartime FB5. Note the pusher propeller.
Chrysalis Photo Library

lacked modern artillery and the necessary shells, and what supplies did reach the front were inadequate. An attempt to relieve Przemysl was made in February 1915, but the Austro-Hungarians were unable to decisively break through the passes of the Carpathian Mountains held by the Russians even with the aid of German reinforcements. With no hope of relief and close to starvation, Przemysl's 100,000 surviving defenders surrendered to the Russians on March 22. However, Russia's hold on the fortress was brief. In early June it was recaptured by German and Austro-Hungarian forces taking part in the Gorlice-Tarnów Offensive. *IW*

Pusher aircraft

As an aircraft powered by an engine with a propeller mounted on the front of the nacelle "pulled" the machine along, it followed that a rear-mounted propeller acted in much the same way but "pushed" the aircraft. A common World

War I configuration, the term applied to aircraft such as the FE2b, Farman F40 and Voisin 3 and tended to indicate a machine with a lower performance than that achieved with the more usual tractor engine configuration. *JS*

Putnik, Radomir (1847–1917)

The Serbian Field Marshal Radomir Putnik had had experience in the Balkan wars of the late nineteenth century, before early retirement in 1895. However, following King Peter's coup of 1903, he returned, becoming chief of staff in 1904—a post he held until 1917—and also serving as war minister prior to World War I. In August 1914 he took field command of the Serbian Army, defeating the Austrian advances at Drina (August 1914) and Save (September 1914), and launching a counterattack at Kolubara (December 1914). However, Serbian forces were not strengthened by the Allies, with the result that, following a further Austrian assault in October 1915, the Serbia army was forced to undertake its own "Great Retreat" in late November 1915. By this stage, Putnik was seriously ill and was withdrawn to France, where he died in May 1917. *MS*

Q

Q-ships

As the German U-boat offensive increased in ferocity, the British Admiralty sought new ways to counter the U-boat menace. Several tramp steamers were converted into decoy ships (known as Q-ships), the first to enter service being the *Victoria* in November 1914. In July 1915 a Q-ship sank a U-boat, and a further ten sinkings were accredited to the 180 British Q-ships employed during the war. They were designed to look exactly like other merchant vessels, but the ships were armed with powerful weapons—hidden deck guns, depth-charge throwers, machine guns, and even torpedoes. *AK*

Below: The four-inch gun hidden under a dummy hatch on the British Q-ship *Baron Rose*. *Chrysalis Photo Library*

Bottom: Q-ship *Coreopsis*. *Chrysalis Photo Library*

RACE TO THE SEA

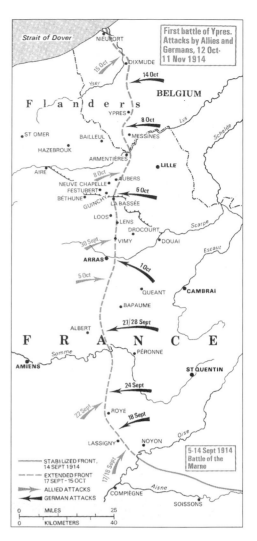

Race to the Sea

Following the First Battle of the Aisne in early September 1914, the only open flank left for a war of maneuver was on the Allied left flank, toward the sea. Both sides ought to take advantage of this open flank and a series of maneuvers and actions began that came to be known as the "Race to the Sea." Initially, the French Sixth and Seventh Armies attacked the German right flank between September 17 and 22, they were beaten off. Maud'huy's Tenth Army was the next to try, but met a similar fate. It was at this point that Sir John French requested that the BEF be restored to its original position on the left of the line. It was withdrawn from the Aisne front and started to move on October 1. French's plan was to outflank the Germans and move forward into Belgium winning the war in a short, glorious campaign. Von Falkenhayn had a similar idea, and his forces were already marching toward the coast with the aim of taking first Ypres and then the channel ports. The two forces met around La Bassée in what was the start of the First Battle of Ypres. *MC*

Right: Troops detraining at Poperinghe, September 30, 1917. *Chrysalis Photo Library*

Opposite, Top: 1st Hertfordshire Yeomanry disembarking at Alexandria, September 20, 1914. *Chrysalis Photo Library*

Opposite, Bottom: 20th Brigade, 7th Division leaving Zeebrugge for Bruges, October 7, 1914. *Chrysalis Photo Library*

Radio

Although the potential of radio—or wireless telegraphy as it was known—to revolutionize communication was widely recognized, the practical limitations of the bulky equipment and the large power source required to operate it meant that the impact of the novel technology was limited. Communication between trenches and rear command posts relied on fragile telegraph lines, carrier pigeons, and runners. At sea, where the technical problems were less severe, the effective use of radio in battle was diminished by the failure to develop rapid means of securely encoding and decoding the Morse code transmissions. However, the use of radio did allow navies to communicate over much longer distances, a vital factor in coordinating both Allied blockades and the German U-boat offensive. *DC*

Railroads

Railroads, as the swiftest method of bulk transport, were of vital importance. The potential of rail was demonstrated during

1912 German maneuvers when von Moltke switched three corps from one flank to another in an afternoon. Mobilization depended on trains, and war could now apparently be fought "by timetable." The important thing was not how many miles of track and locomotives were available, but how dense the network was, and whether the routes served strategic objectives. Railroads tended to follow the degree of national industrialization: Britain's railroads were the best developed, though obviously of limited strategic use. The French and German systems were not far behind. Perhaps the greatest enigma was the Russian system that was least developed, and least dense. German planners had assumed that while they were able to send in excess of 650 locomotives a day westward, the Russians could only get 200 to their western border. These calculations were important in the framing of the Schlieffen Plan and the decision to attack France. Yet even by 1914 the Russian system had made great advances aided by loans from France, and in the event it proved possible to move 360 trains per day, causing a material upset to German plans. Rail continued to be of vital importance throughout the war. For the Battle of the Somme the British had to move over 120 trains per day simply to maintain the offensive on a comparatively narrow sector. At home much of Britain's rail system was put under the national control of the Railway Executive Committee, allowing rolling stock to be moved to France. *SB*

Right: Laying railroad track across the Sinai Desert. *Chrysalis Photo Library*

Above Left: Resupply by light railroad, Ypres, February 1917. *Chrysalis Photo Library*

Above: 190mm guns mounted on an armored train near the Somme, August 28, 1916. *Chrysalis Photo Library*

Left: Battle of Pilckem Ridge. 11th Durham Light Infantry being taken forward by light railroad, July 31, 1917. *Chrysalis Photo Library*

Rasputin, Grigori Efimovich
(1871–1916)

There were few more influential figures in the last years of Tsar Nicholas II's reign than the mystic monk Rasputin. He arrived at St. Petersburg at a critical time; belief in mystical religion was on the increase and he gained an introduction to the royal household. Here he found an influential supported in the Tsarina, Alexandra, as a result of his supposed ability to assist the Tsarevitch, Alexei, who was a hemophiliac. From 1905 he was ever-present at the court and from 1911, confident in the Tsarina's support, he started to interfere in politics. Licentious in his personal behavior,

Rasputin was one factor in the growing alienation of the Russian royal family from the establishment. Rasputin was murdered in 1916 as a result of a plot organized by Prince Felix Yusupov. *MS*

Rathenau, Walter (1867–1922)

One of the most influential of late nineteenth century German industrialists, Rathenau was born in Berlin to a Jewish family. His father, Emil, had founded the *Allgemeine Elektrizitäts Gesellschaft* (AEG—General Electricity Company) in 1883 and Walter Rathenau assumed control of it. In 1916, faced by the threat of the British blockade, the German government appointed Rathenau to organize the country's war economy. He created a system of "war socialism," whereby all men aged between seventeen and sixty had their work determined by the state. With the creation of the Weimar Republic, he formed the Democratic Party, becoming minister of reconstruction in May 1921. In early 1922 he became minister of foreign affairs, helping to improve relations with United States, France, and Russia. However, his political career was to be cut short in June 1922 when he was assassinated by anti-Semitic nationalists. *MS*

Rawlinson, Sir Henry Seymour (1864–1925)

Rawlinson served in Burma, Sudan, and South Africa prior to World War I. He commanded the Fourth Army at the Somme in 1916 and, in 1918, led the force that broke the Hindenburg Line near Amiens. After the war, he served as commander-in-chief in India from 1920 and was created the first Baron Rawlinson. *MS*

Recruiting

The major European armies relied upon conscription for the bulk of their manpower. In France men became eligible to serve at twenty. The "Three Years" law was introduced in 1913 which increased liability to three years in the active army; eleven in the reserve; seven in the

Right: Recruits waiting in line during the rain at the Whitehall Recruiting Office. 1914.
Chrysalis Photo Library

territorial army; and seven in the territorial reserve. This produced a regular peacetime army of about 730,000 that could be rapidly expanded in war. Voluntary enlistments were also taken between the ages of eighteen and fifty. Recruiting committees judged physical fitness and applied height limits, and weight limits for the cavalry. The German system was similar. Service liability with the *Landsturm* began at seventeen, but men were not called to the colors in peacetime until age twenty, when two years' active service commenced. Reserve service was four or five years, with eleven in the *Landwehr* and seven in the second division of the *Landsturm*. A special "Ersatz" reserve was made up of those men who had been excused service for family or economic reasons, or had minor physical defects. Britain was unusual in that it depended on volunteers until the introduction of conscription in 1916. *SB*

Left: Playing on a guilty British conscience.
Chrysalis Photo Library

Above: Draftees from New York City on their way to camp. *Chrysalis Photo Library*

Red Army

The Red Army was created by the Bolsheviks to promote and defend the 1917 Russian Revolution against internal unrest, monarchists, and more moderate revolutionaries. Recruits were a mixture of former members of the Tsarist Russian Army, revolutionary militias, peasants, and industrial workers. Although some Red Army forces were stationed on the Eastern Front before Russia's surrender, they played little role in the fighting against the Central Powers. However, during the subsequent Russian Civil War (1918–21) they established Bolshevik authority throughout the former empire. This was in large part due to the skills of the commissar for war, Leon Trotsky. *IW*

Reparations

The victorious Allies were determined to recover some of the vast cost of the war from Germany in the form of reparations. The Treaty of Versailles set up a committee that would meet in 1921 to determine the full scope of these payments and stated that in the meantime Germany must meet an initial charge of US$5 billion. Deprived of its colonies and most coal-producing regions and with its industry devastated, Germany

was unable to pay more than half of the due amount by 1921. Obliged to devote the bulk of its earnings to paying reparations, the government was forced to print excess money to fund its domestic responsibilities, fueling a massive inflationary spiral and economic collapse. Despite criticism, including that of the leading economist John Maynard Keynes, the Reparation Commission did little to modify the excessive demands when it finally reported in 1924. It did, however, make some provision for the recovery of German industry and for a rising scale of payments to reduce the immediate burden. It noted that reparations, initially one billion marks per year, rising after four years to 2.5 billion, should be met from transportation, excise, and customs taxes. The Reichsbank was to be reorganized under Allied supervision. With the onset of the Great Depression in 1929, German economic recovery ended and it could no longer meet the required payments. A new plan was adopted in 1930 that set a final total of $26.35 billion for reparations to be paid over the next fifty-eight years. It had little effect as a moratorium was agreed for the fiscal year 1931–32, and unpaid reparations were repudiated when Adolf Hitler became chancellor. *DC*

Respirators

All nations were unequipped for gas when it appeared in April 1915. Pad-type masks were quickly adopted as a stopgap measure. In the British instance, GHQ instructed the use of field dressings dipped in bicarbonate of soda, and Lord Kitchener launched an appeal for cotton wool pads and stockinette masks. Yet the first pad-type mask to make any real impact was the chemically impregnated design developed by Lieutenant Leslie Barley. While the French continued to use improved pad and snout designs such as the P2 and M2 into 1916, British and

Right: U.S. medical troops in gasmasks.
Collection of Bill Yenne

Below: British troops wearing gasmasks in the trenches on the Salonika Front.
Chrysalis Photo Library

German technicians produced more innovative solutions. During the summer of 1915 the British made and distributed "hypo helmet" types that were made of impregnated flannel and pulled on over the head like a bag. The improved "tube" model incorporated a pipe for exhaling. By 1916 the British were experimenting with "box" models which featured face pieces with tubes, and separate filter boxes contained in a bag. The final result was the highly effective Small Box Respirator, which was also adopted by the Americans. The German 1915 model mask was produced from September of that year. It consisted of a face piece onto which the filter was screwed directly, the connecting piece being an adaptation of a fitting already in production by the Osram light company. Though reasonably effective its filters did not last as long as those used in box systems. Rubber shortages forced the production of a sheep leather model in 1917. About the same time the French adopted a similar type called the "ARS." *SB*

Rhodesian forces

Rhodesian commitment to the Allied cause lay chiefly with the creation of a number of volunteer units that saw service in several campaigns in Africa. In 1914, some 2,500 Rhodesians formed the Northern Rhodesia Rifles and fought in German East Africa; a second force, some 2,000 men consisting of the Southern Rhodesia Volunteers and police units, took part in the occupation of German Southwest Africa. Other Rhodesians volunteered for service with the British Army on the Western Front. Total casualties were 732 men killed out of the 12,000 who served. Despite Rhodesia's small white population, it sent a greater percentage of men to fight than any other part of the British Empire. *IW*

Richthofen, Manfred von (1892–1918)

Count Manfred von Richthofen was possibly the best-known combat pilot of all time, his success in downing eighty Allied aircraft bringing him fame far beyond his homeland. Nicknamed the "Red Baron" after he began flying a blood-red Fokker Dr I Triplane the highly skilled *Rittmeister* (ring master) gained a fearsome reputation. He remained loyal to the triplane and died while flying it on April 21, 1918, under

Above: Manfred von Richthofen.
Chrysalis Photo Library

circumstances that remain controversial today: convincing cases were made by RFC pilot Roy Brown for an aerial kill and by Australian ground gunners who claimed to have hit the low-flying aircraft. The baron was found dead in the cockpit after the aircraft came to rest, virtually intact. *JS*

Rickenbacker, Edward Vernon "Eddie" (1890–1975)

A race-car driver turned pilot, Eddie Rickenbacker became the highest-scoring American ace of World War I and a national luminary. He would use his celebrity status to carve out a role for himself in American aviation for half a century. Born in Columbus, Ohio, Rickenbacker grew up with an avid interest in things mechanical and a boy's interest in fast machines. He went on the racing circuit when he was barely aged twenty and earned a reputation for speed and coolness. When the United States entered World War I, he tried to organize an aero squadron composed of his racing pals, but when he enlisted, General John J. Pershing requested Rickenbacker as his personal driver. In August 1917, he was transferred to the U.S. Army Signal Corps Aviation Section (which became the U.S. Army Air Service in May 1918) and signed up for flight training. Arriving in France, he flew briefly with a French squadron before joining the 94th Aero Squadron—the legendary "hat in the ring" squadron—in March 1918. Rickenbacker scored his first aerial victory on April 29, and his fifth on May 30, making him the first American-trained American "ace." Grounded

Below: Eddie Rickenbacker.
Collection of Bill Yenne

Right: Captain Eddie Rickenbacker.
Chrysalis Photo Library

briefly with an ear infection, he returned to combat in August as his squadron upgraded to the French-made Spad XIII fighter aircraft, possibly the best Allied fighter of World War I. During the last three months of the war, he distinguished himself by bringing his score to twenty-six, and demonstrated the heroism that earned him the Congressional Medal of Honor. He was also promoted to serve as commander of the 94th Aero Squadron. After the war, Rickenbacker wrote his memoirs, *Fighting The Flying Circus* (1919), organized the Rickenbacker Motor Company, and served as its president until 1928, when he went to Fokker Aircraft Corporation as vice president. Between 1932 and 1935 he served in various posts for American Airways (later American Airlines and North American Aviation). In 1935, he became general manager of Eastern Airlines, a company to whom he devoted most of his remaining career as an aviation executive. During World War II, he undertook several special fact-finding missions for the U.S. Army Air Forces. During one of these, his plane was forced down in the South Pacific, and he and six others spent three weeks in a rubber raft before being rescued. This experience was recounted in his book *Seven Came Through* (1943). *BY*

Rifles

By 1900 all major nations had adopted bolt-action rifles as the main arm of their infantry. The combination of reliable ammunition and magazines, with weapons which were sighted to about 2,200 yards, would be one of the major factors in making the war more deadly than previous conflicts. By British definitions anything under 600 yards was now close range, with up to 1,400 counted as "effective." The penetration achieved by modern pointed projectiles was also remarkable. As a manual of 1911 observed, a rifle bullet could now be expected to go through thirty-eight inches of hard wood; nine inches of brick; or three-quarters of an inch of wrought iron at close range. Speed of operation had also increased dramatically during the last hundred years. In 1814 even the swiftest shot was hard-pressed to get three rounds per minute from his musket: in 1914 the slowest weapons

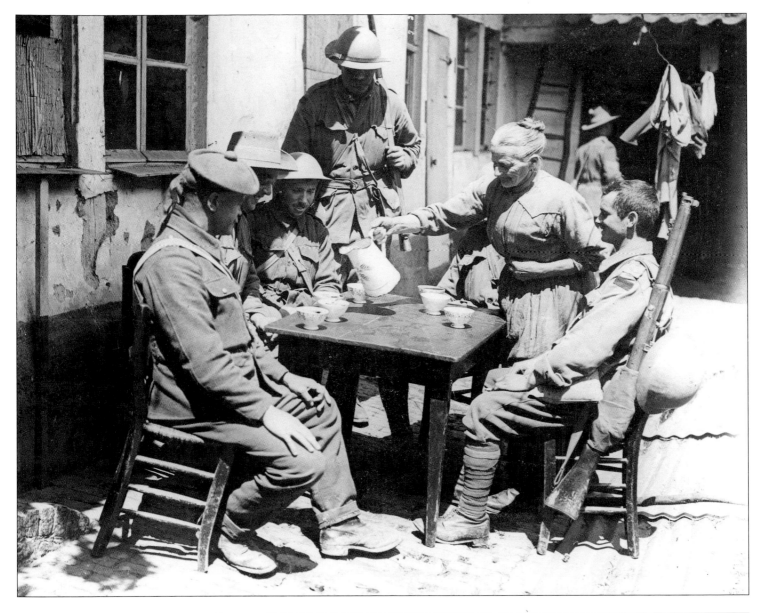

Above: An elderly Frenchwoman giving coffee to British troops at Croix du Bac, near Armentières, May 1916. Note the canvas protection to the rifle mechanism. *Chrysalis Photo Library*

Right: Australian troops of 45th Battalion in action near the Hindenburg Line, September 1918. *Chrysalis Photo Library*

were capable of about eight rounds per minute, with British regular troops claiming fifteen. Many rifles were now charger-loading, allowing the soldier to push several rounds from a clip or charger filling the magazine with one easy movement. There were also experiments with automatic rifles. Various Mauser action rifles armed the Germans, Belgians, and Serbians. The standard German model was the Gewehr 98 or G98, approved in 1898. This was a 7.92mm weapon, 49.2 inches in length, weighed 9.1lb, and had a five-round magazine. Highly accurate to great ranges, it was one of the most influential designs of the period. It could be fitted with a number of different types

of bayonet including the 1905 broad bladed model, Christened the "butcher bayonet" by the Allies. In 1914 many German reservists and Landwehr troops were still using an old type of Mauser, the G88. The standard British rifle was the Short Magazine Lee Enfield, or SMLE: so named because the action of this Enfield-manufactured magazine rifle was designed by James Lee. It was indeed shorter than the models that preceded it, and had been introduced in the wake of the Boer War as a universal arm for cavalry as well as infantry. It was a .303-inch weapon, 44.5 inches in length, weighing 8.2lb with a ten-round magazine. The 1907 model "sword" bayonet had a 16.5-inch blade. In the event the SMLE proved to be one of the best, if not the best, rifle of the war combining relative handiness with speed and ease of operation. Other rifles used in smaller numbers by the British included the old "long" Lee Enfield, and the P14

Left: Sentry wearing a PH mask—called this because the fabric had been impregnated with **Phenate Hexamine.** *Chrysalis Photo Library*

Below: Patrol of 6th Seaforth Highlanders, August 29, 1918. *Chrysalis Photo Library*

Enfield. France was less well served, having adopted the 8mm Lebel infantry rifle in 1886. At the time this had been very advanced, featuring an eight-round under-the-barrel tube magazine. The bayonet was a long stiletto, with a blade cruciform in section. Yet by 1914 the Lebel was looking distinctly slow and old-fashioned. It was also relatively long at fifty-one inches, and heavy, weighing 9.5lb. It was, therefore, rapidly supplemented by Berthier models. Despite being more satisfactory, these initially suffered from a magazine capacity of only three rounds, a figure that was upped to five shots later in the war. Models of other nations included the Russian "3 Line" rifle of 1891; the various types of Mannlicher used by the Austrians and Romanians; the Springfield and P17 Enfield of the Americans. *SB*

Robertson, Sir William Robert (1860–1933)

Although enlisting initially as a private, Robertson was ultimately to rise to the highest rank in the British Army—field marshal—and be awarded a baronetcy.

He enlisted in 1877 in the 16th Lancers and was the first private to pass through Staff College after he received his commission. He was commandant of the Staff College between 1910 and 1913 before serving as Quarter-Master General and Chief of the General Staff; he was Chief of the Imperial General Staff from 1915 until 1918 and was made a field marshal two years later. *MS*

Romanian Army

The Romanian Army—some 100,000 men in peacetime and 860,000 on full mobilization—was ill-prepared to fight a modern conflict when the country declared war in August 1916. There was an acute shortage of machine guns and the standard-issue rifle was of outdated design. Equally, much of the available artillery was of inferior quality (little more than half of the pieces available were of modern design) and short of shells. Many of its conscripts had little more than rudimentary military training and a high proportion of their officers were similarly unskilled. The country's land forces were severely mauled when the Central Powers attacked but the

Left: Romanian infantry in dress uniform in Bucharest before Romania entered the war on August 27, 1916. *Chrysalis Photo Library*

overall quality of the survivors improved from early 1917 thanks to training missions provided by Britain and France. *IW*

Romanian Campaign of 1916

Romania's decision to declare war on Austria-Hungary in late August 1916 proved ill-judged and brought a swift response from the Central Powers. While Romanian forces made hesitant moves to occupy parts of the Austro-Hungarian province of Transylvania, a mixed forces of Austro-Hungarian, Bulgarian, German, and Turkish troops under German General August von Mackensen advanced from Bulgaria into southern Romania at the beginning of September. Despite limited Russian assistance, which slowed Mackensen's advance at the end of the month and for much of October, the invaders were able to seize the Black Sea port of Constanza on the 29th. The focus of Mackensen's advance now shifted northward; in late November he crossed the Danube River in a thrust toward Bucharest, the Romanian capital. In the meantime, a second front had been opened by the Central Powers in Transylvania and along the line of the Carpathian Mountains. Attempts in September by forces under General Erich von Falkenhayn to force the

Romanian-held passes through the mountains failed, but reinforcements allowed him to succeed in mid-November. Von Mackensen and von Falkenhayn linked up on the 26th and, following the three-day Battle of the Arges River in early December, Bucharest was occupied. Subsequent progress was slowed by heavy rains, poor roads, and the belated arrival of significant Russian reinforcements, but by January 7, 1917, the greater part of Romania, including its oilfields, had been occupied by the Central Powers. Only the province of Moldavia in the north remained in Romanian hands, although its defense was in the hands of the already overstretched Russian Army as Romania's forces had been decimated in the recent fighting. *IW*

Roosevelt, Theodore "Teddy" (1858–1919)

One of the most colorful and best-loved of U.S. presidents, Theodore Roosevelt served in that office from 1901 to 1909. A sickly child turned adventurer, he was a vibrant volunteer infantry leader in one war who sought unsuccessfully to do it in another. Born in New York City, he graduated from Harvard in 1880, studied law at Columbia and served in the New York state legislature as a Republican. After the death of his mother and his first wife, Alice Hathaway Lee, Roosevelt spent time on his ranch in Dakota Territory, where he developed a deep affection for the clean air and individualist spirit found on what was still the rugged Old West. Returning to New York City in 1886, he began a career of public service in both city and federal posts. In 1897 he was appointed Assistant Secretary of the Navy by President William McKinley. A supporter of United States' expansion, he worked toward putting the U.S. Navy on a war footing for the coming war with Spain. After the outbreak of the Spanish-American war, he resigned his post to organize a volunteer regiment composed of Western cowboys that was known as the "Rough Riders." His wartime exploits made Roosevelt a popular hero, and helped elect him governor of New York state in 1898. In 1900, he was nominated to run as a vice-presidential

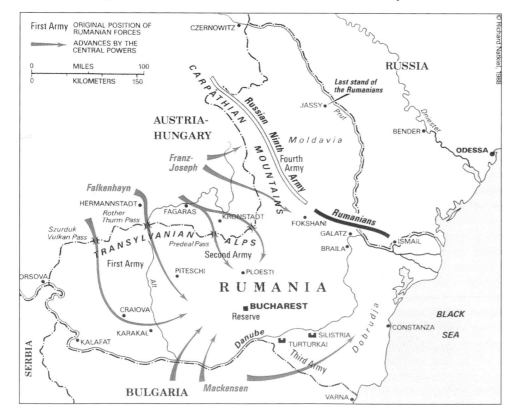

candidate during President McKinley's reelection bid. In September 1901, when McKinley was assassinated, Theodore Roosevelt became the twenty-sixth president. He would be reelected in 1904. During his presidency, Roosevelt successfully wielded the Sherman Antitrust Act to break up monopolies, and pressed for passage of early environmental legislation such as the Reclamation Act of 1902. He established the U.S. Department of Commerce & Labor (now two separate departments), and backed the Meat Inspection and the Pure Food and Drug Acts. He also oversaw the construction of the Panama Canal and was awarded the 1906 Nobel Peace Prize for brokering an end to the

Russo-Japanese War. He chose not to run for president in 1908, but his handpicked successor, William Howard Taft, won. Roosevelt became disillusioned with Taft and ran against him in 1912 on the Progressive Party—the "Bull Moose" Party—ticket. Roosevelt beat Taft, but the two only served to divide the Republican majority. Woodrow Wilson, the Democrat, became only the second Democrat elected since the Civil War. Roosevelt, however, was the only third party presidential candidate in American history to come in second, rather than third. When World War I began, the middle-aged Roosevelt attempted without success to assemble a volunteer force akin to the Rough Riders of 1898.

Though Roosevelt himself did not take part in World War I, five of his six children did. Theodore "Ted" Roosevelt Jr. served as an officer in the 26th Infantry, was gassed at Cantigny and wounded. In World War II, as a general, Ted took part in the Normandy invasion but died of a heart attack five weeks later while with his unit was fighting in France. Archibald Bullock "Archie" Roosevelt, also an officer with the 26th Infantry, was severely wounded in March 1918 and later awarded Croix de Guerre. Like his brother, Archie served again with distinction in World War II. Kermit Roosevelt served initially with the BEF in Mesopotamia, and later with AEF's Field Artillery in the Meuse-Argonne Offensive. Like Ted and Archie, he would serve again in World War II. He died in Alaska in 1943, one year and two days before Ted. Ethel Carow Roosevelt Derby, Theodore Roosevelt's youngest daughter, worked as a nurse with Ambulance Americane. Roosevelt's youngest son, Quentin, joined the Army Air Service in 1917 and was shot down in July 1918 at age twenty in aerial combat over occupied enemy territory in France and was buried by German troops. As Mrs. Roosevelt wrote, the death of Quentin deeply affected the former president. His health declined rapidly, and he died six months later. *BY*

Rosyth

Experience gained from the British response to raids on the English coast at Hartlepool and Lowestoft led to redeployment of the battlecruiser fleet commanded by Vice-Admiral Beatty, together with its attendant lighter forces. At first Beatty's ships were moved to Invergordon on the Cromarty Firth, a natural anchorage with a single entrance. The danger of a blockade by German submarines or mines prompted a second relocation of Beatty's force to Rosyth on the Firth of Forth, across the Forth estuary from Edinburgh. Rosyth served as the base for the battlecruisers for the remainder of the war. *AK*

Left: President Theodore Roosevelt, standing beside the large globe that was an important fixture in his office, February 1903.
Collection of Bill Yenne

Opposite: Map of the 1916 Romanian Campaign.
Richard Natkiel

Royal Navy

In 1914, the British Royal Navy (RN) was the foremost naval power in the world, and its presence was felt around the globe, protecting the interests of the British Empire and its commerce. As the largest fleet in existence it was also a source of immense national pride, and consequently much was expected of it. When the war began, the core of the navy was the Grand Fleet; twenty-four dreadnoughts (eleven more would enter service during the war), ten battlecruisers (plus five more built during hostilities), and numerous cruisers, destroyers, and lighter vessels, including submarines. While the Grand Fleet was kept in the North Sea, where it was ready to engage the German fleet if the opportunity presented itself, many of the thirty-six predreadnought battleships and other less battleworthy warships were used to protect the sea lanes. A significant portion of the fleet was also stationed in the Mediterranean, where it was employed against the Austro-Hungarian and Turkish fleets, and to support British military operations in the region. Although the British were denied a decisive naval clash against the Germans, their pyrrhic victory at Jutland (1916) ensured the British blockade of Germany remained unbroken, a leading contributing factor to Allied victory. *AK*

Right: HMS *Barham* in foreign waters.
Chrysalis Photo Library

Below: HMAS *Sydney* and the Third Light Cruiser Squadron steaming through choppy seas.
Chrysalis Photo Library

Above: Superdreadnoughts of the 1st Battle Squadron in line: in the foreground, *Royal Sovereign*, following *Resolution* and, in the lead, *Revenge*.
Chrysalis Photo Library

Left: British ratings having a meal in one of the mess decks on a battleship.
Chrysalis Photo Library

Above Left: HMS *Invincible*.
Chrysalis Photo Library

Above: Superdreadnought *Royal Sovereign* **firing her fifteen-inch guns.** *Chrysalis Photo Library*

Left: British battleship *Agincourt*.
Chrysalis Photo Library

Rupprecht, Crown Prince
(1869–1955)

Heir to the throne of Bavaria, Rupprecht served as the commander of the German Sixth Army in August 1914 and was overall commander in Lorraine. His failure to breach the French defenses along the Moselle was one factor in the ultimate failure of the Schlieffen Plan. He became a field marshal in July 1916 and served the entire war on the Western Front. In August 1916 he became commander of Army Group Rupprecht, on the northern part of the front. Recognizing the imminence of German defeat, he disobeyed orders and gradually retreated ahead of the Allied Courtrai Offensive in 1918. *MS*

Russian advance through Poland
(1915)

Their recent defeat at the Battle of Tannenberg notwithstanding, the Russians pushed ahead with their plans to advance into Germany from their province of Poland in September 1914. However, their preparations were dogged by confusion and command rivalries, and the Germans were able to

WORLD WAR I: A VISUAL ENCYCLOPEDIA

339

preempt the Russians by advancing deep into Poland. By mid-October they were occupying positions along the west banks of the Vistula and San rivers, within striking distance of Warsaw. The Russian offensive opened with unsuccessful attempts to cross the Vistula at Ivangorod on October 11. This failed but the Austro-Hungarian and German forces, facing a much superior enemy, were ordered to withdraw from October 20. A few days later Russian troops crossed the Vistula, but progress was slow. To make matters worse the Russian forces began to move apart. One went northward to protect Poland from an attack from East Prussia, and one southward toward Austria-Hungary. Using their efficient rail network, the German Ninth Army under General August von Mackensen was moved northward to East Prussia from its positions in southern Poland between November 3 and 9, taking up positions between Posen and Thorn prior to a drive into northwestern Poland. The German attack began on the 11th and the Russians were pushed back and then defeated at the Battle of Lodz. The Russian withdrawal ended with the fall of Lodz itself on December 6 and the building of new positions along the Bzura and Rawka Rivers to the west of Warsaw. The Germans had clearly undermined Russia's plans to invade their homeland, but had not inflicted a decisive defeat on the invaders. *IW*

Russian air forces

Imperial Russia entered the war on August 1, 1914, at a time when her Flying Corps had 244 aircraft and 300 pilots, and the navy 100 pilots and several flying boats and floatplanes. By 1915 the country's first indigenous fighter, the Russo-Baltic RBVZ-S-16, entered service, this being followed by the RBVZ-S-17 and -20 in single and two-seat versions. Foreign types such as the Morane MB and Parasol monoplanes, Spad SVII and Nieuport 11, 17, and 21 fighters, plus Voisin bombers, made up the bulk of Russia's combat aircraft. These were supported by further Russian types including the Lebed-7 and Lebed-10 fighters and the Lebed-12 for reconnaissance duties. Flying boats such as the M-5 and M-9 were supplied to the navy. Pioneers of heavy bombing, the Russians formed the grandly named "Squadron of

Aerial Ships" or EVK (*Eskadrilya Vozdushnykh Korablei*) in late 1914 with the mighty Ilya Mourometz. Based at Jablonna in Poland, these bombers began raiding German forces from February 15, 1915, when an Ilya Mourometz named *Kievsky* dropped 600lb of bombs on a target near Plotsk. This first successful attack by the EVK was followed by others, the force more frequently flying reconnaissance and ground-attack sorties. After the upheaval of November 1917 the Bolsheviks lost some aircraft to the revolutionaries and it was May 24, 1918, before the establishment of the Workers' and Peasants' Red Air Fleet (GU-RKKVF). With no more than 300 aircraft, flown by former Tsarist pilots, the GU-RKKVF formed the 1st Socialist Aviation Gruppa, equipped mainly with foreign aircraft. This unit took part in the Red occupation of Kazan and the attack on the Crimea in 1918, by which time a division had been formed. *JS*

Russian aircraft

Although Russia's aircraft industry was tiny in 1914, it was not short of innovation and a desire to build large. However, the country was obliged to rely on numerous types purchased from abroad while its design and manufacturing base was expanded. A sound scientific base had been established led by N. Ye. Zhukovskii, the "Father of Russian Aviation." Expansion of the industry took time and consequently many of the sorties flown by the Imperial Flying Corps during the early part of the war were undertaken by foreign, mainly French, aircraft. Despite the 1917 revolution the air arm continued to function and operate as a reorganized national "Red" air force against "White" breakaway elements dedicated to restoring the status quo. Among the Tsarist industry's most impressive achievements was the giant four-engined Ilya Mourometz heavy bomber designed by Igor Sikorsky. Fitted with defensive armament and bomb racks, production of these monsters ran to seventy-two. Also responsible for the RBVZ series of aircraft built by the Russo-Baltic factory, Sikorsky's own designs contributed only modestly to the total of 1,769 airframes and 660 aero engines built in Russia during 1916, the bulk being of foreign origins. Several firms produced prototypes of original designs including Hackel, Kasyanenko, and Savelyev. *JS*

Russian Army

On paper at least, the sheer size of the Russian Army in 1914 appeared to make a most formidable force. Estimates suggest that there were some twenty-five million men eligible for service in 1912, and the army was also in the throes of a vast reorganization that aimed to improve its capabilities. This process had been initiated in 1908 in a response to the country's humiliating defeat in the Russo-Japanese War (1904–05) and reached its apogee in 1914 when the war minister, General Vladimir Sukhomlinov, initiated what was term the "Great Program." This centered on increasing recruitment to 585,000 men each year, upgrading artillery units, and modernization of the railroad system. Such reforms were to be completed by 1916, and were viewed with increasing alarm by both Austria-Hungary and Germany. The latter in particular believed that Russia's chief weakness was its slow pace of general mobilization, but Sukhomlinov's reforms seemed to be partly directed toward resolving the problem. In reality, the Russian Army was not as formidable as it seemed. Its manpower was not inexhaustible. Although some twelve million men were mobilized, it probably never fielded more than 2.25 million at any one period, and many of these had to be deployed away from the Eastern Front to protect the vast empire. Despite reforms to the conscription system, it remained haphazard due to the scale of exemptions, bureaucratic incompetence, and financial limitations. This was reflected in the lack of trained officers and NCOs. Equally, supply was often chaotic, with acute shortages of many essential items, not least weapons and ammunition. What was available often reached the front in small amounts due to inefficiency, corruption, and the poor state of the railroad system. Also, the army was short of modern artillery and top-quality communications equipment. At the core of the problem was resistance to Sukhomlinov's reforms from a group of senior officers, who believed that the

Right: Russian troops moving to a forward area on the Balkan Front. They are carrying French pattern steel helmets, September 1916.
Chrysalis Photo Library

ongoing reforms should focus on cavalry and fortresses. Despite these problems, the Russian Army proved remarkable resilient and played a full part in the Allied war strategy between 1914 and 1917, when it finally disintegrated. Aside from successful campaigns in Caucasia and commitments in the Balkans and Greece, it launched a series of offensives on the Eastern Front during these years, either in support of Allied offensives on the Western or Italian Fronts, or to weaken German attacks in the same theaters. In either case, the aim was to draw German troops to the Eastern Front. This ploy invariably worked, although perhaps not on the scale that the Allies had hoped. However, Russia's offensives were usually defeated or any gains, as in the 1916 Brusilov Offensive, quickly lost. This catalogue of failure, in part due to the incompetence of many senior generals, was accompanied by casualties on a huge scale. The prewar army, intensely loyal to Tsar Nicholas II, was virtually destroyed by the end of 1915, and those that refilled the ranks showed less loyalty and poor morale. This decline culminated in the revolutions of 1917 that led to the collapse of the Russian Army. The part played by the Russian Army during the war can be gauged by its casualty list—1.8 million dead, 2.8 million sick or wounded, and 2.4 million captured. *IW*

Russian Civil War

Opposition to the Bolsheviks increased when Russia was forced to give up a huge swathe of territory including Poland, Ukraine, and the Baltic states under the terms of the Treaty of Brest-Litovsk signed in March 1918 by the new revolutionary government. Conflict began in May in Siberia where a large body of Czech troops being evacuated via Vladivostok took control of much of the area from Bolshevik officials. A disparate body of anti-Bolshevik groups, including Tsarist officers, Cossacks, various nationalist bodies, and even Socialist Revolutionaries took up arms against the government. The so-called "White" armies were aided and supplied to a limited extent by small foreign intervention forces sent by the Allies who wanted Russia to rejoin the war. Initially threatened by White armies from all sides, the Red Army, under the control of Leon Trotsky, fought fiercely against a disorganized and badly led opposition. Regions changed hands frequently and atrocities were committed by both sides. Order was maintained in Bolshevik areas by a brutal "Red Terror" regime of intimidation and confiscation. The Whites lacked a clear political and economic alternative to the Bolshevik program, with many peasants fearing that they would restore the monarchy. By

Above: Russian troops halted on a roadside on the Balkan Front, September 1916. *Chrysalis Photo Library*

Right: Map of the Russian Civil War. *Richard Natkiel*

1920 the Red Army had forcible recaptured the bulk of the old Russian Empire, paving the way for the creation of the Union of Soviet Socialist Republics (USSR). Only in Poland were local forces able to repulse the Russians, leading to recognition of Polish territory in the Treaty of Riga (1921). *DC*

Russian forces, Command structure of

Russia was the most autocratic country in Europe, the Tsar having narrowly avoided overthrow as recently as 1905. Shock defeat by Japan in the war of 1904 bode ill for future conflicts, but the Russo-Japanese War provided salutary lessons. The Duma or parliament had been created and a cabinet government appointed, and after 1906 Russia had moved into a period of growth and military reform. By 1914 her naval expenditure slightly exceeded that of Germany, and she had 114 infantry divisions under arms. At the outbreak of war the Russian commander-in-chief, Grand Duke Nicholas, was directly responsible to Tsar Nicholas II. The commander's chief of staff presided over

342

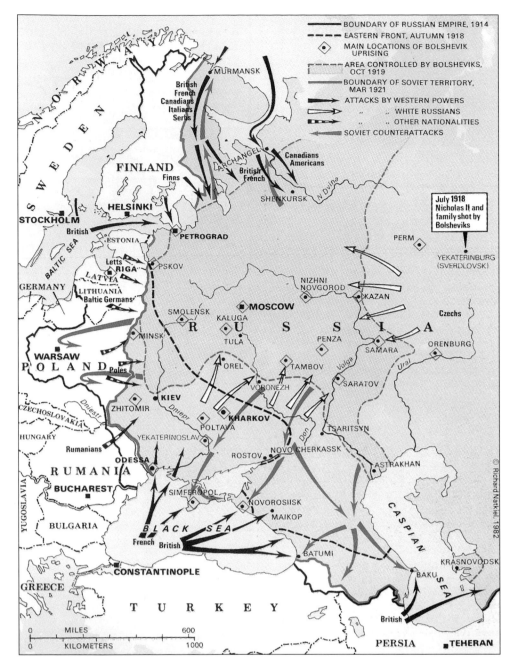

BOUNDARY OF RUSSIAN EMPIRE, 1914
EASTERN FRONT, AUTUMN 1918
MAIN LOCATIONS OF BOLSHEVIK UPRISING
AREA CONTROLLED BY BOLSHEVIKS, OCT 1919
BOUNDARY OF SOVIET TERRITORY, MAR 1921
ATTACKS BY WESTERN POWERS
"   " WHITE RUSSIANS
"   " OTHER NATIONALITIES
SOVIET COUNTERATTACKS

July 1918
Nicholas II and
family shot by
Bolsheviks

© Richard Natkiel, 1982

as production stopped following the Russian Revolution in October 1917. In addition the Russians still had five active predreadnought battleships in each fleet (except the Pacific), and were still building these obsolete vessels as late as 1910. Apart from a skirmish with the battle-cruiser *Goeben* and its consort off Cape Sarych in the Black Sea (1914), Russian naval supremacy in the region meant the Turks refused to give battle. In the Baltic, the odds were more equitable, and the Russians fought several small yet crucial actions against their German foes. *AK*

Russian Revolution

Partial reform introduced under the regime of Tsar Alexander II brought only greater pressure for radical change. In the countryside the abolition of serfdom had created irresistible demands for land reform, while in towns improved access to education generated a large mass of radical unemployed youth. The costly military stalemate on the German Front, together with economic collapse at home, made revolutionary change inevitable. In March 1917 mutinous troops joined rioters demanding bread in St. Petersburg. Government authority collapsed and Tsar Nicholas II abdicated in favor of a committee of the state Duma or parliament led by Alexander Kerensky. The provisional government, supported by the Petrograd Soviet, tried to continue the war effort, despite opposition from the Bolsheviks following the return of Lenin from exile in Switzerland. A failed offensive at the end of June led to mass desertions and the effective collapse of the Russian Army. In the tumultuous months of demonstration and counterdemonstration that gripped the capital the Bolsheviks gained in strength but held back from seizing power. Their opportunity came when Kerensky reacted ambiguously to an attempt by the army General Kornilov to march on the capital and restore order, first offering support but then arming the Soviets to resist. In the event the proposed coup collapsed when the troops were persuaded to back down, leaving Kerensky compromised. Seizing the moment Trotsky mobilized his disciplined units of Bolshevik Red Guards on the night of November 6, seizing control of the Winter Palace and other key sites, arresting members of the provisional government and calling for "all power to the Soviets." *DC*

three branches of staff, the Quartermaster General's Department, the Adjutant General's Department, and the Railway Department. The country was divided into twelve military districts, and the Imperial Nicholas Academy provided officers for the staff. A large land mass and population, combined with a willingness to take casualties, would make the Imperial Russian Army "steamroller" a force to be reckoned with. However, despite apparently meticulous administration, the Russian command system had significant weaknesses. Minister of War General V. A. Sukhomlinov was regarded as corrupt and incompetent, and the General Staff or "Generalni Shtab" was weak and narrow in composition. The supply system was hopelessly inadequate for modern war, and Russian infrastructure poor. The Tsar assumed supreme command in September 1915, and

perforce became inextricably linked with the defeat of 1917. *SB*

Russian Navy

Before the Russo-Japanese War (1904–05) the Imperial Russian Navy was a powerful force, maintaining fleets in the Baltic Sea, the Black Sea, and the Pacific Ocean. The almost complete annihilation of the Baltic and Pacific fleets during the war against Japan left the Russian Navy demoralized, and consequently it was slow to build a new fleet, and to face the challenge posed by the *Dreadnought*. Four dreadnoughts of the "Gangut" class entered service in the Baltic Fleet just before, or soon after, the start of the war, while three "Imperatritsa" class dreadnoughts joined the Black Sea Fleet in 1915. A series of four battlecruisers were never completed,

St. Mihiel, Battle of

The first operation by the AEF First Army as an independent and integral army, St. Mihiel was also an important Allied victory. A prelude to the Meuse-Argonne Campaign, the battle occurred in the St. Mihiel salient, southeast of Verdun, between September 12 and 16, 1918. The object was to eliminate German occupation of the salient as a prelude to the planned Meuse-Argonne Campaign, which would have the objective of capturing Metz and allowing Allied forces to carry the war into Germany. For the battle, three American and one French corps were assigned to First Army. The U.S. V Corps, including the 26th and 4th Divisions as well as the 15th French Colonial Division, would attack to the west. The U.S. IV Corps—composed of the 1st, 42nd, and 89th Divisions—along with I Corps—containing the 2nd, 5th, 90th, and 82nd Divisions—would assault the southeast part of the salient. The French Colonial II Corps would be in the center to exploit any breakthrough that might occur. The French would supply artillery support with 3,000 guns. Overhead, General Billy Mitchell's Air Service would field the largest concentration of tactical air power yet seen in wartime. Counting French and British aircraft, he would have nearly 1,500 planes at his disposal. Although the AEF would suffer 7,000 casualties, St. Mihiel was an outstanding success, with 15,000 prisoners captured and the salient cleared and occupied in five days. *BY*

Below: U.S. 23rd Infantry during the Battle of St. Mihiel.
National Archives via Chrysalis Photo Library

Right: Advancing in the St. Mihiel salient.
National Archives via Chrysalis Photo Library

Below Right: Ammunition wagon northeast of St. Mihiel, Beaumont Ridge September, 15, 1918.
National Archives via Chrysalis Photo Library

Samsonov, Alexander Vasilevich
(1859–1914)

Samsonov served with the Russian Army during the ill-fated campaign against Japan in 1904–05. He was the commander one of the Russian armies that invaded East Prussia in August 1914 (the other was led by Rennenkampf), an army that was decisively defeated at the Battle of Tannenberg on August 26–31 by a German army led by Hindenburg. German strategy envisaged the encircling of Samsonov's army—which was achieved with some 100,000 Russians being captured—and a belief that Rennenkampf would not act to relieve Samsonov. Again, this was proved correct and, after defeating Samsonov, the German Army defeated Rennenkampf at the Battle of the Masurian Lakes. Samsonov committed suicide shortly after his catastrophic defeat. *MS*

Sapping

A "sap" was a trench, often covered or zigzag, from which an approach was made toward an enemy position. The end of the sap was the "sap head." The idea of "sapping" had been in existence since the sixteenth century, and as revived in the World War I could be used as part of mining; to establish lines closer to the enemy; or to reach sniping or listening positions. From their involvement in sapping engineers and miners were often known as "sappers." *SB*

Sarrail, Maurice Paul Emmanuel
(1856–1929)

The French general, Maurice Sarrail was born in Carcassonne. He served as commander of the French Third Army at the First Battle of the Marne, in 1914, before being made commander of Allied forces at Salonika between 1915 and 1917. It was while fulfilling this role that he forced Greek King, Constantine I (the brother-in-law of Kaiser Wilhelm II), to abdicate. After the war, he served briefly (between 1924–25) as High Commissioner in Syria. *MS*

Sassoon, Siegfried Louvain
(1886–1967)

Another of the great poets to have emerged from World War I, Sassoon was born in Kent. He met, and heavily influenced, another of the wartime poets, Wilfred Owen, while both were recovering from military action. Unlike a number of the World War I poets, Sassoon survived the war, although through poems such as *The rank stench of those bodies haunts me still* and *Does it Matter?* he brought home the horrors of trench warfare. Sassoon continued writing, both verse and prose, postwar and his memoirs provide a brilliant view of the war as seen by a young British officer. *MS*

Scapa Flow

For the duration of the World War I, the home base of the Royal Navy's Grand Fleet was the natural anchorage of Scapa Flow, in Orkney. The remote but beautiful islands contained a virtually landlocked deep-water harbor capable of holding the entire fleet several times over. As war approached, the main battle fleet was moved there from Portsmouth, Plymouth, and Chatham. The mainland of Orkney and its largest island of Hoy created a barrier to Scapa Flow, as did a string of islands to the southeast of the mainland (including Lambs Holm, Burray, and South Ronaldsay). The shallow channels of the South Isles were sealed by blockships, torpedo nets, and shore batteries, leaving two entrances to Scapa, through Hoxa Sound to the south and Hoy Sound to the west. The Grand Fleet sailed from Scapa on all of its main sorties, including the one in 1916 which led to the Battle of Jutland. By 1915 the anchorage was well-protected by mines, antisubmarine screens, patrol craft, and shore batteries. No enemy U-boat ever

Below: Russian troops being inspected by General Sarrail soon after landing at Salonika. July 30, 1916. *Chrysalis Photo Library*

Left: Admiral Scheer, commander-in-chief of the German High Seas Fleet at the Battle of Jutland. *Chrysalis Photo Library*

penetrated the anchorage's defensive screen, although the dreadnought battleship *Vanguard* was lost in an accidental explosion as she lay at anchor in July 1917. One of these mines also accounted for the loss of the protected cruiser HMS *Hampshire* in 1916, as it sailed north up the Orkney coast, carrying Field Marshal Lord Kitchener on a diplomatic mission to Russia. At the end of the war, the anchorage also played host to the interned German High Seas Fleet, whose men scuttled their ships in Scapa Flow in 1919. The remains of both German and British battleships still lie beneath Scapa's waters. Scapa also served as the principal base for the British Home Fleet during World War 2. *AK*

Scheer, Reinhard (1863–1928)

Scheer was a protégé of Admiral Tirpitz, and joined the navy in 1870. As a junior officer he assisted Tirpitz in the creation of the High Seas Fleet, and helped develop strategic naval plans. By 1905 he had risen to become a *Kapitän zur See*, and in 1910 he was promoted to the staff as a *Konteradmiral* (rear-admiral). In 1913 he assumed command of the 2nd Battle Squadron (a force of predreadnoughts). Following his promotion to

Vizeadmiral (vice-admiral) he took charge of the more modern 3rd Battle Squadron of dreadnoughts in December 1914. When Admiral Pohl was removed from command in early 1916, Scheer was elevated to the command of the entire High Seas Fleet, hoisting his flag in the dreadnought *Friedrich der Große*. Scheer had developed a reputation as an able, aggressive commander, and his appointment made the clash at Jutland virtually inevitable. Unlike his predecessors, Scheer was willing to risk his fleet in a battle fought on his terms. When it became apparent that the German ambush at Jutland had failed, Scheer displayed considerable skill in extricating his fleet from danger, although he was never allowed to place the fleet in jeopardy again.

Schlieffen Plan
See **Western Front 1914–18**

Scorched earth tactics

Scorched earth tactics involving the destruction or removal of everything in an area to deny its use to the enemy have been known since classical times. The

Below: Demolition by the Germans prior to their retreat from the Somme, 1917. *Chrysalis Photo Library*

best-known employment during World War I was during the German retreat to the Hindenburg Line in March 1917. Booby traps and roadblocks were used to particular effect. *SB*

Serbian Army

The Serbian Army had a fully mobilized strength of around 360,000 men and, while many troops had received limited training, it had a solid professional corps of both officers and men, many of whom had served in the Balkan Wars (1912–13). When war broke out in 1914, the country was still rearming under the direction of Field Marshal Radomir Putnik and, although the standing army was well supplied with modern weapons, many reservists had to make do with older arms. Artillery, much of it French, was of generally modern design but shells were in short supply. Following the loss of much of its equipment in 1915 when the army was forced out of Serbia, it was reequipped by the British and French. *IW*

Above: A column of howitzers being pulled through the mud by troops retiring from Krushivatz. *Chrysalis Photo Library*

Far Left: General Yankovitch of the Serbian Army. *Chrysalis Photo Library*

Left: Serbian troops huddled outside their shelters in a front-line trench during the Battle of Kaimakchalan-Florina, on the Balkan Front. September 1916. *Chrysalis Photo Library*

Serbia, Assault on (1915)

Serbia held considerable strategic importance for the Central Powers, not least because it lay astride the supply route running between Germany and Turkey, as well as Bulgaria, which had sided with Central Powers in October 1915. Serbia had rebuffed a series of Austro-Hungarian invasions in 1914, but faced a much greater threat late the following year. Planned by General Erich von Falkenhayn, the German chief of staff, the invasion force consisted of four armies—one Austro-Hungarian, two Bulgarian, and one German. Operational command rested with General August von Mackensen. The attack began on October 6 and the capital, Belgrade, fell three days later. The Serbian Army fought back with great determination but, caught between enemy armies moving southward from Austria-Hungary and through Montenegro, and westward from Bulgaria, it was forced to retreat to the southwest. What followed was a fighting withdrawal of epic proportions, mostly in the depth of winter. The remnants of the Serbian forces under their commander-in-chief, Field Marshal Radomir Putnik, were finally pushed out of their homeland and retreated into southern Montenegro and Albania during November. Despite the horrors of the "Great Retreat," which included the loss of 200,000 troops and civilians, the remaining Serbian Army, some 85,000 men, survived to fight on. In early 1916 British and French naval vessels were able to evacuate the survivors from various ports in Albania first to Corfu and then to Salonika, which became the base for Serbian operations for the remainder of the conflict. *IW*

Serbia, Operations in (1914)

The bombardment of the Serbian capital Belgrade by Austro-Hungarian gunboats on the Danube River on July 29 heralded the opening of World War I, and was followed by a full-scale invasion on August 12. The Austro-Hungarian invasion force, some 450,000 men under General Oskar Potiorek, was opposed by an equal number of Serbian troops under Field Marshal Radomir Putnik and 40,000 Montenegrin allies. Making skillful use of the mountainous terrain, the Serbians repulsed Potiorek's troops at the Battle of the Jadar River, which

ended on the 21st. A second invasion was launched by the Austro-Hungarians on September 7, but this also ended in defeat—at the Battle of Drina River—and Potiorek was forced to withdraw from Serbia once again. Weeks past while the Austro-Hungarians built up their strength and laid plans for a third invasion. The attack commenced on November 8, and this time the Serbians were forced to abandon Belgrade, which was occupied by Potiorek's troops on December 2. In reality, the Serbian retreat had been planned to tire the Austro-Hungarians and stretch their supply lines to the limit. Sensing these aims had been achieved, Putnik counter-attacked along the line of the Kolubara River on December 2 and the Austro-Hungarian Army collapsed after two days of hard fighting. Serbian losses totaled some 170,000 men, while the Austro-Hungarians suffered more than 225,000 casualties in the campaign. Belgrade was recaptured and Serbia was entirely free of enemy troops by the 15th. Potiorek was dismissed and replaced by Archduke Eugen. There was no further action in this area until October 1915. *IW*

Shcherbachev, Dmitri (1857–1932)

The Russian general Dmitri Shcherbachev commanded IX Army Corps at the start of the war in the east before commanding the Seventh Army during its failed offensive along the River Strypa in early 1915. He again attempted a breakthrough along the Strypa at the start of the Brusilov Offensive in June 1916 with similar lack of success until a minor attack at Jaslowiec on the 4th of the month destroyed the southern Austro-German Army under Bothmer. In April 1917 he took command of Russian forces in Romania, where he remained until the Treaty of Brest-Litovsk ended the war in the east.

Smith-Dorrien, Sir Horace Lockwood (1858–1930)

The British General Smith-Dorrien was born in Hertfordshire. After serving in the Zulu War, India, and Egypt, he served as a battalion commander at the Battle of Omdurman in 1898. Back in Britain after 1907, he was one of the powers behind the creation of the Territorial Army. His role in World War I

was relatively limited—he was relieved of his command of the British II Corps in April 1915 after he had ordered his troops to withdraw following a gas attack at Ypres. He remained in the army until retirement in 1923, being killed seven years later in a road accident. *MS*

Smuts, Jan Christian (1870–1950)

Although ultimately to side with the Boers during the Second Boer War, Smuts, who was born in 1870 in the Cape Colony, received his university education at Cambridge. Becoming a lawyer, he sought a compromise between British and Boer before the war, but then acted as a Boer commander. He assisted in the negotiation of the Treaty of Vereeniging, which settled the war, and then entered politics, being first elected in 1907. He acted as the South African Colonial Secretary. With the outbreak of World War I, he served with the forces that invaded German Southwest Africa (1914–15) before commanding the Allied troops in German East Africa, capturing Dar-es-Salaam in September 1916. In March 1917 he traveled to London and joined the Imperial War Cabinet; while in Europe he undertook negotiations with the Austrians in the hope of brokering a separate peace. He attended the postwar peace negotiations and also helped establish the League of Nations. He became Prime Minister of South Africa in August 1919, holding the post until 1924. He remained active in politics during the interwar years, again becoming Prime Minister in September 1939 (until 1948). During World War II he was an influential figure at a number of conferences. Smuts was made a field marshal in 1941. *MS*

Snipers

"Sniping," in the sense of hunting birds or sharpshooting, had been known in the eighteenth century yet was undeveloped as a military art in Europe in 1914. Many big-game hunters and foresters brought civilian skills and sporting weapons to the front, and ad hoc sniping duels were the result. Elephant guns were used in an attempt to penetrate defensive shields and snipers' loops. By 1915 efforts were in hand both to improve sniping equipment and tactics. The Germans fitted telescopes to their G98 service rifles, and there were experiments with

hyposcopes that allowed rifles to be fired from below the parapet, and "rifle batteries" which allowed one or more weapons to be set up and fired on predetermined targets even at night. By 1916 sniping was highly developed. The British Army established schools of scouting and sniping, and camouflaged "robes" and "crawling suits" of surprisingly modern appearance were produced. Sniper scopes were issued, several per company in most armies. Small factories behind the lines produced dummy figures, camouflage nets, and hides. Tactics were similarly advanced so that snipers now commonly acted in pairs forming an advanced screen in front of the main lines. *SB*

Left: Camouflaged snipers of U.S. 168th Infantry, at Badonviller, May 18, 1918.
Chrysalis Photo Library

Below: Sniper of the London Irish Rifles in Albert using a telescopic sight August 6, 1918.
Chrysalis Photo Library

**Above: AEF 42nd
Division snipers,
Badonviller, May 18,
1918.** *Collection of
Bill Yenne*

**Left: American snipers
from 28th Infantry
Regiment, Bonvillers,
May 22, 1918.** *Chrysalis
Photo Library*

**Below: German sniper's
shield.**
Chrysalis Photo Library

Somme, Battle of the

The Somme proved to be the principal Allied attack of 1916 and the baptism of fire of Britain's "New Armies." The battle lasted from July 1, 1916, until November 18, 1916, but it is the first day that has attracted so much attention throughout the years, principally due to the enormous casualties suffered by the British on that day. In its original planning the offensive was conceived as a joint Anglo-French affair; the French commander-in-chief, General Joffre, saw it as a battle of attrition, designed to weaken the German reserves irretrievably rather than as a means of breaking the German lines on the Western Front. However, by the middle of 1916 this plan had been superseded. On February 21, 1916, the German bombardment opened around the forts of Verdun, and the French were soon locked into a battle of attrition of the German Army chief of staff's making. Von Falkenhayn planned to "bleed France white" and blunting this offensive took almost all the available French manpower. The French urgently needed German reserves to be diverted from the killing fields around Verdun and pressed Haig, the new commander of the BEF following the deposition of Sir John French, to bring his offensive forward in order to achieve this. Haig agreed and brought forward the date of the planned offensive from August 1 to July 1. Haig's initial plan was simple: there would be the most intense bombardment of the German trenches ever seen on the Western Front that would destroy the German front-line defenses and cut their defensive belts of barbed wire, following this the men of Rawlinson's Fourth Army would advance in from their lines around Albert toward Bapaume, supported by diversionary attacks in the north by Third Army under General Allenby and in the south by the French Sixth Army under Fayolle. The opposition was expected to be minimal due to the intense bombardment. Following this the massed cavalry reserve was to break through to Cambrai and Douai, thus splitting the German lines in two. The principal means of breaking through was the preliminary artillery brigade, and the BEF had mustered as many guns as

Above Right and Opposite: Over the top! Somme 1916. *Chrysalis Photo Library*

Right: The Battle of the Somme. *Richard Natkiel*

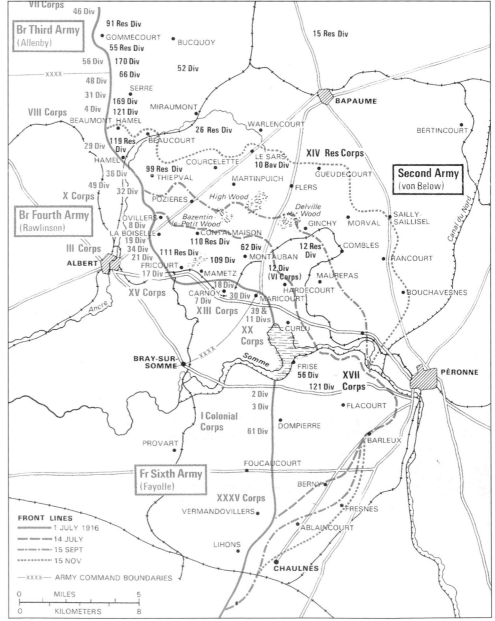

WORLD WAR I: A VISUAL ENCYCLOPEDIA

SOMME, BATTLE OF THE

could be found. There were 1,500 sited on their front, with approximately the same number covering the French Sixth Army's front to the south. However, the German positions on the Somme were formidable. They had been able to dig deep, siting their dugouts far beneath the ground so that it would take a direct hit by a heavy howitzer shell to collapse them. The British artillery also suffered two main drawbacks. First, a considerable proportion of their shells were badly made and did not explode at all. Second, the task that they were allotted, breaking the German wire, was a difficult one even with the best of ammunition. It was possible for shrapnel shells, which made up the vast majority of the British shell stockpile, to break up concentrations of barbed wire. However, the fuse had to be set absolutely right in order to achieve this. The conditions on the front in June 1916 were not suited to this sort of painstaking practice and a depressingly high proportion of the German wire remained uncut when the infantry went forward on July 1. On that morning, twenty-seven divisions went into the attack, eighty percent of them from the British Army. Against them there were only sixteen divisions of the German Second Army. The attack was started by the explosion of seventeen large mines at 7:30am, the first of which went off ten minutes early. Haig had wanted the attack to be at dawn, but the French insisted that it be delayed so that the morning mist, so prevalent on the Somme, could be given time to disperse. The first attacking wave of the offensive went over the top from Gommecourt to the French left flank just south of Montauban. The troops were ordered to advance slowly and in dressed order. Partly this was due to the sheer weight of their equipment, partly because Rawlinson, against Haig's advice, had ordered the slow pace. He did not believe that the untested divisions of the New

Army would be capable of moving in staged rushes. This slow pace, combined with an early lifting of the barrage, gave ample time for the German defenders to leave their dugouts and man their front-line positions. The result was an absolute slaughter of the first attacking waves. On the first day of the Somme the British Army lost over 58,000 casualties, the vast majority in the initial attacking waves. To the south the French made better progress. They had had the advantage of a higher proportion of heavy artillery to their front and they also advanced in small groups, rushing the German front line. However, they consolidated their gains rather than exploiting them and the advance ground to a halt in that sector as well. Despite the slaughter of the first day the offensive continued, making limited gains across the length of the front. The British Fourth Army had secured the first line of German trenches by July 11 and

Far Left, Top: : British Mk. I tank, September 25, 1916.
Chrysalis Photo Library

Far Left, Bottom: Battle of Albert: the attack on La Boisselle. Tyneside Irish Brigade of 34th Division advances, July 1, 1916.
Chrysalis Photo Library

Above and Left: Battle of Albert: 12th Glosters advancing parallel to the Bucquoy-Achiet road, August 21, 1916.
Chrysalis Photo Library

Above: Battle of the Somme: artillery falls on German trenches, July 1, 1916.
Chrysalis Photo Library

Above Left: British heavy tank Mk. I (note tail wheels) advancing in battle at Flers, September 15, 1916. *Collection of George Forty*

Left: Bazentin Ridge, July 14–17, 1916. Officer observing from church ruins.
Chrysalis Photo Library

German reserves started to be transferred from the Verdun front to bolster the line, thus fulfilling at least one of the objectives of the battle. There were also some local successes, such as when the ANZAC Corps managed to take Pozières village on July 23. Due to Haig's conviction that the German Army was on its last legs, the battle was maintained throughout the summer and into November. On November 13 the British made a final effort on the Somme in the Battle of the Ancre, in which they captured the field fortress of Beaumont Hamel. Shortly after this the poor weather conditions meant an end to the offensive. During the attack the British and French had gained less than ten miles, this for the cost of over 420,000 British and over 200,000 French casualties. However, the Germans are estimated to have lost over half a million casualties, particularly among their NCOs and junior officers, which was to cost them dearly in the years to come. *MC*

Above Left: Battle of the Somme: newspaper says "A very satisfactory first day." In fact it was the worst day in British Army history with 58,000 casualties. *Chrysalis Photo Library*

Left: British field guns during the German Somme offensive, March 26, 1918. *Chrysalis Photo Library*

Above: Advancing down a trench with bayonets fixed. *Chrysalis Photo Library*

South African forces

At the outbreak of the war South Africa's armed forces comprised a handful of mounted rifle units and artillery detachments backed by the part-time volunteer Active Citizen Force (ACF). In 1915 the authorities organized an expeditionary corps for overseas service with the ACF forming the nucleus. In total, around 147,000 white South Africans were recruited during the conflict, of which 43,000 served in East Africa and 30,000 on the Western Front. Some 10,000 also enlisted directly into the British forces. Around 85,000 Black South Africans, who were prohibited from bearing arms, served in support and labor units. The South Africans suffered around 18,500 casualties, including 6,600 killed. *IW*

South America, Part played in the war

Though World War I was fought on a much greater geographical scope than any war in history, it was by no means the sort of global conflict that World War II would be. Whereas World War II touched virtually every corner of every continent (except Antarctica), World War I was focused primarily on Europe, Africa, the Middle East, and the Atlantic. Most of the nations of South and Central America felt themselves distant from the conflict and maintained their neutrality. As early as 1914, the neutrality was strained as Britain and France were complaining that Colombia, Ecuador, Peru, and Chile were providing services to the German fleet in violation of their neutrality, and Germany made a similar complaint with regard to Britain's relations with Argentina. Later, German ships were seized briefly in Argentina and interned permanently by Chile. In November 1914, the Royal Navy attacked the German cruiser *Dresden* in Chilean waters in the Battle of Coronel, an action in which two British ships were sunk. A continuing naval battle culminated in the major naval battle off the Falkland Islands. Initially, the war hurt the neutral

nations of South America economically because it hindered trade. Britain imposed its "Black List" under which it boycotted companies with ties to Germany or Germans, of which there were many in South America. Eventually, however, ways were found to circumvent strict neutrality and the South American economies rebounded. Though there were sizable British, French and Italian minorities in Argentina, the Argentine government tenaciously held tight to neutrality, hoping to make money doing business with both sides while avoiding bloodshed. However, when German U-boats sunk two Argentine ships, anti-German demonstrations in Buenos Aires led to a severing of diplomatic relations in September 1917. Chile was essentially the opposite of Argentina, that is, it was pro-German and anti-Allies in spirit, while remaining officially neutral. Of course, Chile's copper mines were eyed keenly by both sides and the Chilean economy flourished. When the United States entered the war, Peru and Bolivia sought to curry favor with the North American Goliath because of their anti-Chilean feelings that dated back to the War of the Pacific in 1879. As with Chile's copper, Peruvian copper and Bolivian tin became important commodities on the world market. Ultimately, Brazil was the only South American country to declare war, although several Central American and Caribbean nations would. All of them declared on the side of the Allies against the Central Powers. Of those that remained neutral, most tended to favor the Allies, with the exception of Chile, which was pro-German, and Columbia, which was strongly anti-American because the United States' role in fomenting the recent Panamanian revolution. Mexico, covered by a separate entry in this encyclopedia (see page 263), was probably the most overtly pro-German nation in the Western Hemisphere, although it stopped short of declaring war. Cuba and Panama, both protectorates of the United States, declared on April 7, 1917 a day after the United States. Brazil followed suit on October 26. Four others were added to the list during 1918: Guatemala on April 21, Nicaragua on May 6, Haiti on July 12 and Honduras on July 19. None of these countries would play a crucial role in the war, but Brazil did contribute ships and supplies to the Allied effort. As noted above, the war also created an increased demand for Brazilian—as other South American—raw materials on the world market. After Brazil entered the war, it became an important source of food imports for Britain, France, and other countries in Europe that had been disrupted by the war. Though Brazil did not declare war until October 1917, the Brazilian League for the Allies had been agitating for war as early as 1915. This was counterbalanced by their having been a large number of persons of German extraction in the Brazilian government—including Foreign Minister Mueller—and a sizable German colony in the south that considered itself part of Germany, not Brazil. Indeed, the immigrant communities—especially British and German—in South America were very vocal about supporting their original homelands, and many individuals returned to Europe to fight with these homelands. Eventually, the same catalyst brought Brazil into the conflict that had been America's last straw. In June 1917, as German U-boats exacted their toll of Brazilian shipping in the Atlantic, the scales tipped, and Brazil revoked its neutrality. War was declared four months later and German assets, especially businesses, were seized. While a handful of Brazilian troops were sent to Europe, it would have been 1919 before a Brazilian military presence in the war would have been noticeable. The Brazilian Navy did prove effective in antisubmarine patrols, especially in the South Atlantic. Brazil's participation in the war put the country in a good position to be a key member of the League of Nations. *BY*

Southwest Africa, Conquest of

Neighboring South African troops invaded German Southwest Africa in February 1915. There were two main thrusts—one under the command of General Louis Botha that advanced from Swakopmund and a second under General Jan Christiaan Smuts from Lüderitz Bay and South Africa itself. The outnumbered German forces fought stubborn rearguard actions but were slowly forced into the colony's interior and had to abandon its capital, Windhoek, which was captured by Botha on May 20. Despite German attempts to reach a compromise settlement, Botha moved northward in search of the remaining enemy forces and these were compelled to surrender on July 9. *IW*

Spee, Count Maximilian von (1861–1914)

This aristocratic Prussian officer rose to command the German East Asiatic Squadron based at Tsingtao in China, and his emphasis on gunnery training resulted in the ships under his command winning the navy's gunnery trophy two times in succession. In August 1914 he sailed his squadron across the Pacific, encountering and destroying a British squadron at Coronel in November 1914. He decided to break into the Atlantic, but he encountered the squadron of Admiral Sturdee at the Falklands in December, and he was killed, while all but one of his five cruisers were sunk. *AK*

Spies

The period leading up to the Great War saw the birth of modern espionage. As early as 1904 Germany inserted agents with false identities into Britain, with the primary objective of reporting on naval dockyards. By 1909 the Committee of Imperial Defense had become concerned enough to institute the establishment of a British Secret Service Bureau. Key figures in the new organization were Captain Vernon Kell of the South Staffordshire Regiment and Captain Mansfield Cumming of the Royal Navy. With the outbreak of war there was spy mania, with enemy agents suspected everywhere and internment of enemy aliens in many countries. British intelligence was now divided between information protection and information collecting . Kell, often known as "K," took the defensive work; Cumming, or "C," was devoted to intelligence-gathering. "M" was the cover of

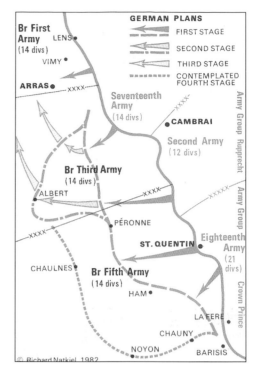

Metropolitan Police Superintendent William Melville, charged with investigating reports of spies. In January 1916 the Directorate of Military Intelligence was formed with the counterespionage section as Military Intelligence 5 (MI5), and the intelligence-gathering arm MI6. Probably the best known spy of the war was Mata Hari (see page 253), a dancer and courtesan recruited by the German consul at the Hague. Captured by the French she claimed that she had also worked for French intelligence in occupied Belgium. She was executed on October 15, 1917. *SB*

Spring Offensive, German (1918)

General Erich von Ludendorff planned a major offensive on the Western Front early in 1918, when Russia's collapse meant that numerical superiority was

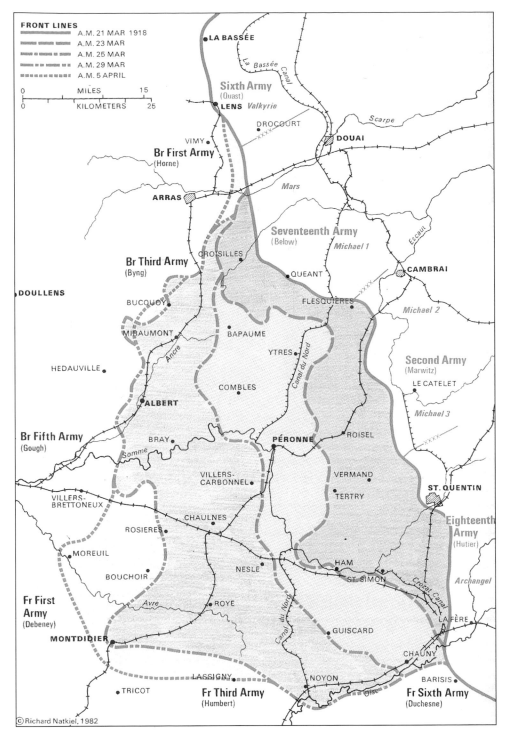

FRONT LINES

	A.M. 21 MAR 1918
	A.M. 23 MAR
	A.M. 25 MAR
	A.M. 29 MAR
	A.M. 5 APRIL

MILES 0 — 15
KILOMETERS 0 — 25

© Richard Natkiel, 1982

finally on the German side. The two major elements of Ludendorff's plan were Operation "Michael," March 21–April 5, and "Georgette," April 9–29. Von Ludendorff hoped to exploit the rifts he saw emerging between the Allied armies, driving a wedge between the French and British forces, while simultaneously severing Allied rail communications with the northern front and recreating the British collapse of March 1918. He failed in all of these objectives. Operation "Michael" began where the British and French armies joined on the old Somme battlefield, as the German Seventeenth, Eighteenth, and Second Armies lined up against British Third and Fifth Armies on March 21 for a surprise attack. Sixty-five German divisions launched a five-hour artillery assault until, under partial cover of gas and smoke and with the misty conditions on their side, German troops advanced across the sixty-mile front. Gough's Fifth Army soon collapsed, exposing Third Army's flank and forcing it to withdraw, abandoning Peronne and the Cambrai salient. German Eighteenth Army drove the splintered remnants of Third Army across the Somme before British and French units were able to plug the gap. Paris itself came under fire on March 25, and the following day Foch was nominated Allied Commander. He would become official commander-in-chief of all Allied forces in France on April 3. Meanwhile, German momentum was beginning to wane. Despite having achieved a fifty-mile salient, only the German Eighteenth Army was still making progress, and when reserve forces challenged their advance at Montdidier, German supply lines began to give. Operation "Michael" was called off with significant loss to both forces. Many specially trained German shock troops had been sacrificed without major achievements, and casualties were running at 163,000 British, 77,000 French and 250,00 Germans. Von Ludendorff's next best option was to attack the British in Flanders, and the "Georgette" assault on the lines south of Armentières began on April 9, as the

Opposite, Above and Above Left: Maps of the German Spring Offensive. *Richard Natkiel*

Opposite, Below: German Offensive 1918. Note overhead wire didn't protect this British trench. *Chrysalis Photo Library*

Left: German column moving toward Amiens, March 1918. *Chrysalis Photo Library*

WORLD WAR I: A VISUAL ENCYCLOPEDIA

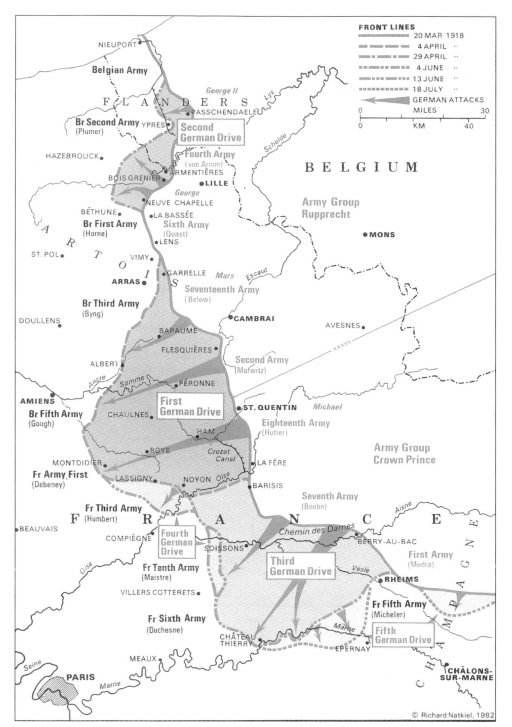

British under Horne came under heavy bombardment from German Sixth Army. On April 10, men from Plumer's Second Army came to Horne's aid, but when Crown Prince Rupprecht launched attacks on either side of Ypres, Second Army forfeited almost all of the ground won at Passchendaele in just three days' fighting. On April 21, Mitry brought his army to the British aid, and Plumer's exhausted divisions could rest. The Germans renewed the offensive on April 24, attempting to cut off Second Army and the Belgians at Mount Kemmel, but despite early advances by German shock troops, Mitry and Plumer stabilized their positions and von Ludendorff's assault was stopped on April 29. The losses incurred by the German Spring Offensive of 1918 crippled both the British and German armies, but when U.S. troops began to arrive in Europe German morale was further depleted. Despite tactical successes, von Ludendorff's Spring Offensive was consigned to history as a strategic defeat as he turned his attention to the impending Third Battle of the Aisne. *MC*

Stockholm Conference

Inspired by the ongoing social upheaval in Russia, which was ultimately to lead to their withdrawal from the conflict, the Stockholm Conference was planned by socialist parties in neutral countries in an attempt to build on ideas of international workers' solidarity in order to end the war. The idea was supported by the Russian government, but opposed by the Allies and the Central Powers, both of which were alarmed by all talk of socialism and attempted to prevent delegates from their countries attending. The planned "conference" ended by being a series of visits to Stockholm by representatives of socialist parties to discuss the situation. *DC*

Stormtroops

The idea of an assault soldier using new weapons and tactics to overcome trenches and stalemate had been born as early as the winter of 1914–15 with the development of the grenade and raiding parties.

Above Left: The limits of the advance. *Richard Natkiel*

Left: German troops rest outside Bapaume, April 1918. *Chrysalis Photo Library*

Parties of *Stoss* (shock) troops were identified within German offensive organizations soon afterward, but new weapons, experience, and training would take a further two years to be assimilated into a battle winning system. In the German Army, *Sturmabteilungen* (shock units) were formed experimentally from 1915, with *Sturmbataillone* (shock battalions) within each army from 1916. Keys to the new methods, used en masse in the Spring Offensive of 1918, were self-reliant small units, in non-linear formations, using a mix of all infantry weapons. Though not called "storm troops" the Allies also worked on developing similar capabilities. *SB*

Straussenburg, Baron Artur Arz von (1857–1935)

Straussenburg joined the Austro-Hungarian army in 1878. After a unremarkable military career, he was appointed Chief of the General Staff by the new emperor, Karl, in succession to Conrad von Hötzendorf. The emperor's rationale was that he felt that von Straussenburg would acquiesce in the monarch's desire for a much stronger personal role in the military decision-making process following the death of the 86-year-old Emperor Franz Josef. Von Straussenburg went into retirement after the war. *MS*

Sturdee, Admiral Sir Frederick Doveton (1859–1925)

Celebrated as one of the luckiest naval commanders of the war, Sturdee began the war as chief of staff to the Admiralty, but clashes with Fisher led to an active assignment. His forces in the South Atlantic caught up with Vice-Admiral von Spee's squadron, and in the Battle of the Falklands (1914) he won a crushing victory. He returned in triumph, despite Fisher's criticism. He went on to command a division of dreadnoughts at the Battle of Jutland (1916), but he was passed over to command the Grand Fleet when Jellicoe was promoted. *AK*

Submarines

In the decades preceding the war, the major maritime powers experimented with submarines, but they were frequently viewed with distaste by the naval hierarchies, and were certainly never viewed as strategic weapons. Germany began to create a U-boat fleet in 1906, when Britain, America, France, and Russia had already created their own nascent submarine forces. Experiments with "Holland" class boats by the British and Americans led to a fleet of more reliable diesel boats. By the outbreak of war, the British boasted a fleet of "D" and "E" class Vickers boats, displacing over 700 tons and capable of submerged speeds of seven knots. Craft such as these rendered earlier petrol-powered submarines obsolete: further developments by both the Germans and Italians created a series of powerful long-range boats, capable of being used as strategic weapons. By 1915, while earlier boats were redesignated as coastal submarines, these later craft became the mainstay of the submarine forces of all the major powers. Improvements in torpedo quality and the abandonment of restrictions on the use of submarines turned these boats into war-winning assets, and the Allies devoted precious resources to combat the strategic threat posed by German U-boats in the Atlantic Ocean. *AK*

Sukhomlinov, Vladimir (1848–1926)

Already approaching age sixty at the outbreak of war Sukhomlinov was initially one of Tsar Nicholas II's most important military advisers, having been appointed war minister in 1909. In that role he had undertaken significant work in overhauling the Russian Army and in modernizing its tactics, often against vested interests. He was influential in ensuring full Russian mobilization in July 1914, but his position was weakened through his personal reputation and his attack on vested interests with the result that he was dismissed in June 1915 after one of his associates had been executed for treason. He was to be arrested in early 1916 and again in September 1917, but went into exile in Germany in May 1918. *MS*

WORLD WAR I: A VISUAL ENCYCLOPEDIA

Above: Landing at Anzac Beach April 25; the evacuation would take place in December.
Chrysalis Photo Library

Suvla Bay and Helles, Evacuation of

When General Charles Munro arrived as General Ian Hamilton's replacement as commander of the Allied forces fighting the stalemated campaign on the Turkish-controlled Gallipoli Peninsula on October 28, 1915, he quickly appraised the situation and argued for total evacuation. This caused considerable controversy, but his superiors were finally won round and their agreement was secured on December 7. The great fear was that the Turkish forces holding the peninsula would cut the withdrawing Allied forces to pieces as they made for their boats. However, Munro was a careful and imaginative commander and made extensive preparations for the two-stage operation. Timetables were issued emphasizing secrecy and ruses were used to make the Turks believe that the Allied trench were still occupied. Nevertheless, thousands of casualties were expected, and much equipment would have to be destroyed or abandoned. Suvla Bay was evacuated first, between December 10–20. Against most expectations, the withdrawal, which was chiefly carried out under the cover of darkness, was an overwhelming success. Some 100,000 troops and 300 artillery pieces were spirited away without any

interference from the surrounding Turks who overlooked the embarkation beaches. The second phase of the withdrawal, the evacuation of those holding positions on Cape Helles, began in late December and continued until January 9, 1916. Over this period some 35,000 men were withdrawn, again without the knowledge of the nearby Turks. The evacuations were a superb feat of military planning— just three men were wounded—yet they could not disguise the total mismanagement of the campaign. *IW*

Suvla Bay, Landings at

By June 1915, it had become clear that the Allied attempts to drive out of their small beach-head at Cape Helles on the Gallipoli Peninsula had failed and that a new strategy was needed to break the deadlock. The local commander, General Ian Hamilton, planned a complex three-pronged operation. First, there was to be a feint by the forces at Cape Helles to keep the Turkish defenders there occupied and draw in any local reserves. Second, the ANZAC troops at Anzac Cove were to break out of their isolated beach-head, drive northward, and link up with the forces committed to the third element of the plan. This consisted of a landing at Suvla Bay on the northern

coast of the peninsula. Once the ANZACs and the Suvla forces had linked up they were to drive across the peninsula, thereby cutting off the Turkish operating farther south at Cape Helles. This was a bold and complex plan that required perfect execution. In reality, very little went right. The operation began on August 6 and the Cape Helles diversion rapidly developed into a costly assault rather that carefully managed diversion. It was called off on the 10th. The drive northward from Anzac Cove was conducted with considerable bravery, but broke down on the first day. Only Suvla offered some initial hope. The assault troops under General Frederick Stopford landed in the face of negligible Turkish opposition but failed to push inland immediately to take the high ground, which was swiftly occupied by significant numbers of Turkish troops led by Mustapha Kemal. Once again the fighting degenerated into stalemate, although the Anzac Cove and Suvla Bay positions were eventually united. *IW*

T

Tanks (Europe)

The idea of the armored vehicle goes back to classical times, and experiments with all of the vital elements necessary for tanks predated 1914: but the combination of tracks, armor, firearms, and the internal combustion engine belongs to the Great War. By 1918 armor theorists would be thinking in terms of the armor, armament, and speed "triangle," and even imagining a strategic role for tank armies. The tank was a British answer to the very specific problems of cutting wire, crossing trenches, and attacking machine guns while remaining protected. As early as 1914 Major E. D. Swinton put forward an idea for a "machine-gun destroyer" and not long after Winston Churchill was urging the development of "armored caterpillar tractors." Several experimental vehicles were produced for the "Landships Committee" but the first really practical design was *Little Willie* put together by Walter Wilson and William Tritton at Foster's of Lincoln. In response to specific War Office specifications improvements were made resulting in the familiar rhomboid which became known as *Mother* in January 1916. After further refinements Mark I was produced in both a "Male" version which included six-pounder guns, and a "Female," which had only machine guns. The debut of the tank on the Somme came in September 1916. Promising

Above Right: August 8, 1918: note fascine and bridges on top of tank. *Chrysalis Photo Library*

Right: British tanks at the Battle of Somme. *Chrysalis Photo Library*

performance led to continual improvement through the Marks II to VIII. In 1918 light Whippet tanks would also be committed. French armor in the form of Schneider and St. Chamond tanks went into action from the spring of 1917, with Renault light tanks seeing service in 1918, some of them with American units. Total production of the German A7V was about twenty vehicles. *SB*

Left: Battle of Amiens: British Mk. V tanks August 22, 1918. *Chrysalis Photo Library*

Below: Third Battle of Ypres, October 12, 1917: British Mk. V tank with a broken track bogged in a shell hole. *Chrysalis Photo Library*

Right: Battle of Polygon Wood: camouflaged tanks and infantry moving up to the attack, September 26, 1917. *Chrysalis Photo Library*

Below Right: Men of U.S. 107th Regiment, 27th Division advancing supported by tanks, Beauquesnes, September 13, 1918. *Chrysalis Photo Library*

Above: French Schneider M16 CA1. It was armed with a 75mm howitzer (visible on front right of tank) and two machine guns. *Collection of George Forty*

Left: Beutepanzer—literally a "booty" tank—a British tank captured by the Germans and impressed into service. *Collection of George Forty*

Above Right: A7V Sturmpanzer; at 30 tons, with a crew of eighteen, it was armed with a 57mm cannon and six MGs. *Collection of George Forty*

Right: French St. Chamond armed with a 75mm gun in nose. *Collection of George Forty*

Right: Battle of Ypres, 1917: tank stranded in shell hole.
Chrysalis Photo Library

Below: Another stranded tank—this one on Westhook Ridge, September 21, 1917.
Chrysalis Photo Library

Tanks (United States)

During World War I, the U.S. Army formed two independent Tank Corps. The first, formed in Europe by General Pershing, was the Tank Corps, American Expeditionary Force, commanded by Colonel Samuel D. Rockenbach of the cavalry. The second, the Tank Corps, United States, was formed in the United States by Secretary of War Newton Baker and commanded by Lieutenant Colonel Ira C. Wellborn, an infantry officer who had been awarded the Medal of Honor for service in Cuba during the Spanish-American War. The standard tank of both corps would be the French-made 7.4-ton Renault light tank, mounting a 37mm gun or a 8mm Hotchkiss machine gun. Some AEF units in the Somme, however, used the British Mark V heavy tank. The first battalion commander and the first brigade commander in the Tank Corps, AEF would be Captain George Smith Patton, Jr. An early advocate of the use of tanks in modern warfare, Patton had previously

been an aide to General Pershing during the 1916 Punitive Expedition into Mexico. As commanding general of the U.S. Third Army in 1944-1945, Patton would go on to be the most famous Allied tank commander of World War II. In February 1918, Patton established the AEF's Light Tank School at Bourg, located five miles from Langres on the road to Dijon. The first ten Renaults were delivered in March, with another fifteen arriving in June. Patton organized the 1st (later 326th) Light Tank Battalion in April, and a second unit, the 327th Tank Battalion, in June. The AEF Tank Corps first saw action in St. Mihiel Offensive in September 1918, with Patton's newly formed 304th Tank Brigade attached to I Corps. Patton fielded a total of 144 Renaults with American crews that were augmented by French tank crews manning 275 tanks that included Renault light tanks, as well as Schneider and St. Chamond heavy tanks. Dogged by mechanical problems, the tanks contributed less than had been hoped to the ultimate victory at St.

Mihiel. Patton pulled his Tank Corps together and it was at full strength for the beginning of the massive Meuse-Argonne Campaign at the beginning of October 1918. Here, the Tank Corps was able to play a bigger role, but again, breakdowns were a major problem. There were twenty-seven American tanks lost to enemy action in the Meuse-Argonne Campaign, but twice that number were written off to mechanical failures. For actions during the campaign, two tank drivers, Corporal Donald Call and Corporal Harold W. Roberts, were awarded the Congressional Medal of Honor. After the war, the two corps were merged, and then, in 1920, the unified Tank Corps was eliminated from the U.S. Army budget by an act of Congress.
BY

Below: French FT17s advancing. The U.S. forces made great use of this excellent, two-man vehicle. It was armed with a 37mm gun.
Collection of George Forty

Above: U.S. FT17 tank and an infantry patrol heading for cover under fire. *National Archives via Chrysalis Photo Library*

Right: U.S. troops and FT17s advance into the Argonne, September 26, 1918. *National Archives via Chrysalis Photo Library*

Below: American armored troops going forward in the Argonne, France, September 26, 1918. *Collection of Bill Yenne*

Above: U.S. FT17 tank crew.
National Archives via Chrysalis Photo Library

Above Right and Right: The Battle of Tannenberg. *Richard Natkiel*

Tannenberg, Battle of

Shortly after the outbreak of war, the commander of Russia's Northwest Army Group, General Yakov Zhilinsky, ordered the two armies under him to capture the German province of East Prussia. Operations began on August 16, with General Paul Rennenkampf's First Army attacking the province from the northeast and the Second Army under General Alexander Samsonov advancing far to the south. Defense of the province rested with General Maximilian von Prittwitz's heavily outnumbered German Eighth Army. Following a minor engagement against Rennenkampf's forces at the Battle of Gumbinnen on August 20, von Prittwitz panicked and ordered the abandonment of East Prussia. This was political unacceptable and, as events proved, militarily unnecessary, and von Prittwitz was hastily replaced by General Paul von Hindenburg, who was called out of retirement, and General Erich von Ludendorff, who had recently won fame for his part in the capture of the Belgian fortress of Liège. The two generals arrived in East Prussia and quickly reevaluated the situation. Although clearly outnumbered, they recognized several factors in their favor. Rennenkampf was advancing extremely slowly and Samsonov was so far to the

south that the two Russian armies were unlikely to link up for some time. Indeed, the bulk of Samsonov forces were moving away from Rennenkampf's

army. Equally, because of the distances involved and the poor state of the rail network operated by the Russians, it was unlikely that they could support each other if one was attacked. Conversely, the German rail system in East Prussia was highly efficient, allowing forces to be switched between the two theaters of operations smoothly and rapidly along interior lines. It was also noted that the Russians were short of essential supplies, not least ammunition. Finally, the German had detailed knowledge of the Northwest Army Group's plans as Russian radio messages were being sent uncoded. Hindenburg and Ludendorff saw that the slow-moving forces of Rennenkampf could be safely masked with little more than a cavalry screen, allowing them to concentrate the greater part of their Eighth Army against Samsonov. In fact, one of von Prittwitz's officers, General Maximilian Hoffmann, had already laid the groundwork for such a plan. One German corps, that of General Hermann von Francois, was sent south by train to take up position on the right flank of the single corps, the XX, that was monitoring the continuing advance of the Russian Second Army. Two other corps, the I Reserve and XVII, marched into position on the German left

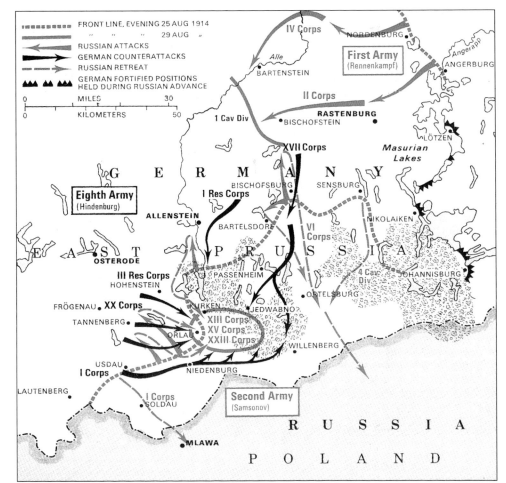

flank where they could oppose the Russian right flank, which was somewhat isolated from the rest of Samsonov's army and strung out along a forty-mile front. The center of Samsonov's army ran into the German XX Corps on August 22 and continued to advance over the following days, thereby inviting German counterattacks on its exposed flanks. The first of these came on the 26th, when the I Reserve and XVII Corps attacked the exposed Russian right, inflicting severe casualties and pushing the survivors back to the border. A day later, Francois cut through the Russian left flank capturing the railway junction at Soldau. With the Russian flanks effectively destroyed or in retreat, the Germans now moved to surround the center. On the 28th Francois and the commander of XVII Corps, General August von Mackensen, were ordered to push northeast and southwest respectively to link up behind Samsonov's center. A day later the encirclement was complete. Russian attempts to break out of the pocket were ineffective, as were attacks by relief forces. The fighting ended on the 30th with the virtual destruction of the Second Army, with only 10,000 men escaping out of 150,000. Samsonov was not one of the survivors—he committed suicide on the 29th. German losses were less than 20,000 men. Tannenberg was hailed as a great victory in Germany and it certainly shook Russia and its allies, yet Russia's reserves of manpower remained enormous. *IW*

Theaters of war

The Great War truly deserved the title of the first "World" war, as it spread around the globe. The **Balkan Front** was first to open with the Austro-Hungarian bombardment of Belgrade from July 29, 1914. Montenegro declared war on Austria on August 5, and Austria began the first invasion of Serbia on August 13. By this time war in the east had become general following Germany's invasion of

Above Left: FT17 in U.S. service August 28, 1918.
Collection of George Forty

Far Left: Armenian girl soldier.
Collection of George Forty

Left: Balkan Front.
Collection of George Forty

WORLD WAR I: A VISUAL ENCYCLOPEDIA

Russian Poland on August 2. Austrian forces entered Poland from Galicia on August 10. Despite long stretches of field works, and periods of stalemate, the **Eastern Front** maintained a degree of fluidity. This was partly due to its length, which ultimately stretched through varied terrain, from the Baltic, through Riga, to the vicinity of Minsk, the Ukraine, Romania, and the Black Sea coast, a distance in excess of a thousand miles. Yet mobility was also influenced by local imbalances of forces and technology, and by Romania's entry into the war on the Allied side on August 27, 1916. This led to the deployment of Bulgarian and German forces and Mackensen's successful campaign in Romania. On the **Western Front** huge armies deployed on relatively narrow fronts and the faltering of the German offensive on the Marne led to the "Race to the Sea," and by late 1914 the digging of trenches from the Belgian Coast to Switzerland. Though comparatively static the Western Front varied considerably in character. In the north the lines met the beaches: in Flanders fields the flat terrain was so near the water table that deep digging was impossible. Around Loos the landscape was dotted with mine works. The Somme was marked by chalk and rolling fields, and further south and east more broken land gave way to the bare fields of the Champagne. The Argonne was more wooded, and the Vosges mountains were at the southern extremity of the Franco-German border. "Sideshows" were legion. Fighting commenced in **Togoland and Southwest Africa** as early as August 1914, with an Indian Expeditionary Force deployed to Mombasa, **East Africa**, in September. Japanese troops were deployed to **China** the same month. In the **Middle East** operations at Basra commenced in November 1914, and soon after British forces were fighting in **Mesopotamia** against the Turks, and in **Egypt** against both the Turks and local tribesmen. Further conflict resulted from the commencement of hostilities between Turkey and Russia. Naval attack in the Dardanelles was followed by Franco-British and Anzac landings in **Gallipoli** in April 1915. The mountainous **Italian Front** opened following Italy's declaration of war in May 1915. Sea and air added new dimensions, with naval actions as far apart as the North Sea, Baltic, South Atlantic, and Far East. *SB*

Left: Grossadmiral von Tirpitz.
Chrysalis Photo Library

Tirpitz, Alfred von (1849–1930)

After joining the Prussian Navy at age sixteen, Tirpitz served on a cruiser during the Franco-Prussian War, then went on to command torpedo-boats and cruisers. After reaching flag rank he commanded a cruiser squadron before becoming the chief of staff of the Baltic Fleet in 1890. The following year he moved to the Naval High Command, where he worked on the development of the High Seas Fleet. An advocate of battleships and gunnery, he argued for a powerful fleet capable of fighting either the French or the Russian battle fleets. In 1896 he became the State Secretary of the Navy, answerable to the Kaiser for naval matters. With Imperial support he ensured the passage of the Naval Bill in 1898 followed by a second in 1899. This funding allowed him to create his navy. Under his supervision the size of the German Navy doubled from nineteen to twenty-eight battleships between 1901 and 1917, and his rapid introduction of a dreadnought program allowed Germany to maintain its position relative to the British fleet, which Tirpitz saw as Germany's main threat. Germany became the world's second largest naval power by 1914, and Tirpitz was the architect of this achievement. AK

Torpedo boats

While the development of the torpedo continued apace, it became inevitable that naval vessels would be introduced which had been specifically designed to carry the weapon. In 1882 the British commissioned the "torpedo ram" *Polyphemus*, which proved highly successful, as did the German torpedo-boat *Zieten*, and the U.S. Navy's *Katahdin*. All these vessels were characterized by a light surface armament, and small, fast hulls (typical displacement was between 200 and 700 tons), allowing the attacker to fire a salvo of three to six torpedoes, then retire to safety. Naval theorists also wanted the craft to be able to attack enemy torpedo boats, so larger vessels with a more powerful armament were also developed, and these eventually evolved into torpedo-boat destroyers, or destroyers. By 1914, torpedo boats were on their way out, replaced by the destroyer, which was a more useful general warship, and its greater size meant it had better seakeeping qualities, range, and endurance. The German High Seas Fleet still employed torpedo boats en masse, as after 1907 German naval construction had concentrated on building dreadnoughts. These torpedo boats were still a potent weapon, particularly when employed close to their home bases, and when operating in squadron-sized groups. *AK*

Torpedoes

Probably the most significant development in naval warfare during the late nineteenth century was the introduction of the torpedo. Robert Whitehead, a British engineer working for the Austrians, produced a prototype compressed-air-powered torpedo in 1866. The key to the Whitehead design was to harness water pressure (which increases with depth) to activate fins, which kept the projectile at a set depth. His first experimental torpedoes were relatively ineffective, but an American officer provided the breakthrough by adding a gyroscopic device which could keep the weapon on course. In 1876 the first torpedo was fired in anger, but it missed. Over the next three decades developments meant that by 1914, torpedoes typically had a top speed of up to forty knots. Torpedo tubes became standard fittings on most warships, while torpedo boats were introduced in 1876 as a custom-built delivery system for the

Above: Hoisting a torpedo aboard a U-boat at Zeebrugge. *Chrysalis Photo Library*

Left: U-boat torpedo stowage.
Chrysalis Photo Library

projectile. The relatively inexpensive torpedo and torpedo boat posed a threat to the supremacy of the battleship, and the introduction of torpedo-firing submarines increased the nervousness of the leading naval powers. During the war torpedoes fired by submarines and small craft accounted for several major warships, including the British armored cruisers *Aboukir*, *Cressy*, and *Hogue*. AK

Townshend, Sir Charles Vere Ferrers
(1861–1924)

Townshend, having served in India, was promoted to the rank of major general in 1915. He led the 6th Indian Division in the campaign in Mesopotamia (Iraq) against Turkish forces. Initially, the Allied offensive proved successful, with Townshend taking Amara and Nasiriya, on the River Euphrates, before capturing Kut, 120 miles from Baghdad, on September 28, 1915. A further advance northward led to his defeat at Ctesiphon,

Above: General Townshend.
Chrysalis Photo Library

twenty-four miles from Baghdad, on November 22, 1915. Townshend then retreated back to Kut, where he surrendered on April 26, 1916, as a result of the failure of three efforts to relieve him. Some 8,000 Allied soldiers passed into captivity. After the war, Townshend was briefly a Member of Parliament before his death. *MS*

Trench construction

Theorists of most nations viewed offensive action as superior to passive defense, and thought that the war would be short. Field works were, therefore ,expected to be of limited use, and nobody planned a trench war. As the British *Manual of Field Engineering* (1911) explained, "field fortification" was a "means to an end," its purpose being to "enable the soldier to use his weapons with the greatest effect" and to "protect him against his adversary's fire." Judicious use of field works would allow areas to be held with reduced garrisons, thereby freeing troops for offensive action elsewhere. Yet in 1914, after both German and French offensive plans had foundered and the attempts of the armies to maneuver round each other in the "Race to the Sea" had proved abortive, there was no "elsewhere." Digging-in all along the front was a visible admission of strategic failure. For immediate digging most infantry were

provided with entrenching tools. French and German examples resembled a short shovel; the American 1910 model a short pointed spade. The British implement was a combined pick and mattock with a detachable metal head fitted to a wooden helve. Full size picks, spades, and other equipment were carried in battalion carts or by engineers. Many trench lines were begun where an advance ended, with each soldier digging his own shallow scrape for prone cover. Further work produced kneeling cover and linked the individual holes together, and finally a full standing cover trench was cut. According to British theory it took troops a few minutes to dig a scrape, about an hour and forty minutes to produce kneeling cover, five hours for proper trenches. Proper fire trenches (*Schutzengraben* in German), were about five feet deep and three feet wide with the dug earth providing a parapet, and a fire step to give defending troops the height to shoot out. Use was made of sods, wood, and other material for revetting. Sandbags were rare initially, but with increasing provision sandbag work became something of an art form, individual bags being used like bricks in elaborate constructions. At intervals

there would be "traverses" or blocks in the trench line to prevent enfilade fire down the trench, and limit the effect of grenades and shells to single bays. In the fully developed trench system, communication trenches linked with a rear support trench, and there were individual posts and bunkers for machine guns, dressing stations, trench mortars, signals, and latrines. Barbed wire was used in ever greater quantity and could be used in a variety of ways. Low-wire and high-wire entanglements were dense linear obstacles; spider wire was odd strands difficult to observe making an area difficult to cross; "knife rests" were prefabricated wooden spars covered in wire which could be moved into place as units. By 1916 it was usual for trench positions to be hundreds of yards deep, and consist of multiple lines of trenches and wire. Lateral lines and communication trenches were used to divide the area into boxes, so that penetration of one part of the line did not compromise the whole. Yet from 1917 there was an increasing move toward more scattered posts, made possible by concrete pill boxes and more machine guns. Such defenses economized on men, and presented less concentrated artillery targets. *SB*

Above: Bulgarian trenches in the Balkans.
Chrysalis Photo Library

Left: Neat trenches of the 15th Yeomanry Battalion, the Suffolk Regiment, in Gaza, summer 1917.
Chrysalis Photo Library

Far Left: Australian troops repairing a communications trench, May 1916.
Chrysalis Photo Library

WORLD WAR I: A VISUAL ENCYCLOPEDIA

Trench warfare

The Western Front, and certain parts of the Eastern Front, congealed into trench lines as early as the end of October 1914. Neither side had planned to fight a trench war, nor did many believe that this could be more than a temporary interlude in a war of movement and aggression. Horrible as the trenches often were, they performed a very useful protective function, and it is indisputable that the periods of open warfare at the beginning and end of the war actually led to more casualties than the relatively static times in between. Some commentators have even gone so far as to suggest that much of trench warfare was a "live and let live" system in which tacit truces and "ritualized" aggression—such as firing artillery at set times—predominated. While this may have been the case in some quiet sectors, it is also a fact that many troops spent much of their time devising ever more sophisticated ways to kill the enemy. Various types of sniping, trench mortars, catapult, grenade, trench club, and dagger were devised by the troops themselves, in addition to whatever horrors could be dreamed up by home inventors. Raids also helped to develop

Above: Mirror periscope in use in trench near Armentières May 18, 1918.
Chrysalis Photo Library

offensive spirits: as early as February 1915 Sir John French was insisting that British troops should engage in constant activity even though they were on the defensive. By 1916 raids had become a deliberate instrument of policy for preventing lethargy, harassing the enemy, raising morale, and gaining mastery of No Man's Land. It is also arguable that raids were indulged in to persuade people and politicians that something was being done at times when all-out attacks were clearly impossible. Raids did help produce ideas like bombing parties and select small assault groups that contained more than one type of weapon, thereby helping to the development of "shock" and "storm" tactics and night offensives. This ultimately contributed to the breaking of trench stalemate. On the other side of the coin, the trenches did produce new "routines" of war. By 1915 it was widely realized that to leave the same unit in the trenches for too long would lead to heavy casualties and demoralization. The French used the rotation of troops to excellent effect

during the Battle of Verdun, and the British became arguably the masters of the idea. Even in a front-line British division a man was unlikely to spend as much as quarter of his time in trenches adjacent to the enemy. Usually a month with such a formation would see a week or less in the front line, with a further week in a reserve line, and the remainder in reserve or rest. Sensible as this was, reserve and rest were likely to include fatigues and training. Equally, frequent rotation also meant many long marches over terrible terrain and many agonizingly slow journeys by train. Daily routines also appeared. Typically a day in the trenches would start with "stand to" when the fire trenches would be manned at dawn, thus being ready at the most likely time of attack. In the British trenches a tot of rum might then be issued to thaw out numb bodies. "Morning hate" with shelling or sniping might serve to remind the enemy of one's existence. Breakfast could then be eaten, cooking depending on whether smoke would give away the position. Inspections, administration, fatigues, burials, and trench repairs would fill much of the rest of the day. Sentries were kept day and night. *SB*

Left: Stretcher bearers at Thiepval September 26, 1916.
Chrysalis Photo Library

Below Left: Tandem bicycle frame used by Germans to generate electricity for trench wireless, September 5, 1918.
Chrysalis Photo Library

Below: Artillery signal rocket rack in a trench held by the East Yorks, January 9, 1918.
Chrysalis Photo Library

Above: Officers of the Staffordshire Regiment in a captured dugout, Beaumont Hamel, November 1916.
Chrysalis Photo Library

Above Right: Reporting to officers in a dugout, November 1916.
Chrysalis Photo Library

Right: Shell bursting among barbed wire, Beaumont Hamel, December 1916.
Chrysalis Photo Library

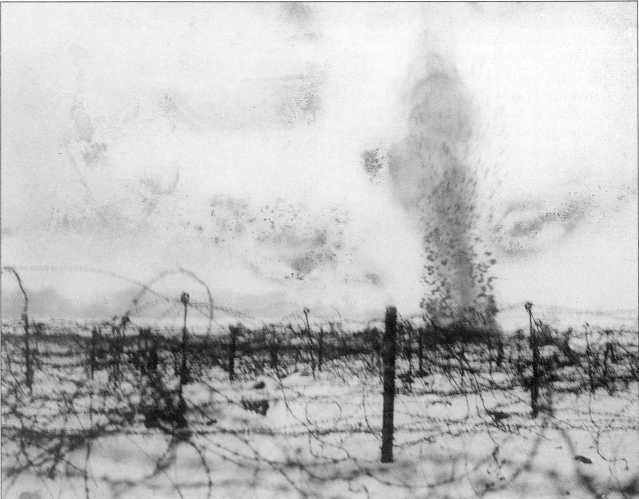

Left: Interior of a dugout of 105th Howitzer Battery, 4th Brigade Australian Artillery near Ypres, August 27, 1917.
Chrysalis Photo Library

Below Left and Below: Conditions in the trenches, particularly when the water table was high, could be made much worse by mud and water as can be seen in these photographs of a working party and Colonel P.R. Robertson, 1st Cameronians, returning to his dugout after doing his rounds, Bois Grenier, January 5, 1915.
Chrysalis Photo Library

Trenchard, Hugh Montague
(1873–1956)

Although now remembered as one of the founders of the Royal Air Force, Trenchard initially served as a soldier. Joining the forces in 1893, he served in India (on the Northwest Frontier with Afghanistan), in South Africa, and in West Africa, before becoming Assistant Commandant of the Central Flying School in 1913. He achieved his wings just before his fortieth birthday and was one of the first twenty pilots in the newly formed RFC—precursor of the RAF—when it was established in 1912. He was the first field commander of the RFC and was Chief of the Air Staff in 1918 when the RAF was created. He was appointed Marshal of the RAF in 1927, two years before his retirement. Under his control, the status of the RAF as a separate element of Britain's armed forces was ensured. From 1931 until 1935 he served as Commissioner of the Metropolitan Police. In 1936 he was created the first Viscount Trenchard of Wolfeton. *MS*

Troopships

The Allied powers made extensive use of troopships during the war, ferrying the British Army across the English Channel from 1914, and Imperial troops to Europe or the Middle East as required. In most cases, converted merchant ships were used, adapting passenger or cargo ships to accommodate and house hundreds of men and their equipment. From 1915 onward, specially converted amphibious landing ships carried landing barges and special lifting equipment to facilitate offloading close to a landing beach. The U.S. Navy employed specially converted passenger vessels as troopships when it ferried the U.S. Army to France in 1917–18. *AK*

Trotsky, Leon (1879–1940)

Born Lev Davidovich Bronstein in the Ukraine of Jewish parentage, Trotsky was one of the pivotal figures in the Russian Revolution of 1917. First arrested in 1898 and sent to Siberia for his political activities, Trotsky escaped and joined Lenin in exile in London in 1902. Returning to Russia for the 1905 revolution (where he acted as president of the St. Petersburg Soviet), he was again sent to Siberia and again escaped. In February 1917, he was in New York when the first revolution of that year occurred. He returned to Petrograd and, by October 1917, was head of the Petrograd Soviet. He was the first commissar for foreign affairs and, as such, played a role in the negotiations of the Treaty of Brest-Litovsk. He then served as commissar for war, creating the Red Army, when the Russian Civil War started. However, Trotsky's influence declined significantly with the death of Lenin in 1924; Stalin was antipathetic to his more international views on revolution and Trotsky was expelled from the Politburo. Initially he was again exiled to Central Asia (in 1927) before being expelled from the country (in 1929). Overseas, however, Trotsky continued to campaign for "permanent revolution" and in 1937, he was sentenced *in absentia* to death. Trotsky was assassinated in Mexico by an ice-pick-wielding murderer, Ramon del Rio, who was acting on behalf of the Soviet secret police. *MS*

Below: Troopship *Mt. Vernon* leaving New York harbor carrying AEF troops in spring 1918. *Chrysalis Photo Library*

Right: Men of the 2nd Scots Guards and 2nd Gordon Highlanders on board SS *Lake Michigan*, October 6, 1914. *Chrysalis Photo Library*

Below Right: The Royal Navy Division en route to Dunkirk aboard *Mount Temple*, October 5, 1914. *Chrysalis Photo Library*

Turkey, War in

Turkey was the most isolated of the Central Powers, with only tenuous lines of communications with its allies in Europe. It was also perceived by the some of the senior figures in the Allied camp as militarily and economically weak. They argued that its early defeat would have several strategic benefits. First, Turkey held the Dardanelles, a vital sea way linking the Mediterranean with the Black Sea, which if opened to Allied shipping would ease the flow of supplies between Russia and Britain and France. Second, the sprawling Turkish Empire bordered or was close to areas that were of key importance to the Allies, particularly the British, whose regional concerns were dominated by the need to protect India and the Suez Canal that linked the vast colony with Britain. Thus Turkey's defeat would remove these worries. It was also recognized that the cohesion of the Turkish Empire was poor. First, the rail network from the heart of the empire to its farther reaches was limited, often confined to single-line tracks, which made the rapid movement of Turkish troops difficult. Second, Turkey contained a number of local peoples, particularly Arabs and Armenians, who wished to establish independent homelands. Thus conventional Allied military operations might be backed by uprisings and guerrilla campaigns by these peoples. Finally, Turkey had long been regarded as a corrupt and efficient regime that might collapse under any degree of external military pressure, and the fighting efficiency of its armed forces was by no means comparable to those of the Allies. Although the Allies conducted prolonged campaigns within Turkish territory from late 1914, they gambled all on a rapid victory. This centered on forcing a way through the Dardanelles to capture Constantinople. However, both a naval attempt and the amphibious assault against the Gallipoli Peninsula failed in 1915–16. These two events highlighted problems that would confront the Allies for much of the war against Turkey—difficult terrain and a harsh climate, operations conducted on a shoestring, and the resilience of the ordinary Turkish soldier. Conventional operations against Turkey centered on three main theaters—Caucasia in the northwest, where Russian forces cooperated with Armenian nationalists; Palestine, where

British-led forces were to act in concert with Arab guerrillas; and Mesopotamia (Iraq), a wholly British theater of operations. Thus the Turks faced three widespread threats, as well as an ongoing commitment to support the other Central Powers in the Balkans. They did suffer significant defeats in Caucasia during 1914–16 that allowed Russian troops to occupy some Turkish territory, but these areas were regained following the collapse of Russia in 1917. In the other two theaters, the Turks were able to contain the threats, albeit it with severe casualties, until early 1917, chiefly by fighting defensive campaigns. However, the British renewed their efforts in both Palestine and Mesopotamia. Turkish losses mounted and soldiers' morale plummeted. Starved of supplies, chiefly due to the reduction of German material aid, and amid growing political turmoil, Turkey concluded an armistice on October 30, 1918. *IW*

Turkish air forces

The outbreak of war found Turkey without an organized air service despite there having been a degree of military air operations beforehand. As a wartime ally of Germany, Turkey received sufficient aircraft such as Albatros and Halberstadt fighters and AEG CIV reconnaissance aircraft, as well as the personnel to man them. The Army Air Service was formed in 1917, and units were soon in action against Russian forces. Turkey also participated in operations in Egypt and the attempted capture of the Suez Canal. Active against the Allied invasion of the Dardanelles, the Turks used among other types, modified Gotha WD13 seaplanes to combat the Short seaplanes of the RNAS opposing them in the Mediterranean area. *JS*

Turkish Army

The Italo-Turkish (1911–12) and Balkan Wars (1912–13) highlighted major weaknesses in the Turkish Army, which had been starved of resources for many years, was riddled with corruption and incompetence, and performed badly during the two conflicts. Attempts were immediately made to rectify these deficiencies, not least the arrival in Turkey of a German military mission under General Otto Liman von Sanders in December 1913 at the behest of the Committee for Union and Progress,

better known as the Young Turks, which had effectively run the country's affairs since 1908. In January 1914 Liman von Sanders was made inspector-general of the Turkish forces, a decision reflecting the parlous state of the country's armed forces, at the behest of Enver Pasha, one of the leading figures in the Young Turks and the country's minister of war. However, Turkey's decision to side with the Central Powers in October 1914 meant that the mission's work had hardly begun before the country went to war. The army was a conscript force that reflected the empire's diverse nature. Arabs, Armenians, Kurds, and Syrians filled the ranks, but Anatolian Turks were considered to be the best and most reliable troops. Members of the Christian and Jewish communities were prohibited from armed service and were enrolled in labor and construction units. Service was through conscription. Around 250,000 men were called up annually but roughly fifty percent of the potential recruits gained exemptions, and probably no more than around 70,000 of the remainder saw service. Under the conditions of the May 1914 Army Act Turkish males were to serve from the age of eighteen, but in reality most became liable on the March 1 after their twentieth birthday. Length of service varied with the branch of the army. Recruits into the infantry, for example, served two years with the regular army (*Nizam*) and twenty-three years split between the regular reserve (*Ikhtiat*), the secondary reserve (*Redif*), and the territorial militia (*Mustahfiz*). The peacetime strength of the *Nizam* was set at around 270,000 officers and men, although this figure was wildly optimistic given the scale of under-recruitment, and expansion on mobilization was supposedly achieved by filling the ranks of the regular army with members of the regular reserve. In August 1914 the army had a paper strength of thirty-six divisions, each with 15,500 men, a figure that was supposed to rise to 19,000 on mobilization. However, these figures were rarely achieved and some divisions were less than one third of their authorized strength, a situation that worsened as the war continued. For example, the three Turkish armies operating in Palestine in 1918 could muster less than 20,000 men in total. There are no really accurate figures on the army's manpower during the war, although estimates suggest that some 3.5 million Turks saw service. Of these some

Above: Turkish cavalry marching in Palestine.
Chrysalis Photo Library

750,000 are believed to have deserted and a further 500,000 were killed, wounded, or hospitalized through various sicknesses, including malaria, cholera, and influenza. The army reached its greatest strength in early 1916 (around 1.5 million men), but suffered a decline thereafter, particularly from the spring of 1917, as the rate of desertion rose rapidly and the supply of replacements dried up in the face of Allied successes in the Middle East. By the most modern standards of the time the Turkish Army was woefully deficient in many areas. Peacetime training for the regular reserve was set at one month per year and one month every two years for the secondary reserve, but these figures were rarely achieved due to financial constraints and the unwillingness of many reserves to take part. Officers of all levels were of variable quality, often having received little more training than the men under them. Some 1,500 had undergone more thorough instruction abroad or at home under German tutelage, but this shortcoming was never really addressed, although it was alleviated to some extent by the presence of German officers—some 200 in 1916 and four times as many by 1917. Many of these occupied technical posts or, at a more senior level, exercised direct

control of Turkish forces in the field. Among such officers were Liman von Sanders, Friedrich Kress von Kressenstein, and Erich von Falkenhayn. Relations between the Turkish and German officers were not always easy, with the former resenting the influence of the latter. Nevertheless, some Turkish senior officers displayed considerable military skills, not least Mustapha Kemal Pasha, who gained fame for his part in the fighting on the Gallipoli Peninsula in 1915–16. Equipment was of variable quality, with much of the most up-to-date being supplied by Germany. With regard to artillery, the chief field guns were Krupp types, supplemented by models supplied by the French firm Schneider-Creusot. Comparatively few heavier designs were available and many of those deployed were often obsolete smoothbores dating from the previous century. The standard rifle was the German Mauser, while machine guns were usually Maxim or Hotchkiss designs. Supply was a constant problem, with everything from uniforms to munitions becoming increasingly scarce. The army was especially ill served by its medical branch, with just 2,500 doctors available for the whole of the war years. Germany's military commitment to its ally in part reflected Turkey's technical weakness—its tiny air force, for example, was under German control and flew German aircraft. Few German units actually fought with the Turks, although the *Yilderim* (Lightning) Force, which

served in the Middle East, did contain German combat units. Despite these many shortcomings, the Turkish Army, especially its individual soldiers, frequently showed great skill, determination, and bravery. However, the quality of the Turkish Army declined markedly from 1917. Heavy casualties and high desertion rates contributed to this, but friction between recruits from the empire's subject nations and ethnic Turks was also a contributing factor. The Turkish Army was chiefly deployed in three main areas: Caucasia, where it faced Russian forces, Palestine, and Mesopotamia, where it was opposed by British-led forces. Other theaters of operations included the Balkans and, most famously of all, Gallipoli. *IW*

Turkish Navy

The arrival of the German battlecruiser *Goeben* and its consort the *Breslau* in Turkish waters in August 1914 precipitated a slide into war for which the Turkish Navy was singularly ill-prepared to fight. The fleet consisted of four old predreadnoughts, supported by two light cruisers and a handful of lighter forces. A contemporary described it as "a weird collection of scrap-iron." Two Turkish battleships were torpedoed by British submarines, but the German warships ensured the Turks retained a powerful squadron, and they contested the control of the Black Sea until the commissioning of the Russian dreadnoughts in 1915. *AK*

U-boat campaign

The Germans were slow to realize the full strategic potential of their U-boat fleet, but given the Allies' clear superiority in surface warships, the development of a powerful U-boat (*Unterseeboote*) fleet proved a logical course of action. When the war began the German Navy had a small fleet of U-boats, many of which were coastal vessels. Nevertheless, while a massive U-boat construction program was initiated, these first U-boats scored some significant successes against British naval targets. On September 5, 1914, the scout cruiser *Pathfinder* was sunk off the Firth of Forth, and just over two weeks later the *U-9* sank the cruisers *Aboukir*, *Hogue*, and *Cressy* off the Dutch coast. Fearful of attacks on an anchorage which lacked anything but the most rudimentary defenses against underwater attack, the Grand Fleet was temporarily moved from Scapa Flow until the anchorage could be properly defended by submarine nets, mines and patrol craft. The loss of the seaplane carrier *Hermes* in October and the predreadnought battleship *Formidable* in January 1915 further demonstrated the potential of the

U-boats. As new vessels became available, the Germans were able to venture further afield, and stepped up their attacks on Allied merchant ships. At first these attacks had been carried out in compliance with the terms of the Hague Convention, with the U-boat surfacing and ordering its victim to stop. After allowing the crew to abandon ship, the merchant vessel was then sunk. By 1915, these niceties had been replaced by the more effective but less chivalrous tactic of sinking the target without warning. In 1915 the Germans declared that the waters surrounding the British Isles formed an exclusion zone, and any vessel inside the area was liable to be attacked, whatever its nationality. This introduction of restricted U-boat warfare resulted in a dramatic increase in the number of Allied surface ships lost to submarine attacks, while other mine-laying submarines operating off major Allied ports caused further losses. As numbers of operational U-boats increased, so too did Allied losses. In all, a total of 306 German and twenty-seven Austro-Hungarian U-boats sailed on operational patrols during the war, and of these, at least 190 were lost in action, through mines, depth-charging, gunfire,

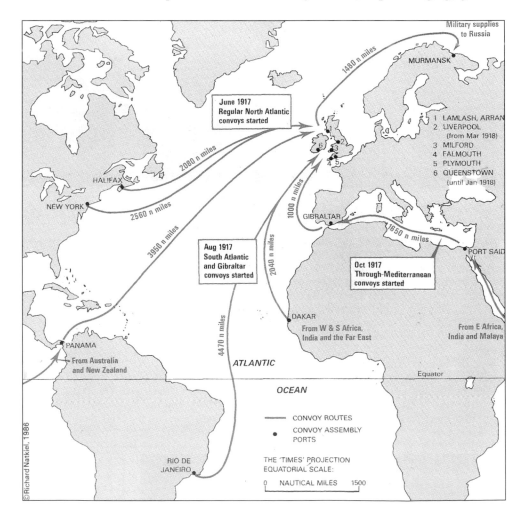

Far Right, Bottom: U-boats savaged British supply lines across the Atlantic and it was only in 1917 that the tide would turn against the Germans. *Chrysalis Photo Library*

Right: Sea routes to Britain at the time of World War I. *Richard Natkiel*

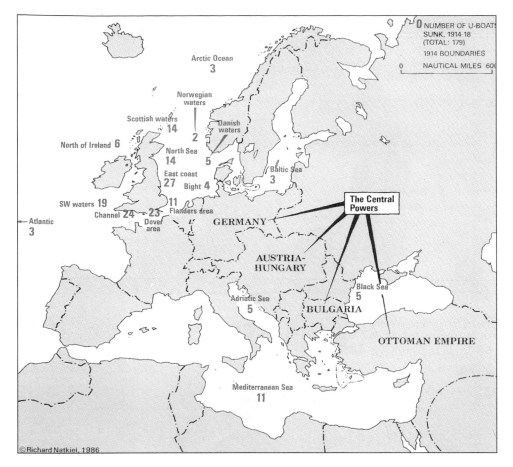

torpedoes, or other causes. By 1916 the Allies had begun to commission a fleet of antisubmarine vessels, and improved antisubmarine barrages helped limit the effectiveness of the onslaught. The height of the campaign came in 1916, when the Germans initiated a fresh campaign against Allied shipping in the western approaches to Britain. In the four months from October 1916 to January 1917, U-boats sank almost 500 ships. Since August 1914, the British merchant fleet alone had lost 2,000 ships, at a cost of 65 U-boats. In December 1916 the Germans initiated "unrestricted" U-boat warfare, in an attempt to starve Britain into submission. If losses remained at their January level

Left: Numbers of U-boats sunk 1915–18. *Richard Natkiel*

Below: The Italian steamer *Stromboli* seen from a U-boat. At the start of the war U-boats would allow the crew of a ship to disembark before torpedoing. *Chrysalis Photo Library*

U-BOAT CAMPAIGN

(368,000 tons of shipping), this would have been achieved within six months. Losses rose from 540,000 tons in February to 594,000 tons in March, and Britain faced a humiliating defeat, as one in four ships crossing the Atlantic was sunk. The tide turned in May 1917, when the British initiated the convoy system, and new directional hydrophones improved the chances of detecting enemy submarines. The entry of American into the war, and the employment of a large numbers of antisubmarine vessels, airships, and escorts also led to a dramatic drop in losses, while the attrition among the German U-boat service increased. Although the campaign continued until the end of the war, the crisis had been averted, and Britain's survival was assured. *AK*

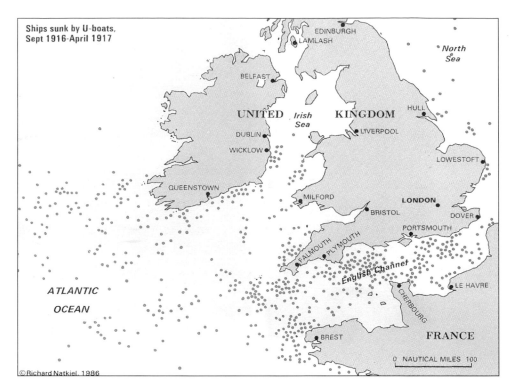

Top: *U8* was sunk on March 4, 1915; here the crew can be seen getting out of the conning tower and into boats. *Chrysalis Photo Library*

Above: USS *Covington* sinking off Brest after being torpedoed by German submarine U-86. July 2, 1918. *Chrysalis Photo Library*

Right and Above Left: Ship losses to submarines around the coast of the UK. *Richard Natkiel*

Left: Krupp's yard with submarines and a destroyer. *Chrysalis Photo Library*

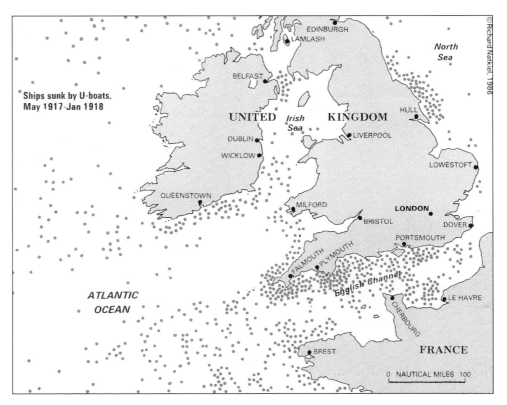

Ships sunk by U-boats, May 1917–Jan 1918

© Richard Natkiel, 1986

U-BOAT CAMPAIGN

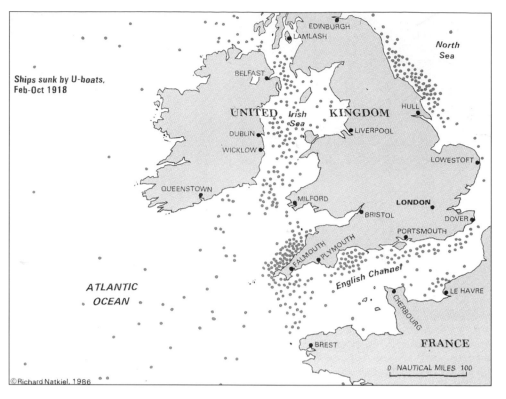

Ships sunk by U-boats, Feb-Oct 1918

© Richard Natkiel, 1986

Above: The USS *Santee*, after being struck by a German torpedo on her maiden voyage. *Collection of Bill Yenne*

Below: American tanker *Illinois* sinking into the English Channel after being fired on and sunk by a German submarine from which this photograph was taken, March 18, 1917. *Chrysalis Photo Library*

Bottom: The Cunard liner *Ausonia* sinking after being torpedoed 600 miles out in the Atlantic Ocean, 1918. *Chrysalis Photo Library*

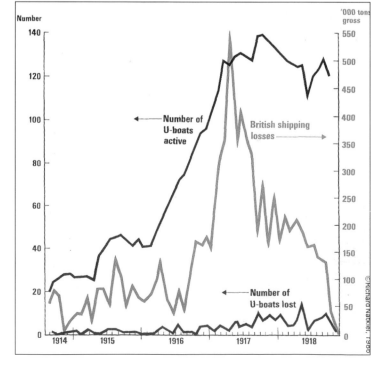

U-boats

Due to opposition from Tirpitz, Germany was slow to embrace submarine warfare, but in 1906 *Unterseeboot No. 1 (U-1)* was built in Kiel. This prototype led to others, and by 1914, the German Navy had six diesel-powered U-boats available (*U-19* to *U-24*). Earlier craft were small coastal boats, of little offensive value. When the war began the navy ordered seventeen, then fifty more. These early U-boats displaced 1,200 tons and were capable of speeds of seventeen knots on the surface, and seven knots under water. As an example of the early boats, *U-9* was completed in 1910, and displaced 611 tons, and was operated by a crew of twenty-eight men. She was fitted with four torpedo tubes, capable of firing eighteen-inch (45cm) torpedoes. By

Top: Officers of the watch on the top of the conning tower. *Chrysalis Photo Library*

Above: The largest classes of U-boat were very big indeed and the U-cruisers had a range of over 12,000 miles. This is a cruiser of the "U139/141" class. *Chrysalis Photo Library*

Left: Crew on deck giving a good idea of the size of the smaller UB type boats. *Chrysalis Photo Library*

Opposite, Top Right: Ship losses to submarines around the coast of the UK. *Richard Natkiel*

Opposite, Bottom Left: Ship tonnage lost to submarines during the war. *Richard Natkiel*

1915, 900-ton diesel-electric boats were introduced into service, with a far greater range. Unlike their predecessors, these later boats were capable of operating far out into the Atlantic Ocean. In addition, the Germans made use of minelaying boats (the "UC" class) capable of laying up to eighteen mines at a time. Apart from these oddities, the later-war patrol U-boats proved to be some of the most effective weapons in the German arsenal. *AK*

Left: U42 alongside *U35* in the Mediterranean, May 1917. *Chrysalis Photo Library*

Right: U-boat crew signaling to an aircraft. *Chrysalis Photo Library*

Below: *U35* about to submerge, May 1917. *Chrysalis Photo Library*

Bottom: *U42* comes alongside *U35*. *Chrysalis Photo Library*

Udet, Ernst

Unlike many of his contemporaries Ernst Udet survived the war and his record of sixty-two aerial victories made him the second highest scoring ace after von Richthofen. He flew with Jastas 15, 37, and 11 before becoming CO of Jasta 4 and during his service with that unit, between May 20 and September 26, 1918, Udet scored thirty-four victories before receiving the wounds that effectively put him out of the war. *JS*

United States air forces

The non-availability of any American scout or "pursuit" type suitable for combat in 1917 led to the U.S. Air Service purchasing aircraft of French origin to equip its units sent to Europe. Starting life as the flying branch of the Signal Corps, the USAS was formed after American pilots had flown in combat attached to French and British squadrons in France, starting in April. The first two USAS units, the 17th and 48th Aero Squadrons, flew British Sopwith Camels while Nieuport 28s, largely rejected by the French, were snapped up to equip the 94th and 95th. First in action on April 14, 1918, the

94th marked the day with two victories over their German rivals, Jasta 64. The subsequent arrival of men of the 27th and 147th Squadrons enabled the formation of the 1st Pursuit Group which encompassed the 94th and 95th. With American nationals also flying the SE5a and Sopwith Dolphin, as well as the Camel, the New World was well represented on the Western Front by mid-1918. From July conversion of the USAS squadrons from the Spad VII to the Spad XIII had begun although individual pilots opted to stay with their RFC or French units until the end. Some USAS units stayed loyal to the Spad VII, which was flown operationally by the 41st, 103rd, 138th, 139th, 141st, and 638th squadrons. *BY*

United States aircraft

When the United States entered the war, the Aviation Section of the U.S. Army Signal Corps had only 250 aircraft. None of these was suitable for combat, and no practical American-designed warplane was anywhere near production. Aviation may have been born in America, but was nurtured in Europe, and by 1917, the United States was no longer a first-rate power in terms or aeronautical technology.

When General Billy Mitchell formed the first AEF Air Service combat squadrons in Europe in 1917, they were equipped with French Nieuports and Spads. The British-designed de Havilland DH-4 was license-built in America by various companies—including Boeing. It was probably the only aircraft built in the United States that actually served in combat and then only marginally. Where the United States did excel during the 1914–18 period was with the excellent Liberty aircraft engine, and with the Curtiss JN-4 Jenny. While the Jenny was no combat aircraft, it was a reliable trainer. Curtiss built them fast enough, and in sufficient quantities, that American airmen were thoroughly prepared to take their place alongside Europe's best pilots. The JN series, especially the JN-4, had the distinction of being produced in larger numbers than any other American airplane of the 1914–18 period or before. Only eleven JN-1 and JN-2 aircraft and two JN-3s had been built, with two delivered to the navy as floatplanes, and the rest delivered to the U.S. Army through 1916 to equip its 1st Aero Squadron. However, nearly 8,500 JN-4s were built, including 2,765 examples of the JN-4D, the most widely produced variant. *BY*

Opposite: Oberleutnant Ernst Udet with his Fokker DVII.
Chrysalis Photo Library

Above: RE18 of Escadrille Lafayette looping.
Official U.S. Air Force via Chrysalis Photo Library

Left: Alexei Shiukov with his Morane Parasol aircraft.
Chrysalis Photo Library

WORLD WAR I: A VISUAL ENCYCLOPEDIA

403

U.S. Army

The U.S. troops in Europe were organized within what was called the AEF (American Expeditionary Force; see page 22), which was primarily composed of U.S. Army troops—with U.S. Marine Corps units attached. The AEF was under the command of General John J. Pershing, whose rank increased from major general (two stars) to general (four stars) as he took command of the AEF in the field. AEF had a Quartermaster Corps, an Air Service, and various administrative organizations, but ground combat forces were contained with its First Army, which was directly under Pershing's command. AEF organization was theoretically capable of containing several U.S. Army numbered armies as they became administratively necessary in the chain of command between the AEF itself and the constituent divisions. First Army remained under General Pershing's direct command until October 1918. At that time, with the First Army embroiled in the Meuse-Argonne Campaign,

Right: American officers of the 305th Machine Gun Battalion, 77th Division consulting a map with a British staff officer, Watten, May 19, 1918. *Chrysalis Photo Library*

Below: Strange camouflage supposed to conceal him while climbing trees. A member of Company "F," 24th Engineers, Army Engineer Corps, he stands in front of a building at American University in Washington, D.C. that is camouflaged to represent a fence and trees. *Collection of Bill Yenne*

Above: The homecoming parade for the AEF's 364th Infantry, Los Angeles, CA, April 22, 1919.
Collection of Bill Yenne

Second Army was created and given responsibility for the reduced St. Mihiel Salient for an eventual thrust against Metz. General Hunter Liggett was given command of First Army, and General Robert Lee Bullard was given command of the Second Army. In the AEF chain of command, both, in turn, reported to General Pershing. Because of the need to coordinate tactics and operations of a number of national armies involved in the war effort, the Allies had created a unified Allied command for the Western Front in April 1918. This plan called for a supreme Allied commander to head the unified command. He would be Marshal Ferdinand Foch, chief of the French general staff. Under him were the three non-French national commanders— Field Marshal Sir Douglas Haig of Britain, King Albert I of Belgium, and General Pershing of the United States— all of who retained considerable command authority. The basic building block of the AEF (as with most armies) was the division. During World War I, the U.S. Army consisted of twenty Regular Army divisions, numbered 1st through 20th; seventeen National Guard divisions, numbered 26th through 42nd; and eighteen National Army divisions) (Regular Army divisions created during and for the war), numbered 76th through 93rd. Of the latter, the 92nd and 93rd

were "Colored" or African-American divisions. A total of forty-two of the above divisions had reached AEF (and its two constituent numbered armies) by the time of the Armistice. The 1st Division was the first to arrive in France (June 1917) and the first to have its troops enter combat (October 1917). The 2nd Division was the second to arrive in France (October 1917), but the fourth to have troops in action (March 1918). Both the 26th and 42nd Divisions arrived in France in November 1917 and had troops in combat in February 1918. At the end of 1917, the AEF had five divisions in France, the above four plus the 41st Division. The 32nd Division arrived next (February 1918), followed by the 3rd and 77th Divisions in April 1918. Nine divisions (the 5th, 27th, 35th, 82nd, 4th, 28th, 30th, 33rd, and 80th) arrived during May 1918. Though the decision had been made to commit AEF troops as integral units, it was to be several months before division-strength units entered the line. For example, smaller component units of the 1st, 2nd, 26th, and 42nd Divisions had all seen combat though March 1918, but it was not until the end of April that the 1st Division became the first American division to go into combat as a division. Both the 2nd and 3rd Divisions followed in June 1918, and the 26th, 42nd, 32nd, 27th, 4th, 28th, and 30th Divisions were all in the line as complete units by the end of July. By the time of the Armistice, twenty-eight of the forty-two divisions

sent to Europe had seen combat. Of these twenty-eight, all but four had, by November 11, entered the line as integral division-strength units. *BY*

U.S. artillery

The U.S. Army entered World War I with 900 artillery pieces, including only 544 three-inch (75mm) guns. As was the case with aircraft, tanks, and other specialized equipment, the AEF was dependent upon the Allies for much of its artillery. The most common and most important AEF artillery piece was to be the so-called "French 75." Technically this was the French-made 75 mm Model 1897 field gun, of which more than 17,000 were supplied to the AEF. It was an inventive advancement in the gunner's art insofar as its recoil system consisted of two hydraulic cylinders, a floating piston, a connected piston, a head of gas, and a reservoir of oil, thus permitting a soft, smooth operation. The French 75 could throw a sixteen-pound shrapnel shell or an 11.75-pound high explosive round 9,000 yards. Interestingly, there were still French 75s in U.S. Army inventory in World War II, and the gun remained in use around the world until the latter part of the twentieth century. Other French artillery that was available to the AEF included the Schneider 105mm howitzer, with a range of 6,000 yards; the Model 1897 105mm gun, with a range of 13,400 yards; the Model 1898 155mm howitzer, with a range of 7,650 yards; and the Schneider 155mm howitzer, with a range of 10,500–13,300 yards. British equipment included the Mk. I eighteen-pounder, with a range of 7,000 yards; the 4.5-inch howitzer, with a range of 7,000 yards; the thirteen-pounder, with a range of 5,900 yards; the sixty-pounder with a range of 10,300 yards; the 12.5-pounder mountain gun, with a range of 5,800 yards; the twenty-pounder mountain howitzer, with a range of 5,800 yards; and the six-inch howitzer, with a range of 10,000–11,600 yards. Indigenous production of artillery pieces in the United States was practically nil through 1917 and did not reach significant numbers until the summer of 1918. From April 1917 through July 1918, only a hundred complete units had been produced in the United States. However, American industry geared up quickly, producing 420 units in October, the peak month, and 357 in November. The total produced from August 1918 through April 1919 would be 2,977,

which was roughly equal to what had been manufactured in Britain or France and used by American units. In terms of artillery ammunition, the United States had 1.4 million rounds on hand in April 1917, and production of additional supplies did not get underway until early 1918. By August, production was exceeding two million rounds monthly. As with artillery pieces, the peak was hit in October 1918, with 3.07 million rounds. Through April 1919, twenty million artillery shells were made in the United States. Ironically, much of this inventory was stockpiled, eventually used in Europe during World War II, especially during the difficult battles of the winter of 1944-1945. Perhaps the most famous of American artillerymen to serve in World War I was Captain Harry S. Truman, who commanded Battery D of the 129th Field Artillery, 35th Division, Kansas and Missouri National Guard. Arriving in France with the 35th Division in May 1918, he would later serve as President of the United States from 1945 to 1953. *BY*

Above Left: A U.S. 75mm gun crew. *Collection of Bill Yenne*

Left: A U.S. 155mm howitzer battery near Samongneux, November 3, 1918. *Collection of Bill Yenne*

Below: A 340mm gun manned by AEF Coast Artillery Corps firing in the vicinity of Nixeville, September 26, 1918. *Collection of Bill Yenne*

Left: A twelve-inch coastal defense gun and crew, Ft. Andrews, Boston. *Collection of Bill Yenne*

Below Left: 40th Division review at Camp Kearny, San Diego, March 9, 1918. *Collection of Bill Yenne*

Right: President Wilson before Congress, announcing the break in the official relations with Germany on February 1, 1917. *Collection of Bill Yenne*

been the largest engineering project in American history, but it was paid for mostly by the private sector—albeit with generous governmental incentives (such as land grants). Of the overall total expenditure on World War I, the largest proportion, sixty-four percent, went to the U.S. Army. Of this, forty-four percent was spent on the logistical expenses through the Quartermaster Corps, twenty-nine percent on ordnance and thirteen percent on payroll. In addition to the sum actually spent on the war, the U.S. government loaned $8.85 billion ($87.6 billion in turn-of-the-twenty-first-century dollars) to various Allied governments. Of the nations involved in the war, only Germany, the British Empire, and France spent more than the United States, although the Austro-Hungarian Empire spent nearly as much. The expenditures by the United States were calculated to have been 9.6 percent of the United States' national wealth. The equivalent figures for other nations were fifty percent for Germany, forty-five percent for the United Kingdom, and thirty-nine percent for France. The United States' expenditures were about one-eighth the total cost of the war and about a fifth of the cost to the Allied nations. During the period of World War I, national debt as a proportion of national wealth grew from 0.5 percent to eleven percent in the United States, from 1.5 percent to fifty percent in Germany, from four percent to forty percent in the United Kingdom and from ten percent to forty percent in France. *BY*

United States, Economic effects of the war on the

The American participation in World War I was the most expensive thing that the U.S. government had ever undertaken. It was observed at the time that the cost of the war had been slightly less than the entire federal budget for the years 1791 through 1916. Estimates of the total cost to the United States vary, but it has been suggested that the total cost to the U.S. economy was in the area of about $325 billion in turn of the twenty-first century dollars. To finance the war, the U.S. government increased income and excise taxes, instituted a war-profit tax, and sold war bonds. Treasury disbursements for the twenty-five months from April 1917 through April 1919 (when the troops had been brought home from Europe and demobilization was completed) totaled $23.5 billion. Of this, $1.65 billion were

considered to have been unrelated to the war, leaving a total cost to the federal government of $21.85 billion, which translates to $216 billion turn of the twenty-first century dollars. The cost to both sides in the American Civil War of 1861–65—previously the most expensive undertaking in American history—had been slightly less than half this sum in constant dollar terms. By comparison in turn of the twenty-first century dollars, the American Revolution cost the United States about one billion dollars and the Vietnam War cost $500 billion. By this measure, America's most expensive war, World War II, cost the United States almost three trillion dollars. The cost of the Panama Canal, the most expensive engineering task yet undertaken by the United States had been $635.6 million in turn of the twenty-first century dollars. The construction of the first transcontinental railroad, completed in 1869, had

United States, Entry into the war by the

President Woodrow Wilson had been reelected in 1916 on a platform of keeping the United States neutral and out of "Europe's War." He wanted to maintain U.S. neutrality, and public opinion supported that stance. Initially, American sympathy with the Allies was by no means unanimous, and there was a strong pro-German sympathy. However,

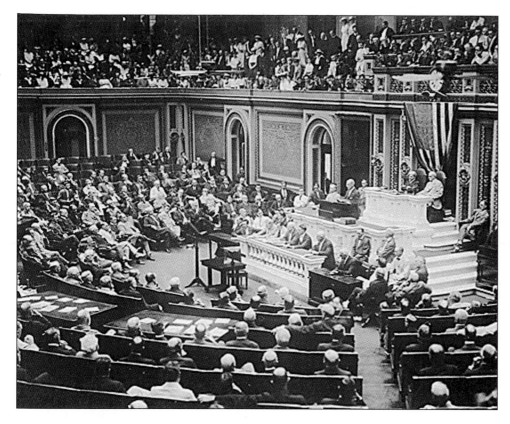

this point of view gradually changed, due primarily to Germany's unrestricted submarine warfare against merchant shipping. When the openly antagonistic Zimmermann Telegram was made public, it would be the straw that broke the camel's back. The first major blows to American neutrality had been the sinking of the passenger liners *Lusitania* and *Sussex*. The British-registered *Lusitania* was sunk off the Irish coast by a German U-boat on May 7, 1915, with the loss of 1,195 lives, including those of U.S. citizens. After that, public opinion shifted toward the Allies in an overwhelming way. Germany eventually conceded liability for the sinking of the *Lusitania* and promised to stop sinking passenger ships without warning. The immediate crisis between the United States and Germany subsided, but the die had been cast. Then, on March 16, 1916, a German U-boat sank the unarmed liner *Sussex* with the loss of further American lives and a further promise by Germany to stop sinking unarmed passenger ships. By the end of 1916, Germany began unrestricted submarine warfare in an effort to break British control of the seas and an American entry into the war on the side of the Allies was seen as only a matter of time. With Britain in control of the ocean routes to the United States, Germany announced in January 1917 that its U-boats would be cleared to attack shipping in the Atlantic without regard to origin—including American

vessels. With the sinking of the American liner *Housatonic*, the United States finally broke off diplomatic relations with Germany in February 1917. In March, more American ships were sunk, the Zimmermann Telegram was made public, and war was declared by the United States against Germany on April 6, 1917. *BY*

United States' involvement in the peace conference

The role played by the United States at the postwar peace conference was proportionally greater than the role that the United States had played in the war prior to the summer of 1918. President Woodrow Wilson became one of the leading figures partially because of the force of his charismatic and articulate presence, and partly because of the unselfishness of his Fourteen Points that were the basis of the peace plan. Essentially, the idealism of these proposals was seen as giving him the moral high ground among Allied leaders. Announced in Wilson's address to a joint session of Congress on January 8, 1918, the Fourteen Points were:

(1) Abolition of secret diplomacy by open covenants, openly arrived at.
(2) Freedom of the seas in peace and war, except as the seas may be closed in whole or part by international action for enforcement of international covenants.

(3) Removal of international trade barriers wherever possible and establishment of an equality of trade conditions among the nations consenting to the peace.
(4) Reduction of armaments consistent with public safety.
(5) Adjustment of colonial disputes consistent with the interests of both the controlling government and the colonial population.
(6) Evacuation of Russian territory by foreign troops, with the proviso of self-determination.
(7) Evacuation and restoration of Belgium.
(8) Evacuation and restoration of French territory, including the Alsace-Lorraine claimed by and occupied by Germany.
(9) Readjustment of Italian frontiers along clearly recognizable lines of nationality.
(10) Autonomy for the peoples of Austria-Hungary.
(11) Evacuation and restoration of territory to Serbia, Montenegro, and Romania, granting of seaports to Serbia, and readjustment and international guarantee of the national ambitions of the Balkan nations.
(12) Self-determination for non-Turkish peoples under Turkish control and internationalization of the Dardanelles.
(13) An independent Poland, with access to the sea
(14) Creation of a general association of nations under specific covenants to give mutual guarantees of political independence and territorial integrity.

The final point, which called for the creation of the eventual League of Nations, was the most radical and the most controversial. Ironically, most of the Allies would finally agree to the creation of the League of Nations and would join it—but the United States would not. Another irony was that Wilson's Fourteen Points were accepted by the new German chancellor, Maximilian of Baden, as the basis of peace negotiations—but they were largely rejected by the Allies as the treaty ending the war was being drafted. In June 1919, when the United States, France, Britain, and Italy convened at Versailles to draft the treaty, most of Wilson's points were swept off the table. Belgium was restored, Alsace-Lorraine returned, Poland created, and Austria-

Hungary dismembered, but most of the other points were ignored or diluted. This was especially true of the notion of colonized peoples being allowed to govern themselves. Germany's colonies were stripped away, but France, Britain, and Italy all had extensive colonial empires. The Bolsheviks, who overthrew the Russian Empire, also rejected the notion of freeing the Tsar's subject nations—from the Ukraine to Central Asia—and kept these colonies as part of the new "Soviet Union." *BY*

U.S. military actions

The principal military actions during World War I that involved the United States included the Battle of Belleau Wood (often referred to by the name of the town of Chateau-Thierry), the Battle of St. Mihiel, and the climactic Meuse-Argonne Campaign. These three actions are all covered in detail separately (see pages 66, 344, and 261 respectively). In addition to these actions involving division-size American units, the AEF had troops active in a defensive role in other sectors of the front, especially in the Ypres-Lys, Oise-Aisne, and in the Somme, where they operated in support of British units. They had also served in a defensive role in the Aisne-Marne, which would be the scene of their great offensive actions. The United States declared war in April 1917, and the first AEF was slow to get into combat. However, once that began to happen, the AEF participation in the war mushroomed. From April 1917, it would be two months before the first troops arrived in France, six months before the first troops entered combat and twelve months before the first division-size unit was in action. However at the end of May 1918, there would be three divisions in the line. In July, there were ten, and by September, the number had more than doubled to twenty-two. In addition to the full divisions in the line, units from a total of forty-two AEF divisions had seen combat by the end of the war, although units from only four had seen combat by the first anniversary of the United States' declaration of war in April 1918. The first significant AEF action was the 1st Division offensive at Cantigny in the Somme on May 25, 1918. The second would be the Battle of Belleau Wood, took place between June 1 and June 26, 1918, on the Aisne-Marne Sector of the Western Front, in a

thick forest northwest of the French town of Chateau-Thierry near the Marne River. Part of the Second Battle of the Marne, Belleau Wood was the battle that truly caused the Allies to come to respect the AEF as a serious fighting force. The Battle of St. Mihiel occurred in the salient of the same name, southeast of Verdun between September 12 and 16, 1918. Relatively small by comparison to what was to come, it was a major victory that established the Americans as a force equal to any on the Western Font. It was,

of course, merely a prelude to the Meuse-Argonne Campaign, which followed ten days later. This campaign began with an American offensive on September 26, 1918, and ended with the Armistice on November 11, 1918. Casualty figures tell the story of the intensity of involvement. AEF battle deaths for the three weeks beginning with Cantigny averaged 323. In the succeeding weeks leading up to Belleau Wood, they averaged 248. For the four weeks centering on the Battle of Belleau

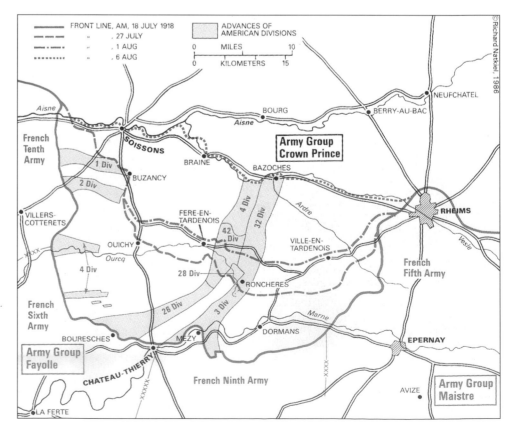

Left: Gun crew in the Argonne. *Chrysalis Photo Library*

Right: U.S. Marines toward the end of the Meuse-Argonne campaign. *Chrysalis Photo Library*

Below: Men of the 369th Infantry, 93rd Division in trenches outside Maffrecourt, May 5, 1918. *Chrysalis Photo Library*

Below Left: Map showing the St. Mihiel offensive. *Richard Natkiel*

Right: Men of the 30th Division moving forward under fire during the Battle of Cambrai, November 1917. *Chrysalis Photo Library*

Below: U.S. infantry in the trenches, January 20, 1918. *National Archives via Chrysalis Photo Library*

Wood, they averaged 2,013. In the weeks between Belleau Wood and the Meuse-Argonne Campaign, including the Battle of St. Mihiel, they averaged 918 per week. It is illustrative of the dramatically increasing level of American involvement that the weekly average of battle deaths leapt to 5,922 for the first three weeks of the Meuse-Argonne Campaign. As the tide turned and the German resistance crumbled, the average for the next four weeks would drop to 2,768, which was still greater than during the Belleau Wood period. The total casualty figure for the AEF was 300,041, which represented seven percent of total U.S. Army strength and fourteenth percent of those sent overseas with the AEF. The U.S. Department of Defense calculates that the United States suffered 53,402 battle deaths, 63,114 deaths from other causes (such as disease), and 204,002 persons wounded. U.S. Army battle deaths were the largest, numbering 50,510, followed by 2,461 Marines and 431 sailors. The U.S. Army suffered 193,663 wounded, the U.S. Marine Corps had 9,520 wounded and the U.S. Navy 819 battle-related injuries. By the time of the Armistice, the AEF had twenty-eight divisions which had seen combat. Of

these, all but four had, by November 11, entered the line as integral division-strength units. According to Colonel Leonard P. Ayres, Chief of the Statistics Division of the U.S. Army General Staff, the 77th Division held the record for the number of miles advanced against the enemy with forty-four. The 2nd Division was next with thirty-seven, followed by the 42nd Division with thirty-five, the 1st Division with fifty-one, the 89th Division with thirty, and the 3rd Division with twenty-five miles. Colonel Ayres credits the 2nd Division with having captured 12,026 enemy prisoners or nineteen percent of all captured by the AEF. The 1st Division was second with 6,469; followed by the 89th Division with 5,061; the 33rd Division 3,987, and the 26th Division with 3,148 prisoners taken. *BY*

Left: Infantry of 27th Division making their way through barbed wire, Somme, September 13, 1918. *National Artchives via Chrysalis Photo Library*

Below: U.S. troops at Badouviller, March 17, 1918. *Chrysalis Photo Library*

Left: Mountain of boots worn out by U.S. troops at the Salvage Depot, Tours, March 10, 1918. *National Archives via Chrysalis Photo Library*

Below: Three German prisoners entertaining U.S. troops at Nonsard, September 9, 1918. *National Archives via Chrysalis Photo Library*

Right: U.S. troops enjoy German beer in a captured trench. *National Archives via Chrysalis Photo Library*

Left: The U.S Navy submarine *L1*.
Collection of Bill Yenne

U.S. Navy

At the beginning of World War I, the Royal Navy's Grand Fleet and the German Imperial Navy's High Seas Fleet were the world's premier naval forces. The U.S. Navy was a second-tier force, but its resounding victory over the Spanish fleet at Manila Bay in 1898 had made it a world class, second-tier naval force. By 1917, the U.S. Navy's "Great White Fleet," as it was known in the early years of the century, had been repainted in battleship gray, and was ready for action. When the United States entered World War I, the great naval battles between the Grand Fleet and the High Seas Fleet had been fought, the High Seas Fleet had been neutralized and the German naval strategy had turned from surface ships to unlimited submarine warfare. The war at sea had turned from the thundering guns of capital ships to the uneasy patrols to protect convoys from the silent threat from below. The United States, a two-ocean nation, had traditionally required a two-ocean fleet. Organizationally, therefore, the U.S. Navy had consisted of two distinct fleets—the Pacific Fleet and the Atlantic Fleet. The Panama Canal now provided a means of transit between oceans, but the fragility of the canal in times of war was obvious, so the two fleets remained. They were commanded separately before World War I, but in 1918, Admiral Henry T. Mayo, commander of the Atlantic Fleet, was promoted to the role of Commander of the U.S. Fleet, with his successor and the Pacific Fleet commander reporting to him. In 1917, the U.S. Navy accepted a British Admiralty invitation to send four battleships to join the British Sixth Battle Squadron on patrol duty in the Atlantic. The Atlantic Fleet selected six, so as to allow them to rotate. All of them were the new dreadnought-type battleships that were based on the British battleship of that name. They each sported multiple turrets of twelve-inch or fourteen-inch guns. The oldest was USS *Delaware* (BB28), commissioned in 1910. There would also be USS *Florida* (BB30) of 1911, as well as both members of the "Wyoming" class, USS *Wyoming* (BB32) and USS *Arkansas* (BB33). Finally, there were both of the much newer "New York" class, USS *New York* (BB34) and USS *Texas* (BB35). Other battleships that would eventually serve in conjunction with the Grand Fleet included USS *Florida* (BB30), USS *Utah* (BB31), USS *Nevada* (BB36), USS *Oklahoma* (BB37), and USS *Arizona* (BB39). The latter was the same ship whose loss at Pearl Harbor in December 1941 became a rallying call in World War II. The U.S. Navy would be actively involved in convoy escort duty and laying the North Sea Barrage, but never came in direct contact with the High Seas Fleet. There was, however, a good deal of contact with the German U-boat force. A number of U-boats were sunk by the U.S. Navy, and the first American warship loss of the twentieth century was to a U-boat—the destroyer USS *Jacob Jones* (DD-61), commissioned in February 1917. After patrol duties on the U.S. east coast, she served on convoy escort duty in the vicinity of the United Kingdom, where, between May and December 1917, she saved many survivors of merchant ships sunk by U-boats. On December 6, she was en route from Brest to Cobh (then Queenstown) on Ireland's east coast she was torpedoed and sunk with the loss of 64 men. *BY*

Above Right: **An Atlantic convoy seen from USS *Pocahontas*. In the foreground, two destroyers.** *U.S. Naval Historical Center via Chrysalis Photo Library*

Below Right: **USS Wyoming (BB32), lead ship of the "Wyoming" class of 1911.** *Chrysalis Photo Library*

Right: The USS *Leviathan* leaving Hoboken, New Jersey. *Collection of Bill Yenne*

U.S. troops, Transport to Europe of

The task of transporting the AEF to Europe during World War I was the largest sealift task, indeed the largest transportation task of any kind, that had ever been undertaken by the U.S. government. Indeed, more U.S. military personnel would be transported between June 1917 and June 1919 than had served in the U.S. military during the half century since the Civil War. When the United States entered the war, the U.S. Navy's sealift capability was virtually non-existent, so the government began by chartering U.S.-flag ships and by July 1917 there were seven troopships and six cargo ships with a total deadweight capacity of 94,000 tons in service. Further vessels were added and by the time of the Armistice the total tonnage had increased to 3.25 million tons, of which nearly eighty percent was earmarked for freight. The additional tonnage came from new ships manufactured by the Emergency Fleet Corporation, as well as from ships chartered from neutral carriers such as the Netherlands, Japan, and various Scandinavian merchant fleets. Of course, German ships that had been in American ports in April 1917 were commandeered, renamed, and put to work. The transport fleet moved 7,453,000 tons of cargo to Europe between June 1917 and April 1919. Starting from a mere 16,000 tons moved in June 1917, the total tonnage passed a quarter million with 289,000 transported in March 1918, and exceeded half a million with 536,000 in July 1918. The peak would be the 829,000 tons moved in November 1918. According to Colonel Leonard P. Ayres, Chief of the Statistics Division of the U.S. Army General Staff, between June 1917 and November 1918, the fleet transported 2,077,226 troops to Europe, and from that date through June 1919, 1,623,251 were returned to the United States. The substantial difference between the two numbers includes those killed in action, as well as the sizable number that would remain in Europe on occupation duty. The number of AEF troops being transported to Europe increased steadily from 14,100 in July 1917 to 306,350 in July 1918, which was the peak month and the only month to exceed 300,000. The number exceeded 200,000 for the months from May through September 1918, but dropped to 180,326 in October. In November, 30,201 were sent to Europe, and 26,245 were brought home. On the return, the numbers also steadily increased, exceeding 200,000 in March 1919 and reaching a peak of 364,183 in June 1919. Of the troops going to Europe, nearly four out of five, or a total of 1,656,000, embarked from the Port of New York. Of the remainder, 288,000 shipped out from Newport News, Virginia and 46,000 from Boston. The Americans sent overseas arrived in almost equal proportion in Britain in France, with 844,000 passing through Liverpool, 791,000 debarking at Brest, and 62,000 arriving via London. The use of British ports necessitated sealift to transport the AEF across the English Channel to France. This fleet began with 7,000 tons in October 1917, and grew to more than a 300,000 tons by the end of 1918. *BY*

Below: The first U.S. Army contingent to reach the United Kingdom, 1917. *Chrysalis Photo Library*

Right: Staff of 342nd Infantry Regiment at Southampton, September 27, 1918—left to right, Colonel C. E. Stoddart, Captain A. J. Stillwell (Vinegar Joe of World War II fame), and Captain C. L. Darlington. *U.S. Signal Corps via Chrysalis Photo Library*

Below Right: Convoy of American troopships and escorts at sea—*George Washington* leading *America* and *Dr. Kalb*, May 18, 1918. *Chrysalis Photo Library*

VENIZELOS, ELEUTHERIOS

Venizelos, Eleutherios (1864–1936)

A Greek statesman, Venizelos was initially trained as a lawyer before being elected to the Cretan chamber of deputies while that island was still under Turkish rule. He was one of the leaders of the Cretan revolt of 1896 and initially served the new Greek governor, Prince George, as Minister of Justice, before leading a guerrilla war against the regime. In 1909 he traveled to Athens and was appointed Greek Prime Minister in 1910, a post he held until 1915. A strong Greek nationalist, he extended the country through the Balkan League (against Turkey in 1912 and against Bulgaria in 1913). Pro-Britain and France at the start of World War I, he disagreed with the more equivocal King Constantine I, and set up a rival, pro-Allied, government at Salonika. He forced Constantine to abdicate in 1917, but his failure to significantly increase Greek territory at Versailles led to his defeat at the 1920 election. Venizelos held the post of Prime Minister on three further occasions postwar, but was forced into exile in 1935 when he supported a further revolt on Crete. He died in exile in Paris the following year. *PW*

Verdun, Battle of

Fought between February 21 and December 15, 1916, Verdun was the longest battle of World War I. It is estimated that 200,000 men died on either side of the lines during the ten months of fighting there. The city of Verdun, an ancient Roman fortress reinforced by Napoleon to include two rings of forts, held no strategic value for its German attackers. General Erich von Falkenhayn planned his attack on the city with the aim of "bleeding the French Army white," forcing France to choose between surrender and a prolonged and bloody defense in which her army would be sacrificed. Originally scheduled for February 10, 1916, and delayed by bad weather, the German assault preempted Allied plans for a year of offensives in the West. The bad weather alone bought the French the time they needed to set up defensive artillery positions and to prepare the city for attack. The guns that had once defended Verdun had been sent to the fronts in 1915, and the French Second Army garrisoned there consisted of only one active division and three reserves. In the days following February 10,

reinforcements in the form of one active and two reserve divisions were shipped into the city, and German hopes of a swift victory diminished. Lined up against the French was the German Fifth Army under Crown Prince Wilhelm. Ten divisions strong, it boasted 542 heavy guns, including the howitzers that had broken the Belgian forts of Namur and Liège, 300 field guns, 152 trench mortars, and over two and a half million shells. Verdun was a battle dominated by artillery, and it became the first real air campaign as German balloons and aircraft provided the intelligence that guided their fire. When Operation "Judgement" finally launched on February 21, only two French battalions were firmly dug into their positions. These were the 56th and 59th Chasseurs à Pied, whose prudent commander, the retired Colonel Emile Driant, had angered General Joseph Joffre the previous year with what Joffre felt to be impertinent objections to the disarming of Verdun. On the morning of February 21, a barrage of artillery German pulverized the French lines along an eight-mile stretch on the east bank of the Meuse. Despite the valiant efforts of the French defenders, including Emile Driant, who died a hero's death in the early days of the fighting, by February 24 the entire outer trench line was in German control. The next German objectives were the Forts Vaux and Douaumont, and Douaumont fell suddenly on February 25 when a German commander bluffed its defenders into surrender. Its fall demoralized French troops, and Verdun seemed close to collapse when, later the same day, Joffre tasked General Henri-Philippe Pétain with the city's defense. Unfashionably over-opinionated and denied advancement by the prewar army, Pétain emerged from Verdun a national hero. His first move was to transform Verdun's main access road into the designated supply route that became the city's lifeline during the months of fighting. Next, he turned his attention to improving artillery tactics, holding the German troops on the east bank of the Meuse under a volley of fire that forced von Falkenhayn to rethink his strategy to avoid stalemate. On February 28, the Germans broadened their front to take in

Above Right: The Battle of Verdun. *Richard Natkiel*

Right: Artillery on the march to the Verdun Front, June 1917. *Chrysalis Photo Library*

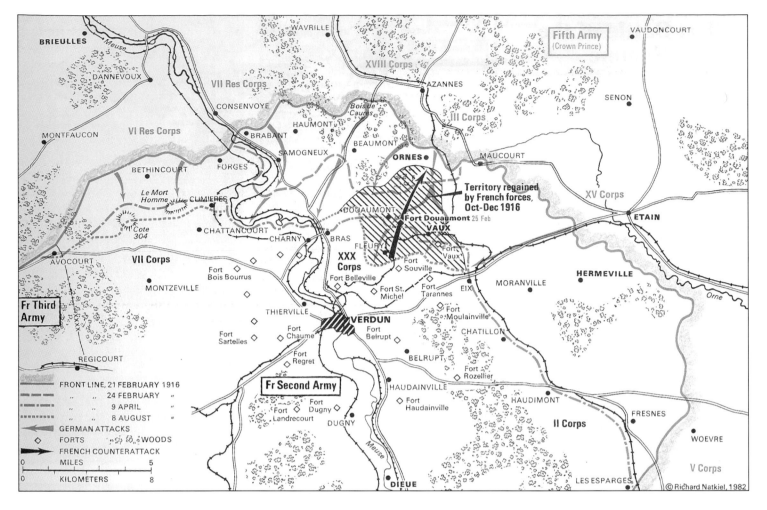

the west bank of the Meuse, with Mort-Homme and Hill 304 as their objectives. Despite 6th Division's advances of March 5, however, the French 92nd Division held on at Mort-Homme. German progress was little better on the east bank. Fort Vaux remained elusive—although the village of Vaux had changed hands thirteen times in March 1916, the fort remained under French command. April brought a new wave of attacks across both banks of the Meuse, but these were called off after four days due to bad weather. Throughout this period, for every German attack Pétain launched a counteroffensive, heightening the death toll and showing von Falkenhayn that his battle of attrition would not end without heavy German casualties. By now, Joffre was becoming increasingly frustrated with Pétain's defensive fighting. Promoting Pétain to army group commander, he installed General Robert Nivelle in Verdun in late April 1916, hoping for a change of tactics. Pressured by Joffre into premature action, on May 17 Nivelle attempted to recapture Douaumont. Using the German tactic of artillery bombardment preceding infantry advance, he took the Fort on May 22 only to have it reclaimed the following day by the Germans. The coming weeks brought further losses for the French. Mort-Homme fell on May 29 and on June 2 three German corps advanced across a three-mile front to take Fort Vaux. There, Major Raynal and his 500 men fought valiantly, but were forced to surrender to 50th Division through thirst. The impulsive Nivelle immediately sought to retake the fort, but his efforts resulted only in casualties among his 2nd Zouaves and Regiment Colonial du Maroc. For the Germans, victory at Verdun seemed within sight. With Fort Vaux taken, they struck out toward Fort Souville, the village of Fleury, and Thieaumont farmstead—vantage points that would offer them a clear line of fire onto the Meuse bridges, dooming Verdun. On June 21, German artillery opened fire on the eastern bank of the Meuse. The following day, they fired shells containing phosgene gas, debilitating the French artillery and allowing the *Alpendivision* to advance on Fort Souville. Had they reached the Meuse bridges, one third of the French force would have been cut off and the French cause lost. However, in the heat of June 23 the German attackers were forced to fall back for lack of water and

the crisis passed. The final German offensive came on July 11, 1914, but the fighting at the Somme had weakened their resources and the attack was beaten off by Nivelle's guns. Fifth Army now relapsed into "aggressive defense" and at last the French Second Army was able to assume the offensive. For the first time in the Battle of Verdun, artillery supremacy lay with the French when, on October 22, Nivelle's guns opened fire on the German lines. Throughout October and November much captured ground was regained. On October 24, Nivelle's chief subordinate, General Charles Mangin, successfully retook Fort Douaumont, deploying two 400mm rail guns. On November 3 Fort Vaux was also recaptured. The final attack of the Battle of Verdun took place on December 15. Having regrouped his forces, Mangin renewed the attack across a broader front, taking many prisoners and 2.5 miles of land. The Battle of Verdun was finally over. *MC*

Versailles, Treaty of

Treaty of June 28, 1919 between the Allied Powers and Germany setting out the terms for peace. Its main provisions were the transfer of disputed regions to France, Belgium, Poland, Czechoslovakia, and Lithuania, strict limitations on the future size of the German Army and Navy, the payment of reparations totaling £6,600 millions, the surrender of all colonies to League of Nations mandate, a fifteen-year occupation of the Rhineland, a ban on the union of Germany and Austria, and an acceptance of Germany's guilt in causing the war. The harshness of these terms caused Germany to sign only under protest and was a continuing source of bitterness and dispute in the years that followed. *DC*

Vimy Ridge, Battle of

The attack on Vimy Ridge was conceived as part of the Arras offensive of 1917. The ridge was the highest point in the area and strategically vital for the siting and aiming of artillery. On the morning of April 9, 1917, the Canadian Corps under General Sir Julian Byng went over the top. The attack was supported by an accurate creeping barrage and within half an hour the Canadian 1st Division had captured the first line of German positions. By the time an hour has passed the German

second line had also fallen By April 12 the entire of the ridge was in Allied hands. *MC*

Vittorio Emanuele III, King
(1869–1949)

The son of Umberto I in Naples, Vittorio Emanuele became king of Italy in 1900. Despite parliamentary opposition, he forced Italy into World War I on the Allied side. After the war and faced by political chaos and the rise of Mussolini's Fascist party, Vittorio Emanuele made Mussolini Prime Minister in 1922, paving the way ultimately to the totalitarian state with Mussolini as *Il Duce* and the king as a constitutional figurehead. Despite the military reverses during the second half of World War II, the king continued to back Mussolini until 1944 and *Il Duce*'s fall. For the next two years, the Italian monarchy continued with Vittorio Emanuele as nominal king but with his son, Umberto II, as Lieutenant-General of the Realm. Following, the king's abdication in 1946, he went into exile, dying in Egypt. *MS*

Vittorio Veneto Offensive (1918)

In mid-June the Austro-Hungarians launched a two-pronged offensive to break through the Italian defenses along the Piave River that had formed following the previous year's Battle of Caporetto. This was to be a purely Austro-Hungarian affair as German forces were occupied by events on the Western Front. Two armies under Field Marshal Svetozar Boroevic von Bojna moved directly against the Piave while the Eleventh Army commanded by Field Marshal Franz Conrad von Hötzendorf opened the attack by advancing through the Trentino toward Asiago. The Austro-Hungarian troops involved, demoralized, short of supplies, and close to mutiny, made few gains during what was named the Battle of the Piave River. By the 23rd, they were back holding the positions they had occupied before the offensive. Conrad was sacked in July and replaced by Archduke Josef. It was clear to the Allies that Austria-Hungary was close to collapse and likely to seek an armistice if faced by a major counterattack. However, the Italian chief of staff, General Armando Diaz, made no immediate moves to capitalize on the Piave battle, despite the protestations of his own government and his country's allies.

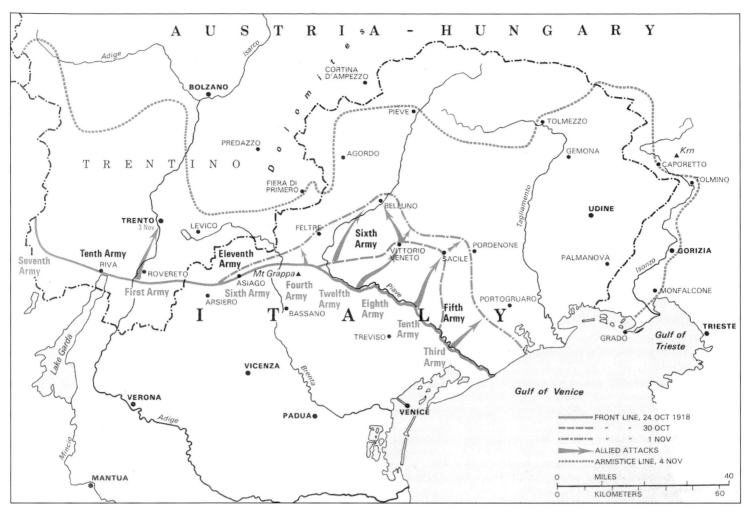

Above: **The Vittorio Veneto Offensive.** *Richard Natkiel*

Throughout the summer and early fall, as the Austro-Hungarian position became even more parlous, Diaz marshaled his forces until he had a significant superiority in both troops and artillery. Finally, on October 23, the Italians advanced, beginning with a diversionary attack around Monte Grappa close to Asiago on the Trentino sector of the front, which was held by Austro-Hungarian forces under Archduke Josef. This succeeded in drawing some Austro-Hungarian reserves from the main focus of the Italian attack, which was toward the town of Vittorio Veneto across the Piave River. This part of the offensive opened on the 24th but the Italian Eighth Army, which was spearheading the drive toward Vittorio Veneto, faced surprisingly strong resistance from the Austro-Hungarian Sixth Army. Two additional Italian armies, the Tenth and Twelfth, which contained British and French divisions and were commanded by generals from the same two countries, advanced to the right and left of the Eighth Army, secured bridgeheads across the Piave, and forced the Austro-Hungarians to retreat. Vittorio Veneto was captured on the 30th and Austro-Hungarian resistance collapsed over the next few days, partly hastened by severe Allied air attacks. As the Italian armies swept forward, Austro-Hungarian troops surrendered in their tens of thousands, some 300,000 in just ten days. The Allied forces recorded just 38,000 casualties in the same period. A ceasefire was announced on November 2, by which time Allied forces had captured much of the southern Trentino and were holding positions halfway between the Piave and Tagliamento rivers. Austria-Hungary agreed an armistice the next day, ending its part in the conflict. *IW*

Voie Sacrée, La

Known in 1916 as *La Route*, under Pétain *La Voie Sacrée* became the designated supply route for Verdun. Whole divisions of Territorials maintained the fifty-mile route, while the best fighter squads protected it from aerial attack as 90,000 men, 50,000 tons of supplies, and 12,000 trucks traveled back and forth from Bar-le-Duc to Verdun. *MC*

Volunteers

Declaration of war in 1914 led to many displays of patriotism. In Vienna Chief of Staff Conrad greeted war as the only way to hold together the empire. Film shows excited gatherings in Berlin, London, and Paris. Yet the picture of unalloyed enthusiasm has been questioned. Recent French research shows that questionnaires prepared by the Minister of Public Education revealed that almost as many greeted the news of mobilization with consternation or resignation as enthusiasm or patriotism. Nevertheless volunteers did flock to the colors: the German Army already had a class of one-year volunteers and these were joined by many young men and students. Britain, with its non-conscript army, was dependent on volunteers. Lord Kitchener's call to arms, "Your King and Country Needs You" was issued as early as August 7, 1914, although the famous pointing poster was not produced until later. While the Territorial Army continued to recruit well, "Kitchener Volunteers" were enlisted to make up "Service Battalions" for existing regiments. These went to form whole New Armies which would take to the field in 1915 and 1916. Almost two million joined the army voluntarily before the introduction of conscription. *SB*

War Graves Commission

The Commonwealth War Graves Commission was established as the Imperial War Graves Commission in May 1917 to continue the work of organizing and maintaining soldier's graves that had begun in 1915. It was led by Fabian Ware who had come to France in September 1914 with a Red Cross unit and had recognized that proper arrangements for graves were important for morale both among the troops and back home. The War Office established the Graves Registration Commission under the command of Ware as part of the army, charged with recording and marking the graves of those killed, and as soon as military conditions permitted, making arrangements for the construction of permanent cemeteries and appropriate memorials. The commission also compiled and published records and handled requests for information from relatives. Wherever identification was possible, individual named headstones were set up, while memorials commemorated the huge numbers of unidentified. Covering the war dead of Australia, New Zealand, Canada, South Africa, India, the United Kingdom, and its colonies, the commission is responsible for 587,526 identified burials and a further 559,318 commemorated on memorials. The commission marked the eightieth anniversary of World War I's end by establishing an online Debt of Honor register which has received several hundred thousand hits each day, reflecting the huge worldwide interest in the issue. American war graves overseas are maintained by the American Battle Monuments Commission, which maintains twenty-four overseas burial grounds containing war graves, including those of 30,921 casualties of the World War I. *DC*

War Memorials, United States

There are dozens of memorials to the U.S. troops who fought in World War I, who are buried at numerous cemeteries—especially Arlington National Cemetery, Virginia. However, the principal memorials and cemeteries that are specifically dedicated to World War I troops are the twelve official memorials and eight official national cemeteries administered by the American Battle Monuments Commission. The Commission was established by Congress immediately after the war at the request of General John J. Pershing to honor the accomplishments of the American Armed Forces where they had served. Several of these are in the Aisne Department of France, which is where most of the combat involving American troops occurred. After World War II, additional memorials were added in Europe, the Pacific, and in the United States. Those discussed here are those that were established to honor the veterans and war dead of World War I. The AEF's Memorial, located on Pennsylvania Avenue between 14th and 15th Streets in Washington D.C., commemorates the two million American military personnel who made up the AEF of World War I. It consists of a stone plaza fifty-two feet by seventy-five feet, an eight-foot statue of General Pershing on a stone pedestal. The Audenarde American Monument is located in the town of Oudenaarde (Audenarde), Belgium, to commemorate the services and sacrifices of the 40,000 American troops who, in October and November 1918, fought in the vicinity as units attached to the group of armies commanded by King Albert I of Belgium. Some are buried in the Flanders Field American Cemetery at nearby Waregem, Belgium. The Bellicourt American Monument near St. Quentin (Aisne Department), France commemorates the achievements and sacrifices of the 90,000 American troops who served in battle with the British armies in France during 1917 and 1918. The tunnel beneath it was one of the main defense features of the Hindenburg Line which was broken by the American troops in a brilliant offensive in September 1918. The Cantigny American Monument is located in the village of Cantigny (Somme Department), France, to commemorate the first offensive operation by American forces in May 1918. The Chateau-Thierry American Monument is located on a hill two miles west of Chateau-Thierry, France near the Aisne-Marne American Cemetery and Memorial and the Oise-Aisne American Cemetery and Memorial. It commemorates the achievements of the American forces that fought in this region. The Chaumont Marker is a bronze plaque located at the entrance to Damremont Barracks, Chaumont, France. This was the location of General Pershing's General Headquarters of the AEF. The Kemmel American Monument is located on the Kemmelberg (Mont Kemmel) near Ieper (Ypres), Belgium, overlooking the bitterly contested Ypres battlefield. It commemorates the services and sacrifices of the American troops who, in the late summer of 1918, fought nearby in units attached to the British Army. The Belleau Wood Monument is marked by a flagpole in the center of the road leading through Belleau Wood, on the high ground to the rear of the Aisne-Marne American Cemetery and Memorial south of the village of Belleau (Aisne Department), France. It commemorates the valor of the U.S. Marines who captured this area in 1918. The Montsec American Monument is located on the isolated hill of Montsec (Thiaucourt Department), France near the St. Mihiel American Cemetery and Memorial outside the town of St. Mihiel. It commemorates the achievements of the American soldiers who fought in this region in 1917 and 1918. Slightly damaged during World War II, it has been repaired. Trenches used during the fighting are still visible. The Naval Monument at Brest, France stands on the ramparts of the city overlooking the harbor which was a major base of operations for American naval vessels during the war. The original monument built on this site to commemorate the achievements of the U.S. Navy during World War I was destroyed by the Germans on July 4, 1941, prior to the United States' entry into World War II. The present structure is a replica of the original and was completed in 1958. The Sommepy American Monument stands on Blank Mont Ridge, three miles northwest on Sommepy-Tahure (Marne Department), France. The Tours American Monument located in the city of Tours, France, commemorates the efforts of the 650,000 men who served during World War I in the Services of Supply of the AEF who worked behind the battle lines. The Aisne-Marne American Cemetery and Memorial lies south of the village of Belleau (Aisne Department), France near Chateau-Thierry. It contains the graves of 2,289 American dead, most of whom fought in the vicinity and in the Marne valley in the summer of 1918. The Brookwood American Cemetery and Memorial is located near the town of Brookwood, Surrey, England. It contains the graves of 468 American military dead from World War I. Close by are military cemeteries and monuments of the British Commonwealth and other

Allied nations. The Flanders Field American Cemetery and Memorial lies on the southeast edge of the town of Waregem, Belgium is the final resting place of 368 American military dead. The Meuse-Argonne American Cemetery and Memorial is located east of the village of Romagne-sous-Montfaucon (Meuse Department) near Verdun. Covering 130 acres, it holds the largest number of American war dead in Europe. Most of the 14,246 buried here gave their lives during the Meuse-Argonne Offensive. The Oise-Aisne American Cemetery and Memorial is at Fereen-Tardenois (Aisne Department), near Chateau-Thierry. Its thirty-six acres contain 6,012 Americans who died while fighting in this vicinity. The Somme American Cemetery, located near St. Quentin and Cambrai, contains the graves of 1,844 American military dead. Most lost their lives while serving in American units attached to British armies or in the operations near Cantigny. The St. Mihiel American Cemetery and Memorial is located at Thiaucourt, France and contains the graves of 4,153 American military dead from the great offensive which resulted in the reduction of the St. Mihiel salient. The Suresnes American Cemetery and Memorial is located in the Paris suburb of Suresnes and contains the graves of 1,541 American military dead from World War I and twenty-four graves of American unknown dead from World War II. *BY*

Watson, James Gerard (1867-1951)

Having served briefly as the American ambassador to Germany before World War I, James Gerard Watson is best recalled for his vociferous verbal assaults on the German people and German-American U.S. citizens. Born in New York City, he was appointed to the New York Supreme Court in 1908, and picked by Woodrow Wilson in 1913 as his first ambassador to Spain. Later that year, he was reassigned as U.S. ambassador to Germany, and he was in this post when World War I broke out in Europe. Returning to the United States later in 1914, Watson made an unsuccessful run for the U.S. Senate. He is perhaps best recalled for an especially

Right: James Gerard Watson.
Collection of Bill Yenne

inflammatory speech that he gave on November 25, 1917, to the Ladies Aid Society of St. Mary's Hospital in New York City. Watson described what he called the "German Peril," the threat that a half million German-Americans would revolt within the United States if the AEF undertook a serious offensive against German troops in Europe. He then advocated hanging German-Americans "from lamp posts." In 1920, Watson was an unsuccessful candidate for the Democratic Party's Presidential Nomination. *BY*

Weizmann, Chaim Azriel (1874–1952)

The first president of the state of Israel, was born near Pinsk in Russian Poland, but was educated as a scientist in his native land and in Germany and Switzerland before emigrating to Britain in 1904. An ardent Zionist, part of his rationale for moving to Britain was a belief that the country was more likely to support the creation of a Jewish homeland. In 1917 his dreams were fulfilled when as a result of advice that he had been asked to give, the Balfour Declaration stated British support for the creation of a Jewish state in Palestine providing that the rights of the existing non-Jewish populations were safeguarded. The declaration was the foundation for the League of Nations' Mandate for Palestine agreed in 1920. Weizmann became head of the World Zionist Movement in 1920 and, in 1929, of the Jewish Agency for Palestine. In 1948,

four years before his death, he became the new country's first president. *MS*

Western Allies, Command structure of the

As a constitutional monarchy the British head of state and armed forces was King George V. Unlike the French head of state, President Raymond Poincaré, he took little practical part in the war: key roles in British government were played by his prime ministers, successively Asquith and Lloyd George. Initially the secretary of state for war was Earl Roberts, but on his death in November 1914 was succeeded by Lord Kitchener. As the Cabinet was too large for efficiency a smaller War Council was formed from the Committee of Imperial Defence. This included not only the Prime Minister and secretary of state for war but First Lord of the Admiralty Winston Churchill. Following the formation of the coalition government a new War Committee came into existence from November 1915. In this, ministers Asquith, Lloyd George, Bonar Law, Balfour, and McKenna were prominent. Later, under Lloyd George, a four-man War Cabinet was formed. The chiefs of the Imperial General Staff were successively William Robertson and Sir Henry Wilson. The vaguest part of the Allied command structure was the relationship of British and French forces. Initially Sir John French was told to cooperate with the French, but not made subordinate to them. Only after the Rapallo Conference of November 1917 was a Supreme Allied War Council formed, with Foch as overall commander for the Western Front. Ironically this was at a time when the French were less obviously the leading power, as Britain had now taken up a significant part of the line and U.S. troops were arriving in numbers. *SB*

Western Front 1914–18

Following weeks of diplomatic activity the war on the Western Front began on August 4, 1914, when German troops from seven armies swept into Luxembourg and Belgium as part of the Schlieffen Plan. This was a plan formulated by the eponymous German Chief of the General Staff (1891–1905) which called for a sweeping move by massed forces on the right flank of a German advance through neutral Belgium and down to Paris from the North,

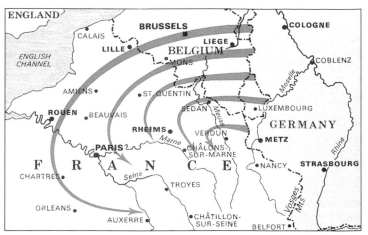

enveloping it and thus ending the war within six weeks of mobilization. Fortunately for the Allied forces this plan failed, partly due to its own inherent difficulties of timetable, partly because the current German Chief of the General Staff, Helmuth von Moltke, had weakened the crucial right flank to provide additional protection for his forces in Alsace and Lorraine. This resulted in a major German advance in August and September 1914, but one that failed to achieve its final goals. The timetable had gone awry by the end of the first week when the Belgian Army put up a much stiffer resistance than expected, though this rebounded upon the civilian population. Instead, they put up a stiff fight, which delayed the rigid German campaign schedule. The Germans then pressed on into northern France where they were further delayed by actions of the BEF, notably at Mons and Le Cateau, and Lanrezac's Fifth Army at the Battle of Charleroi. Although the Germans won all of these encounters, the delay was fatal to their attempts to win the war

quickly as it gave the French commander-in-chief, General Joseph Joffre, time to gather his reserves and start the construction of the French Sixth Army around Paris. It was at this point that the Germans made another serious error. German General Alexander von Kluck turned his First Army to the southeast of Paris, rather than the west as he was supposed to in the Schlieffen Plan. This was in order to turn the flank of the French Fifth Army and to support Bülow's Second Army. Von Kluck had assumed that the BEF was destroyed and

Above: The Schlieffen Plan. *Richard Natkiel*

Below: Royal Engineers taking wire up to the front, October 10, 1917. *Chrysalis Photo Library*

discounted the existence of the French Sixth Army under Maunoury. On September 5 the French General Joseph Gallieni quickly assembled the newly formed Sixth Army and, coordinating with Fifth Army's commander, assaulted von Kluck's exposed flank. In the process of defending himself, von Kluck redirected his corps westward, allowing yet another dangerous gap to open between him and von Bülow. These

errors cost the Germans any further progress and they withdrew back to safe positions north of the Marne River, where they resisted attempts by the French to dislodge them in the Battle of the Aisne (September 12–13). Then began the period known as the "Race to the Sea." Each side sought take opportunity of the open flank toward the sea in order to take advantage of the room to maneuver and the chance to win the war

Above: French civilians returning to their homes, Le Cateau, November 17, 1918. *Chrysalis Photo Library*

Below Left: The Western Front at the end of 1914. *Richard Natkiel*

quickly. This led to a series of sharp engagements culminating in the Battle of First Ypres from October 22, as the BEF found themselves under immense pressure from German attacks trying to force their way through to the Channel Ports. The British line held and the year ended in stalemate, with the lines now set for the vast remainder of the conflict. The beginning of 1915 saw Joffre eager to drive the German invader from German soil and in order to achieve this he had launched a series of attacks in the Champagne region in the middle of December 1914. These continued through the first three months of the year, but with little territorial gain and heavy French losses. The Allied troops were yet to realize that those on the defensive in this conflict held the upper hand due to strongly entrenched positions and the disruptive power of artillery barrages and machine guns. Despite these setbacks the Allies attacked again in March, with a

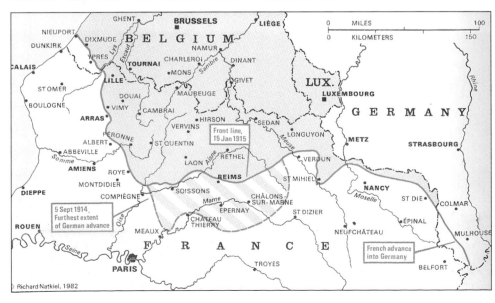

Right: German retreat to the Hindenberg Line. British and French troops in reserve lines at Le Verquier, April 25, 1917. *Chrysalis Photo Library*

Below: The Western Front at the end of 1916. *Richard Natkiel*

British offensive in the Artois region. They broke through initially at Neuve Chapelle but failures in communications and a lack of reserves ensured that these local gains were not exploited and the opportunity vanished. In April the Germans attacked the Ypres Salient again, employing gas for the first time on the Western Front. The Allied line in the salient held, but they suffered large casualties and been pushed back a distance of about four miles. While the Second Battle of Ypres was still raging, the British and French launched yet another offensive in the Artois region, with the British First Army attacking toward Aubers Ridge and Festubert, while the French Tenth Army attacked toward Vimy Ridge. These assaults also failed at a cost of 300,000 Allied casualties. There was one further major Allied offensive this year, once more in the Artois and Champagne regions. Joffre believed that the German reserves had been stripped from the line to reinforce the Eastern Front and, now that the French Colonial and British New Army divisions were starting to arrive, he would have overwhelming superiority in numbers. Both offensives made limited gains, but the same flaws associated with earlier attacks were apparent, a lack of reserves and a breakdown in communications once the troops had gone over the top. The Allied losses were over 250,000 casualties and the fall out from the battle cost the commander-in-chief of the BEF, Sir John French, his job. Sir Douglas Haig replaced him in September. The

Germans had learned from the localized breakthroughs that had occurred during the various Allied assaults of 1915 and spent the winter of 1915–16 strengthening their lines. In particular they instituted an elastic defense system, which allowed them to give up ground in order to mass reserves and break the momentum of attacks around a network of reserve trenches and machine gun posts. The beginning of 1916 saw the German commander-in-chief, Erich von Falkenhayn, put into action his plan to "bleed white" the French Army. He intended to isolate a section of the frontline that the French would not allow to fall, and then assure that the area was ringed by the heaviest artillery coverage available. His target was the ancient French fortress of Verdun, which his

troops first assaulted on February 21 after the most concentrated bombardment of the war. The campaign carried on for five terrible months, during which 300,000 Germans and 460,000 French became casualties. Although the campaign was certainly bleeding the French armies white, it also had the effect of draining the German Army as well. What Verdun also ensured was that the French would be unable to launch a major offensive throughout 1916, and the role of Allied aggressor on the Western Front was now allotted to the BEF, bolstered by the arrival of numerous divisions from Kitchener's New Army, inadequately trained and equipped yet full of enthusiasm. Pressed by Joffre to launch an assault that would draw away German reserves from the Verdun battlefield, Haig launched the Battle of the Somme on July 1, 1916, a month earlier than he had hoped. The British Third and Fourth Armies, together with the French Sixth Army, launched their offensive against some of the heaviest German fortifications on the entire Western Front. The German wire and front lines were supposed to have been destroyed by the largest artillery bombardment ever, and the troops were simply to walk across and occupy the positions. However, the bombardment hadn't worked and the attacking troops were cut down in their thousands. The BEF lost 58,000 casualties on the first day of the Somme, the majority in the first few waves. Despite these horrendous losses the campaign

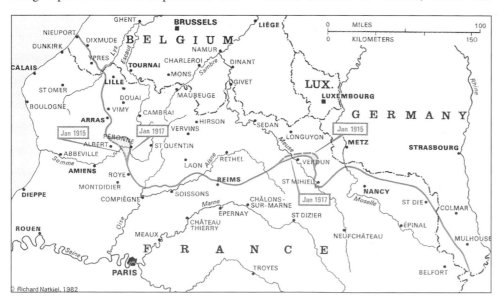

© Richard Natkiel, 1982

continued until November, by when 420,000 British, 200,000 French, and 450,000 Germans had become casualties for the sake of an Allied advance of a few miles. The Battle for Verdun ended in December after the French, under Robert Nivelle, had counterattacked the German positions and took almost all the ground they had lost at the beginning of the year. December also saw the fall of Joffre as French commander-in-chief, to be replaced by the victor of Verdun, Nivelle. The Germans had had a change of command earlier in the year. In August the victors of the Eastern Front, Hindenburg and Ludendorff, had replaced von Falkenhayn. Between February and April 1917 the Germans implemented Operation "Alberich." A voluntary withdrawal from their positions between Arras and Soissons to a carefully sited and prepared line known to the British as the Hindenburg Line. This move was

designed to reduce the dangerous salients that had been created in the German front by the attacks of 1916 and to straighten the line, thus freeing vital reserves to defend against future Allied attacks. The Germans were beginning to feel the strain on their manpower reserves after the terrible battles of attrition of the previous year. This planned withdrawal severely damaged the chances of success of an offensive planned by the new French commander-in-chief, Robert Nivelle. He planned an ambitious offensive by the Northern Army Group between the Somme and the Oise, with the BEF attacking the smaller German salient around Arras. The German withdrawal ensured that these attacks would be falling on strongly prepared positions. The British attacked at Arras on April 9 with the spectacular capture of Vimy Ridge by the Canadian Corps. The first day saw good gains, but

thereafter the battle bogged down into another attritional confrontation ending on April 14 with around 84,000 British casualties. Nivelle launched his own offensive on April 16. This attack ground to a halt on its first day, and by the time the assault was called off one month later, 220,000 more casualties had been added to the already overlong list of French losses for the war. The failure of this attack had a profound effect on the morale of the French Army, with mutinies, described by the participants as "strikes" breaking out along the length of the Western Front. Nivelle was dismissed and the hero of Verdun, Marshal Pétain, assumed command of the French Army. He managed to keep the French divisions

Below: A track through the mud near Passchendaele, January 11, 1918.
Chrysalis Photo Library

in the line and began to improve conditions and morale, but it was clear that the French Army as an offensive force had ceased to exist for the time being. The British launched yet another assault at Ypres with a series of great mine explosions that completely destroyed the German front lines. For once, the British inflicted more casualties than they received and pushed forward. However, the breakthrough that the Battle of Messines offered proved to be illusory, and when the Third Battle of Ypres started in July it proved to be as bad a bloodbath as any other Western Front encounter, with over 400,000 British casualties. Finally, in November, a new method was used against the German lines at the Battle of Cambrai. Hundreds of tanks were used. They broke the Hindenburg Line completely and advanced five miles. However, the reserves were not in place and the Germans counterattacked regaining all their lost ground. Reinforced by troops from the Eastern Front, the last great German offensive in the west was launched on March 21, 1918, with Operations "Michael," "Georgette," "Blücher," and "Yorch." "Michael" opened with an unprecedented 6,000-gun bombardment and the Germans at one point advanced fourteen miles in one day. "Georgette" was launched in the Ypres Salient, and came very close to breaking through to the Channel ports before it was stopped. "Blücher" and "Yorch" were launched on May 27, and by May 30 they had managed to advance forty miles, taken 40,000 prisoners and were only fifty-six miles from Paris before they were finally stopped around Rheims. With the failure of these assaults the strategic balance swung in favor of the Allies and they were not slow in exploiting it. The first attacks were made in July by the French west of Rheims. This was followed by a British offensive at the Amiens Bulge and a general offensive toward the Hindenburg Line. The Americans under General John Pershing attacked the St. Mihiel Salient south of Verdun and then attacked through the Argonne west of Verdun. By the end of October the Germans were retreating on all fronts and in danger of suffering an internal collapse. The Armistice was signed on November 11, with the bulk of the Allied forces poised in Belgium and on the German frontier, occupying positions very similar to those that they had held in September 1914. *MC*

Above: British soldier crawling back to the trenches after being wounded, Arras, December 1916. *Chrysalis Photo Library*

Left: A shave after coming out of the front line, Beaumont Hamel, November 1916. *Chrysalis Photo Library*

Below: View over the Douvre Valley showing a bombardment in progress on Messines, June 8, 1917. *Chrysalis Photo Library*

Nominated for president by the Democrats in 1912, he might have lost to incumbent Republican William Howard Taft had popular former President Theodore Roosevelt not launched a third-party candidacy. As it was, Roosevelt beat Taft, but only to come in second. Wilson was elected with forty-two percent of the vote. Among the highlights of Wilson's first term were reductions in a tariff system that was virtually unchanged since the Civil War, the Sixteenth Amendment to the U.S. Constitution, which provided for a permanent, graduated income tax. He also played a role in creating the Federal Reserve System to stabilize the national banking structure. When World War I began, Wilson actively tried to use diplomacy to get the warring parties to stop, and in 1916, he ran successfully for reelection by promising to keep the United States out of the faraway and unpopular conflict. Unrestricted German submarine attacks on U.S. ships and the Zimmermann Telegram finally pushed the president to denounce Germany on April 2, 1917, for waging "a war against all nations." On April 6, Congress declared war. Still an idealist, Wilson imagined World War I as a "war to end all wars" in which a permanent era of peace could be won. He drafted his Fourteen Points' peace plan calling for "open covenants of peace, openly arrived at," and advocated the League of Nations. It was Germany's acceptance of his proposals that helped bring about the Armistice. On December 4, 1918, three weeks after the Armistice, Wilson sailed to France to head the American delegation to the peace conference. It was the first time in history that a president had left the United States while in office. Woodrow Wilson quickly became the leading figure at the peace conference, but at home, his enemies in Congress were maneuvering against him. During the early months of 1919, Wilson guided the conference and urged creation of his League of Nations. He fought an uphill battle against Allied diplomats, who thought him naive, but he ultimately won their respect. Back home, he would not be so successful. He battled the Senate for approval of the League of Nations, and undertook an nationwide speaking tour to drum up popular support. Wilson suffered a serious stroke in September 1919 while returning to Washington from the West Coast. Two months later, the Senate rejected the League. Wilson

spent the last year of his second term in virtual seclusion, having been largely debilitated by the stroke, the full details of which were not made public at the time. Wilson's belief in international cooperation through an association of nations led to the creation of the League of Nations and ultimately to the United Nations. For his efforts, he was awarded the 1919 Nobel Peace Prize. After leaving office in 1921, he became a recluse. He died in 1924 and was buried in the National Cathedral in Washington, D.C. *BY*

Wireless at sea

The origin of wireless dates to 1888, when Sir William Crookes declared that electromagnetic waves could be used for communications. In 1896 the Royal Navy commissioned the Italian inventor Marchese Guglielmo Marconi to produce a working wireless telegraph for use at sea, an improvement of the cable telegraph systems already in use around

the world. In 1897 the German Professor Slaby began work with the German Navy for the same purpose, and although both inventors produced working models, Marconi produced the first workable naval transmitter in 1899. The U.S. Navy also conducted experiments with wireless equipment, and by 1901 the British issued Marconi wireless sets to all their major warships. Both Germany and America relied on Slaby-Arco wireless sets, and by 1905 most major navies used wireless communications to some extent or other. In 1907 the Royal Navy changed from telegraph wireless messages to audio communications, and signaling instructions were issued to regulate radio traffic, as signaling procedures became increasingly important. During the war almost every type of warships (including submarines) carried wireless sets, and while reception and transmission ranges increased, so too did the risk of the enemy intercepting messages, as both sides came to employ listening stations.

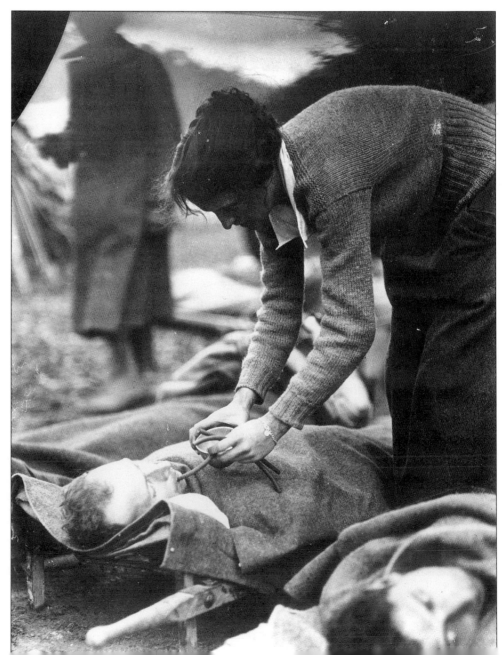

Above: Women workers on the railway.
Chrysalis Photo Library

Left: American Red Cross worker Miss Anna Rochester feeding Sergeant W. B. Hyer of 166th Infantry at Souilly Examination Hospitals, Meuse, France October 14, 1918.
National Archives via Chrysalis Photo Library

Women

Women played vital roles in the total mobilization of civil society required to sustain the unprecedented military activity of World War I. Although there were women in the small antiwar movements, most women supported and encouraged the recruitment campaigns. In Britain the Organization of the White Feather shamed men who were not in uniform by handing them a symbolic white feather. Women were recruited in auxiliary branches of the navy, army, and air force, and in the naval and marine forces in America, performing back up roles that released men for active service. The Women's Royal Naval Service, for example, had some 5,000 ratings and 450 officers by November 1918. Through the Red Cross and other groups thousands of women nurses and ambulance drivers made up much of the medical support tending to the wounded. Many more women took on paid work, providing the labor force to sustain wartime industry and munitions' production. Women were mobilized as farm laborers in Britain through the Women's Land Army. Across America countless women's groups were set up to promote the war effort, headed by the Women's Committee of the Council for National Defense. They organized war relief both at home and in allied nations, boosted patriotism and encouraged recruitment, supplied labor to health care, industry and agriculture, promoted the sale of

Below: Major General Leonard Wood addressing officer candidates at Fort McPherson, GA.
Collection of Bill Yenne

Liberty Bonds, and numerous other activities. *DC*

Wood, Leonard (1860–1927)

A U.S. Army doctor who favored a strong military posture during World War I, Leonard Wood was one of the leading American political figures in the early twentieth century. Born in Winchester, New Hampshire, he was educated at the Harvard Medical School and joined the U.S. Army in 1885 as a surgeon. He served mainly in the southwest during the Apache campaign, and in 1898, he was a co-founder with Theodore Roosevelt of the Rough Riders volunteer unit. He commanded the Rough Riders in Cuba during the Spanish-American War of 1898, and thereafter served as the U.S. military governor of Cuba though 1902. He is also credited for playing a major role in developing procedures for the eradication of yellow fever. After service in Cuba, he served in the Philippines through 1908 and was Chief of Staff of the U.S. Army from 1910 to 1914. His advocacy of a strong military put him at loggerheads with President Wilson, whose reaction to World War I was to keep the United States neutral and non-belligerent. In 1920 Wood was considered the leading contender for the Republican presidential nomination but the party chose Warren G. Harding. In 1921 Wood was appointed to serve as the governor-general of the Philippines, but his notion that the Filipinos should rule the Philippines themselves was controversial among conservatives in the United States. *BY*

York, Alvin Cullum (1887–1964)

Generally regarded as the greatest individual American hero of World War I, Alvin York was awarded the Congressional Medal of Honor for bravery during the Meuse-Argonne Campaign. Born in rural Fentress County, Tennessee, York was regarded as the best marksman in the county. He formed strong religious convictions thanks to the influence of his girlfriend, Gracie Williams, and was a conscientious objector at the beginning of World War I. His church did not specifically forbid military service, so he was drafted in 1917. He soon impressed officers with his amazing shooting ability, but for moral reasons, he declined to shoot at targets shaped like people. York decided eventually that Matthew 22:21, which speaks of "rendering unto Caesar the things which are Caesar's," allowed him to serve in combat, and he shipped out with the 328th Infantry Regiment of the 82nd Division. In October 1918, York, now a corporal, took part in the Meuse-Argonne Campaign as part of G Company of the 328th. On October 8, near Chatel-Chehery, the going got particularly rough. York's platoon suffered heavy casualties—including three other NCOs—and he assumed command. Armed with his Springfield rifle and a Colt .45 automatic pistol, York personally attacked the machine-gun nest which was pouring deadly and incessant fire on his platoon. He knocked out more than a dozen machine guns, and

kept going. Before he was through, he had killed twenty-five enemy troops—and he returned to American lines with 132 prisoners, including four officers. York was promoted to sergeant and was awarded the French Croix de Guerre and Medaille Militaire, along with the Congressional Medal of Honor and other decorations. He was to be the most highly decorated American of World War I. Said Supreme Allied Commander, Marshall Ferdinand Foch, "What you did was the greatest thing accomplished by any private soldier of all the armies of Europe." Back home, the returning hero received a gift of a 400-acre farm from the people of Tennessee. He married Gracie Williams and settled down to put his wartime experience behind him, commenting, "It's over. Let's just forget about it." York steadfastly resisted making product endorsements, saying resolutely that "this uniform ain't for sale." In 1941, however, he finally agreed to allow Hollywood to make a movie based on his diary—but only if Gary Cooper played the lead. Gary Cooper did, in fact, play the lead in *Sergeant York*, which took the Academy Award for Best Picture and earned Cooper the Oscar for Best Actor. Trivia buffs will recall that "Sergeant" York was actually a corporal at the time of the Meuse-Argonne Campaign, and that this film was the first of two in which Cooper would be cast as a Medal of Honor recipient. The second would be *The Court Martial of Billy Mitchell* (1955). *BY*

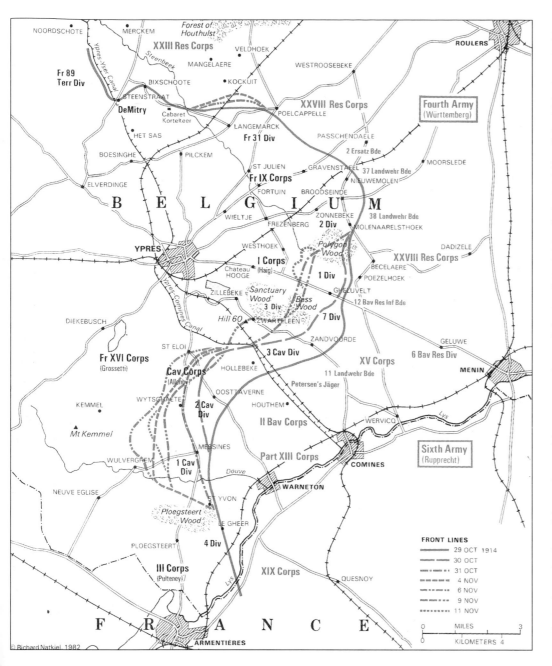

Despite breaking through the Belgian defenses to the north of the lines, they suffered heavy losses, particularly within their war-raised volunteer divisions who proved no match for the BEF's rifles in the central sector. On October 24, progress was halted when the Belgians blew up the sea dykes, flooding the region. Six divisions of the Group Fabeck renewed the offensive on a narrower front on October 31, breaking through Haig's I Corps at Gheluvelt before hastily assembled reinforcements pushed them back. The final offensive came on November 11, with Ypres as its objective. Breaking through at Nuns Wood on the southern end of the line, the Germans were held off by a group of cooks and batmen and the crisis passed. The period of fighting designated "First Ypres" ended on November 22, 1914, as the Allies entrenched themselves along what would become known as "the Salient." Among the battle's dead were an estimated 41,000 of Germany's ill-prepared volunteer forces, victims of the "Massacre of the Innocents." *MC*

Ypres, Second Battle of (1915)

Fought between April 22 and May 25, 1915, the Second Battle of Ypres was the Germans' only Western Front offensive of the year. Designed partly to distract attention from German movement toward the Eastern Front, Second Ypres was also the testing ground for a lethal new weapon—chlorine gas. On April 22, 1915, the German Fourth Army attacked with 160 tons of chlorine. French Algerian and territorial divisions fled in terror at the appearance of the yellow-green gas cloud, and German forces took over four miles of the Allied line before meeting resistance from a Canadian division. In a makeshift measure, Lieutenant Colonel Ferguson of 28th Division proposed that water soaked cloths be tied around men's faces to dissolve the chlorine, and further attacks against Canadian positions the following day proved less devastating in their effect. Against Sir John French's wishes, the Allies were forced to withdraw, surrendering the highest ground of the Salient and losing up to three miles of ground by the time of the final German gas assault on May 25, 1915. That Allied losses in the Second Battle of Ypres were almost twice as great as those of the Germans is largely attributable to the part played by chlorine. *MC*

Ypres, First Battle of (1914)

The First Battle of Ypres can be divided into the four distinct battles of La Bassée, Armentières, Messines, and Ypres. Raging from October 18 to November 22, 1914, it ended in stalemate. The fighting began on October 20, when fourteen infantry divisions from the German Sixth and Fourth Armies attacked along a twenty-mile front.

Above: The First Battle of Ypres.
Richard Natkiel

Left: First Battle of Ypres, 1914. The 2nd Battalion Royal Warwickshire Regiment being transported by bus to Ypres, November 6, 1914.
Chrysalis Photo Library

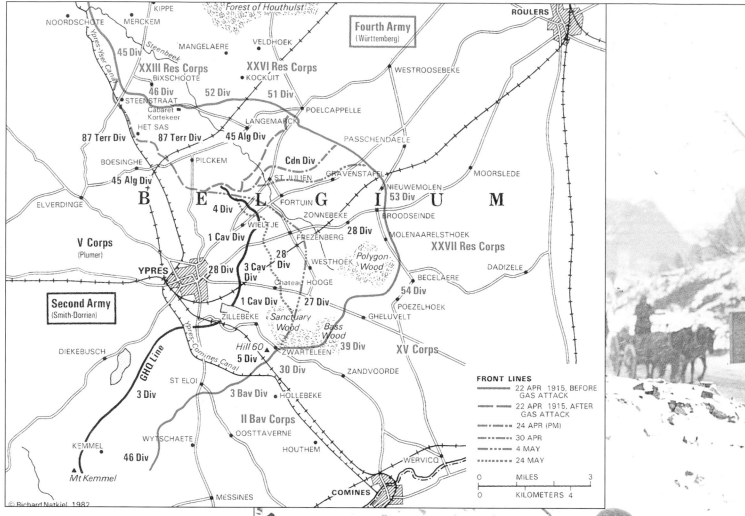

Ypres (Passchendaele), Third Battle of (1917)

Despite opposition from all quarters, General Haig remained convinced that a major assault on Ypres would result in Allied victory. So began the Third Battle of Ypres, or Passchendaele as it is also known, fought from July 31 to November 6, 1917. When British Fifth Army advanced on July 31, it became clear that the Germans had prepared on an unprecedented scale. Furthermore, ten days of Allied shelling had rendered the marshy salient all but impassable, and the offensive was halted by the evening of August 4. The next major attack, the Battle of Langemarck, began on August 16, but yielded little ground and Haig transferred the main burden of the offensive to Plumer's Second Army. Plumer renewed the campaign in early September, with short infantry advances supported by artillery fire. Polygon Wood, Broodseinde, and Gheluvelt all fell before the Germans changed their

Above: The Second Battle of Ypres. *Richard Natkiel*

Right: Menin Road, Ypres, winter 1917–18.
Chrysalis Photo Library

WORLD WAR I: A VISUAL ENCYCLOPEDIA

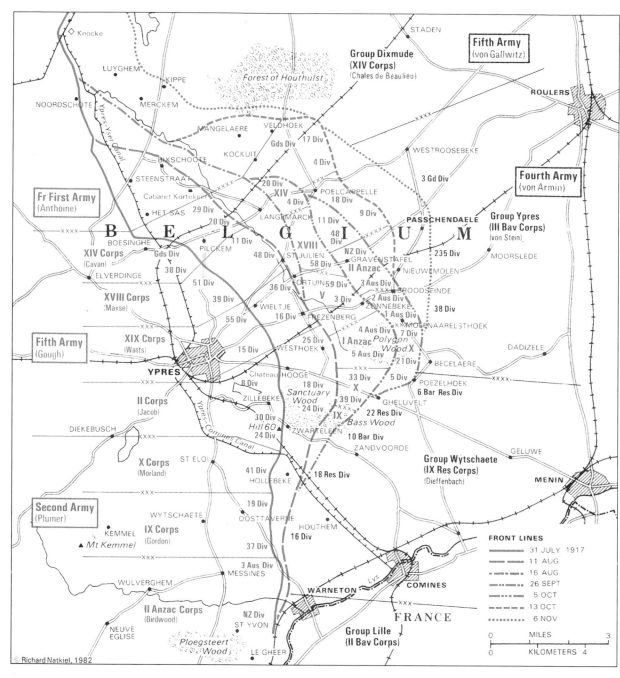

own tactics and stalemate emerged. Despite pressure to halt the offensive, Haig remained determined to reach Passchendaele and on October 12, II ANZAC Corps began the First Battle of Passchendaele: 3,000 Australians died there before their attack was aborted. The Second Battle of Passchendaele followed on October 26, and the Canadians, under a skeptical General Sir Arthur Currie, finally took the ravaged village on November 6, 1917, at a total cost of over 310,000 Allied casualties. *MC*

Above: The Third Battle of Ypres. *Richard Natkiel*

Above Right: Battle of Polygon Wood: camouflaged tanks and infantry moving up to the attack along the Menin Road east of Ypres, September 26, 1917. *Chrysalis Photo Library*

Right: The ruins of Ypres—all that was left of the Cloth Hall in 1916. *Chrysalis Photo Library*

Right: Passchendaele: men of 16th Canadian Machine Gun Company manning shell holes on Passchendaele Ridge, November 14, 1917.
Chrysalis Photo Library

Far Right: Relieving battalion (4th Dorsets) marching up to the line at evening near Ypres, September 5, 1917.
Chrysalis Photo Library

Below: Dead Germans in trench, Battle of Ypres, July 31, 1917.
Chrysalis Photo Library

Yser, Battle of

The Battle of Yser broke out on July 10, 1918, taking the British forces under Rawlinson by surprise. Having gleaned intelligence of the British intention to renew the assault on the Ypres Salient in July 1918, by July 9 Crown Prince Rupprecht had fortified his own lines to a strength considerably superior to that available to the attacking force. The Crown Prince then pushed his advantage further, attacking the British Fourth Army as they waited in their advance position by the Yser. Catching the British off their guard, he drove them back across the river, and seized control of the commanding ground on the right bank. *MC*

Yudenich, Nikolai (1862-1933)

Yudenich became deputy chief of staff to the Caucasus Army in 1907 and was chief of staff to General Mishlaevski by November 1914. He defeated the Turks at Sarikamish in December 1914 and was promoted in January 1915. He achieved further success at Malazgirt in August 1915, before capturing Erzurum, Trabzon, and Erzincan between February and July 1916. His position was, however, weakened by the growing domestic crisis in Russia and, after the February Revolution, was forced to retire. After the October Revolution, he fled to Finland from Petrograd, before leading the anti-Bolshevik forces against Petrograd. Although initially successful, Yudenich was defeated and he went into exile in France. *MS*

WORLD WAR I: A VISUAL ENCYCLOPEDIA

Z

Zeebrugge, Raid on

Together with Ostend, the Belgian port of Zeebrugge was a major base for German coastal U-boats during the war, and the two were linked together by a canal system. In 1918 the British devised a plan to "put a cork" in the port. A similar and simultaneous attempt to block Ostend ended in failure two weeks later, when the old cruiser *Vindictive* was scuttled in the harbor, but failed to prevent its use by U-boats. The Zeebrugge raid was launched on St. George's Day 1918. While the *Vindictive* and two support vessels landed their crews on the long protective mole which sheltered seven small German torpedo-boats, the block-ships *Intrepid* and *Iphigenia* were sailed into the canal entrance and scuttled. Their approach was covered by the cruiser *Thetis*, but heavy fire prevented them from scuttling where they would be most effective. The landing parties achieved little, but suffered heavy casualties, although German reinforcements were prevented when the explosive-laden submarine *C3* destroyed the mole's approach viaduct. Although the navy lost 500 men, the raid was a qualified success, and hindered U-boat activity for several months, while a follow-up attack on Ostend in May proved successful. *AK*

Zeppelins

Awesome though they were in terms of size, Germany's giant rigid airships to which Count von Zeppelin had given his name were, despite becoming the world's largest aerial weapons, fatally flawed. Zeppelins nevertheless carried out bombing raids on England starting on January 19–20, 1915, when two navy ships bombed King's Lynn in Norfolk, and on May 31, 1915, London's East End was bombed in daylight for the first time by an army Zeppelin. This and other early daylight sorties found an element of success as there was no practical defense against them. Not until September 2–3, 1916, was a Zeppelin shot down (by Lieutenant Leefe Robinson). Sporadic raids in daylight continued but the Germans were eventually forced to switch to night attack in deference to the increasing defenses. While many raids were successful and without losses, the damage inflicted was fairly widespread although London with its clearly defined river estuary, was a natural target and relatively easy to find in darkness with rudimentary navigational aids. Zeppelin crews lacked any means of bomb aiming and the indiscriminate nature of the raids caused an outcry in Britain and, in due course, the implementation of

Right: Aerial view of the entrance to the Bruges Canal at Zeebrugge showing the sunken *Thetis*, *Intrepid*, and *Iphigenia* and a dredger at work. *Chrysalis Photo Library*

Opposite, Below: The British attack on Zeebrugge, April 1918. *Richard Natkiel*

Opposite, Below: First flight of Zeppelin LZ1, July 2, 1900. *Chrysalis Photo Library*

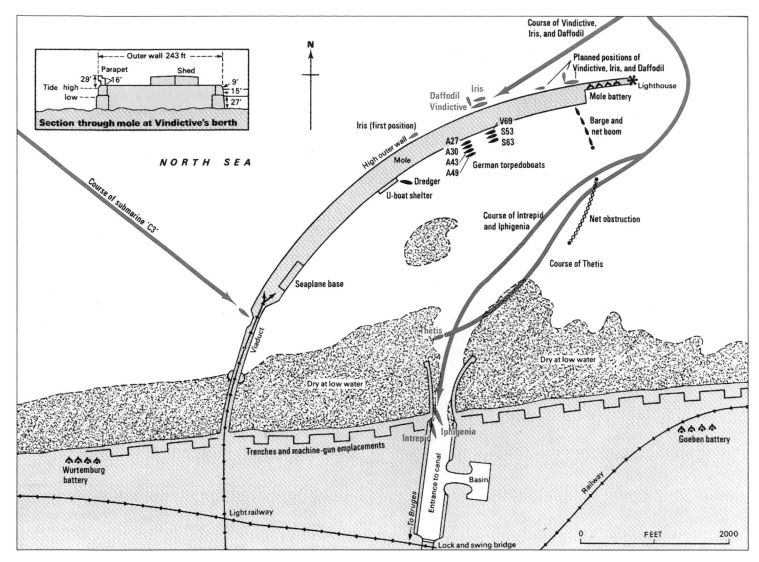

Section through mole at Vindictive's berth

Outer wall 243 ft

Parapet 16'

Shed

29'

Tide high low

9'

15'

27'

N

NORTH SEA

Course of Vindictive, Iris, and Daffodil

Planned positions of Vindictive, Iris, and Daffodil

Iris

Daffodil
Vindictive

Lighthouse

Mole battery

Iris (first position)

V69
S53
S63

A27
A30
A43
A49

German torpedoboats

Barge and net boom

High outer wall

Mole

Course of submarine 'C3'

Dredger

U-boat shelter

Course of Intrepid and Iphigenia

Net obstruction

Course of Thetis

Seaplane base

Viaduct

Thetis

Dry at low water

Dry at low water

Trenches and machine-gun emplacements

Intrepid Iphigenia

Goeben battery

Wurtemburg battery

Entrance to canal

Basin

Railway

Light railway

To Bruges

Lock and swing bridge

0   FEET   2000

effective countermeasures. In total nineteen Zeppelins were to succumb to the defenses and adverse weather conditions with the loss of 389 crewmen. Other Zeppelins were destroyed on the ground during Allied raids on their sheds in Germany. With Zeppelins on strength for the duration of the war, Germany had built a total of 115 by 1918, gradually increasing engine power and carrying capacity. Streamlining of the drag-inducing gondola and suspended engine nacelles was also achieved to some degree, the *L48* of 1917 incorporating several such refinements. With their multiple 200–260hp Maybach engines giving the relatively lightweight ships a high-altitude capability (the late-war *L71* had a service ceiling of 22,967ft), the German crews initially enjoyed some immunity from interception. But defending British fighters did eventually pose a serious threat, as did AA guns working with searchlights. Filled with highly combustible hydrogen gas, the Zeppelins were dangerously susceptible to the incendiary bullets loaded into the guns of RFC and RNAS fighters. For their part the giant dirigibles were by no means defenseless and as well as mounting machine guns in the suspended gondolas,

some intrepid souls were perched on top of the envelope with a brace of water-cooled Maxim machine guns to ward off interceptors. An airship represented a very stable gun platform, virtually free of weight restrictions and the gondolas were adequately equipped to defend against low-flying aircraft—or so it was believed. All Zeppelins carried their crews and bomb load in the gondola and provided they had sufficient fuel and favorable weather conditions, flights could be made over very long ranges, at typical speeds of between 50mph and 70mph. Bomb loads varied but weapons of up to 600lb in weight were capable of causing considerable damage. Among the more spectacular Zeppelin flights attempted was that mounted by *L59*, which set out to resupply German forces in Africa in the spring of 1918. On April 7 the airship caught fire and went down off the Italian coast into the Strait of Otranto. *JS*

Below: Drawing of the Zeppelin raids on London.
Chrysalis Photo Library

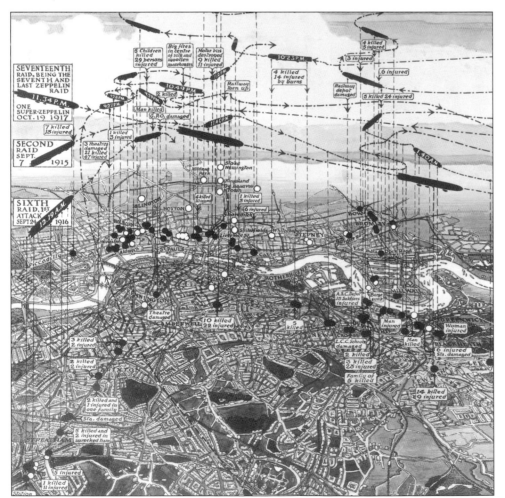

Zimmermann Telegram

In January 1917, British cryptographers deciphered a telegram from German Foreign Minister Arthur Zimmermann to the German Minister to Mexico, von Eckhardt, offering U.S. territory to Mexico in return for joining the German cause. It also proposed a German military alliance with Mexico and Japan against the United States. Zimmermann held out to the Mexican Government the possibility of German assistance to regain New Mexico, Arizona, and California. This message helped draw the United States into the war. The telegram had a major impact on American opinion. According to David Kahn, author of *The Codebreakers*, "No other single crypto-analysis has had such enormous consequences . . . never before or since has so much turned upon the solution of a secret message." On the evening of Saturday, February 26, 1917, President Woodrow Wilson received the decoded text of the secret message from Acting Secretary of State Frank Polk. The President was shocked by the threat to American security. The next day he proposed to Congress the arming of United States' ships against German attacks, and on March 1 he announced the discovery of the Zimmermann Telegram. Arthur Link, President Wilson's biographer, wrote that, "No other event of the war . . . so stunned the American people . . . American Congressional and public revulsion to the Zimmermann Telegram was a major turning point in the attitude about intervening with the Allies against Germany, and the first of a series of rapid ourselves. Please call the President's attention to the fact that the ruthless employment of our submarines now offers the prospect of compelling England in a few months to make peace.

Far Left: German Foreign Minister Arthur Zimmermann who sent the telegram to the German Ambassador in Mexico. *Collection of Bill Yenne*

Left: This is the original Zimmermann Telegram as written in code. *Collection of Bill Yenne*

Below: The Zimmermann Telegram decoded. *Collection of Bill Yenne*

steps culminating in the American entry into the war in April 1917." The text of the message is as follows:

"We intend to begin on the first of February unrestricted submarine warfare. We shall endeavor in spite of this to keep the United States of America neutral. In the event of this not succeeding, we make Mexico a proposal or alliance on the following basis: make war together, make peace together, generous financial support and an understanding on our part that Mexico is to reconquer the lost territory in Texas, New Mexico, and Arizona. The settlement in detail is left to you. You will inform the President of the above most secretly as soon as the outbreak of war with the United States of America is certain and add the suggestion that he should, on his own initiative, invite Japan to immediate adherence and at the same time mediate between Japan and

TELEGRAM RECEIVED.

FROM 2nd from London # 5747.

"We intend to begin on the first of February unrestricted submarine warfare. We shall endeavor in spite of this to keep the United States of America neutral. In the event of this not succeeding, we make Mexico a proposal of alliance on the following basis: make war together, make peace together, generous financial support and an understanding on our part that Mexico is to reconquer the lost territory in Texas, New Mexico, and Arizona. The settlement in detail is left to you. You will inform the President of the above most secretly as soon as the outbreak of war with the United States of America is certain and add the suggestion that he should, on his own initiative, invite ~~will be~~ Japan to immediate adherence and at the same time mediate between Japan and ourselves. Please call the President's attention to the fact that the ruthless employment of our submarines now offers the prospect of compelling England in a few months to make peace." Signed, ZIMMERMANN.